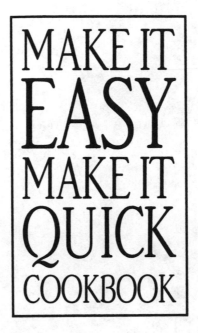

MAKE IT
EASY
MAKE IT
QUICK
COOKBOOK

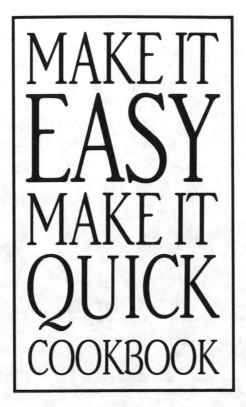

MAKE IT EASY MAKE IT QUICK COOKBOOK

LAURIE BURROWS GRAD

GALAHAD BOOKS
New York

Published in 1991 by

Galahad Books
A division of LDAP, Inc.
386 Park Avenue South
Suite 1913
New York, NY 10016

Galahad Books is a registered trademark of LDAP, Inc.

Published by arrangement with Jeremy P. Tarcher, Inc.

Library of Congress Catalog Card Number: 90-86015

ISBN: 0-88365-773-2

Printed in the United States of America.

CONTENTS

ACKNOWLEDGMENTS

The author wishes to thank the following people for their advice, counsel, support, and discerning taste buds:

—Mary Carey, a truly special friend, who fought to decipher my hieroglyphics and transpose them into the real thing, copy after copy after copy. . . .

—Millie Loeb, my wonderfully helpful editor, who, without undue pressure, helped me find the right direction.

—My publisher, Jeremy Tarcher, who tried to please, and did.

—My agent, Dominick Abel, the big-deal maker in New York.

—My official testers, for their show of friendship and support: Bob Broder, Catherine Bergstrom, Michelle Naumberg, Fred Roberts, and Barbara Tenenbaum.

—And my unofficial testers, for their aid and abettance.

—Gary, Steve, Marty, Bob and all the people at *Hour Magazine* for their continued support.

—All my friends at *Los Angeles Magazine*.

—Judi Kaufman, who provided valuable wisdom.

—Dan and Leora Garner, for the gracious loan of their kitchen.

—Linda Burrows, who waded steadfastly through the manuscript, in her ninth month of pregnancy.

—Carolyn Spencer, who made an extra effort to help.

—Joan Leemhorst, who thoroughly copy edited.

—All my supportive friends, for encouragement and for just being there: Sandy, Betsy, Diane, Barbara G., Barbara T., et al.

—My mom, Ruth Burrows, the gourmet, for introducing me to bouillabaisse, my dad, Abe Burrows, the writer, for introducing me to a short sentence, and my brother, Jim Burrows, the director, who told me I should never be an actress or listen to my parents!

—My super-patient family, for their indulgence and support in my kitchen experiments.

PART ONE

MAKE IT EASY COOKING

INTRODUCTION

I love to cook. I also love to eat and serve food that looks as delicious as it tastes. However, as a working woman with a family, I have neither the hours nor the energy to spend in the kitchen making believe I am another Julia Child. Don't misunderstand me, I love Julia Child—her style, her wit, and especially her cooking. But there just isn't the time. I assume that my life isn't particularly unusual and that, like me, you too are busy with a schedule full of commitments. But that doesn't mean our desire for good food goes away. In fact, it can increase, since there is something very pleasing about a well-prepared, beautifully presented meal after a long day jammed with activities. But again, the issue is time. How are we to find it? The Make-It-Easy style of cooking described in this book is an answer to this dilemma.

For the past two years I have been demonstrating Make-It-Easy cooking on the nationally syndicated television show, *Hour Magazine*. In doing so, I have become expert at just about every trick in the cook's repertoire for making life easier in the kitchen. The response to the television segment, in the form of thousands of letters asking for recipes or suggesting even newer and better ideas, indicates the incredible interest in this approach to food preparation.

What has been most appealing to viewers is that Make-It-Easy Cooking emphasizes quality. It doesn't mean visits to the Colonel or the deli or a retreat to canned or frozen dinners. Instead, I will show you how to create meals that look complicated, taste fantastic, and can be prepared with the greatest of ease in the least amount of time—using fresh ingredients.

The assembled recipes—a combination of tried-and-true favorites and many that are more unusual and exotic—emphasize a balance between high- and low-calorie foods, expensive and inexpensive ingredients, and a variety of international flavors. In these pages you will find everything from *Scandinavian Gravlax* and almost-instant pâtés to an *Ice Cream Cookie Freakout* and *Zabaglione*.

What makes the new wave of easy cooking possible are the food processor and the blender. The processor, especially, is a magical and wondrous invention that, once mastered, will save you hours. In fact, if you make only one new investment for your kitchen, I would strongly advise that you consider this piece of equipment, especially since the price of good processors has been greatly reduced during the past few years. However, a good blender is a suitable substitute. It may not be able to julienne or finely chop, but it can purée a pâté, process a cold soup, and whip up a chocolate mousse, acting as a tremendous time-saver.

Obviously, the key to Make-It-Easy cooking is cutting the preparation time. Most recipes take less than 20 minutes to prepare, some ten or 15, and a few, miraculously, can be whipped up in only five. The cooking times vary in length from 5 minutes to 2–3 hours, although most dishes are done in under 60 minutes. I save the recipes with longer cooking times, the soups and the stews, for weekends, when I can wait for a pot to boil. No matter how long the simmering, the preparation time is always short.

In order to get the most out of *Make-It-Easy in Your Kitchen*, I suggest reading the chapter introductions before proceeding with the recipes. I've tried to include in them a wealth of general information, along with specific tips on purchasing and storing ingredients. For instance, if you read these sections you will discover how to select and perfectly season a wok and how to prepare just about every conceivable kind of crumb pie-crust for a spur-of-the-moment dessert. You will also find other recipes, such as *Perfect White Rice the Chinese Way* and *Raspberry Vinegar*, which can be used in an array of dishes.

All of this is aimed at inspiring you, since there is something so satisfying about preparing fabulous dishes—especially ones that are put together quickly—that previously seemed too difficult or time-consuming. In fact, the entire book has been designed to ease your experimentation.

ABOUT THE RECIPES

Each recipe includes both its preparation time and its cooking time, followed by a list of ingredients, and step-by-step instructions given in an understandable and concise manner. To simplify menu planning, entrées and main-dish salads are followed by *Accompaniments*. If these suggested accompaniments are italicized (for example, *Perfect Baked Potatoes*), the recipes can be found in the book. Most recipes include a section called *Variations*. Some of these are specific ideas for lowering the price of the dish or its calorie count; others illustrate how changing one or two ingredients leads to the creation of an entirely different dish, but one that is just as appealing.

At the close of most recipes you will find *Make-It-Easy Tips*. These are those marvelous pieces of wisdom—concerning how to use your equipment most efficiently, the secrets of culinary chemistry, reheating and freezing—that can make any cooking experience more satisfying and successful. I know that each time I learned one of these tricks—how I could chop onions by hand without crying, prevent the blueberries from sinking to the bottom of the batter, and tenderize meat without using preparations full of strange chemicals, it was a revelation. I will pass on this information and much more, in the hope that you, too, will be happily surprised. Many of the tips are repeated over and over again as they apply to specific recipes, since I assume no one wants to read a cookbook as if it were a novel.

So thumb through and then select one dish that is especially appealing but that you never considered trying before. Once you learn that you can Make-It-Easy in Your Kitchen, you will see that great food can be made from scratch in less time than you ever imagined. The result will be a sense of achievement, and the discovery of a way of cooking that reflects the way we live now and would like to eat.

A NOTE ON INGREDIENTS
Some ingredients appear over and over again in recipes throughout the book, so Make-It-Easy general information about them and tips regarding them belong here at the beginning. What you will find below is the accumulated knowledge of experienced cooks.

Herbs
Fresh herbs can make all the difference—a point I will stress repeatedly throughout the book. Keeping them on hand is really rather simple. The food processor can chop large bunches at once, and they can be frozen in small containers or plastic bags. Frozen herbs may not look as bright and green as fresh, but they taste much better than the dried variety. If you are using dried herbs, crumble them between your

fingers just before adding them to recipes to release their optimum flavor. In general, 1 *tablespoon* freshly chopped herbs is equivalent to 1 *teaspoon* dried herbs.

Seasoning

In all the recipes in this book, with the exception of the baking chapter, I have limited the amount of salt to ½ teaspoon. Even this is optional. I have adopted this approach because the medical evidence seems to suggest that salt isn't very good for us, and it is easy to substitute other spices or herbs or even lemon juice to heighten the flavor of food. In contrast to the substitutes for sugar, there is no controversy about chives or dill or onions and garlic. They taste good and are good for us. If you are concerned about the deleterious effects of salt, remember that soy sauce, mustard, canned chicken or beef broth, smoked meats, and many other ingredients contain high levels of sodium.

Adding ground pepper is another easy way to heighten flavor. It is just as easy to turn a peppermill a few times to get freshly ground pepper as it is to give a few shakes of the flat, flavorless, ready-ground pepper in the can. White pepper is simply black pepper with the outer husks removed. The white is less pungent and spicy than the black and is aesthetically more pleasing in an all-white sauce.

Butter, Margarine, and Oil

I recommend unsalted butter (also called sweet butter). It has a more delicate taste. I also suggest it because the addition of salt can often camouflage a poor or rancid taste in the butter. It allows you, once again, to keep the sodium content down.

Unsalted margarine can be used in place of unsalted butter if you wish to avoid saturated fats. Read the labels carefully and select one that lists liquid corn, safflower, sunflower, or soy bean oil (all polyunsaturated fats) as the first ingredient.

There is a wide variety of oils on the market. A good Italian olive oil should be reserved for light salads, whereas the chartreuse-colored, heavier, thicker, and more pungent olive oil can be used in limited amounts for some of the new and unusual salads or in sautéing, where a stronger flavor is required. The liquid vegetable oils such as corn, cottonseed, soy bean, safflower, and sunflower, which are higher in polyunsaturated fats, are more healthful to use and lighter in taste. Oil is a great help when added to butter for sauté-ing. The higher smoking point of the oil prevents the butter from burning. In Chinese cooking, I recommend peanut oil for stir-frying, and oriental sesame oil, which adds a nutty flavor to cooked dishes and salads.

Eggs, Cheese, and Dairy

Large or extra-large eggs should be used for the recipes in this book. Jumbo eggs will add too much liquid. Since I find no taste difference between brown and white eggs, I purchase the brown ones one week and the white ones the next. By alternating colors, I can remember to use the older eggs up before starting on the new ones.

Stale, dried-out, and over-aged packaged, grated Parmesan cheese in the can bears no resemblance to freshly grated. It takes only a few seconds for the food processor to grate a block of cheese, which can then be kept in a covered container for at least a week. A hand grater works almost as easily. Although it may not be as Make-It-Easy, it defi-nitely qualifies for "make it better."

Swiss cheese, Monterey Jack cheese, Muenster cheese, brick cheese, even mozzarella cheese can be used interchangeably in recipes in this book. Cheddar can also be substituted, but its stronger taste keeps it from being interchangeable. Grate the cheese in large batches in the food processor or by hand. It will keep in sealed plastic bags for several weeks. Garlic-herb cheeses such as Boursin, or the delicious, less expensive copies, Rondele and Alouette, are useful as instant ap-petizers, stuffing for mushrooms, or unusual fillings for rolls. The new soft version of cream cheese or whipped cream cheese makes preparing a dip or spread easy. If unavailable, soften the cream cheese in the food processor or blender.

Light cream is a thing of the past and has been replaced by half-and-half. Heavy cream and whipping cream are one and the same. Whenever possible, stay away from the ultra-pasteurized cream, which lasts longer but does not whip well or taste as good. The nondairy cream substitutes are a dreadful conglomeration of chemicals, preser-vatives, and saturated fats that are to be avoided.

Flour and Bread Crumbs

I recommend an all-purpose unbleached flour, which is a blend of hard and soft wheat flours and is high in gluten. Either pre-sifted or not, the unbleached variety is preferable to the bleached. Self-rising flour is plain flour mixed with baking powder and salt. Use self-rising flour within 2–3 months of purchase since it tends to lose its effectiveness after this time.

Packaged bread crumbs may seem Make-It-Easy but this is another case where you should not sacrifice quality. If a food processor or blender is available, make dry crumbs from toasted bread, either white or whole wheat, or soft bread crumbs from slices of fresh bread. It should take about 1 minute. Avoid stale bread. Stale bread produces stale-tasting crumbs. One slice of bread produces about ½ cup fresh crumbs. Cracker crumbs can be used in place of bread crumbs. Use unsweetened, unsalted soda crackers and pulsate in food processor or blender until they become crumbs, but are not pulverized. Store bread crumbs in sealed containers or plastic bags for short-term storage or place in sealed containers in freezer for long-term storage.

Broth, Stock, and Soup

Since Make-It-Easy cooking does not allow time for preparing fresh stock, I find canned chicken or beef broth (without gelatin) an adequate substitute. I learned this tip from chefs and cooking authorities who found the taste difference negligible. If the recipe calls for strong broth, I use the undiluted variety. When using canned broth, always salt to taste after adding broth, since the broth contains large quantities of salt. I find that powdered stock or bouillon cubes are mostly chemicals, and I prefer not to use them. I also abstain from using any canned, creamed, gookey soups laden with preservatives. As a substitute for fish broth, I favor bottled clam juice, especially when cooking *Quick and Easy Cioppino* or similar fish and shellfish stews. If there is extra time to whip up some homemade stock, place the finished product in an ice-cube tray and use the frozen cubes as flavor enhancers.

Wines

I find the best and most readily available white wine to use in cooking is dry vermouth. Vermouth in itself is not a variety of wine. It is actually a wine that has been treated in a certain way, usually with the addition of distilled alcohol, and herbs and spices. Vermouth can be kept for a longer period of time once opened and is often less expensive to use in cooking than most white wines.

As a substitute for red wine, particularly when I want a sweeter taste for a stew or pot roast, I often use Marsala, Madeira, port, or sweet vermouth, which have longer shelf-life than an opened bottle of wine.

ON STORING AND FREEZING

In the introduction to most chapters, and in the *Make-It-Easy Tips* following the recipes, you will find specific information about storing ingredients once you have them home. For example, taking the chicken out of the supermarket package and wrapping it properly will keep it fresh for an extra day. In Appendix B, you will find a freezer chart listing every major ingredient and type of dish along with their freezer life spans. Since I advise cooking many recipes in double batches or, if you have a small family, freezing one-half of what you have prepared, this freezer chart can be very helpful.

CHAPTER ONE

APPETIZERS
AND
HORS D'OEUVRES

Crudités

Vegetable Basket

Guacamole

Caper Dip

Yogurt Vegetable Dip (Indian Style)

Hot Crab Dip

Hummus Bi Tahini (Chick Pea Spread)

Liverwurst Pâté

French Chicken Liver Pâté

Mushrooms Stuffed with Garlic-Herb Cheese

Drumettes

Carpaccio

Celery Root Rémoulade

Hot Baked Sausages

Baked Artichoke Hearts

Double Salmon Mousse

Gravlax (Scandinavian Salmon Marinated in Dill)

The preparation of appetizers can be made incredibly easy if you just remember that they were originally designed to be appetite stimulators. They are meant to whet the appetite in anticipation of taste thrills to come. *Hors d'oeuvre*, the French words for appetizer, means "outside the meal," or little tidbits to start the juices flowing.

Appetizers should be uncomplicated little samples. All your guests, not only the ones on diets, will thank you for not pre-stuffing them with extra calories, and you'll have extra time to put into the preparation of the main meal.

If you are planning a very special occasion or the boss is coming to dinner unexpectedly, you can transform most of the following appetizer recipes into first courses. The cocktail hour can be limited, and a lovely, easy, more formal dinner can proceed. (On most occasions, however, first courses require too much work, time, energy, and extra dishes to qualify for a Make-It-Easy dinner.)

Appetizers and hors d'oeuvres come in a variety of sizes, shapes, and temperatures. The cold dip may appear to be the easiest to prepare, but cutting up the multitude of colorful vegetables to accompany that dip makes it a more difficult procedure. Hot canapés often involve working with complicated pastry, and hours of time-consuming activities and are, therefore, almost eliminated from a Make-It-Easy schedule.

Your goal is to find the easiest dishes to prepare that fit into your menu plan and the time of year. Obviously, hot appetizers are more appealing on a cold winter night, and cold appetizers can be prepared beforehand, giving you more time to spend with your guests.

For a large cocktail party, finger foods are easy to serve without using too many plates or too much cutlery. In addition to *crudités* (raw vegetables), chicken wing *Drumettes*, *Carpaccio* (raw steak slices), and prosciutto ham wrapped around a variety of fruits and vegetables make excellent nibbles at a large party, or delicious small bites before a dinner.

Keep in mind that, even though appetizers may be kept simple, the garnish surrounding them is all important. The addition of a few sprigs of parsley, some tiny sour pickles, and assorted crackers to a plain piece of pâté makes this an appealing and special treat. Baskets make especially attractive serving containers for appetizers such as raw vegetables, crackers, or cheeses.

The simplest appetizer, of course, is cheese and crackers served on a board, in a basket, or on a platter. The appetizers that follow are designed for those who want to serve something special but still want to keep it easy.

Crudités and a Vegetable Basket

Crudités are crisp fresh raw vegetables served as an appetizer, often with a dip. If eaten alone, they are perfect for the dieter, and with a dip they will satisfy those who want something a bit richer. The Make-It-Easy trick to cutting up raw vegetables is to choose those vegetables that need as little work as possible. The list below provides a basis for making the easiest crudité basket possible. The use of a large serrated slicer or smaller decorating knife can make the vegetables even more attractive and takes no more time than regular slicing. The vegetables can be cut up in advance and chilled in ice water to crisp them and keep them crunchy.

When really in a hurry, stick to cherry tomatoes, with the stems on (your guests can easily manage to remove them).

VEGETABLE BASKET
Line a small basket (with or without a handle) with several soft lettuce leaves or a colorful napkin. Boston and curly leaf lettuce are easy and attractive choices. A few sprigs of parsley take up enough room to make the vegetables stand up. Pick from the following assortment of

vegetables, depending on seasonal availability and color preference, and arrange in a decorative fashion in the basket.

If the basket is still full enough after the cocktail hour, use it as a centerpiece, bolstered with a few more sprigs of parsley.

1. *Cherry Tomatoes:* Wash, but leave stems on. They look prettier and guests do not mind removing them.
2. *Unpeeled Zucchini, Cucumber, or Crookneck Squash:* Slice into spears or circles with serrated slicer if available. They are colorful and particularly attractive when alternated, green and yellow.
3. *Snow Peas:* Wash and, if possible, remove strings by pulling from the top down the sides.
4. *Broccoli Florets* (or Cauliflower Florets): Wash the broccoli and cut off the florets (the stems can be peeled and sliced and used as a vegetable at another time).
5. *Turnip Slices:* Peel and slice.
6. *Medium-Size Mushrooms:* The easiest way to clean them is to dip a mushroom brush or paper towel into lemon juice and brush or wipe away the dirt, leaving the mushrooms clean and impervious to discoloration. Serve them whole.
7. *Red Radishes:* Wash and remove ends. They are colorful and easy to clean. A radish flowering tool can be used for an even prettier arrangement.
8. *Daikon (Japanese Radish):* Peel only a thin layer and slice with a serrated knife into strips and slices.
9. *Green and Red Peppers:* Wash and cut into wedges, removing seeds.

Radish decorator

10. *Scallions:* Cut off root ends and leave greens on. They look beautiful as part of the basket arrangement.

11. *Celery:* If you have a little extra time, use celery or, if available, fennel (finocchio, fenucchi) for an interesting taste addition.

12. *Thin Asparagus:* Very thin asparagus can be eaten raw as a crudité. Just wash, break off the tough fibrous stem ends, and arrange in a basket.

13. *String Beans:* Wash, and break off tips if desired.

14. *Jicama:* A crunchy Mexican vegetable with a sweet taste, similar to a water chestnut; peel, and slice with a serrated knife to resemble french fries, or cut into thin pieces.

Jicama

Daikon

Guacamole

SERVES: 4
Preparation time: 10 minutes

The Ingredients:
　　1　ripe avocado, peeled
　　1　tablespoon fresh lemon juice
　　⅓　cup finely chopped red onion
　　⅓　cup finely chopped green pepper
　　¼　teaspoon chili powder, or to taste
　　¼　teaspoon salt, or to taste
　　1　ripe tomato, sliced in half, squeezed of seeds, and finely chopped
　　　　Garnish: Chopped scallion stalks or corn or taco chips

The Steps:
1. Mash avocado with lemon juice to prevent discoloration.
2. Fold in onions, green pepper, chili powder, and salt, and stir until smooth.
3. Add chopped tomatoes, and serve immediately. Garnish with chopped scallion greens and surround with corn or taco chips.

Variation:
Lime juice can be substituted for lemon juice.

Make-It-Easy Tips:
√ Use a pastry blender to chop guacamole ingredients.
√ Serve guacamole with avocado pit in center; it will help prevent discoloration.
√ To remove seeds from tomato easily, slice tomato in half and gently squeeze it until the seeds fall out.
√ Ripen avocados quickly by storing in a brown paper bag. Check daily.
√ The guacamole can be chilled for 2 hours before serving but for not much longer or it may discolor.

Caper Dip

SERVES: 6–8
Preparation time: 10 minutes
Chilling time: 1–2 hours

For the smoothest consistency, use a food processor or blender.

The Ingredients:
   3 scallions, white part only, finely chopped
   1 4-ounce jar small capers, drained and chopped
   ½ cup dairy sour cream
   ½ cup mayonnaise
      Salt and freshly ground pepper to taste

The Steps:
   1. In food processor, blender, or by hand, chop scallions and capers together until just minced.
   2. Transfer to a bowl, stir in sour cream and mayonnaise, and chill for 1–2 hours.
   3. Season to taste with salt and freshly ground pepper, and serve chilled with vegetable crudités.

Variations:
   Any leftover dip can be used as a sauce for cold poached fish or poultry.

   For an extra special dip, try using homemade *Basic Blender Mayonnaise, see* page 247.

Make-It-Easy Tip:
   √ Chop and reserve scallion greens as garnish or flavoring. Store in refrigerator or freezer.

Yogurt Vegetable Dip (Indian Style)

SERVES: 4
Preparation time: 10–15 minutes
Chilling time: 1–2 hours

In most Indian *raitas* (relishes), the cucumber is salted to extract the moisture. Since there is only a small cucumber used in this recipe, I bypassed the salting step. This is a fantastic low-calorie dip to serve with vegetable crudités.

The Ingredients:
        1 small cucumber, peeled, seeded, and finely chopped
        2 radishes, finely chopped
        3 tablespoons finely chopped scallions (green and white included)
        1 teaspoon fresh lemon juice
        ¼ teaspoon ground cumin, or to taste
           Pinch of cayenne pepper
           Pinch of salt
        1 cup plain low-fat yogurt
           Salt and freshly ground pepper to taste

The Steps:
        1. Chop vegetables in food processor, blender, or by hand.
        2. Pour vegetables into a bowl and add remaining ingredients. Mix well.
        3. Chill 1–2 hours
        4. Taste, and adjust seasoning if necessary. Serve chilled with vegetable crudités.

Variations:
    Yogurt vegetable dip can also be served as a *raita*, an Indian relish that accompanies spicy dishes such as curry.
    Any leftovers can be added to a basic vinaigrette salad dressing, which will make it creamy, but still not high in calories.
    For thicker variation, add ⅓ cup sour cream.

Hothouse cucumbers

Make-It-Easy Tip:
√ Substitute ⅓ of a European hothouse hydroponic cucumber for the small cucumber. It needs no peeling and has fewer seeds.

Hot Crab Dip

SERVES: 6–8
Preparation time: 10 minutes
Cooking time: 15 minutes

Frozen crab is used in this recipe since it is to be cooked. If fresh crab is reasonably priced, by all means use it.

The Ingredients:
　12 ounces cream cheese
　　1 6-ounce package frozen snow crab or king crab, thawed, drained, and flaked
　½ small onion, minced (2–3 tablespoons)
　　1 tablespoon lemon juice
　　2 teaspoons white horseradish
　½ teaspoon Worcestershire sauce
　½ teaspoon salt, or to taste

½ teaspoon freshly ground white pepper, or to taste
¼ cup slivered almonds
Garnish: Crudités, sesame crackers, or corn chips

The Steps:
1. Using a food processor, blender, mixer, or by hand, combine cream cheese, crabmeat, onion, lemon juice, horseradish, Worcestershire sauce, salt, and pepper.
2. When well mixed, place in an oven-proof dish and refrigerate.
3. When ready to serve, preheat oven to 375°, top crab dip with almonds, and heat until bubbly, 10–15 minutes.
4. Serve hot, garnished with crudités, sesame crackers, or large-size corn chips.

Variation:
The crab dip can be reheated or served cold the next day.

Make-It-Easy Tips:
√ Whipped cream cheese, which is easier to blend, can be substituted for solid bars of cream cheese, eliminating the need for a food processor or blender.
√ To thaw crabmeat quickly, place sealed package of frozen crabmeat in warm water for half an hour.

Hummus Bi Tahini (Chick Pea Spread)

SERVES: 8
Preparation time: 10 minutes

This easy to prepare Middle-Eastern specialty is an exotic and interesting taste addition to an hors d'oeuvres table.

The Ingredients:
1 15½-ounce can garbanzo beans (chick peas), drained, washed, and drained again
¼ cup *tahini*, also called sesame paste (available in some supermarkets, Middle Eastern groceries, or by mail order—*see* Appendix A)
Juice of 1 lemon

    1 large garlic clove, peeled
  2–3 tablespoons olive oil
      Salt to taste
      Garnish: Fresh coriander or parsley, and Pita toast or
      crackers

The Steps:
  1. Combine drained beans, *tahini*, lemon juice, garlic, and olive
     oil in food processor or blender, and process until smooth. If
     gummy and too thick, add a little water to thin. Taste, and
     add salt if necessary.
  2. Mound on a flat plate and serve at room temperature; garnish
     with fresh coriander or parsley and Pita toasts or crackers.

Make-It-Easy Tip:
  √ Squeeze lemons at room temperature to release the most amount
    of juice.

EASY PÂTÉS
The preparation of a true French *pâté de campagne* (Country Pâté)
can be a whole-day affair. In order to Make-It-Easy, pâtés should con-
sist of liver spreads, fish spreads, vegetables, or even leftover meat
dishes processed until smooth with the aid of a food processor,
blender, or even a Foley food mill or ricer. Keep in mind that pâtés are
usually rich enough so that a little goes a long way.

Liverwurst Pâté

SERVES: 8
Preparation time: 10 minutes
Chilling time: 1 hour

This decorative and delicious hors d'oeuvre can be garnished to suit
your holiday or festive mood.

The Ingredients:
  ½ pound liverwurst, at room temperature
  1 teaspoon grated onion
  ¼ cup mayonnaise

Liverwurst pâté

Regular version   Christmas version

Frosting:
3 ounces cream cheese, softened
1 tablespoon mayonnaise
Garnish: Sliced stuffed olives and strips of pimiento

The Steps:

1. In a food processor, blender, or with a wooden spoon, mash liverwurst. Blend in onion and ¼ cup mayonnaise, and shape into a smooth round. Chill until firm.
2. To prepare frosting, use food processor, blender, or combine by hand. Mix cream cheese with 1 tablespoon mayonnaise until smooth.
3. Frost chilled pâté as if you were frosting a cake, covering the mound entirely. Then decorate with sliced stuffed olives and strips of pimiento in whatever design desired.

Variations:

Decorate pâté for Christmas using strips of pimiento as tree branches and stuffed olive slices as ornaments.
Crisp bacon bits can be added to liverwurst mixture.

Make-It-Easy Tip:

√ To ready the pâté quickly for frosting, place in freezer for 10–15 minutes.

French Chicken Liver Pâté

SERVES: 6–8
Preparation time: 25 minutes
Chilling time: 6 hours or overnight

Although this chicken liver mousse takes some time to prepare, the results are well worth the effort. Once you have tried the recipe several times (which is guaranteed to happen once you've tasted it), you'll find it easier to make. It is extra rich, so a little will serve a large group.

The Ingredients:
½ pound chicken livers
¼ pound (1 stick) unsalted butter, softened
3 tablespoons grated onion
½ teaspoon salt, or to taste
¼ teaspoon dry mustard
⅛ teaspoon ground cloves
Fat pinch of nutmeg
Pinch cayenne pepper
1 teaspoon dry sherry
2 teaspoons Bourbon
Garnish: 1 loaf of thin baguette-size French bread, sliced into rounds, or crackers

The Steps:
1. Lightly oil a small loaf pan (about 7″ x 4″ x 2″) or similar shallow mold.
2. Fill a medium saucepan ⅔ full with water. Bring to boil. Add chicken livers. When the water returns to the boil, cook livers for 12–15 minutes over medium heat; drain and set aside.
3. While livers are cooking, place butter, onion, salt, mustard, cloves, nutmeg, and cayenne in a food processor or blender and process until combined.
4. Add the warm livers to butter mixture and continue to process until smooth; add sherry and Bourbon and process another few seconds.
5. Pour the liver paste into the oiled pan, cover, and chill 6 hours or overnight.

6. When ready to unmold, place pan in sink filled with 2–3 inches of warm water and count slowly to five; run a knife around edges. Turn upside down on platter and shake to unmold.
7. Serve garnished with sliced French bread rounds, or crackers.

Make-It-Easy Tips:
√ This French liver pâté keeps well for at least 5 days in the refrigerator, so it can be made several days ahead.
√ If leftover liver pâté is frozen, make sure to stir around well by hand or in the food processor or blender to restore texture after defrosting.
√ Mold can be sprayed with non-aerosol vegetable shortening instead of oil.

Mushrooms Stuffed with Garlic-Herb Cheese

SERVES: 4–6
Preparation time: 5–10 minutes

The Ingredients:
12 large mushroom caps, stems removed
Lemon juice
2 4-ounce packages garlic-herb cheese (Alouette, Rondele, or Boursin)
Garnish: Parsley sprigs

The Steps:
1. Clean mushrooms with paper towel or mushroom brush dipped in lemon juice to prevent discoloration.
2. Fill the caps generously with cheese and serve garnished with little parsley sprigs on top, if desired.

Make-It-Easy Tip:
√ Use an egg carton to transport stuffed mushrooms to office or picnic luncheon.

Drumettes

SERVES: 6
Preparation time: 15 minutes
Cooking time: 25–30 minutes

Drumettes are the meaty portion of chicken wings with the tips severed so that they look like mini-drumsticks. They are available in most supermarkets today and make great hors d'oeuvres for adults and great snacks for kids.

The Ingredients:
¼ pound (1 stick) unsalted butter, melted
14 chicken drumettes
1 cup buttermilk
1½ cups cereal crumbs

The Steps:
1. Preheat oven to 400°.
2. Melt butter in 9″ x 13″ baking dish.
3. Dip drumettes in buttermilk and then in crumbs, pressing crumbs onto chicken. Place in pan in a single layer.
4. Bake for 25–30 minutes or until golden all over.
5. Serve hot, at room temperature, or chilled.

Variations:
Substitute 6–8 chicken thighs for the drumettes. Cook for 40–45 minutes and serve as a main course, picnic dish, or put in lunch bags the next day.

Make-It-Easy Tips:
√ Use packaged cornflake crumbs for cereal or substitute any of the unsweetened cereals and crush for 2–3 seconds in a food processor or blender.
√ If you have the time, place breaded chicken in refrigerator for 10–15 minutes before baking since this helps crumbs to adhere.
√ You can substitute the following for buttermilk: Add 1 tablespoon vinegar or lemon juice to 1 cup fresh milk and allow to

stand 5 minutes. You can also purchase dried buttermilk in many supermarkets. Or you can freeze a quart divided into one-cup portions to defrost and use as needed if no one in your family drinks buttermilk.

Carpaccio

SERVES: 6–8
Preparation time: 15 minutes
Chilling time: 2–3 hours

The name for this dish of sliced raw beef is somehow attributed to the Venetian Renaissance painter, Carpaccio. The sauce-topped slices of meat should be eaten as finger food.

The Ingredients:

12 slices boneless shell steak (1½ pounds), cut into ¼-inch-thick slices (some meat markets may call shell steaks New York Strip, Kansas City Strip, or plain strip steak)

Mustard Mayonnaise Sauce:

1 cup mayonnaise
2 tablespoons minced *cornichons* (sour pickles)
2 tablespoons freshly minced parsley
4 teaspoons Dijon mustard
1 teaspoon lemon juice
½ teaspoon salt, or to taste
¼ teaspoon freshly ground white pepper
Garnish: Parsley sprigs, lemon wedges, freshly cracked pepper

The Steps:

1. Place steak slices between 2 sheets of waxed paper and pound with a flat mallet until wafer thin; transfer the beef slices to a platter and chill until ready to serve.
2. Prepare the sauce by combining all ingredients in a small bowl. Mix until smooth and chill for 2–3 hours.
3. To serve attractively, arrange chilled meat slices on a platter and spread about 1 tablespoon of sauce over each slice; garnish platter with parsley sprigs, lemon wedges, and freshly cracked pepper.

Variation:
Serve the beef with *Spinach Mayonnaise* (*see* Chapter 8).

Make-It-Easy Tip:
√ If food processor is available, use it to slice the beef very thin. Place meat in freezer until just semi-frozen (or, if frozen, defrost to this state), and then slice with thin blade of the processor.

Celery Root Rémoulade

SERVES: 6
Preparation time: 15–20 minutes
Chilling time: 1–2 hours

Celery Root Rémoulade is a traditional French dish. Celery root, or celeriac as it is sometimes called, has an interesting taste, especially when mixed with this mayonnaise dressing. Prepare during the fall and winter months when it is more readily available.

The Ingredients:
1 pound celery root (celeriac or celery knob), peeled
Rémoulade:
1 cup mayonnaise
1 hard-cooked egg, chopped
2 tablespoons finely minced parsley
1 tablespoon finely minced sour pickles (called *cornichons* in France)
1 tablespoon finely chopped capers
1 tablespoon finely minced chives or scallion stalks
1 teaspoon Dijon mustard
1 teaspoon finely minced fresh tarragon or ½ teaspoon dried tarragon crumbled
2 teaspoons lemon juice
½ teaspoon salt, or to taste
¼ teaspoon anchovy paste
¼ teaspoon freshly ground white pepper, or to taste
Garnish: Parsley sprigs and crisp sesame wafers

Celery root

The Steps:

1. Prepare the rémoulade in a food processor, blender, or by hand by combining all rémoulade ingredients and blending until smooth.
2. Cut celery root into julienne strips (matchstick shapes) by hand, in food processor, or with hand food-grinder.
3. Toss the celery root strips with the rémoulade until coated, and chill for 1–2 hours.
4. Taste, and adjust seasoning if necessary. Serve on a lettuce-lined platter garnished with parsley sprigs. Spread on crisp sesame wafers.

Variation:

Serve Celeriac Rémoulade as a salad course for lunch or dinner.

Make-It-Easy Tips:

√ Any leftover sauce can be refrigerated for several weeks. Use it on eggs for a quick Eggs à la Russe, with shrimp or crabmeat for a spread, or as a dip with vegetable crudités.

√ The sauce is prepared first so that the cut celery root can be tossed immediately with the sauce to keep it from discoloring.

√ To julienne a round vegetable easily by hand, peel, slice in half, cut into thin slices, stack the slices and cut the stack into thin strips. Julienne matchstick strips will be formed.

√ If using a food processor, it is not necessary to chop egg, parsley, pickles, capers, and chives separately. Cut up roughly in large pieces, place in food processor, and chop together.

Hot Baked Sausages

SERVES: 10–14
Preparation time: 10–15 minutes
Cooking time: 35–45 minutes

Any variety or combination of sausages can be used, so select your favorites.

The Ingredients:

12 Italian sausages (6 hot and 6 sweet), or 3–4 Polish *kielbasa*, or 6 Spanish *chorizos*, or 6 Portuguese *linguiças*

8 long, thin, pale green peppers or 6 dark green bell peppers, cut into eighths

3 medium onions, peeled and cut into eighths

The Steps:

1. Preheat oven to 375°. Lightly oil a large foil-lined roasting pan with vegetable oil.
2. Cut sausages into ½-inch slices and place in pan.
3. Add peppers and onions to pan.
4. Place in preheated oven and bake uncovered for 35–45 minutes, stirring occasionally.
5. Slip under the broiler and brown for a few minutes, if necessary.

6. Serve the sausages hot, on little plates with forks or large toothpicks.

Variations:

The cooked sausages can be frozen or reheated. Use leftovers for fantastic hero sandwiches.

Serve baked sausages as a main course for 6–8 people with lots of Italian bread and an Italian salad.

Make-It-Easy Tip:

√ Line the pan with aluminum foil to save on clean-up chores.

Baked Artichoke Hearts

SERVES: 6–8
Preparation time: 10 minutes
Cooking time: 15 minutes

The Ingredients:

1 14-ounce can artichoke hearts (8 per can), drained and cut in half horizontally
16 round melba sesame crackers
¼ pound (1 stick) unsalted butter, melted
½ teaspoon salt, or to taste
¼ teaspoon freshly ground pepper
⅛ teaspoon freshly crushed garlic
2–3 teaspoons sesame seeds

The Steps:

1. Preheat oven to 350°. Very lightly butter an attractive oven-proof dish that can accommodate 16 rounds and can be used for serving.
2. Place one artichoke half, cut side up, on each sesame round and arrange in the prepared dish.
3. Add salt, pepper, and garlic to the melted butter and generously spoon the seasoned butter into the artichoke crevices, allowing some to run on the rounds.
4. Sprinkle with sesame seeds and bake for 10 minutes.

5. Just before serving, run under broiler for 2–3 minutes to brown. Serve hot.

Make-It-Easy Tips:
√ Use only the canned artichokes packed in water. Avoid the marinated variety.
√ Garlic can be crushed with a food processor or in a garlic press a few cloves at a time, and stored for several weeks in the refrigerator in a small, tightly-capped jar with a few tablespoons of oil.

Double Salmon Mousse

SERVES: 6–8
Preparation time: 15 minutes
Chilling time: 6–8 hours or overnight

The addition of smoked salmon gives this Salmon Mousse a strong, smoky taste. A fish mold is not necessary for the recipe but provides a very attractive result. If using a ring mold, serve with the *Cucumber Dill Sauce* in a bowl in the center.

The Ingredients:
4 thin slices smoked salmon, cut into small pieces
½ cup boiling water
2 tablespoons lemon juice
1 thick slice onion, cut in half
1 envelope plain gelatin
1 15½-ounce can salmon, drained and flaked
½ cup mayonnaise
1 tablespoon freshly snipped dill or 1 teaspoon dried dill
¼ teaspoon paprika
    Pinch of cayenne
1 cup heavy cream
¼ teaspoon salt, or to taste
¼ teaspoon freshly ground pepper
    Garnish: Pitted black olives, sliced capers, watercress, dill sprigs, cherry tomatoes, *Cucumber Dill Sauce* (*see* Chapter 2)

Salmon mousse

The Steps:

1. Lightly oil a 4-cup fish mold or ring mold.
2. In food processor or blender, place smoked salmon, boiling water, lemon juice, onion, and gelatin and process until smooth.
3. Add salmon, mayonnaise, dill, paprika, and cayenne; continue to process until smooth.
4. While machine is running, add cream, blending until smooth.
5. Taste for seasonings, adjust with salt and pepper, pour into prepared mold and chill for 6–8 hours or overnight.
6. Unmold and serve garnished with olives, capers, watercress, dill sprigs, cherry tomatoes and *Cucumber Dill Sauce*.

Accompaniments:

Dark pumpernickel bread with sweet butter and/or sesame seed crackers.

Variations:

On a warm summer night, this dish will serve as a main course with a tossed green salad, black pumpernickel bread, chilled white wine, and a bowl of summer fruits.

Double Salmon Mousse makes a great luncheon or brunch dish with baked eggs and French bread.

A more traditional Salmon Mousse can be prepared without the smoked salmon.

Make-It-Easy Tips:

√ A blender or food processor is essential for this recipe.
√ When adding liquid to blender while it is running, remember to keep a towel near the opening to catch splatters.
√ To unmold easily, dip mold in a sink filled with 3″ of warm water for a few seconds.

Gravlax
(Scandinavian Salmon Marinated in Dill)

SERVES: 8–10
Preparation time: 10 minutes
Marinating time: 3–4 days

Although the marinating time is long for this dish, the preparation time is short and the result is sensational and very low in calories. It's the Scandinavian version of Japanese *sushi*. The raw fish is "cured" with salt, sugar, and lots of fresh dill. You can't substitute dried dill weed in this recipe; the fresh is essential.

The Ingredients:
     2–2½ pounds salmon, filleted
        3 tablespoons sugar
     1½ tablespoons coarse salt (also called Kosher salt)
        1 teaspoon whole white peppercorns
        ½ teaspoon freshly ground white pepper
        4 large bunches fresh dill
          Garnish: Lemon wedges, dill sprigs, capers, *Mustard Dill Sauce* (see page 47), dark pumpernickel bread

The Steps:
   1. Lay salmon on sheet of waxed paper. Sprinkle with half the sugar, salt, peppercorns, and pepper; turn, and sprinkle the other side. Press down firmly on salmon to make sure seasonings permeate fish.
   2. In shallow, nonmetallic pan, spread out 2 bunches of fresh dill. Place salmon on top. Then arrange remaining 2 bunches of dill over salmon creating a sandwich effect.
   3. Cover well with foil or plastic wrap; place a weight on top (use a heavy pot lid, brick, canned foods or a combination of these) and refrigerate.
   4. Turn salmon twice a day (in the morning and at dinner time) for 3–4 days.
   5. When ready to serve, remove all dill and peppercorns. Lightly pat dry with paper towels. Thinly slice on the bias and serve garnished with lemon wedges, dill sprigs, capers, *Mustard Dill Sauce*, and dark pumpernickel bread.

Accompaniments:

Gravlax can be served as part of a smorgasbord of Scandinavian hors d'oeuvres or as part of an international array.

Variation:

Leftover gravlax makes a wonderful sandwich on dark pumpernickel or rye with *Mustard Dill Sauce*. (Gravlax will keep for 3–4 days after "curing".)

Make-It-Easy Tip:

√ The easiest weight to use on the gravlax is a cast-iron pot or pot lid filled with canned goods. My alternate method is to use an iron bacon press, which also works efficiently.

CHAPTER TWO

BASICS AND SAUCES

Creme Fraîche

Double Cream

Reduced-Calorie Sour Cream

Mustard Dill Sauce
  (Gravlaxas)

Hollandaise with Ease

Marinara Sauce

Pesto

Creamy Horseradish Sauce

Dill Watercress Sauce

Cucumber Dill Sauce

Low-Calorie Yogurt Dill
  Sauce

Cucumber Raita

Homemade Vanilla Extract

In this section you will find a group of basics, those sauces and flavorings that accompany many of the other recipes in the book. For example, the Pesto sauce is called for three or four times, and the Marinara can become a basic part of your cooking repertoire for a wide variety of dishes.

Crème Fraîche

YIELD: 2 cups
Preparation time: 5 minutes
Marinating time: 12–24 hours

Crème Fraîche is a French sour cream prepared here from buttermilk and cream. Because of its high butterfat content, it can be used in cooking since it will not curdle like sour cream. Its tartness makes it a wonderful topping for fruit desserts, cakes, or mousses.

The Ingredients:
  1 pint heavy cream
  2 tablespoons buttermilk

The Steps:
  1. Place cream in glass container or jar. Add buttermilk, stir lightly, and cover.
  2. Allow jar to stand at room temperature until thickened to the consistency of sour cream. (This can take anywhere from 12 to 24 hours, depending on the temperature of the room. The warmer the room, the faster it will turn to Crème Fraîche.)
  3. Crème Fraîche will continue to thicken as it chills. It will keep for about 10 days under refrigeration.

Double Cream

YIELD: 4 cups
Preparation time: 5 minutes
Marinating time: 12–24 hours

Double Cream is a thicker version of Crème Fraîche, similar to the clotted English Devonshire cream. It needs only 5 minutes of preparation and the same 12–24 hours to thicken at room temperature as Crème Fraîche. Chill it and use it in place of whipped cream as a topping for fresh fruit or as an unusual and fabulous accompaniment to chocolate cake.

The Ingredients:
  3 cups heavy cream
  1 cup buttermilk

The Steps:
  1. Combine cream and buttermilk in a glass jar. Stir, cover, and allow to sit at room temperature for 12–24 hours or until thickened to the consistency of sour cream. (The timing depends on the temperature of the room.)
  2. The Double Cream will continue to thicken as it chills. It will keep for about 10 days under refrigeration.

Reduced-Calorie Sour Cream

YIELD: 2¼ cups
Preparation time: 10 minutes

This puree can be used as a dip, flavored with chives, freshly chopped vegetables, curry, garlic, or whatever special flavors you like. Add a dollop to a cold, low-calorie soup, thicken a sauce with it, add it to a salad dressing, or use it in place of mayonnaise in egg, tuna, or chicken salad.

The Ingredients:
  1 pint cottage cheese or pot cheese
  ½ cup buttermilk

The Steps:
  1. Place cottage cheese in food processor or blender and puree until smooth.
  2. Add buttermilk gradually through the feed tube or top of the blender and process until thick. Desired thickness is obtained by varying the amount of buttermilk.
  3. Remove, and refrigerate in a covered container.

Mustard Dill Sauce (Gravlaxas)

YIELD: 1 cup
Preparation time: 10 minutes
Chilling time: 2–3 hours

Mustard Dill Sauce is the perfect accompaniment to *Gravlax (Salmon Marinated in Dill)* and can also be used with cold poached fish, smoked salmon, or even roast lamb. If possible, use fresh dill for a better flavor.

The Ingredients:
- ¼ cup dark mustard (spicy mustard, Dijon mustard, or dark-style mustard)
- 3 tablespoons dark brown sugar
- 2 tablespoons white vinegar
- 1 teaspoon dry mustard
- ⅓ cup vegetable oil
- 2–3 tablespoons freshly snipped dill (or 2–3 teaspoons dried dill)

The Steps:
1. In food processor or blender, mix the dark mustard, brown sugar, vinegar, and dry mustard and process for a few seconds.
2. While machine is running, pour oil into container jar in steady stream until sauce is thick and smooth.
3. Pour sauce into small bowl. Add dill, and chill for 2–3 hours or until ready to use.

Make-It-Easy Tips:
√ The sauce will keep for several weeks under refrigeration, so make double the amount and keep for use with fish or lamb dishes.
√ Chop large bunches of fresh dill when it's most plentiful in the spring and summer months and freeze it in small containers for use year 'round.
√ The sauce can be prepared by hand with a wire whisk, but the food processor or blender makes the preparation Make-It-Easy style.

Hollandaise with Ease

SERVES: 3–4
Preparation time: 10 minutes

The easiest way to prepare Hollandaise Sauce is in a blender or food processor. It takes just a few minutes to process and, once prepared, can be reheated in a double boiler or kept warm in a Thermos jar that has just been rinsed with hot water.

The Ingredients:
4 ounces (1 stick) unsalted butter
3 large egg yolks
2 tablespoons fresh lemon juice
½ teaspoon salt
¼ teaspoon freshly ground white pepper or pinch of cayenne pepper

The Steps:
1. Melt butter in small saucepan until bubbling hot.
2. Place egg yolks, lemon juice, salt, and pepper in blender jar or food processor bowl. Cover and mix for a few seconds until just combined.
3. Remove top and, with machine running, pour hot butter into machine in slow, steady stream.
4. When butter is incorporated, serve the sauce immediately or keep warm in double boiler. Do not let sauce boil or it will curdle and separate.

Variations:
Hollandaise Sauce can be served with asparagus, broccoli, cauliflower, leeks, or with artichokes as a dipping sauce.

Add 2 tablespoons Dijon mustard with the egg yolks for a *Sauce Moutarde*, or add 1 tablespoon freshly snipped dill or other herbs for heightened flavor.

Make-It-Easy Tips:
√ Eggs separate more easily when cold.
√ It is best to cook with eggs (whole or separated) when they are at room temperature.

Leftover egg whites can be frozen in small containers. Be sure to mark number of eggs and date they were put in container and frozen.

Although blender or food processor hollandaise is almost fool-proof, occasionally you may end up with a thin, watery liquid instead of thick hollandaise. This can happen if the container or bowl was not properly dried, or the butter was poured in too rapidly. To rectify this disaster, pour the liquid into a dry bowl. Then wash and thoroughly dry the processor bowl or blender container. Place an additional egg yolk in the container and, while the machine is running, pour the hollandaise mixture into the container in a slow, steady stream. Process until thickened.

Marinara Sauce

YIELD: 3–4 cups
Preparation time: 20–25 minutes
Cooking time: 40 minutes

Use Marinara Sauce over cooked pasta, adding sausages, meatballs, mushrooms, green peppers, or whatever desired. It can also be used as the base for *Quick and Easy Cioppino,* an Italian shellfish stew (*see* Chapter 5). Prepare the sauce in large batches and freeze in small containers for future use.

The Ingredients:
  ¼ cup olive oil
  2 cups finely chopped onion
  2 cloves garlic, finely chopped
  1 large carrot, grated or chopped
  4 cups canned Italian plum tomatoes, coarsely chopped
  1 tablespoon freshly chopped parsley
  1 teaspoon dried oregano, crumbled
  1 teaspoon dried basil, crumbled
  ½ teaspoon salt, or to taste
  ½ teaspoon freshly ground pepper, or to taste

The Steps:

1. Heat oil in a large skillet and sauté the onion, garlic, and carrot over medium heat until soft and golden brown.
2. Add tomatoes, parsley, oregano, basil, salt, and pepper. Partially cover, reduce heat, and simmer 10 minutes.
3. Adjust seasoning with salt and pepper to taste, and continue to cook, partially covered, for 30 minutes.

Make-It-Easy Tip:

√ It is best to freeze the Marinara Sauce in small (8-ounce), durable plastic containers so that you can defrost what you need without having to thaw the whole recipe.

Pesto

YIELD: 1 cup
Preparation time: 15–20 minutes

Pesto is a great Make-It-Easy aid. Once made, it can be frozen and later defrosted and used in a variety of dishes. Pesto is very rich so only 2–3 tablespoons are necessary for each recipe. It makes a wonderful pasta topping, a tangy addition to soups, a flavor booster for sautéed mushrooms, or a sauce for seafood. Once you've tasted Pesto, you'll want to try it on everything!

The Ingredients:

1 cup tightly packed fresh basil leaves (stems removed), washed and dried on paper towels. (Only *fresh* basil will do.)
½ cup olive oil
3 tablespoons freshly grated Parmesan cheese (or use a combination of Parmesan and Romano or use Pecorino cheese)
2 tablespoons pine nuts (*pignoli*) or chopped walnuts
3 small cloves garlic, peeled
1 tablespoon freshly chopped parsley
½ teaspoon salt, or to taste
¼ teaspoon freshly ground white pepper

The Steps:

1. In the bowl of food processor or in blender container, place all ingredients; process in a pulsating motion, turning machine on and off until well blended and smooth.
2. Place in container with a ¼″ layer of olive oil covering the Pesto, cover, and refrigerate or freeze until ready to use.
3. When ready to use, discard the layer of oil, measure out the Pesto, and proceed with the recipe. (Put another ¼″ layer of oil on the remaining Pesto before storing.)

Make-It-Easy Tips:

√ Grate the cheese and parsley in the food processor or blender before proceeding, and have all the ingredients ready to use.

√ Prepare Pesto in large batches in summer months when fresh basil is plentiful; double or triple the recipe, and freeze for use year 'round.

√ Remember to keep a ¼″ layer of oil on top of stored Pesto at all times. Pesto can be stored for several months in the refrigerator or in the freezer indefinitely. (If freezing, omit the cheese and add later, which will extend the freezer life of the Pesto.)

Creamy Horseradish Sauce

YIELD: 2 cups
Preparation time: 5–10 minutes
Chilling time: 2 hours

Creamy Horseradish Sauce accompanies roast beef, pot roast, vegetables, or smoked fish.

The Ingredients:

¼ cup prepared white horseradish, drained and squeezed dry
1 tablespoon sugar
2 teaspoons Dijon mustard
1 teaspoon white vinegar (or lemon juice)
½ teaspoon salt
Pinch paprika
1 cup heavy cream, whipped

The Steps:

1. Mix the horseradish, sugar, mustard, vinegar, salt, and paprika together until smooth.
2. Gently fold whipped cream into horseradish mixture and chill for 2 hours.

Make-It-Easy Tips:

√ Prepare the day you plan to serve sauce since whipped cream does not keep well.

√ Chill both bowl and beaters to prevent cream from turning, and to produce a lighter and fluffier whipped cream.

Dill Watercress Sauce

YIELD: 2¾ cups
Preparation time: 15 minutes
Chilling time: 2–3 hours

Dill Watercress Sauce accompanies cold poached fish like salmon or halibut, or cold seafood. It can be used by itself as a dip for vegetable crudités.

The Ingredients:

¾ cup chopped watercress
¼ cup freshly snipped dill (or 2–3 teaspoons dried dill to taste)
2 tablespoons freshly chopped parsley
½ teaspoon freshly minced garlic
1 cup mayonnaise
1 cup sour cream
2½ tablespoons fresh lemon juice
½ teaspoon salt, or to taste
¼ teaspoon freshly ground white pepper, or to taste

The Steps:

1. In a food processor or blender, chop watercress, dill, parsley, and garlic, pulsating until just chopped but not pureed.

2. In a bowl, combine chopped ingredients with mayonnaise, sour cream, lemon juice, salt and pepper to taste, and stir until smooth.
3. Chill 2–3 hours.
4. Serve the sauce, chilled, with cold fish, seafood, or as a dip.

Make-It-Easy Tips:
√ The sauce may be prepared 2–3 days in advance. It will keep in the refrigerator for 4–5 days.
√ Leftover watercress wrapped in a towel and placed in a plastic bag will keep fresh for 4–5 days.

Cucumber Dill Sauce

YIELD: 2½–3 cups
Preparation time: 10 minutes
Chilling time: 2 hours

Serve with *Salmon Mousse* or poached fish.

The Ingredients:
1 cup mayonnaise
1 cup sour cream
2 tablespoons freshly snipped dill or 1½ teaspoons dried dill
2 tablespoons lemon juice
½ teaspoon salt, or to taste
Freshly ground white pepper
1 large (or 2 small) cucumbers, peeled, seeded, and chopped

The Steps:
1. In a bowl, combine mayonnaise, sour cream, dill, lemon juice, salt, and pepper until smooth.
2. Fold in chopped cucumber and chill for 2 hours or until ready to use. (Sauce will keep for 2–3 weeks in the refrigerator.)

Make-It-Easy Tips:
√ To seed a cucumber, cut it in half and core with a zucchini corer or with a serrated grapefruit spoon.

√ It is easy to chop cucumbers in a food processor, but remember to pulsate until just chopped, *not* pureed.

√ The European hothouse hydroponic cucumber, which is "burpless" and almost seedless, is especially easy to use since it needs no peeling and little seeding.

Low-Calorie Yogurt Dill Sauce

YIELD: 1¾ cups
Preparation time: 5–10 minutes

Use this dill sauce as a salad dressing, low-calorie dip for vegetable crudités, or as a side sauce for low-calorie fish dishes.

The Ingredients:
    2 scallions (green and white parts included)
    1 tablespoon freshly snipped dill (or 1 teaspoon dried dill)
    1 teaspoon Dijon mustard
    ½ teaspoon capers, drained (optional)
    ½ teaspoon lemon juice
    ½ teaspoon salt, or to taste
    ¼ teaspoon freshly ground pepper
    1¼ cups plain low-fat yogurt

The Steps:
    1. In food processor, blender, or by hand chop scallions.
    2. Add remaining ingredients, and blend until smooth.
    3. Chill until ready to use.

Make-It-Easy Tip:
    √ The sauce can be prepared 2–3 days in advance and will keep for 4–5 days in the refrigerator.

Cucumber Raita

YIELD: 3–4 cups
Preparation time: 15 minutes
Marinating time: ½ hour

Raita is a refreshing accompaniment for strong Indian curries. It can be served with any spicy dish as a cooling side sauce. Although the preparation time may seem long, once the cucumbers have been salted to release excess moisture, you can focus your attention on the rest of the meal.

The Ingredients:
2 large cucumbers, peeled, seeded, and grated (or 1 European hothouse hydroponic cucumber, grated)
1 teaspoon salt
1 pint plain yogurt
2 tablespoons minced scallions (green and white included)
¼ teaspoon sugar
¼ teaspoon cumin powder
¼ teaspoon freshly ground white pepper
⅛ teaspoon paprika
Garnish: Freshly chopped coriander or parsley

The Steps:
1. Place cucumber in colander, sprinkle with salt, and allow to stand for 30 minutes; press dry with paper towels.
2. In a bowl, combine yogurt, scallions, sugar, cumin, freshly ground white pepper, and paprika and stir well.
3. Fold in the cucumber; mix well and chill.
4. When ready to serve, taste, and adjust seasoning if necessary. Garnish with chopped coriander or parsley.

Make-It-Easy Tip:
√ When selecting cucumbers, pick unwaxed, slender, firm ones with a bright green color. Fat cucumbers are often soft and mushy on the inside.

Homemade Vanilla Extract

YIELD: 1 pint
Preparation time: 5 minutes

This is especially useful during the Christmas holidays, when pungent vanilla imparts a special flavor to all those holiday baked goodies. It is prepared by mixing brandy with vanilla beans, and letting the mixture marinate for several weeks. This vanilla extract will keep for years, getting just a little bit better each year!

The Ingredients:
   2 vanilla beans
   1 pint brandy

The Steps:
   1. Slice vanilla beans down the center so that seeds are exposed, and drop into the bottle of brandy. Shake, cover, and allow to marinate for several weeks, shaking every few days. (It may be necessary to pour off a small amount of brandy to accommodate the vanilla beans.)
   2. Use this homemade vanilla extract whenever vanilla extract is called for in a recipe.

CHAPTER THREE

EGGS AND CHEESE

Frittata
Make-It-Easy Cheese Soufflé
Dutch Babies
Spinach Quiche
Vegetable Cheese Pie

Omelets and baked-egg dishes need not be relegated to the breakfast, brunch, or lunch hour. They make inexpensive and interesting Make-It-Easy suppers when accompanied by a salad and toasted herb bread.

Frittata

SERVES: 4–6
Preparation time: 20–25 minutes
Cooking time: 16–18 minutes

A *frittata* is an Italian vegetable omelet that can be served hot for lunch, brunch, or as a light supper, or served cold the next day as an hors d'oeuvre or snack.

The Ingredients:
 2 tablespoons unsalted butter
 2 tablespoons olive oil
 ½ pound mushrooms, thinly sliced
 3 shallots or 2 scallions (green and white included), minced
 6 eggs
 2 tablespoons half-and-half
 ½ teaspoon salt, or to taste
 ½ teaspoon freshly ground pepper, or to taste
 ¼ cup freshly grated Parmesan cheese
 1 tablespoon freshly chopped parsley
 ¼ teaspoon dried oregano, crumbled
 ¼ teaspoon dried basil, crumbled
 3 tablespoons grated Parmesan cheese

The Steps:
1. Preheat broiler.
2. Heat butter and oil together in a 10" oven-proof skillet; sauté the mushrooms and shallots over medium-low heat until soft and lightly golden, 5–10 minutes.
3. In a bowl, beat eggs with half-and-half, salt, and pepper until well mixed. Add ¼ cup cheese, parsley, oregano, and basil and continue to beat until smooth.
4. Pour egg mixture into skillet, stir once, and then cook without

stirring until the bottom is lightly browned and the eggs are
beginning to set; tip skillet to allow eggs to run to the edges.
5. Sprinkle with remaining 3 tablespoons cheese and place under
broiler, 5″–6″ from flame for 3–4 minutes to brown top.
6. Serve hot, sliced in wedges, or cold as an hors d'oeuvre.

Accompaniments:

Herbed Pita Toast, Spinach Salad with Creamy Dressing.

Variations:

Additional vegetables can be added or substituted to taste: One
9-ounce package frozen artichokes, cooked and drained;
chopped black or green olives; ½ cup frozen chopped spinach,
thawed and squeezed dry; sautéed green pepper strips; sautéed
minced garlic; diced cooked potatoes; shredded cheese; diced
leftover ham, turkey, shrimp, or crabmeat, or even crisp bacon.
Be creative and invent your own.

The Frittata may be baked with a topping of tomato sauce or, for
a Mexican version, topped with green chile salsa, sprinkled
with cheese, and broiled until browned.

Make-It-Easy Cheese Soufflé

SERVES: 6–8
Preparation time: 15 minutes
Cooking time: 50 minutes–1 hour

The advantage of this easy dish is that it is assembled a day ahead. All
that's needed is to pop it into the oven for a perfect lunch, brunch
dish, or light supper.

The Ingredients:

1 tablespoon unsalted butter for greasing
8 slices bread, crusts removed, and cut into cubes (Pepperidge
Farm or similar thin-firm bread)
¾ pound Swiss cheese, cubed (or ½ pound Cheddar cheese and
¼ pound Swiss cheese)

¼ cup crumbled bacon bits or ½ cup cooked diced ham (optional)
3 tablespoons unsalted butter, melted
8 large eggs
2 cups whole or low-fat milk
1 teaspoon Dijon mustard
½ teaspoon Worcestershire sauce
½ teaspoon paprika
½ teaspoon salt
¼ teaspoon freshly ground white pepper
 Pinch cayenne pepper

The Steps:

1. Butter a deep, 10″ round baking dish or a 10″ x 6″ x 2″ rectangular baking dish or other dish of similar size.
2. Beginning with the bread, layer the bread and cheese cubes in the prepared dish until used up. If bacon or ham are to be added, layer them with the cheese.
3. Pour melted butter over layered bread and cheese.
4. Whisk the eggs with the milk. Add mustard, Worcestershire, and seasonings and whisk until combined. Pour over bread and cheese, cover, and refrigerate overnight.
5. The next day, preheat the oven to 350° and bake for 50 minutes to 1 hour or until golden brown and bubbly.
6. Serve immediately, sliced into squares or wedges.

Accompaniment:

Spinach Salad.

Variations:

Cheddar, Monterey Jack, or other cheeses can be substituted for Swiss.

Whole wheat or other whole grain bread, sourdough, or even French bread can be substituted for white bread.

Lightly sautéed mushrooms, onions, and green peppers can be added to the layers in Step 2.

For a spectacular first course, the soufflé can be assembled in 6–8 small au gratin dishes and served individually. The cooking time should be changed to 35–40 minutes for individual small dishes.

Make-It-Easy Tip:
√ The easiest way to grate cheese is in a food processor, but, if grating by hand, make sure the cheese is well chilled and rub a small amount of oil on the grater to prevent sticking.

Dutch Babies

SERVES: 3–4
Preparation time: 15 minutes
Cooking time: 15–20 minutes

"Dutch Babies" is the unusual name given to this oversized puffy pancake, which can be topped with the traditional Hot Swedish Lingonberries or other preserves, or used as a base for sausages, bacon, or other breakfast and brunch meats.

The Ingredients:
3 tablespoons unsalted butter
3 eggs, at room temperature
½ cup sifted all-purpose flour
½ teaspoon salt
½ cup whole milk, at room temperature
Garnish: 2 tablespoons unsalted butter, melted; 1 tablespoon lemon juice; confectioners' sugar

The Steps:
1. Preheat oven to 450°. Butter bottom and sides of a cold, heavy, 10″ skillet with 3 tablespoons butter.
2. In a food processor, blender, or with an electric mixer, beat eggs.
3. Gradually add flour and salt, and continue to beat.
4. Add milk, and beat until smooth.
5. Pour batter into skillet and bake for 15–20 minutes or until golden brown. (The pancake will be uneven and puffy.)
6. Cut into serving pieces, drizzle with melted butter, lemon juice, and a sprinkling of confectioners' sugar, and serve immediately.

Variations:

> For sweet variations, top with berries, jelly, jam, honey, nuts, cinnamon, or raisins
>
> For non-sweet variations, serve with butter, sausages, bacon, ham, grated cheese, chilies, or pimientos

Spinach Quiche

YIELD: 2 quiches; 6 servings in each quiche
Preparation time: 15–20 minutes
Cooking time: 30–35 minutes

Quiche is a perfect luncheon, brunch, or supper dish, or it can be cut in thin slivers to use as an hors d'oeuvre.

The Ingredients:

- 2 tablespoons unsalted butter
- ¼ cup chopped onion
- 2 10-ounce packages frozen chopped spinach, thawed and squeezed dry
- ½ teaspoon salt, or to taste
- ¼ teaspoon freshly ground white pepper
  Fat pinch nutmeg
- 4 eggs
- 1 cup half-and-half
- 1 cup heavy cream
- ½ cup grated Swiss or Monterey Jack cheese
- 2 frozen 9″ pie shells, thawed

The Steps:

1. Melt butter in a large skillet. Sauté onions over medium heat until soft, about 5 minutes.
2. Add spinach and continue to cook, stirring often, until no liquid is left in the skillet.
3. Add the salt, pepper, and nutmeg; stir well and allow to cool slightly, about 5 minutes.
4. Preheat oven to 375°.
5. Beat eggs and creams together and gradually add to spinach

mixture, stirring until smooth; add the cheese and stir to combine.
6. Pour mixture into pie shells. Place pie shells on a cookie sheet
   and bake for 30–35 minutes or until inserted knife comes out
   clean.
7. Serve the quiche hot or at room temperature.

Accompaniments:
Cold Cucumber-Avocado Soup and sliced tomatoes.

Variations:
Use tiny pie shells for individual quiches and bake 25–30 minutes.
Crisp-fried bacon bits, sautéed mushrooms, or chopped tomatoes
can be added for variety.

Make-It-Easy Tips:
√ Spinach Quiche can be frozen once cooked and reheated right
  from the freezer in a 325° oven for 30 minutes or until hot.
√ Check metal tin holding frozen pie shell to see if there are any
  tiny holes in the bottom. (This happens occasionally.) If that is
  the case, place quiches on a foil-lined cookie sheet.

Vegetable Cheese Pie

SERVES: 6–8
Preparation time: 20 minutes
Cooking time: 40 minutes

Vegetable Cheese Pie is a great way to use up leftover cooked vegetables. Combine them with cheese and create an inexpensive vegetarian
dinner, lunch, or brunch dish. Choose vegetables with an eye to color
as well as taste.

The Ingredients:
1 9″ deep-dish frozen pie crust
3–3½ cups cooked vegetables (carrots, corn, broccoli, green
beans, zucchini, peas, etc.)

1½ cups grated Cheddar cheese
6 cherry tomatoes, halved
1 medium onion, finely chopped
1 clove garlic, finely minced
¼ teaspoon salt, or to taste
¼ teaspoon freshly ground pepper, or to taste
¼ cup freshly grated Parmesan cheese
1 tablespoon unsalted butter, diced into bits

The Steps:
1. Preheat oven to 400°.
2. Prick pie crust 3 or 4 times with a fork and bake for 10 minutes.
3. Remove from oven and reduce heat to 350°.
4. Mix cooked vegetables with Cheddar cheese, cherry tomatoes, onion, garlic, salt, and pepper and place in crust.
5. Sprinkle with Parmesan cheese, dot with butter, and bake for 30 minutes or until hot and lightly golden.
6. Serve pie hot, cut into wedges.

Accompaniment:
Tossed Salad with Red Onions.

Variations:
Swiss Gruyère cheese can be substituted for Cheddar, or use half Swiss, half Monterey Jack cheese.
Thawed frozen vegetables can be added if desired.

Make-It-Easy Tips:
√ Cut cherry tomatoes easily with a serrated knife.
√ For a more attractive presentation place the partially thawed pie crust in a glass or ceramic pie plate and proceed with recipe.

CHAPTER FOUR

SOUPS

Beef Barley Soup

Split Pea Soup

Quick and Easy Vegetable
  Beef Soup

Easy French Onion Soup

Hot Avgolemono Soup

Hot Oriental Mushroom Soup

Stracciatella con Spinaci

Leftover Turkey Soup

Cold Cucumber-Avocado
  Soup

Cucumber Yogurt Soup

Chilled Dilled Zucchini Soup

Cold Curried Pea Soup

Spanish Gazpacho

Leftover Salad Soup

HOT SOUPS

On cold nights, hot soup is the perfect way to start, and sometimes even complete, a meal. A rich soup such as beef barley or split pea served piping hot with bread on the side can be filling enough for dinner. Prepare the soups in double batches, freeze in family-size containers, and dinner can be ready in a matter of minutes.

When using canned stock, make sure to taste before adding salt since most are high in salt. And, if you want to make canned stock richer, try boiling it with some inexpensive chicken parts like backs and necks, a cut-up onion, a peeled and cut-up carrot, a few sprigs of parsley, and several peppercorns. Strain and use the stock for soups or stews.

Garnishing hot soups, even simple and easy ones, is important even if it's just some toasted almonds, grated cheese, strips of pimiento, sliced mushrooms, chopped green onions, thin-sliced lemons, minced eggs, or the traditional standby, chopped parsley.

Beef Barley Soup

SERVES: 8–10
Preparation time: 20–25 minutes
Cooking time: 2 hours

Beef Barley Soup is so filling it will make a complete dinner when served in deep soup plates with bread and salad as accompaniments.

The Ingredients:

4 pounds beef short ribs or flanken
4 medium onions, coarsely chopped
3 large carrots, sliced
2 10½-ounce cans onion soup plus 2 cans of water
2 10½-ounce cans beef bouillon plus 1 can water
1 10¾-ounce can chicken broth plus 1 can water
1 cup pearl barley
1 bay leaf
½ teaspoon minced garlic
½ teaspoon salt, or to taste
¼ teaspoon freshly ground pepper

The Steps:
1. Place all ingredients in deep soup pot; bring to a boil, skim off accumulated scum from the surface with a large spoon; cover, reduce heat, and simmer slowly for 2 hours or until meat is very tender.
2. Remove bay leaf and discard, taste for seasoning, adjust with salt and pepper if necessary, and serve hot, bones and all, garnished with freshly chopped parsley.

Accompaniments:
  Light Beer Bread or hot crusty French bread.

Variation:
  If you don't want the bones in the soup, remove from soup and allow to cool; pull off meat and shred into the soup; discard bones and fat.

Make-It-Easy Tips:
  √ Double the recipe and freeze the soup in family-size containers for quick and easy dinners.
  √ If possible, chill the soup overnight so that the fat will congeal at the top. It can be removed easily the next day.

Split Pea Soup

SERVES: 8–10
Preparation time: 25 minutes
Cooking time: 4 hours

Although the cooking time is long, the ingredients for split pea soup just get tossed in, covered, and cooked until ready. Prepare in large batches and freeze for great winter suppers.

The Ingredients:
  6 cups chicken broth
  2 cups water
  Ham bone, with some meat left on

  1 slice thick bacon, chopped
  2 stalks celery, coarsely chopped
  2 carrots, peeled and coarsely chopped
  2 onions, coarsely chopped
  1 pound split peas
  1 bay leaf
  ½ teaspoon salt, or to taste
  ½ teaspoon freshly ground pepper, or to taste
  ⅛ teaspoon oregano, crumbled
  2 tablespoons freshly chopped parsley
  2 teaspoons freshly chopped chives or scallion stalks
  1 cup diced ham or ½ pound Canadian bacon, cubed (optional)

The Steps:
  1. In a large kettle, combine broth, water, ham bone, bacon, celery, carrots, onions, peas, bay leaf, salt, and pepper.
  2. Bring to a boil, skim off accumulated scum forming on the top, cover, and simmer 3–4 hours.
  3. Remove bone, skim fat off soup, detach meat shreds and return to soup.
  4. Add oregano, parsley, chives, and extra ham or Canadian bacon if desired, and simmer covered over very low heat 1 hour longer.
  5. Remove bay leaf and discard; taste, and adjust seasoning as necessary; serve as a soup course or even as a whole supper.

Accompaniments:
Sliced knockwurst or hot dogs can be added in the last half hour to create a traditional Split Pea Supper. Serve with herbed crusty French or Italian bread.

Variations:
Ham hocks are a great substitute if you don't happen to have a ham bone on hand. Have the butcher crack one into 3 pieces. Ham hocks will create a layer of scum on the top of the soup as it begins to boil. Skim off the layer and discard.

And . . . if you don't wish to use ham and bacon, use the carcass of a smoked turkey as the basis of the soup.

Substitute dried lentils for the split peas for a hot lentil soup.

Make-It-Easy Tips:
√ Kitchen shears are handy for chopping bacon. Line up the slices and cut across. Turn and cut the other way.

√ If bones are still too hot to shred meat in Step 3, allow to cool or use thick rubber gloves to protect hands.

√ Split Pea Soup is best prepared a day or two in advance to allow the flavors to mellow.

Quick and Easy Vegetable Beef Soup

SERVES: 8–10
Preparation time: 20 minutes
Cooking time: 2½ hours

This soup is more than a first course. It is a full, one-pot dinner for a family, with meat, vegetables, and starch all included. I recommend preparing the soup a day ahead to allow the fat to congeal after refrigeration for easy removal the next day.

The Ingredients:
3½ pounds beef flanken
1 28-ounce can crushed tomatoes packed in puree
2 10½-ounce cans undiluted beef bouillon
1½ cups water
2 large carrots, peeled and roughly chopped
2 stalks celery, roughly chopped
1 large onion, roughly chopped
2 new potatoes, peeled and cut into chunks
Salt and freshly ground pepper to taste
Garnish: *Creamy Horseradish Sauce* (*see* Chapter 2) or grated horseradish

The Steps:
1. Place beef in a large soup pot or deep casserole and cover with tomatoes, bouillon, and water. Bring to a boil, cover and simmer over low heat for 1–1½ hours or until meat is tender.
2. Add carrots, celery, and onion, cover again, and continue to cook over very low heat for 30 minutes.

3. Add potatoes, cover and cook for only 12–20 minutes or until potatoes are just tender but not overcooked. (Prepare soup a day in advance to this point, if possible.)
4. Remove excess grease from top and reheat until just boiling.
5. Taste, and adjust seasoning with salt and freshly ground pepper. If too thick, add additional bouillon or water.
6. Serve soup first, reserving meat. Then follow with meat as a main course, garnished with *Creamy Horseradish Sauce* (*see* Chapter 2) or grated white horseradish.

Accompaniment:

Custardy Corn Bread.

Variations:

For a slightly sweetened flavor, add 2–3 tablespoons ketchup in Step 2.

Flanken is short ribs cut from the ends of the rib roast and the plate. Larger short ribs can be substituted but must be cooked slightly longer.

Add one 10-ounce package frozen mixed vegetables for a chunkier-style soup.

Make-It-Easy Tips:

√ To degrease soups or stews quickly: Skim the surface, and then wrap a few ice cubes in heavy-weight paper towels and run them over the top of the soup. Remove any excess with a wet lettuce leaf.

√ If potatoes are cut in advance, place in a bowl of acidulated water (water with 2 teaspoons lemon juice) to keep from discoloring.

Easy French Onion Soup

SERVES: 8
Preparation time: 20 minutes
Cooking time: 20 minutes for the bread
40 minutes for the soup

The preparation of a traditional French onion soup can be a long and complicated procedure involving long-simmering stocks, homemade breads, and several hand-chopped onions. With a few Make-It-Easy Tips, the help of a food processor to do the chopping, and some canned broth, I've worked out a recipe for an easy French onion soup that may not be totally traditional but is always a success.

The Ingredients:

    1 small French bread, cut into 1" thick slices
    4 tablespoons (½ stick) unsalted butter
    6 cups thinly sliced onions (3–4 large onions)
    1 cup red wine
    6 cups strong undiluted beef broth
    ½ teaspoon salt, or to taste
    ½ teaspoon freshly ground pepper, or to taste
    2½ cups grated Swiss Gruyère cheese

The Steps:

1. Toast bread slices in preheated 350° oven for 20–25 minutes or until golden. (Bread slices can be done a few days in advance and kept in an airtight container or bag until ready to use.)
2. Melt butter in large saucepan; add onions and sauté over medium-low heat until soft and golden, about 15 minutes.
3. Add wine and allow to boil for a minute. Then add broth and bring to a boil again. Cover, reduce heat, and simmer slowly for 15–20 minutes.
4. Preheat oven to 450°.
5. Adjust seasonings in soup with salt and pepper to taste. Place a slice of toasted bread in the bottom of each of 8 onion soup crocks. Pour soup over bread and top with a generous sprinkling of cheese.
6. Place crocks in oven until cheese is melted and bubbly brown, about 5 minutes, and serve immediately.

Variations:

Serve the soup as a complete light supper with a salad and Parmesan melba toast on the side.

For a sweeter flavor, Marsala or port wine can be substituted for red wine.

Sourdough or Italian bread can be substituted for the French bread.

Onion goggles

Make-It-Easy Tips:
√ When chopping or slicing onions, use ski goggles or those funny new onion goggles to ward off tears. As an alternative, freeze onions half an hour before slicing and the funes will not be as strong.

√ If tops don't brown when soup is in oven, run under a hot broiler for 2 minutes, watching carefully.

√ The soup can be cooked ahead through Step 4 and then refrigerated or frozen. When ready to use, reheat and proceed with the recipe.

Hot Avgolemono Soup

SERVES: **4**
Preparation time: 10–15 minutes
Cooking time: 20 minutes

Avgolemono is a Greek egg-and-lemon sauce used here as the base for a soup that is flavorful and low in calories. If the egg yolks are at room temperature and the hot liquid is added very gradually there is no danger of curdling.

The Ingredients:
   6 cups strong chicken broth, skimmed of fat
  ¼ cup raw rice
   2 egg yolks, lightly beaten, at room temperature
   2 tablespoons lemon juice
   1 teaspoon arrowroot (or cornstarch)
     Pinch cayenne
  ¼ teaspoon freshly ground white pepper
     Garnish: Freshly chopped parsley, thin lemon slices

The Steps:

1. In saucepan, bring broth to boil. Add rice and cook uncovered until rice is tender, about 15 minutes.
2. Place egg yolks in a bowl and whisk in lemon juice, arrowroot, and cayenne pepper.
3. Add a few drops of hot broth to egg mixture and whisk to combine. Continue to add a few drops until egg mixture can be stirred into the broth mixture without curdling.
4. Once the egg mixture is added to the broth, stir over very low heat until slightly thickened. (Do not allow the soup to boil.)
5. Season with freshly ground pepper and serve the soup hot with a generous sprinkling of freshly chopped parsley and thin slices of lemon.

Accompaniment:

Plain melba toast crackers.

Make-It-Easy Tips:

√ The soup can be kept warm in the top of a double boiler for 1–2 hours prior to serving.
√ Leftover egg whites can be frozen in ice-cube trays. After freezing, remove from the trays and store in a sealed plastic bag in the freezer.
√ The starch in the arrowroot helps prevent curdling.

Hot Oriental Mushroom Soup

SERVES: 4–6
Preparation time: 10 minutes
Cooking time: 20 minutes

This clear soup can be served as the beginning of a low-calorie dinner.

The Ingredients:

6 large Chinese or Japanese dried mushrooms, soaked in very hot water to cover for ½ hour
4 cups strong chicken broth
¼ cup Madeira (Marsala or other slightly sweet wine can be used)
Garnish: Chopped scallion stalks

The Steps:

1. When mushrooms are soft, squeeze dry of liquid with your hands. Cut away and discard hard stem portion and slice into julienne strips. (Discard the soaking liquid as well.)
2. Bring broth to a boil, add mushrooms and wine, reduce heat, cover and simmer for 20 minutes.
3. Sprinkle with chopped scallion stalks and serve hot.

Variations:

Soup can be thickened with 1 tablespoon cornstarch, which has been completely dissolved in 2 tablespoons cold water.

An oriental egg-drop soup can be created by bringing the thickened soup to a rolling boil and, while stirring the soup with a fork with one hand, gradually pouring 2 beaten eggs into the boiling soup in a steady stream with the other hand, scrambling with the fork.

Make-It-Easy Tip:

√ Soup can be prepared in advance through Step 2 and reheated just before serving.

Stracciatella con Spinaci

SERVES: 4
Preparation time: 10 minutes
Cooking time: 5–10 minutes

Stracciatella is the Italian version of egg-drop soup, here with spinach added for color and flavor. This clear soup is low in calories.

The Ingredients:

3 cups chicken broth
¼ cup finely chopped spinach leaves or ¼ cup frozen chopped spinach, thawed and squeezed dry
½ teaspoon grated lemon peel
⅛ teaspoon ground nutmeg
¼ teaspoon salt, or to taste

¼ teaspoon freshly ground white pepper, or to taste
2 eggs, lightly beaten
2–3 tablespoons freshly grated Parmesan cheese

The Steps:

1. Bring chicken broth to a boil. Add spinach and cook, stirring, over medium heat for a minute or two.
2. Add lemon peel and nutmeg; stir to combine.
3. Add salt and pepper to taste. (The broth may be heavily salted so you may not need to add salt at all.)
4. While soup is at a rolling boil (be careful to watch that it does not boil over) and, while stirring the soup with a fork with one hand, gradually pour eggs into soup in a stream with the other hand, scrambling with the fork.
5. Quickly stir in cheese and serve immediately with extra cheese on the side.

Accompaniment:

Crusty French bread.

Variations:

Coils of very thin pasta can be cooked in the stock until *al dente*.
For a chinese egg-drop soup variation: Boil the broth with a slice of fresh ginger (if available) and a scallion for 10 minutes. Add 1–2 teaspoons soy sauce in place of the lemon peel and nutmeg and continue with the recipe omitting the Parmesan cheese.

Leftover Turkey Soup

SERVES: 10–12
Preparation time: 25 minutes
Cooking time: 2–3 hours

This is the last gasp for the cooked turkey, when little is left but the bones. It's easy to prepare—just toss in the bones, vegetables, and seasonings, boil and serve.

The Ingredients:

1 turkey carcass, with some meat clinging to the bones
Leftover giblets (if available)

3 large carrots, coarsely chopped
2 large onions, coarsely chopped
2 stalks celery, coarsely chopped
1 parsnip, peeled, coarsely chopped (optional)
  Bouquet garni
Bouquet Garni:
4 sprigs parsley
2 celery leaves
2 sprigs fresh dill (optional)
6 peppercorns
¼ teaspoon leaf thyme
1 bay leaf
6 cups chicken broth
  Water
½ teaspoon salt, or to taste
½ teaspoon freshly ground pepper, or to taste
1 cup wide noodles or ½ cup raw rice

The Steps:

1. Break up carcass, if necessary, to fit in large soup kettle, adding any leftover giblets. Add carrots, onions, celery, and parsnip.
2. Place parsley, celery leaves, dill, peppercorns, thyme and bay leaf on a small square of cheesecloth, bring corners together and tie securely with string to make a Bouquet garni. Add to soup kettle.
3. Add chicken broth and enough water to cover ingredients, bring to a boil, cover, and cook slowly for 2½–3 hours.
4. Allow to cool slightly, remove carcass, strip meat from bones and return meat to kettle. Remove and discard Bouquet garni, squeezing juices into soup.
5. Adjust seasonings, bring to a boil, add noodles or rice and cook uncovered until rice or noodles are tender.
6. Serve soup hot, sprinkled with freshly chopped parsley.

Variations:

Any vegetables or herbs desired can be added to the soup to taste.
Soup can be served clear without the vegetables; or vegetables can be strained or pureed into the soup for a thick and nutritious treat.

Make-It-Easy Tips:

√ Making a Bouquet garni is easy, and you don't have to go fishing around in hot soup trying to find little pieces of celery or peppercorns. Just remove, squeeze out juice, and toss away. A metal tea ball infuser can also be used to hold the Bouquet garni.

√ Chicken broth is used rather than just water to give extra flavor to the soup; vary the amount of broth and water to taste.

COLD SOUPS

Cold soups are especially refreshing on hot summer days or nights. With the help of a food processor or blender, leftover cooked vegetables and salads can be easily transformed into cold soups. Add some chicken broth, seasoning, curry powder, or cream for a richer soup, if desired. Puree until smooth, and chill. Remember to taste soups after chilling because the cold will diminish the intensity of the seasoning.

Garnishes for cold soups are particularly important; take into account color, texture, and taste. Chopped watercress, chives, basil, and dill are all good toppings, especially when sprinkled over a dollop of regular or reduced-calorie sour cream or yogurt. Chopped vegetables such as radishes, tomatoes, cucumbers, and red and green peppers are also appealing garnishes as are thin slices of lemons, limes, oranges, apples and other fruits.

Cold creamy soups need not be fattening. Yogurt and buttermilk can be used for richness without adding too many extra calories. Even finicky eaters who refuse buttermilk or yogurt will like the light tang these dairy products add to cold soups.

Cold Cucumber-Avocado Soup

SERVES: 4–6
Preparation time: 10–15 minutes
Chilling time: 4–6 hours

A food processor, blender, or hand-held food mill are essential for this recipe.

The Ingredients:
    1 large cucumber, peeled, seeded, and cut into 2" pieces
    1 large ripe avocado, peeled
    2 scallions (green and white included), chopped
    1 cup chicken broth
    ¾ cup dairy sour cream
    2 tablespoons lemon juice
    ½ teaspoon salt, or to taste
    ¼ teaspoon freshly ground white pepper
    Garnish: A dollop of sour cream and chopped chives or scallion stalks

The Steps:
1. In food processor or blender, combine cucumber, avocado, and scallions until chopped, pulsating on and off.
2. Add broth, sour cream, and lemon juice, and continue to process until smooth.
3. Season with salt and pepper to taste, and chill 4–6 hours.
4. Taste for seasoning after chilling; serve soup in chilled soup bowls garnished with a dollop of sour cream and chopped chives or scallion stalks.

Variation:
European hothouse hydroponic cucumbers, which do not need peeling or seeding, can be substituted.

Make-It-Easy Tips:
√ Wrap cucumbers in plastic and they will keep fresh for about a week in the refrigerator.
√ This soup should not be prepared a day in advance because the avocado will discolor it.

Cucumber Yogurt Soup

SERVES: 4
Preparation time: 10 minutes
Chilling time: 4–6 hours or overnight

A food processor or blender is essential for Cucumber Yogurt Soup.

The Ingredients:
    2 large cucumbers, peeled, seeded, and roughly chopped or 1
      large European hothouse hydroponic cucumber, roughly
      chopped
    1 clove garlic, crushed
    1 cup plain low-fat or whole-milk yogurt
    ⅔ cup dairy sour cream
    1½ tablespoons freshly snipped dill, or 1½ teaspoons dried dill
      weed
    ½ teaspoon salt, or to taste
    ½ teaspoon freshly ground white pepper, or to taste
      Garnish: ¼ cup chopped walnuts

The Steps:
    1. Place cucumber and garlic in food processor or blender con-
       tainer and process briefly to combine.
    2. Add yogurt, sour cream, dill, salt and pepper to taste, and con-
       tinue to process until smooth.
    3. Chill for 4–6 hours or overnight.
    4. When ready to serve, taste, and adjust seasoning if necessary;
       serve the chilled soup garnished with chopped walnuts.

Variations:
    For a low-calorie variation, use 2 cups of yogurt instead of yogurt
    plus sour cream, and substitute chopped dill for the walnut
    garnish.

Make-It-Easy Tip:
    √ To seed cucumbers easily, peel, slice in half horizontally, and seed
    with a serrated grapefruit spoon.

Chilled Dilled Zucchini Soup

SERVES: 6
Preparation time: 15 minutes
Cooking time: 25 minutes
Chilling time: 6 hours or overnight

Chilled Dilled Zucchini Soup is a very rich soup and should be followed by a light entrée such as roast chicken, and tomatoes with *Laurie's Basic Vinaigrette* dressing.

The Ingredients:

        4 medium zucchini, cut in slices ½″ thick
        2 14¼-ounce cans chicken broth
        1 bunch scallions (green and white included), chopped
      ½ teaspoon salt, or to taste
      ½ teaspoon freshly ground white pepper
        2 8-ounce bars of cream cheese, softened
        1 cup dairy sour cream
    1½ tablespoons freshly snipped dill or 1½ teaspoons dried dill
        1 tablespoon freshly chopped chives or scallion stalks
           Salt and freshly ground pepper to taste
           Garnish: Dairy sour cream, freshly snipped dill, and paprika

The Steps:

1. Combine zucchini, chicken broth, scallions, salt, and pepper. Bring to a boil in large saucepan. Cover, reduce heat, and simmer slowly for 20–25 minutes or until zucchini is soft. Allow to cool for 10–15 minutes.
2. In a food processor or blender, combine cream cheese, sour cream, dill, and chives and process until smooth.
3. Add the slightly cooled zucchini mixture, liquid and all, and continue to process until smooth.
4. Chill for 6 hours or overnight.
5. Adjust to taste with salt and ground pepper, and serve soup chilled, garnished with a dollop of dairy sour cream, freshly snipped dill, and a sprinkling of paprika.

Variations:

1 teaspoon curry powder can be added in Step 2.

To reduce calories, substitute two 8-ounce packages Neufchatel (low-calorie cream cheese) and 1 cup low-calorie sour cream.

Make-It-Easy Tip:

√ It is important to allow the hot cooked zucchini mixture to cool before adding to the sour cream, which tends to curdle if mixed with boiling liquid.

Cold Curried Pea Soup

SERVES: 4
Preparation time: 10 minutes
Cooking time: 10 minutes
Chilling time: 4–6 hours or overnight

Even if you don't like peas I guarantee you'll like the strong curry flavor of this pea soup.

The Ingredients:

1 10¾-ounce can strong chicken broth
1 10-ounce package frozen peas
1 tablespoon chopped chives or scallion stalks
1 teaspoon lemon juice
1 teaspoon curry powder, or to taste
½ teaspoon salt, or to taste
¼ teaspoon freshly ground pepper, or to taste
½ cup half-and-half
Garnish: Chopped chives, scallion tops

The Steps:

1. In a small saucepan, bring broth to a boil. Add peas, bring to a boil again; cover, and simmer for 10 minutes.
2. Add the chives, lemon juice, curry powder, salt, and pepper, and puree in food processor or blender.
3. Chill for 4–6 hours or overnight.
4. Add cream, adjust seasoning, and serve in chilled soup plates garnished with chopped chives or scallion stalks.

Variations:

Fresh or frozen chopped broccoli can be substituted for the peas.
For a lower-calorie version, substitute low-fat buttermilk for the half-and-half.
This pea soup can also be served hot.

Spanish Gazpacho

SERVES: 4–6
Preparation time: 15 minutes
Chilling time: 6 hours or overnight

The Ingredients:

1 medium cucumber, peeled and coarsely chopped
½ green pepper, seeded and coarsely chopped
1 small red onion, coarsely chopped
1 clove garlic, peeled and cut in quarters
1 16-ounce can tomatoes, roughly chopped
1 6-ounce can vegetable juice (I use V-8)
3 tablespoons red wine
2 tablespoons olive oil
2 tablespoons lemon juice
1 egg yolk
1 teaspoon Worcestershire sauce
Salt and freshly ground pepper to taste
Garnish: Croutons, chopped cucumbers, scallions, tomatoes, and green peppers

The Steps:

1. Place cucumber, green pepper, onion, and garlic in food processor or blender and pulsate until finely chopped.
2. Add tomatoes, vegetable juice, red wine, olive oil, lemon juice, egg yolk, and Worcestershire sauce.
3. Process until very smooth, and chill for 6 hours or overnight.
4. Adjust seasoning with salt and pepper to taste and serve soup well chilled, garnished with bowls of croutons, chopped cucumbers, scallions, tomatoes, green peppers, or whatever vegetable desired.

Make-It-Easy Tips:
√ Double the amount of cucumber, green pepper, and onion in Step 1 and use half the chopped amount for garnishes.
√ The soup gets thicker, stronger, and more flavorful as it chills, so be sure to prepare a day or two in advance.
√ If preparing in blender, it is necessary to blend in 2 batches and to strain the soup.
√ If soup is to be served immediately, float an ice cube in each bowl to chill it quickly.

Leftover-Salad Soup

SERVES: 4
Preparation time: 10 minutes
Chilling time: 2–3 hours

It's always a shame to throw away leftover salad but most people don't like it the next day. This recipe takes soggy greens and wilted vegetables along with the dressing and tranforms them into a spicy, cooling soup.

The Ingredients:
2–3 cups leftover salad (greens, tomatoes, onions, bell peppers, cucumbers, etc., complete with dressing)
1 cup chicken broth
Salt and freshly ground pepper to taste
Garnish: Dairy sour cream or plain yogurt, chopped chives or scallion greens

The Steps:
1. Place salad in food processor or blender container with ¼ cup of the broth and process a few times, on and off, to combine.
2. Add remaining broth and continue to process until smooth. (If too thick, add more broth; if too thin, add a few more greens.)
3. Taste at this point. If soup is too bland, vinegar, chopped onions, minced garlic, and salt and pepper will help improve the flavor. Add those to taste, and process until smooth again.
4. Chill for 2–3 hours or until ready to serve.

5. When ready to serve, taste, and add salt and pepper if necessary. Remember that chilling diminishes flavor so always taste cold food just before serving! Serve in chilled bowls garnished with a dollop of sour cream or yogurt and chopped chives or scallions.

Variations:

Add ½ teaspoon minced garlic and ¼ cup minced onion as a flavor booster.

Add any salad vegetables available, as desired.

Make-It-Easy Tip:

√ Refrigerate leftover salad well covered to prevent flavor loss.

CHAPTER FIVE

ENTRÉES

Whole Chicken Cooked in a Clay Pot
Vertically Roasted Chicken
Cuban Chicken
Poulet à Ma Mère
Baked Chicken Chinese Style
Cousin Bette's Chicken
Chicken Breasts Moroccan
Mustard Grilled Boneless Chicken Breasts
Easy Chicken Marengo
Chicken with Artichoke Hearts
Roast Turkey Breast
Turkey Tostados
Turkey and Bulgur
Rock Cornish Game Hens Véronique
Braised Rock Cornish Game Hens
Medium-Rare Roast Beef
Marinated Flank Steak
Broder's Triangle Tip
Brisket Like My Mother Makes
Sweet and Sour Brisket
Spicy Shish Kebab
Deviled Short Ribs
Deviled Beef Bones
Roast Leg of Lamb with Rosemary and Garlic
Marinated Butterflied Leg of Lamb
Lamb with Dill
Rack of Lamb with Fresh Mint Sauce

Barbecued Lamb Riblets
Pork Chops with Mustard Dill Sauce
Sweet and Sour Pork Chops
Pork Loin Polynesian
Potted Pork with Fruit
Special Spareribs
Make-It-Easy Ham
Wiener Schnitzel a la Luchow
Veal and Water Chestnuts
Ragout de Veau
Fluffy Light Meat Loaf
Chinese Ground Beef Loaf
Baked Whole Salmon
Haddock "Blacksmith Shop"
Marinated Grilled Swordfish Steaks
Herb Broiled Fish Fillets
Fish with Butter and Capers en Papillote
Chinese Baked Fish
Fish Fillets Véronique
Braised Fish in Wine and Dill Sauce
Quick and Easy Cioppino
Super-Easy Shrimp Soufflé
Shrimp al Pesto
Curried Scallops
Oriental Flavor Ceviche
Chicken with Hoisin and Nuts
Stir-Fried Beef and Black Bean Sauce
Lamb with Scallions
Ground Pork with Cellophane Noodles, Szechwan-Style
Stir-Fried Shrimp

CHICKEN

We are all aware of the attributes of chicken as a main dish. It is economical, low in calories, low in cholesterol, and exceedingly versatile hot or cold.

Of the many methods of cooking chicken, I find sautéing the easiest when preparing for company. I can sauté the chicken in the morning or the night before, prepare the sauce, and refrigerate until dinner time. The only chore left is to pop the dish into the oven for 10 minutes and serve.

When selecting chickens, look for uniform color. Whether the color is yellow or white makes no difference. Yellow chickens are preferred in the Northeast so they are bred accordingly, whereas other parts of the country demand a white hue. Make friends with the butcher; he (or she) can be a great help. If coaxed, the butcher may even agree to chop up one of the less expensive whole chickens.

Since fresh poultry is extremely perishable, remove it from the store wrapper as soon as you arrive home. The giblets should be removed and refrigerated separately. Wrap the chicken loosely in plastic wrap or waxed paper. Avoid washing until just before using. Moisture and heat create a perfect environment for chickens to go bad. Just before cooking, remove excess fat from the neck area, wash and pat dry with paper towels, and proceed with the recipe.

Whole Chicken Cooked in a Clay Pot

SERVES: 4
Preparation time: 15 minutes
Cooking time: 1¼ hours

Cooking with wet terra-cotta clay dates back to the ancient Etruscans. The unglazed pot is totally immersed in water for about 20 minutes before cooking. When the heat of the oven reaches the clay cooker, the absorbed water heats up causing an instant flush of steam that keeps moisture surrounding the food that is cooking. The food is self-basted and kept moist and juicy so that no extra fats or oils are necessary. No browning of meats in oil or butter is required so the food is low in calories and healthful. The other advantage to clay pot cooking is that a whole one-pot dinner (meat, vegetables, starch) can be assembled in the clay cooker, closed, and totally cooked without basting or watching.

The Ingredients:

    1 Ovenbrique, Romertopf, Gourmetopf or similar brand unglazed terra-cotta pot large enough to hold a chicken plus vegetables
    1 whole roasting chicken (3–4 pounds)
    1 teaspoon *herbes de provence*, crumbled (or combination of crumbled dried basil, oregano, thyme, and chives)
    1 teaspoon salt (clay cooking requires more salt)
    ½ teaspoon freshly ground pepper
    3 medium carrots, peeled and sliced
    2 medium onions, quartered
¾–1 cup dry vermouth or white wine
    Salt and pepper to taste

The Steps:

1. Presoak pot, top and bottom, in water for 15–20 minutes.
2. Wash chicken, pat dry with paper towels, and season inside and out with one-half of the herbs, salt, and pepper.
3. Place carrots and onions in bottom of clay pot.
4. Put chicken on top of vegetables and sprinkle with parsley and remaining seasonings.
5. Pour wine around the sides, cover and *place in cold oven*. (Clay pots must be put in a cold oven or they will crack from the intense sudden heat of a preheated oven.) Set oven to 475° and cook for 1 hour and 15 minutes.
6. Remove from oven, baste chicken, and return to oven without lid for 10 minutes if additional browning is desired.
7. Remove chicken and vegetables to a platter and season to taste with salt and pepper.
8. Remove fat from remaining sauce and serve in gravy boat.

Accompaniments:

Plain white rice, and a mixed green salad with *Yogurt Dressing*.

Variation:

Small unpeeled red or new potatoes can be added to the clay pot. They brown well and can be served with a little of the defatted sauce.

Gravy strainer

Make-It-Easy Tips:

√ When buying a clay cooker, make sure it is large enough to accommodate a large roaster so that you can use it for company as well as family meals. Try the *Potted Pork with Fruit* (*see* page 137) or use your favorite poultry or meat dish and adapt it to clay cookery.

√ The easiest way to remove excess fat from gravy is with a gravy strainer. It is a pitcher with the spout based at the bottom. The gravy is poured in, the fat quickly rises to the top, the gravy is poured off from the bottom and the fat remains in the pitcher.

√ If time is a problem, immerse the clay pot in the morning and leave all day. The meal can then be quickly assembled without additional waiting.

Basic Vertically Roasted Chicken

SERVES: 4
Preparation time: 10–15 minutes
Cooking time: 1 hour

There are many advantages to using the Spanek or any style of vertical roaster for turkey, duck, game hens, or chicken. The fowl is placed in a vertical position on a tempered steel "Eiffel Tower" frame which conducts heat to sear the inside of the bird while allowing the juices to flow downward into the breast area. Poultry is cooked at high temperatures to create a perfectly browned bird without the necessity of turning the bird.

Excess fats drip off making it a dieter's dream, since the birds can be perfectly browned without the addition of extra butter or oil. Carving is facilitated by leaving the poultry on the rack and carving it neatly off the roaster. For sources to purchase the roaster, *see* Appendix A.

The Ingredients:

    1 whole fryer chicken (or duck or game bird)
    2 tablespoons fresh lemon juice
    1 tablespoon unsalted butter, softened (optional)
  ½ teaspoon minced garlic
  ½ teaspoon paprika
  ¼ teaspoon dried oregano, crumbled
  ¼ teaspoon dried leaf thyme, crumbled
  ½ teaspoon salt, or to taste
  ¼ teaspoon freshly ground pepper
 ¾–1 cup white wine
 ¾–1 cup chicken broth
 2–3 tablespoons unsalted butter, melted (optional)

The Steps:

1. Preheat oven to 450°.
2. Dry chicken inside and out with paper towels and rub with lemon juice. Massage with butter, if desired; season inside and out with minced garlic, paprika, oregano, thyme, salt, and pepper.
3. Remove top ring from the Spanek vertical roaster and place chicken over center hollow section of rack making sure top of roaster fits through neck opening of bird. Put excess skin around neck of bird over top and down inside roaster. Replace the top ring of roaster over skin, which is tucked in. (If using alternate brand of vertical roaster follow manufacturer's instructions.)
4. Mix white wine with chicken broth and pour into roasting pan to a depth of ¼". This will prevent the juices from cooking away. (Reserve remaining liquid.) Place vertical roaster in pan and place on lower rack of the oven. Cook for 15 minutes at 450° to sear bird, inside and out.
5. Reduce heat to 350° and continue to cook for 15–20 minutes *per pound.*
6. About halfway through roasting process, baste with optional

1. The vertical roaster

2. Fit the chicken on the roaster.

3. Replace the roaster ring.

4. Apply baster half way through cooking.

5. The roast is ready for carving.

6. Carve the thigh first.

7. Separate the thigh from the leg.

8. Remove the wish-bone.

9. Peel down the breast.

melted butter or use the Spanek basting tray, which allows the butter to melt on top of the bird and flow down the sides; check liquid level and replenish with reserved liquid, if necessary.

7. Remove bird from oven and carve from rack.
8. Skim fat from the sauce and serve clear juices alongside the bird.

Accompaniments:

Lemon Rice, and steamed carrots.

Make-It-Easy Tips:

√ This recipe can be used when roasting a chicken on a regular horizontal rack, but the results will not be the same because the juices will not drip down into the breast meat as they do when chicken is positioned vertically.

√ Sprinkling paprika on chicken before cooking helps to give the bird a golden brown color.

√ Fresh lemon juice is just as easy to squeeze as opening a bottle of poor-tasting, chemically laden bottled lemon juice.

Cuban Chicken

SERVES: 4
Preparation time: 10 minutes
Cooking time: 40–45 minutes
Marinating time: 3 hours

The Ingredients:

Juice of 1 large lime
1 whole clove garlic, peeled and lightly crushed but still intact
½ teaspoon dried oregano
½ teaspoon salt, or to taste
¼ teaspoon freshly ground pepper
1 3-pound chicken, trussed (tied up)
2 tablespoons unsalted butter
1 tablespoon olive oil (Spanish is preferable)
½ cup dry white wine

1 large onion, thinly sliced
Garnish: Freshly chopped parsley or watercress

The Steps:

1. In deep bowl, combine lime juice, garlic, oregano, salt, and pepper. Marinate chicken at room temperature for 3 hours, turning occasionally. (If the weather is hot, marinate in refrigerator for 6 hours or overnight and bring to room temperature before cooking.)
2. Remove chicken from marinade, discard garlic, and reserve remaining marinade for sauce.
3. In large deep casserole or Dutch oven, heat butter and oil together and brown chicken on all sides.
4. Reduce heat, add wine, onion, and reserved marinade.
5. Cover and cook over low heat for 40–45 minutes or until tender, basting occasionally.
6. Serve hot, garnished with freshly chopped parsley or watercress.

Accompaniments:

Plain Brown Rice, and a salad of greens, tomatoes, Spanish olives, Spanish onion slices with *Laurie's Basic Vinaigrette* dressing.

Variations:

Cuban Chicken can be prepared with cut-up chicken parts as well but the cooking time should be reduced to 30–35 minutes or until tender.

For a larger crowd, use a 5–6 pound chicken, double the sauce, and cook for 45 minutes to 1 hour, or until tender and the juices run clear when thigh is pierced.

For a reduced calorie count, brown the chicken in a non-stick skillet in only 1 tablespoon oil and use a gravy strainer or similar device to skim off the fat on the sauce before serving.

Make-It-Easy Tips:

√ The easiest way to truss a chicken is with a trussing needle. Just sew the chicken closed with kitchen twine.

√ An easy way to crush and peel garlic is to wrap a whole clove in waxed paper and smash with the side of a cleaver or heavy knife. The peel can be removed easily and the garlic remains intact so it can be removed after marinating.

Poulet à Ma Mère

SERVES: 8
Preparation time: 15–20 minutes
Cooking time: 50 minutes

This particular chicken dish is so named because it came from my mother, Ruth Burrows, who perfected it as the perfect company dish. Although it may appear to have many steps, it is basically a Make-It-Easy recipe.

The Ingredients:
    3   tablespoons unsalted butter
    1   tablespoon olive oil
    2   2½–3 pound chickens, cut into serving pieces and patted dry with paper towels
    ½   cup port wine (or use Marsala or sweet vermouth)
    2   cups chicken broth
    1   tablespoon freshly minced tarragon or 1 teaspoon dried tarragon
    ½   teaspoon salt, or to taste
    ¼   teaspoon freshly ground pepper
    ¾   cup dairy sour cream or *Crème Fraîche* (*see* Chapter 2)
        Garnish: Parsley sprigs

The Steps:
1. Preheat oven to 350°.
2. In a large skillet, melt butter and oil together; sauté chicken pieces, a few at a time, until golden brown, adding more butter if necessary.
3. Remove browned chicken pieces from skillet. Blot on paper towels to remove excess grease and place in single layer in an oven-proof casserole.
4. When all the chicken has been removed from the skillet, pour off any remaining fat. Add port and stir, scraping up any browned particles on the bottom of the pan.
5. Add broth, tarragon, salt, and pepper; stir, and pour sauce over chicken in casserole.
6. Place casserole in oven and bake uncovered for 40–45 minutes or until tender.

7. Remove casserole from oven, transfer chicken to plate, and allow sauce to cool for 5–10 minutes.
8. Gradually whisk sour cream or *Crème Fraîche* into the sauce until smooth.
9. Return chicken to casserole in single layer and place in oven again just to warm the sauce. (Be careful not to leave casserole in too long or the sour cream may curdle.)
10. Serve chicken hot, garnished with parsley sprigs.

Accompaniments:
Lemon Rice, and *Spinach Salad.*

Make-It-Easy Tips:
√ The chicken can be prepared ahead through Step 7 and refrigerated until ready to serve. Bring sauce and chicken pieces to room temperature before proceeding.
√ *Crème Fraîche,* because of its high butterfat content, will not curdle when heated. *See* Chapter 2 for recipe.
√ To save time and energy, use a very large casserole and prepare sauce in Steps 7 and 8 in a corner of the pan, tipping it towards you.
√ When browning chicken, place a heavy pot lid over the chicken to press it down. This procedure quickens the browning and keeps the grease from splattering all over the stove. If you don't have such a lid, a metal colander inverted over the top of the chicken will serve as a shield but won't assist in the browning.

Baked Chicken Chinese Style

SERVES: 4
Preparation time: 10 minutes
Cooking time: 1 hour

The Ingredients:
3–4 pounds chicken, cut into serving pieces and patted dry with paper towels
2–3 pieces bacon, cut into ½″ pieces (optional)

Sauce:

⅓ cup soy sauce

2 tablespoons ketchup

2 tablespoons dry sherry

1 tablespoon peanut oil

1 teaspoon dry mustard

1 clove garlic, minced

1 teaspoon sugar

1 large slice gingerroot, minced, or ½ teaspoon ground ginger

¼ teaspoon freshly ground pepper

2 large scallions (green only) cut into ½″ pieces

The Steps:

1. Place chicken pieces in large roasting pan in single layer.
2. Prepare sauce by combining soy sauce, ketchup, sherry, oil, mustard, garlic, sugar, ginger, pepper, and scallions.
3. Pour the sauce over the chicken, cover, and refrigerate overnight to marinate, turning once.
4. Preheat oven to 375°.
5. Add optional bacon to pan and bake chicken for 30 minutes *per side*, brushing occasionally with the sauce.
6. Serve chicken hot over white rice.

Accompaniments:

Plain White Rice, the Chinese Way, and *Stir-Fried Spinach.*

Variation:

This Chinese Chicken is wonderful served cold the next day for lunch or at a picnic.

Make-It-Easy Tips:

√ To cut down on excess grease and calories, blanch bacon by dropping into boiling water for 2 minutes and then draining.

√ Excess fat can be removed from sauce before serving with a gravy strainer, skimmer, or other type of fat separator.

√ Store peeled ginger, covered with dry sherry, in a jar in the refrigerator. It will keep for several months.

Cousin Bette's Chicken

SERVES: 6–8
Preparation time: 10 minutes
Cooking time: 35–40 minutes

Cousin Bette's Chicken is not from the Balzac novel but comes from a cousin named Bette in Ohio. It is simple to prepare with a three-ingredient sauce.

The Ingredients:
    4 chicken breasts, split in half
    1 12-ounce jar currant jelly
    ¼ cup light brown sugar
    2 tablespoons orange juice
      Salt and pepper to taste
      Garnish: Freshly chopped parsley

The Steps:
1. Preheat oven to 375°.
2. Place chicken breasts, skin side up, in a single layer in oven-proof baking dish.
3. In small saucepan, combine currant jelly, brown sugar, and orange juice; heat for 2–3 minutes; paint chicken breasts with mixture. Add any excess to baking dish.
4. Cover pan and bake for 20 minutes; remove cover and continue to bake until chicken is tender and crusty brown on top, 15–20 minutes longer.
5. Taste, and adjust seasoning if necessary. Serve chicken hot with sauce poured over top. Garnish with freshly chopped parsley.

Accompaniments:
Apricot Rice and a mixed green salad with *Laurie's Basic Vinaigrette* dressing.

Make-It-Easy Tip:
√ Chicken can be prepared with boned chicken breasts with skins on but must then be basted often and cooked only 20 minutes, or until tender.

Chicken Breasts Moroccan

SERVES: 6
Preparation time: 20–25 minutes
Cooking time: 20–25 minutes

The Ingredients:

1½ lemons
  6 medium-size chicken breasts, halved, washed, and patted dry with paper towels
 ½ teaspoon salt, or to taste
 ¼ teaspoon freshly ground pepper
  2 tablespoons unsalted butter
  2 tablespoons olive oil
  4 large shallots, minced (or 4 large scallions, white only, minced)
  1 clove garlic, minced
 ½ cup dry white wine (or dry vermouth)
 ¼ cup freshly chopped parsley
  1 teaspoon dried oregano, crumbled
 ½ cup chicken broth
    Garnish: Fresh coriander or parsley

The Steps:

1. Preheat oven to 350°.
2. Peel the lemons and cut the lemon rind into julienne strips (matchstick size); squeeze juice from lemon and reserve.
3. Sprinkle chicken with salt and pepper.
4. In large oven-proof pan that can go on top of the stove, heat the butter and oil. Brown chicken breasts on both sides over medium high heat until golden; remove with slotted spoon.
5. Sauté shallots and garlic in remaining fat over medium-low heat and cook until soft, about 5 minutes.
6. Deglaze pan with wine by scraping up browned particles from bottom of the pan. Bring to boil and cook over high heat until the wine is reduced to half its volume.
7. Return chicken to pan, sprinkle with parsley and oregano; add chicken broth, lemon juice, and lemon peel strips. Cover and place in oven for 20–25 minutes or until tender (DO NOT OVERCOOK).
8. Serve chicken hot, garnished with coriander or parsley.

Accompaniments:
Couscous, and *Tossed Salad with Red Onions.*

Variations:
A 3–3½ pound whole chicken cut into serving parts can be used or, for a more elegant version, substitute boneless chicken breasts.

Leftover chicken can be served cold the next day accompanied by a lemon mayonnaise.

Make-It-Easy Tips:
√ A lemon "zester," a gadget with 4–5 small openings at the top, will cut the lemon into julienne strips.
√ Peeled lemons are easier to squeeze, and release more juice.
√ Lemons will yield more juice when they are at room temperature.

Mustard Grilled Boneless Chicken Breasts

SERVES: 4
Preparation time: 5 minutes
Marinating time: 10–15 minutes
Cooking time: 8–10 minutes

These boneless chicken breasts are marinated in lemon juice and mustard and then grilled indoors or outdoors until seared on the outside and juicy on the inside without any added butter or fat. The results are delicious and incredibly low-calorie.

The Ingredients:
4 boneless chicken breasts
¼ cup Dijon mustard
¼ cup lemon juice
1 teaspoon Worcestershire sauce
Salt and pepper to taste

The Steps:
1. Paint chicken breasts on both sides with mustard.
2. Sprinkle lemon juice and Worcestershire sauce over chicken

and allow to marinate at room temperature for 10–15 minutes.
3. Preheat broiler or outdoor grill.
4. Grill chicken for 3–4 minutes a side or until just tender.
5. Season to taste with salt and pepper and serve hot.

Accompaniments:

Potatoes Boiled in Jackets, and a mixed green salad with *Low-Calorie Buttermilk Dill Dressing.*

Variations:

Grainy imported mustard, called *Moutarde à l'Ancien,* can be substituted for Dijon mustard. The most popular brand in the U.S. is *Moutarde de Meaux Pommery.*

The leftover chicken can be served cold with *Mustard Mayonnaise.*

Make-It-Easy Tip:

√ Chicken can be marinated for several hours, covered, in the refrigerator.

Easy Chicken Marengo

SERVES: 6–8
Preparation time: 15 minutes
Cooking time: 35–40 minutes

Chicken Marengo is a stew with a delicate flavor that is inexpensive to prepare.

The Ingredients:

  6 boneless and skinless chicken breasts, cut into 1½"–2" square pieces
½ cup all-purpose flour
  1 teaspoon dried tarragon, crumbled
½ teaspoon salt, or to taste
½ teaspoon freshly ground white pepper
  2 tablespoons unsalted butter
  2 tablespoons olive oil

½ cup dry white wine

2 cups drained and chopped canned tomatoes (two 16-ounce cans or one 28-ounce can should yield 2 cups drained and chopped tomatoes)

12 mushrooms, sliced

1 2.2-ounce can sliced pitted black olives

1 small clove garlic, minced

Salt and pepper to taste

Garnish: Freshly chopped parsley

The Steps:

1. Preheat oven to 350°.
2. Combine flour with tarragon, salt, and pepper and dip chicken pieces in seasoned flour to coat on all sides.
3. Heat butter and oil in large skillet; brown chicken pieces a few at a time until golden (adding more butter if necessary). Remove to an oven-proof casserole.
4. Add wine to skillet and deglaze by scraping up brown particles from the bottom of the pan.
5. Add tomatoes, mushrooms, olives, and garlic, and stir to combine; pour sauce over chicken pieces, and cover. Place in oven and bake for 35 to 40 minutes.
6. Taste, and adjust seasoning if necessary. Serve chicken garnished with freshly chopped parsley.

Accompaniments:

Rice Pilaf with Pine Nuts, and *Spinach Salad with Creamy Dressing.*

Variation:

Cooked shrimp can be added during the last 10 minutes of cooking.

Make-It-Easy Tips:

√ Chicken Marengo can be reheated successfully and is, therefore, an excellent dish to make in large quantities and freeze for future use in foil or plastic containers.

√ Chicken is more easily cut if semi-frozen.

√ Flour and seasonings can be shaken together in a plastic bag. Add chicken pieces and shake. Remove chicken to a colander or strainer and shake off excess flour.

Chicken with Artichoke Hearts

SERVES: 4–6
Preparation time: 20 minutes
Cooking time: 40 minutes

The Ingredients:
    1 3-pound chicken, cut into pieces
    ½ teaspoon paprika
    ½ teaspoon salt, or to taste
    ¼ teaspoon freshly ground pepper
    2 tablespoons unsalted butter
    1 tablespoon olive oil
    2 6-ounce jars marinated artichoke hearts, drained
    ¼ pound mushrooms, sliced
    2 tablespoons all-purpose flour
    ⅔ cup strong or undiluted chicken broth
    ⅓ cup dry white wine or dry vermouth
    ¼ teaspoon dried rosemary, crumbled
       Garnish: Freshly chopped parsley

The Steps:
    1. Preheat oven to 375°.
    2. Sprinkle chicken pieces with paprika, salt, and pepper.
    3. Heat butter and oil in a large skillet and brown chicken on both sides over high heat. With slotted spoon, remove chicken pieces to oven-proof casserole, leaving excess fat in the pan.
    4. Arrange artichoke hearts in casserole between pieces of chicken.
    5. Over medium-low heat, sauté the mushrooms in remaining fat in skillet. Sprinkle flour over mushrooms, stir well, add chicken broth, white wine, and rosemary, stirring until smooth over low heat.
    6. Pour mushroom sauce over chicken and artichokes, cover, and bake for 35–40 minutes or until chicken is tender.
    7. Taste, and adjust seasoning if necessary. Serve chicken garnished with freshly chopped parsley.

Accompaniments:
Plain White Rice, the Chinese Way, and *Broccoli Florets Vinaigrette.*

Variations:
If desired, ¼ cup minced onions, shallots, or scallions can be sautéed with mushrooms in Step 5.

For a very elegant dinner, boned chicken breasts with or without skins can be used. Cook these in the casserole only 15–20 minutes, depending on the size, or until tender.

Make-It-Easy Tip:
√ See the tip under *Poulet à Ma Mère* for the best way to brown chicken.

TURKEY
Roast turkey seems destined to be a November holiday dish no matter how you slice it. I find, however, that turkey breasts or thighs can be easily roasted and used as the basis for unusual variations such as Oriental turkey salad or *Mexican Turkey Tostado.*

When selecting a turkey or turkey parts, choose a fresh one if available. Avoid the frozen "butterball" turkeys, which actually contain little or no butter. For the most part, they are injected with saturated fats and are more expensive. The best way to thaw a frozen bird is to refrigerate it 1–2 days, depending on size. If time does not permit, thaw in sealed wrapper outside the refrigerator in a bowl or sink filled with cold water, changing the water often to hasten the procedure.

When trussing a large bird, sew up with a large trussing needle using kitchen twine, or use oversized pins to clip shut.

Roast Turkey Breast

SERVES: 10
Preparation time: 10 minutes
Cooking time: 1½ hours

For those who prefer only white meat of turkey, Roast Turkey Breast is an ideal entrée. It is easy to prepare and serves a large group. The leftovers make fantastic sandwiches as well as the basis for an excellent turkey salad, hot or cold.

The Ingredients:

       1 5–6 pound turkey breast
       2 tablespoons unsalted butter
     ½ teaspoon paprika
     ½ teaspoon salt, or to taste
     ¼ teaspoon freshly ground pepper
       2 shallots or scallions (white part only), minced
     ½ cup dry white wine
     ½–1 cup chicken broth
         Garnish: Orange slices, parsley sprigs

The Steps:

1. Preheat oven to 350°.
2. Rub butter on skin of turkey breast; season with paprika, salt, and pepper, and scatter shallots or scallions over all sides of bird.
3. Place turkey in a roasting pan (lined with aluminum foil to save on clean-ups) and pour wine and broth around the bottom of the pan. (There should be about ½" of liquid in the pan.)
4. Roast turkey in oven for 1½–2 hours or until juices run clear when meat is pierced. Length of time depends on the size of the bird. In general, roast for 20 minutes per pound or until an inserted meat thermometer registers 160–165°. Using a pastry brush, paint every half hour with the liquids, which can be replenished with additional chicken broth, if necessary.
5. If desired, gravy can be strained, defatted and thickened by boiling down to half its original volume.
6. Serve turkey garnished with orange slices and parsley sprigs.

Accompaniments:

Noodle Pudding, and a mixed green salad with *Laurie's Basic Vinaigrette* dressing.

Variations:

To reduce calories, omit the butter, and baste more often with the natural liquids. Defat gravy, and serve with steamed vegetables and plain white rice.

Leftovers: Cold turkey sandwiches are a favorite around our

house—thin slices of turkey with lots of *Thousand Island Dressing* and some cole slaw on rye bread.

Roast Turkey Breast meat can also be used in casseroles or in the proverbial turkey salad.

Make-It-Easy Tip:

√ Shallots or scallions can be put through a garlic press to extract their juice and crush them.

Turkey Tostados

SERVES: 3–4
Preparation time: 15 minutes
Cooking time: 6–12 minutes

Tostados make a fun dinner where guests or family can help themselves to a variety of toppings.

The Ingredients:

    ¼ cup vegetable oil
    6 small corn tortillas
    1½ cups canned refried beans, warmed
    1½ cups shredded cooked turkey
    ¾ cup Mexican chile sauce with tomatoes (or Jalapeño sauce to taste)
    2 cups shredded lettuce
    ¾ cup shredded Monterey Jack or Cheddar cheese
    1 medium onion, finely chopped
    2 tomatoes, roughly chopped
    2 pimientos, cut into thin strips
    1 2¼-ounce can sliced black olives, drained
    1 ripe avocado, cut into 12 slices
    1 cup dairy sour cream

The Steps:

1. Heat oil in heavy skillet over medium high heat; fry tortillas on both sides, one at a time, until crisp. (Each should take 1–2 minutes.) Drain on paper towels.

2. On each tostado shell, spread ¼ cup refried beans.
3. Top with ¼ cup shredded turkey and 2 tablespoons Mexican chile sauce.
4. Garnish each tostado with lettuce, cheese, onion, tomatoes, pimientos, black olives, avocado, and sour cream, piling them as high as you want. Serve immediately.

Accompaniments:
Tossed Salad with Red Onions.

Variations:
Guacamole (*see* Chapter 1) can be added to the tostado instead of the avocado slices.

Tostados can be served for supper or lunch.

Make-It-Easy Tips:
√ Crisp tortillas, called tostado shells, are available in supermarkets and can be used, but must be heated in a 350° oven for 3–5 minutes to crisp.
√ A tostado party is a fine idea. Put everyone to work chopping the ingredients and then everyone can enjoy making his or her own tostado.
√ Cover leftover pimientos in jar with vegetable oil and refrigerate to prevent spoilage.

Turkey and Bulgur

SERVES: 6–8
Preparation time: 20 minutes
Cooking time: 1 hour

Bulgur (cracked wheat) adds an unusual and nutty flavor to this casserole.

The Ingredients:
3 tablespoons unsalted butter
1 pound mushrooms, thinly sliced
1 small onion, finely chopped

  1 cup bulgur (cracked wheat)
2½ cups chicken broth, or turkey stock if available
  ½ cup heavy cream
  ½ cup slivered almonds or pine nuts
  1 tablespoon lemon juice
  1 tablespoon freshly chopped parsley
  1 teaspoon chopped chives or scallion stalks
  1 teaspoon Worcestershire sauce
  ½ teaspoon salt, or to taste
  ½ teaspoon freshly ground pepper
  3 cups cooked turkey, cubed
  2 tablespoons unsalted butter

The Steps:

1. Preheat oven to 350°. Generously butter a 2-quart casserole.
2. In large skillet, melt 3 tablespoons butter and sauté mushrooms and onions over medium heat until soft and golden.
3. Add bulgur and stir until grains are coated, about 2 minutes.
4. Add broth, cream, nuts, lemon juice, parsley, chives, Worcestershire, salt, and pepper; stir in turkey.
5. Pour into prepared casserole, cover, and bake for 40 minutes.
6. Remove cover, dot with butter, and bake uncovered 20 minutes.
7. Serve casserole hot. (It can be reheated.)

Accompaniment:

Snow-Pea Salad, or its variation made with sugar snap peas.

Variation:

Brown or white rice can be substituted for the bulgur.

Make-It-Easy Tips:

√ Casserole can be cooked, cooled, and frozen for future use.
√ Use an egg slicer to slice mushrooms quickly and easily.

ROCK CORNISH GAME HENS

Rock cornish game hens are easy to prepare and attractive to serve. They can be stuffed and roasted, braised, or split in half and broiled for a company or family meal. Cornish game hens are readily available frozen but, more recently, fresh ones, which are especially tasty, are appearing on the market.

Whole rock cornish game hens are a great help in Make-It-Easy cooking. Each of these 1-pound birds can be roasted and served without any time-consuming slicing or carving. That chore is left to the guests, except that you'll probably find everyone using his or her fingers!

Rock Cornish Game Hens Véronique

SERVES: 4
Preparation time: 15 minutes
Cooking time: 1 hour

The Ingredients:
    4 Rock Cornish Hens, 1 pound or less each (if frozen, thoroughly thawed)
    2 medium onions, quartered
1½ teaspoons dried tarragon, crumbled
    ¼ teaspoon paprika
    ½ teaspoon salt, or to taste
    ¼ teaspoon freshly ground pepper, or to taste
3–4 tablespoons unsalted butter, melted
    2 cups dry white wine or dry vermouth
      Salt and freshly ground pepper to taste
    ½ pound seedless grapes

The Steps:
1. Preheat oven to 350°
2. Place 2 quarters of onion in cavity of each hen.
3. Sprinkle hens with tarragon, paprika, salt, and pepper and brush with melted butter.
4. Place hens in roasting pan and bake for 20 minutes, basting with the pan juices.
5. Pour wine over hens and continue to cook for 20–30 minutes or until golden and tender, basting often.
6. Remove to a warm platter and discard onions.
7. Heat pan juices on top of the stove; reduce to thicken. Taste, and adjust seasoning with salt and pepper. Add grapes, pour sauce over the hens, and serve hot.

Accompaniments:
Rice Pilaf with Pine Nuts, and *Carrots and Parsnips Combined.*

Make-It-Easy Tips:
√ The onions are added for flavor, but can be eaten at family dinners, or reused to make stock.
√ Frozen hens should be thoroughly thawed overnight in the refrigerator or placed in a bowl of water at room temperature for several hours.

Braised Rock Cornish Game Hens

SERVES: 4
Preparation time: 15 minutes
Cooking time: 35–40 minutes

The Ingredients:
2 1-pound Rock Cornish Game Hens, split (if frozen, thoroughly thawed)
¼ cup flour seasoned with ½ teaspoon salt and ¼ teaspoon freshly ground pepper
2 tablespoons unsalted butter
2 tablespoons olive oil
1 large onion, finely chopped
¼ pound mushrooms, sliced
½ cup dry white wine
¼ cup chicken broth
Garnish: Freshly chopped parsley

The Steps:
1. Dredge hens with seasoned flour; shake off excess.
2. In Dutch oven or large casserole, heat butter and oil together; sauté onions and mushrooms over medium heat until soft and golden, 5–7 minutes; remove with a slotted spoon.
3. Brown split hens on both sides in same pan over high heat until golden. Remove hens and set aside with vegetables.
4. Add wine to deglaze the pan, scraping the browned particles into the sauce; return hens, onions, and mushrooms, cover, and simmer slowly for 35–40 minutes or until tender.

5. Serve hens with sauce poured over tops; garnish with a sprinkling of freshly chopped parsley.

Accompaniments:
Lemon Rice, and a mixed green salad with *Green Goddess Salad Dressing.*

Variation:
Chicken parts can be substituted for the game hens.

Make-It-Easy Tips:
√ Hens can be prepared ahead, up to the point where you have deglazed the pan and returned the chicken and vegetables to it. Cool slightly and refrigerate. When ready to proceed with cooking, bring to room temperature and simmer for only 25–30 minutes or until tender.

√ Split the hens open by yourself with a heavy knife or cleaver or ask your friendly butcher to do this for you.

BEEF
After bringing beef home from the market, remove wrapping immediately, and dry meat with paper towels. Wrap loosely in waxed paper or foil before storing to avoid spoilage.

If possible, thaw all frozen meat in the refrigerator to prevent the loss of juices.

When purchasing tougher cuts of meat, try tenderizing them with slices of fresh papaya. The natural enzyme in unripe papaya, called *papain,* is the important ingredient in commercial meat tenderizers. By using fresh papaya you can obtain tender meat without the added salt, sugar, and chemicals that are in packaged tenderizers.

Chopped meat should be ground right before use. The butcher will usually be glad to grind the meat for you while you wait. That way you can be assured of freshness.

Perfect Medium-Rare Roast Beef

SERVES: 4–6
Preparation time: 10 minutes
Cooking time: Depends on size

Variations of this easy method of cooking beef have been suggested by many food authorities in the last few years. It can also be used for leg of lamb cooked to a perfect pink medium rare.

The Ingredients:

Rib roast, 1–2 ribs (brought to room temperature before cooking; this takes about 2 hours)
½ cup chili sauce
1 tablespoon Worcestershire sauce
½ teaspoon salt, or to taste
¼ teaspoon freshly ground pepper
1 tablespoon A-1 Sauce (optional)

The Steps:

1. Preheat oven to 500°.
2. Season roast with a mixture of chili sauce, Worcestershire, salt, pepper, and optional A-1 Sauce.
3. Place roast in pan fat-side up and roast in oven for 36 minutes (which is 18 minutes per rib; a three-rib roast would cook 54 minutes).
4. At the end of that time, turn oven off immediately and do *not* open the door of the oven. Leave the door closed for 2 hours. After that, the roast is done!

Accompaniments:

Tomato Pie, and *Caesar Salad.*

Variations:

Use leftover beef ribs for *Deviled Beef Bones* (*see* p. 124) and use the meat for sandwiches or stir-fry with vegetables Chinese-style.
For leg of lamb, cook for 15 minutes per pound for rare, 18 minutes for medium rare, and 22 minutes for well-done in a pre-

heated 500° oven. Turn oven off and, without opening oven door, allow lamb to cook undisturbed for an additional 3 hours.

Make-It-Easy Tips:
√ The rib roast will keep for an hour after the prescribed 2 hours. To reheat, place in a preheated 200° oven for 10 minutes.
√ If you forget to remove roast from refrigerator beforehand, add 21 minutes to cooking time per rib.

Marinated Flank Steak

SERVES: 6–8
Preparation time: 15 minutes
Marinating time: 12–24 hours
Cooking time: To taste

The Ingredients:
1 cup vegetable oil
½ cup soy sauce
⅓ cup red wine vinegar
¼ cup lemon juice
3 tablespoons Worcestershire sauce
2 tablespoons Dijon mustard
1 teaspoon freshly ground pepper
1 large onion, sliced
1 clove garlic, minced
2 pounds flank steak (or use London broil or Tri-Tip*)

The Steps:
1. Combine oil, soy sauce, vinegar, lemon juice, Worcestershire, mustard, pepper, onion, and garlic in a bowl.
2. Place steak in a shallow dish or bowl, pour marinade over it, cover, and refrigerate. Marinate for 12–24 hours.
3. When ready to cook, preheat broiler or outdoor grill.

* For description of Tri-Tip, see the following recipe.

4. Remove meat from marinade and grill to desired doneness, basting occasionally.
5. Cut meat on the bias into thin slices, and serve hot.

Accompaniments:
Broad Noodles with Spinach, and *Raw Mushroom Salad.*

Make-It-Easy Tips:
√ Two jumbo plastic food-storage bags (not garbage bags) are excellent for marinating meat. Place meat and marinade in bag, tie up with twist tie, place in another bag, tie up again, and feel free to turn the bag at any time without messing up your hands or the refrigerator.

√ If broiling meat indoors, put one or two pieces of dried bread in bottom of pan. They will soak up excess fat and thus cut down on smoking or possible fires.

Broder's Triangle-Tip

SERVES: 4–6
Preparation time: 15–20 minutes
Cooking time: 30–45 minutes

Tri-Tip, sometimes referred to as bottom butt, is a thick, triangular, uneven piece of beef, similar in texture to flank steak. When cut on the bias, it turns into juicy, tender slices of steak. Use the Tri-Tip outdoors on the grill, indoors in the broiler, or braise it, as in the following recipe.

The Ingredients:
  2 pounds Tri-Tip
4–6 tablespoons unsalted butter
  1 medium onion, thinly sliced
  1 green pepper, thinly sliced
  8 medium mushrooms, sliced

2 cups red wine
2 tablespoons Worcestershire sauce
½ teaspoon freshly minced garlic
½ teaspoon salt, or to taste
¼ teaspoon freshly ground pepper
⅛ teaspoon dried oregano, crumbled
⅛ teaspoon dried basil, crumbled
⅛ teaspoon dried thyme, crumbled
Garnish: Toasted French bread, freshly chopped parsley

The Steps:

1. Heat Dutch oven or deep skillet; sear Tri-Tip, fat side down. Turn and brown on other side. Remove.
2. Add butter to pan, reduce heat and, when butter is melted, sauté onions and peppers until soft and translucent, about 8–10 minutes.
3. Add mushrooms, and continue to sauté for 4–5 minutes or until golden.
4. Add wine, Worcestershire, garlic, salt, pepper, and dried herbs and stir to combine.
5. Return Tri-Tip to pan, fat side down, bring liquid to a boil, cover, and simmer slowly for 30–45 minutes, depending on desired degree of doneness. Baste occasionally.
6. Remove meat from pan, slice, and serve over toasted, buttered French bread garnished with chopped parsley. Taste sauce, adjust seasoning, and pour over meat slices.

Accompaniments:

Italian Zucchini Bake, and a mixed green salad with *Laurie's Basic Vinaigrette* dressing.

Variation:

Tri-Tip is almost better the next day, sliced and served on toasted sourdough or rye bread.

Make-It-Easy Tip:

√ In the morning, when thawing meat for dinner, first wrap in plastic wrap and then in several sheets of newspaper. When you arrive home later in the day the meat will still be chilled instead of mushy and warm.

Brisket Like My Mother Makes

SERVES: 8
Preparation time: 15 minutes
Cooking time: 3–4 hours

Brisket is one of the best meats to use for potting. The first cut, also called a flat or thin cut, is less fatty and tends to be drier. It should be cooked a shorter time than the second cut, which is also called the front, point, or thick cut. The second cut is fattier, juicier, and less expensive.

The Ingredients:

      3 tablespoons unsalted butter
      2 large onions, coarsely chopped
      2 carrots, peeled and coarsely chopped
     ½ teaspoon salt, or to taste
     ¼ teaspoon freshly ground pepper
     ¼ teaspoon freshly minced garlic
     ¼ teaspoon paprika
    4–5 pound brisket
     ¾ cup dry red wine
        Salt and freshly ground pepper

The Steps:

1. Heat butter in Dutch oven or deep skillet; sauté onions and carrots over medium-low heat for 10–15 minutes, or until soft; remove vegetables with a slotted spoon.
2. Increase heat; rub salt and pepper, garlic, and paprika onto both sides of brisket, and sear on all sides.
3. Add wine to deglaze skillet, scraping up browned particles from bottom of pan. Return vegetables to pan; reduce heat to simmer, cover, and cook slowly for 3–4 hours or until fork tender, turning every hour.
4. Remove meat from gravy, cool slightly, and cut in thin slices.
5. Defat gravy and puree in a food processor, blender, or through a strainer or food mill until smooth; taste, adjust seasoning if necessary, and serve with sliced meat.

Accompaniments:
   Barley Casserole, and *Spinach Salad.*

Variations:
   Similar cuts of meat for potting can be substituted for brisket, such as chuck or rump roast.
   Although my mother does not approve, I occasionally add ¼ cup chili sauce along with the wine.
   Serve the brisket hot, or cold without gravy but with white horse-radish or *Creamy Horseradish Sauce* (*see* Chapter 2). For those watching their caloric intake, serve it with strong mustard.

Make-It-Easy Tips:
   √ Prepare the brisket 1–2 days ahead. When ready to serve, slice the cold meat (it's easy to slice when cold), pack the slices back together in heavy-duty foil, and heat the foil-wrapped meat for 10 minutes in a 325° oven. The cold gravy can be defatted easily and reheated.
   √ If time is a problem, sauté the brisket and transfer it to a crock pot, which will continue to cook the meat unattended.
   √ Store onions separately from potatoes. Onions release a gas that hastens the spoilage of potatoes.

Sweet and Sour Brisket

SERVES: 6
Preparation time: 20 minutes
Cooking time: 3 hours

This brisket is best prepared a day in advance and reheated, sliced, in the gravy.

The Ingredients:
   4–5 pound first-cut brisket
   ½ teaspoon salt
   ¼ teaspoon freshly ground pepper
   ¼ teaspoon freshly minced garlic

¼ teaspoon paprika
1 tablespoon unsalted butter
1 tablespoon vegetable oil
1 large onion, finely chopped
1 8-ounce can tomato sauce
½ cup beef broth
½ cup water
6 ginger snap cookies, crushed

The Steps:

1. Season meat with salt, pepper, garlic, and paprika.
2. Heat butter and oil in large Dutch oven or casserole, brown meat over high heat on all sides.
3. Before last side is completely brown, add onions to bottom of pan and allow to soften as meat continues to brown.
4. Add tomato sauce, beef broth, and water. Cover, reduce heat to simmer, and cook slowly for 3 hours, turning every 45 minutes.
5. Remove meat and cool for 20 minutes before slicing.
6. Add crushed ginger snaps to gravy and heat through.
7. Serve brisket slices in warmed gravy.

Accompaniments:

Potatoes Boiled in Jackets, and *Carrot Puree in Artichoke Bottoms*.

Variation:

Second-cut brisket can be used but should be cooked slightly longer.

Make-It-Easy Tips:

√ Turn the meat with wooden spoons or tongs so as not to pierce it and thus lose precious juices.
√ Brisket is best prepared a day in advance and reheated in gravy.

Spicy Shish Kebab

SERVES: 4–6
Preparation time: 15 minutes
Cooking time: 15 minutes

This Spicy Shish Kebab has a Middle-Eastern flavor. The easiest way to cook shish kebab is to place the meat and vegetables on separate skewers. This way the meat cooks to desired doneness and the vegetables don't overcook and fall off.

The Ingredients:

2½ pounds boneless sirloin (or similar tender cut of beef)

Marinade:

Juice of 2 lemons
¼ cup olive oil
2 tablespoons grated onions
2 tablespoons chili powder
2 teaspoons curry powder
1 teaspoon ground coriander
1 teaspoon ground ginger
½ teaspoon salt, or to taste
1 clove garlic, minced

Skewer Vegetables:

2 tomatoes, quartered
Red or green pepper
Large mushroom caps
Garnish: Coriander or parsley sprigs

The Steps:

1. Combine all ingredients for marinade in large bowl. Add beef and marinate for *only* 2 hours at room temperature. (The marinade is very spicy, so timing is important.)
2. Remove meat from marinade and thread on skewer(s); thread vegetables on separate skewer(s).
3. Preheat broiler or outdoor grill.
4. Grill meat for 5–7 minutes a side for medium rare, and grill vegetables for 3–4 minutes a side.
5. Serve meat and vegetables together garnished with sprigs of coriander or parsley.

Accompaniments:
Apricot Rice, and *Cucumber Raita.*

Variation:
Boneless lamb can be substituted for beef.

Make-It-Easy Tip:
√ Onions are not included as a vegetable because they require parboiling and peeling which are tedious chores. If you have the
time, by all means include onions with your vegetables.

Deviled Short Ribs

SERVES: 4
Preparation time: 15 minutes
Cooking time: 2 hours

These Beef Short Ribs are braised in a spicy chili-and-onion-flavored
sauce.

The Ingredients:
1–2 tablespoons vegetable oil
3 pounds short ribs, cut into serving-size pieces
2 medium onions, chopped
½ cup chili sauce
½ cup beef broth
3 tablespoons cider vinegar
1½ tablespoons light brown sugar
1 teaspoon Dijon mustard
2 teaspoons Worcestershire sauce
1 clove garlic, minced
1 teaspoon dry mustard
1 teaspoon chili powder
1 teaspoon paprika
½ teaspoon salt, or to taste
¼ teaspoon freshly ground pepper

The Steps:
1. Preheat oven to 350°.
2. In large Dutch oven or deep casserole, heat oil; brown ribs all over; discard accumulated fat.
3. In large bowl, combine onion, chili sauce, broth, vinegar, sugar, Dijon mustard, Worcestershire, garlic, dry mustard, chili powder, paprika, salt, and pepper; pour over ribs, tossing to combine.
4. Cover and bake for 2 hours, removing the cover for the last ½ hour so meat will brown.
5. Taste, and adjust seasoning, if necessary. Serve ribs hot with sauce.

Accompaniments:
Southern-Style Cheese Grits, and *String Bean Salad.*

Make-It-Easy Tips:
√ Double the recipe and freeze in foil containers in family-size portions for future use.
√ To peel a clove of garlic easily, crush it lightly with the flat side of a cleaver or heavy knife and skin will separate.

Deviled Beef Bones
(For Beef or Pork Ribs)

SERVES: 4–6
Preparation time: 15 minutes
Cooking time: 20 minutes

The Ingredients:
¼ cup (½ stick) unsalted butter, melted
2 tablespoons white vinegar
6 cooked beef ribs or 8–10 cooked pork ribs
1½ cups fine dry bread crumbs
water
Sauce:
½ cup mustard (¼ cup spicy brown plus ¼ cup Dijon)
3 tablespoons molasses

2 tablespoons white vinegar
3 tablespoons Worcestershire sauce
½ teaspoon Tabasco
½ teaspoon salt, or to taste
¼ teaspoon freshly ground pepper

The Steps:

1. Preheat broiler to hot. Line a broiling pan with foil.
2. In a small saucepan, melt butter with vinegar and dip bones in mixture to coat.
3. Then dip bones in crumbs coating all over, and place in prepared pan. Pour water into pan to a depth of ½ inch to prevent smoking.
4. Combine sauce ingredients together in bowl.
5. Broil bones for 5 minutes, 6"–8" from heat; then begin basting with sauce, continuing to baste and broil for 20 minutes, or until golden brown.
6. Serve ribs hot or at room temperature.

Accompaniment:
Rice Salad Niçoise.

Variation:
Any combination of mustards can be used.

LAMB

Several years ago, all our lamb was cooked well done. It was greyish looking and often tough. Lately we have come to appreciate lamb cooked rare (slightly red), or medium rare (rosy pink)—lamb that is moist and flavorful, with an attractive appearance.

Although chops are still very popular, they are more expensive and fattier than leg of lamb. The leg can be roasted whole or cut into "lamb steaks," which are chops from the leg that are less expensive than loin or rib chops and much leaner. The leg can also be butterflied (deboned by the butcher), producing a piece of meat similar in shape to a thick steak. Butterflied lamb is particularly tasty when marinated and grilled outdoors.

When buying lamb, look for the tender young lamb that has pink meat versus the dark red meat of old lamb. Young lamb also has white fat versus the yellow fat of older lamb, and young lamb has redder bones versus the whiter, drier ones of older lamb.

Roast Leg of Lamb with Rosemary and Garlic

SERVES: 8
Preparation time: 10–15 minutes
Cooking time: 1½–1¾ hours

The flavor of fresh rosemary and garlic make this super-easy roast leg of lamb delicious.

The Ingredients:
1 5–6 pound leg of lamb, with fell (the tough outer skin) and most of fat removed
2 tablespoons lemon juice
1–2 tablespoons olive oil
½ teaspoon salt, or to taste
½ teaspoon freshly ground pepper, or to taste
2 cloves garlic, peeled and thinly sliced
6–8 sprigs fresh rosemary (if unavailable, use 1 teaspoon dried rosemary)

The Steps:
1. Preheat oven to 350°
2. Wipe lamb with paper towels, rub with lemon juice, massage in olive oil, and sprinkle with salt and pepper.
3. Using tip of sharp knife, make slashes in flesh of lamb and insert slices of garlic and sprigs of rosemary.
4. Place lamb on an oiled rack in a roasting pan; insert a meat thermometer into meatiest part of leg, avoiding the bone. Place in oven for 1½–1¾ hours or until a meat thermometer registers 130°–135° for pink, medium-rare, lamb. (Remove the lamb from oven and allow to stand for 10 minutes at room temperature.) If you prefer lamb more well done, continue to cook to desired degree of doneness. However, I think lamb is at its best served pink. Try it once, you just might like it.

5. Remove garlic and rosemary sprigs, carve the lamb, and serve sliced.

Accompaniments:
Orzo with Mushrooms and Onions, and *Greek Salad.*

Make-It-Easy Tips:
√ If using dried rosemary, crumble the dried leaves between your fingers to release flavor and insert in the slits in the meat.

√ A rosemary herb plant can be grown indoors, adding a fresh scent to the kitchen.

√ Squeeze additional lemon juice to rub on your fingers to remove garlic smell.

Marinated Butterflied Leg of Lamb

SERVES: 6–8
Preparation time: 15 minutes
Marinating time: 24–48 hours
Cooking time: 30–40 minutes

There are many recipes for butterflied leg of lamb—lamb that has been boned and left open so that the meat resembles a steak. It may look jagged and lopsided but, after marinating and grilling, it provides incredibly tasty meat slices. This recipe is adapted from one by the late Michael Field, noted cooking teacher and cookbook author, who serves the lamb with a Greek avgolemono sauce (egg and lemon). I serve *Hot Avgolemono Soup* first, and then the lamb.

The Ingredients:
1 6–7 pound leg of lamb, butterflied, with fell (tough outer skin) removed
Marinade:
⅔ cup olive oil
3 tablespoons lemon juice
2 large onions, thinly sliced
2 cloves garlic, finely minced

    2 tablespoons freshly chopped parsley
    2 bay leaves, crushed
    1 teaspoon dried oregano, crumbled
    ½ teaspoon salt, or to taste
    ½ teaspoon freshly ground pepper
       Garnish: Sprigs of fresh mint or parsley

The Steps:

1. Place lamb in a plastic jumbo food storage bag. (Don't use garbage bags.) Combine marinade ingredients in large measuring cup, pour over lamb in the bag, tie up securely. Place in another bag and tie up. (The storage bag keeps marinade closely around meat and allows you to turn it easily.)
2. Marinate lamb for 24–48 hours, turning twice a day.
3. Preheat broiler or outdoor grill and bring lamb to room temperature.
4. Broil or grill lamb for 15–20 minutes a side, basting occasionally, or until medium rare (light pink).
5. Slice lamb on the bias and serve hot, garnished with sprigs of fresh mint or parsley.

Accompaniment:

Pasta al Pesto, and *Greek Salad.*

Variations:

Leftover medium-rare lamb can be used on sandwiches with spicy mustard, stir-fried with Chinese vegetables, or dipped in mustard and then bread crumbs and broiled until golden.

Make-It-Easy Tips:

√ The lamb can be marinated in a shallow, nonmetallic baking dish, if desired.

√ If pressed for time, marinate lamb for 12 hours. It will not be as tender or juicy, but still satisfactory. If dinner is put off, it can easily marinate for three days.

Lamb with Dill

SERVES: 8
Preparation time: 15 minutes
Cooking time: 3 hours, 18 minutes

Lamb with Dill is juicy, flavorful, and low in calories. The dill flavor comes from the seed, rather than the leaves of the dill plant. The lamb is cooked in a very hot oven for the first 18 minutes, and then the oven is turned off and the lamb cooks undisturbed for the remaining 3 hours.

The Ingredients:

1 5–6 pound leg of lamb, with fell (tough outer skin) and most of fat removed
1 large onion, thinly sliced
1 clove garlic, minced
½ teaspoon salt, or to taste
½ teaspoon freshly ground pepper
1 quart buttermilk
1 tablespoon dill seed
2 large onions, thinly sliced
8–10 small red or new potatoes, scrubbed but unpeeled
⅓ cup beef broth
⅓ cup red wine
Salt and pepper to taste

The Steps:

1. Place lamb in large deep bowl, and cover with 1 onion, garlic, salt, and pepper. Pour buttermilk over the lamb, sprinkle with dill seed, cover, and marinate in refrigerator for 2–3 days, turning twice a day, if possible.
2. When ready to cook, preheat oven to 500°
3. Lay 2 sliced onions in bottom of roasting pan, remove lamb from marinade, draining off excess, and place on bed of onions and surround with potatoes.
4. Add broth and wine to pan, place in oven, and roast for 18 minutes.
5. Turn oven off immediately and allow lamb to stand undis-

turbed in oven for 3 hours *without* opening the door of the oven. (This amount of time will produce medium-rare lamb; for rare, cook only 15 minutes in hot oven and, for well done, cook 20 minutes.)

6. Strain gravy and remove excess fat. Taste, and adjust seasoning with salt and pepper. Serve alongside carved lamb with roasted potatoes and onions.

Accompaniment:

Perfect Baked Potatoes and, shredded cabbage with *Low-Calorie Buttermilk Dill Dressing.*

Variation:

Carrots and celery can be added to bed of onions when roasting lamb.

Make-It-Easy Tips:

√ When marinating lamb, it is easy to do tied up in 2 plastic jumbo food storage bags where the meat can conveniently be turned without messing up hands or utensils.

√ Once the lamb has been cooked at a high temperature for 18 minutes, the oven is turned off and you can forget about dinner until ready to serve. The lamb can sit an additional 1–2 hours after the prescribed 3 hours and then can be reheated for 10 minutes in a 325° oven.

Rack of Lamb with Fresh Mint Sauce

SERVES: 4–6
Preparation time: 15 minutes
Cooking time: 30–35 minutes

This is an expensive and elegant dinner dish that I reserve for very special occasions, serving the lamb with a refreshing mint sauce on the side. A rack is a section of rib or loin chops all in one piece—uncut.

The Ingredients:

2 racks of lamb (1¾–2 pounds each), well trimmed (rib or loin section)

Marinade:

¼ cup brandy

½ teaspoon dried thyme, crumbled

¼ teaspoon dried oregano, crumbled

¼ teaspoon dried basil, crumbled

½ teaspoon salt, or to taste

¼ teaspoon freshly ground pepper

Dip:

¼ cup flour

1 egg lightly beaten with 1 tablespoon milk or half-and-half

1 cup dry bread crumbs

Sauce:

½ cup olive oil

½ cup red wine vinegar

6–8 fresh mint leaves

½ teaspoon salt, or to taste

¼ teaspoon freshly ground pepper

The Steps:

1. Place lamb in shallow dish. Combine marinade ingredients and pour over lamb; cover and marinate at room temperature for 2–3 hours or in refrigerator overnight. Bring to room temperature before cooking.
2. Preheat oven to 450°.
3. Dip lamb in flour, shaking off excess, then dip in egg mixture and, finally, roll in bread crumbs, coating evenly.
4. Bake lamb, fat side up, for 30–35 minutes or until top is crusty and golden brown (meat will be medium rare).
5. While meat is cooking, combine ingredients for sauce in blender or food processor and process until just smooth but with the mint in chunky pieces.
6. Carve lamb into chops and serve hot, with sauce on the side.

Accompaniments:

Potatoes Boiled in Jackets, and *Tomatoes Filled with Peas.*

Variation:

If fresh mint is unavailable, use mint jelly as an accompaniment.

Make-It-Easy Tip:

√ Have butcher cut through bone connecting ribs so that chops can be easily cut after roasting.

Barbecued Lamb Riblets

SERVES: 4–6
Preparation time: 15 minutes
Cooking time: 1 hour

Lamb Riblets are "spareribs" from the breast of lamb. They are an inexpensive and juicy substitute for pork or beef spareribs.

The Ingredients:
    3 pounds breast of lamb, well trimmed of fat
    1 clove garlic, smashed
Sauce:
  ¾ cup ketchup
    2 teaspoons Dijon mustard
  ½ teaspoon minced garlic
    2 teaspoons Worcestershire sauce
  ½ teaspoon chili powder
    2 tablespoons corn oil
    2 tablespoons vinegar
    1 tablespoon soy sauce
  ½ teaspoon salt, or to taste
  ¼ teaspoon freshly ground pepper

The Steps:
1. Preheat oven to 350°.
2. Rub lamb all over with garlic; place lamb, fat side up, in a roasting pan and bake for ½ hour.
3. Combine sauce ingredients in bowl and stir until smooth.
4. Turn lamb, brush lightly with sauce, and return to oven for 20 minutes.
5. Increase heat to broil, lavish on sauce, and broil, not too close to the heat source, until crisp and meat is tender, basting occasionally.
6. Slice lamb riblets into serving pieces and serve hot.

Accompaniments:
Sweet Potato Soufflé, and *Spinach Salad*.

Variations:

This recipe can be used for pork or beef ribs; adjust cooking times accordingly.

To remove excess grease, parboil lamb for 20 minutes, drain, and proceed with Step 3.

Make-It-Easy Tips:

√ Lamb can be cooked earlier in the day, wrapped in foil, refrigerated, and reheated in a low-temperature oven.

PORK

Pork is often neglected as a main course because it is thought to have a high calorie count. Actually, today's pork is much leaner and has almost the identical fat content and calorie count as beef.

Pork is easy to prepare, either as chops, roasted whole as a loin, or cooked as spareribs on the barbecue. When cooking pork roasts, rely on a meat thermometer to determine for health reasons whether it is fully cooked. The old recommended 185°F. temperature is no longer necessary, and the new leaner pork will be dried out if cooked that long. An internal temperature of 165°F. for lean loin roasts, or 170°F. for more marbled cuts of pork, should be sufficient.

Pork Chops with Mustard Dill Sauce

SERVES: 4–6
Preparation time: 20 minutes
Cooking time: 1 hour

The chops are coated with a creamy dill sauce to make a very elegant dinner entrée.

The Ingredients:

6 pork chops, cut 1″ thick
3–4 tablespoons Dijon mustard
2 tablespoons unsalted butter
1 large onion, thinly sliced

  3 tablespoons all-purpose flour
1½ cups beef or chicken broth
 ¾ cup heavy cream
 1 teaspoon freshly snipped dill or ⅓ teaspoon dried dill
 ½ teaspoon salt, or to taste
 ½ teaspoon freshly ground white pepper
  Garnish: Freshly snipped dill or chopped parsley

The Steps:

1. Lay chops on sheet of waxed paper and brush 1 side generously with Dijon mustard.
2. Melt butter in a large heavy skillet; add chops, mustard side down, and cook over medium-high heat until lightly browned; brush top side with mustard, turn the chops, and brown on the other side; remove the chops from skillet with slotted spatula.
3. Add onions to pan and cook over medium heat until golden brown, about 5 minutes. (It may be necessary to add a tablespoon of butter if no fat remains in the skillet.)
4. Remove skillet from direct heat and add flour, stirring well to combine.
5. Add broth, and return to heat, stirring constantly; when boiling, add cream.
6. Add dill, salt, and pepper; return chops to pan, cover, reduce heat, and simmer slowly for 50–60 minutes or until tender. Turn once during cooking.
7. Taste, and adjust seasoning if necessary. Serve chops hot, with sauce poured over them.

Accompaniments:
Baked Potato Skins, and *Raw Mushroom Salad.*

Variations:
Veal chops can be substituted for pork chops but should be cooked only 20 minutes or until just tender.

Make-It-Easy Tip:
√ Dried dill can be substituted, but fresh is better. To ensure having fresh dill year 'round, chop large bunches when available and freeze in small plastic bags or containers.

Sweet & Sour Pork Chops

SERVES: 4–6
Preparation time: 20 minutes
Cooking time: 45 minutes

This is an easy pork chop recipe that can be assembled a day ahead and reheated.

The Ingredients:
¼ cup all-purpose flour
½ teaspoon salt, or to taste
½ teaspoon freshly ground pepper
½ teaspoon ground ginger
6 pork chops, cut 1" thick, trimmed of fat
1 tablespoon unsalted butter
1 tablespoon vegetable oil
1 small onion, finely chopped
1 clove garlic, finely minced
½ cup hot beef broth
¼ cup chili sauce
3 tablespoons cider vinegar
1½ tablespoons light brown sugar
Garnish: Freshly chopped parsley

The Steps:
1. Combine flour, salt, pepper, and ginger; dip chops in flour mixture, shaking off any excess.
2. In large Dutch oven or deep skillet, heat butter and oil together and brown chops on both sides over high heat.
3. Add onions and garlic and cook over medium heat until they are soft, about 5 minutes.
4. Pour off excess accumulated fat in skillet; add beef broth, chili sauce, cider vinegar, and brown sugar. Stir to combine, bring to a boil, cover, and simmer slowly for 45 minutes or until chops are tender. (It may be necessary to add additional beef broth. Check the liquid level periodically and add broth when necessary.)
5. Taste, and adjust seasoning as necessary. Serve chops hot, garnished with freshly chopped parsley.

Accompaniments:
>*Green Rice*, and a mixed green salad with *Laurie's Basic Vinai-grette* dressing.

Variations:
>Sweet & Sour Pork Chops can be baked, covered, in a 375° oven for 45 minutes instead of cooking on top of range.
>
>½ teaspoon freshly grated ginger can be substituted for dried ginger.

Make-It-Easy Tips:
>√ The chops can be cooked earlier in the day, and then refrigerated or frozen.
>
>√ Garlic should be cooked only until golden. When browned or burned, it develops a bitter and unpleasant taste.

Pork Loin Polynesian

SERVES: 6
Preparation time: 15 minutes
Cooking time: 1½–2 hours

The Ingredients:
>Half a loin of pork (3–4 pounds), boned, and tied securely
>½ teaspoon salt
>¼ teaspoon freshly ground pepper
>¼ teaspoon ground rosemary
>**Sauce:**
>¼ cup soy sauce
>¼ cup ketchup
>2 tablespoons honey
>1 large clove garlic, finely minced
>¼ teaspoon powdered ginger
>Garnish: Preserved kumquats and sprigs of watercress

The Steps:
>1. Preheat oven to 350°.

2. Place pork on rack in shallow roasting pan and sprinkle with salt, pepper, and rosemary and roast for 20 minutes.
3. Combine sauce ingredients in bowl and mix together; baste the pork loin frequently with mixture to give it a caramel glaze; cook for an additional 1½ hours or until a thermometer registers 160°F.
4. Transfer pork to a platter and allow to stand for 10 minutes; this will increase the temperature to 165°F. Serve sliced, garnished with preserved kumquats and sprigs of watercress.

Accompaniments:

Baked Spinach with Cheese, and *Curried Brown Rice Salad with Fruit.*

Variations:

Leftover pork can be shredded in an *Oriental Salad* (*see* Chapter 7, Braised Daikon, Variations) with vegetables.

The glaze is also wonderful on roast leg of lamb.

Freshly ground ginger (½ teaspoon) can be substituted for powdered ginger.

Make-It-Easy Tips:

√ The easiest way to grind rosemary is with a mortar and pestle. If unavailable, wrap the rosemary leaves in waxed paper and crush with a rolling pin.

√ To prevent sticking, oil the rack with a brush before roasting pork.

√ When measuring sticky liquids, such as honey, syrup, or molasses, lightly oil the inside of the measuring cup before using and easily rinse out with very hot water after measuring.

Potted Pork with Fruit

SERVES: 4–6
Preparation time: 20 minutes
Cooking time: 1½ hours

As discussed in the recipe for *Whole Chicken Cooked in a Clay Pot,* the wet terra-cotta clay keeps natural cooking juices in, the food is self-basted, fats are kept to a minimum, and a one-pot, no-fuss dinner is created.

The Ingredients:

  1 Ovenbrique, Romertopf, Gourmetopf or similar brand unglazed terra-cotta pot

  1 loin of pork (3½ pounds) well trimmed of fat, with bones cracked for easy carving

  1 clove garlic, crushed but still intact

  1 teaspoon salt, or to taste

  ½ teaspoon freshly ground pepper

  ¼ teaspoon freshly grated ginger

  1 large onion, thinly sliced

  2 large carrots, peeled and thinly sliced

  ¾–1 cup port wine

  12 pitted prunes

  3 ounces dried apples (soaked in boiling water, optional step)

  ¼ cup heavy cream

The Steps:

1. Presoak a clay pot, top and bottom, in water for 20 minutes.
2. While the pot is soaking, rub the trimmed loin of pork well with garlic. Sprinkle both sides with salt, pepper, and ginger.
3. Place onion in bottom of pot. Add pork, fat side up, and surround with carrots. Pour wine around meat and vegetables and insert a meat thermometer into thickest part of the meat.
4. Cover with the presoaked top and place in a *cold* oven. (Clay pots will crack from the sudden heat of a preheated oven.) Set oven to 475° and cook pork for 1 hour.
5. After 1 hour of cooking time, remove pot from oven and distribute prunes and apples around meat. Re-cover pot and continue to cook for an additional ½ hour or until meat thermometer registers done.
6. Remove meat and vegetables to a platter, and keep warm. Skim fat from gravy (or use device to remove fat) and place defatted gravy in small saucepan. Add cream, and stir until slightly thickened. Serve sauce with pork, vegetables, and fruit.

Accompaniments:

Plain Brown Rice, and a mixed green salad with *Laurie's Basic Vinaigrette* dressing.

Variations:

A boneless loin of pork may be substituted for the loin with ribs attached.

Additional dried fruits, such as peaches or apricots, can be added.

Make-It-Easy Tips:

√ A small amount of ginger can be grated easily by using the smallest holes of a kitchen grater or a small lemon- or nutmeg-grater.

√ Use a Gravy Strain or similar brand of fat-straining pitcher to remove fat. It is a pitcher with the spout based at the bottom. The gravy is poured in, the fat rises quickly to the top, the gravy is poured off from the bottom, and the fat remains in the pitcher.

Special Spareribs

SERVES: 6
Preparation time: 15 minutes
Cooking time: 1½ hours

The Ingredients:

4 pounds small, meaty, pork spareribs
Basting Glaze:
¼ cup Bourbon
¼ cup soy sauce
¼ cup brown sugar
¼ cup orange juice
1 tablespoon Dijon mustard
1 tablespoon vinegar
¼ teaspoon minced garlic

The Steps:

1. Preheat oven to 350°.
2. Place spareribs in foil-lined roasting pan (to save on clean-ups) and bake, fat side up, for 15 minutes; turn and bake an additional 15 minutes; pour off accumulated fat.
3. Meanwhile, combine glaze ingredients in saucepan; cook over low heat, stirring constantly, until smooth.

4. Generously glaze ribs with sauce and return to oven for ½ hour, basting after 15 minutes; turn and lavish remaining sauce on ribs and bake for 30 minutes longer or until glazed and golden.
5. Glaze once again, and serve spareribs hot.

Accompaniments:
Southern-Style Cheese Grits, and sliced tomatoes with Spinach Mayonnaise.

Variations:
Beef ribs can be substituted for pork ribs.

Make-It-Easy Tips:
√ Store brown sugar in a sealed container in the refrigerator to prevent caking.
√ Use a thick brush to baste ribs.

Make-It-Easy Ham

SERVES: 6–8
Preparation time: 10 minutes
Cooking time: 1 hour

The recipe for this ham comes from a friend in the South who insists that the real secret is the Coca Cola. I've tried ginger ale, diet colas and even Dr. Pepper with success, proving that the secret is in the bubbles.

The Ingredients:
    1 3–pound ham
    ¼ cup Dijon mustard
  6–8 whole cloves
    ⅓ cup apricot preserves, orange marmalade, or peach preserves
    ¼ cup maple syrup
    1 cup red wine
    ⅓ cup cola drink

2 tablespoons cider vinegar
Garnish: *Mustard Mayonnaise* (*see* Chapter 8)

The Steps:
1. Preheat oven to 350°. Line baking pan with foil.
2. Place ham in pan, fat side up; coat with mustard and stud with cloves.
3. Mix preserves and syrup together and spread on ham.
4. Combine wine, cola, and vinegar; pour over ham, and bake ham for 1 hour, basting every 15 minutes.
5. Remove ham from oven, allow to rest 15 minutes, and serve with *Mustard Mayonnaise.*

Accompaniments:
Baked Acorn Squash, and *Cabbage Salad with Caraway Seeds.*

Variations:
Ham can be served as a luncheon entrée with *Spinach Quiche* or *Frittata* (*see* Chapter 3).

Leftover ham can be stir-fried with Chinese vegetables or used as a base for pâtés or simply in sandwiches with *Mustard Mayonnaise.*

Make-It-Easy Tips:
√ Make sure to line the pan with foil because the glaze on the ham will stick forever to your pan.

√ When purchasing a canned ham, select only a refrigerated one. Hams must be refrigerated at all times, although some supermarkets ignore this fact.

VEAL
Veal is a wonderful and versatile meat. It is easy to prepare either sautéed as scaloppine, or braised in stews; it is also delicious as a roast. Veal adapts itself to a wide variety of sauces. Of all the meats, it is the lowest in both calories and cholesterol.

The only drawback is that veal is very expensive. Scaloppine has become a luxury dinner. However, a pound of veal can serve four people. Veal stews are much less expensive than scaloppine and veal provides a lighter flavor than beef. Ground veal is even less expensive and can be used for meat loaves, meatballs, or even burger patties.

Wiener Schnitzel à la Luchow

SERVES: 4
Preparation time: 15 minutes
Cooking time: 10 minutes

This recipe is an easy variation of the Wiener Schnitzel served at the famous New York restaurant, Luchow's. The traditional topping for Schnitzel à la Holstein is a fried egg and anchovy fillets. Luchow's uses scrambled eggs and asparagus.

The Ingredients:
      3 tablespoons unsalted butter
      4 8-ounce veal cutlets, pounded thin and wiped dry
      1 cup beef broth
      6 eggs
      1 tablespoon chopped chives (or finely minced scallion greens)
      ½ teaspoon salt, or to taste
      ½ teaspoon freshly ground pepper, or to taste
      2 tablespoons unsalted butter
     10 medium-size mushrooms, sliced
        Garnish: Hot cooked asparagus, 16 stalks (optional)

The Steps:
   1. In a large skillet, heat 3 tablespoons butter; brown veal over high heat for only a minute on each side. (Do not overcook.) Remove to a warm platter.
   2. To make gravy, add broth to pan, scraping up browned particles from the bottom; taste for seasoning and adjust.
   3. In small bowl, beat eggs with chives, salt, and pepper.
   4. In another skillet, heat 2 tablespoons butter and sauté mushrooms for 4–5 minutes until golden.
   5. Add egg mixture to mushrooms and cook over moderate heat, scrambling the eggs until just soft but not overcooked.
   6. Pour the eggs over the browned cutlets and top with the broth gravy.
   7. Garnish platter with asparagus and serve immediately, good and hot.

Accompaniment:
Potatoes boiled in Jackets.

Variations:
Boned and skinned chicken breasts or pork tenderloins can be used for a less expensive version, but they must be cooked longer.

Make-It-Easy Tip:
√ Wiener Schnitzel a la Luchow must be prepared at the last minute.

Veal and Water Chestnuts

SERVES: 6
Preparation time: 25 minutes
Cooking time: 1⅓ hours

Veal and Water Chestnuts is a very rich and creamy entrée to be served over plain white rice with only a simple green salad.

The Ingredients:
4 tablespoons (½ stick) unsalted butter
2 pounds boneless veal, cut into 1" cubes
1 pound mushrooms, sliced
1 medium onion, finely chopped
1 clove garlic, finely minced
¼ cup dry white wine
1 cup beef broth
2 8-ounce cans sliced water chestnuts, drained
½ teaspoon salt, or to taste
¼ teaspoon freshly ground pepper
Pinch of nutmeg
Pinch of cayenne
1 cup heavy cream
Garnish: Freshly chopped parsley

The Steps:

1. Preheat oven to 375°.
2. Melt butter in a Dutch oven or large, deep skillet; brown veal on all sides over high heat; remove with slotted spoon.
3. Add the mushrooms, onion, and garlic, and sauté over medium heat until golden.
4. Add wine to deglaze pan, scraping browned particles from bottom of pan.
5. Return veal to pan; add broth, water chestnuts, salt, pepper, nutmeg, and cayenne. Bring to boil; cover, and place in oven for 1¼ hours or until tender.
6. Stir in cream and continue to cook, uncovered, for 20 minutes longer.
7. Taste, adjust seasoning if necessary, and serve hot, garnished with freshly chopped parsley.

Accompaniments:

White rice, and tossed green salad with *Laurie's Basic Vinaigrette* dressing.

Variations:

Whole or quartered water chestnuts can be substituted for sliced. Beef can be substituted for the veal.

Make-It-Easy Tips:

√ This dish can be prepared a day or two in advance, or even frozen and reheated before serving.

Ragoût de Veau (Casserole of Veal)

SERVES: 6–8
Preparation time: 20 minutes
Cooking time: 1½ hours

The Ingredients:

2 tablespoons unsalted butter
1 cup thinly sliced onions
1 clove garlic, minced
⅓ cup all-purpose flour

½ teaspoon salt, or to taste
½ teaspoon freshly ground pepper, or to taste
¼ teaspoon paprika
3 pounds boneless veal (veal stew meat), cut into 1½"–2" cubes
2 tablespoons unsalted butter
1 tablespoon olive oil
½ cup port, Marsala, or other sweet red wine
1 16-ounce can tomatoes, drained and roughly chopped
½ cup chicken broth
½ teaspoon thyme, crumbled
18 pitted olives, 9 black, 9 green (or use only black olives)
Salt and freshly ground pepper to taste
Garnish: Freshly chopped parsley

The Steps:
1. Preheat oven to 325°.
2. In Dutch oven or large casserole, heat butter; sauté onions and garlic over medium heat until soft and lightly golden; remove to a bowl and set aside.
3. Combine flour, salt, pepper, and paprika; add veal cubes and toss to coat all over.
4. Add remaining butter and oil to casserole; sauté veal over medium/high heat until golden.
5. Add wine to deglaze pan, scraping brown particles up from bottom; add tomatoes, broth, and thyme. Bring to boil, cover, and bake for 1½ hours or until veal is tender.
6. Add olives, cover, and continue to bake for 10 minutes longer to heat through.
7. Taste, and adjust seasoning with salt and pepper. Serve garnished with freshly chopped parsley.

Accompaniments:
White rice, and Salad of Asparagus Tips with Mustard Dressing

Variation:
Beef can be substituted for the veal.

Make-It-Easy Tips:
√ This Ragout can be prepared up through Step 5 and refrigerated for 2–3 days, or frozen for several months.
√ To avoid tears when slicing onions, place onion in freezer for 20 minutes prior to slicing.

MEAT LOAVES

The announcement of "meat loaf tonight" is generally not going to bring down the house. As a matter of fact, it might bring down the spirits of the diners if it's of the all too common variety—heavy, mealy, a real loser. The following easy recipes, however, are guaranteed to clear meat loaf's bad name forever!

When buying meat for a meat loaf, ask your butcher (whenever possible) to grind the various meats together. If he can't, do so yourself in a meat grinder or food processor—you'll taste the difference!

Meat loaf is an economical, easy to prepare meal for family or company. Take a test run on your family. You'll see how easy it is to make and how great it is the next day as leftovers!

For variety, bake the meat loaf in muffin tins or mini-loaf pans for individual loaves. Remember that the smaller loaves take only one-half to three-quarters of the time to bake.

Fluffy Light Meat Loaf

SERVES: 3–4
Preparation time: 15 minutes
Cooking time: 50 minutes–1 hour

Fluffy Light Meat Loaf is light in texture and yet high in fiber. If time permits, prepare it in the morning, cover, and allow the flavors to mellow until ready to cook.

The Ingredients:

    1 pound ground beef
    1 6-ounce can tomato paste
   ½ cup oatmeal
    3 tablespoons finely chopped green pepper or celery
    2 tablespoons bran
    2 tablespoons wheat germ
    1 small onion, finely chopped
    1 tablespoon freshly chopped parsley
    1 egg, lightly beaten
   ¼ teaspoon finely chopped garlic

½ teaspoon salt, or to taste
¼ teaspoon freshly ground pepper
Chili sauce

The Steps:

1. Preheat oven to 350°.
2. Combine all loaf ingredients, using your hands.
3. Form into loaf and place in a 9" x 5" x 3" loaf pan, cover with a layer of chili sauce (or ketchup if desired), and bake for 50 minutes to 1 hour. (Do not overbake since part of the secret of fluffiness is shorter cooking time.)
4. Serve the meat loaf sliced and hot.

Accompaniments:

Perfect Baked Potatoes, and *Broccoli Florets Vinaigrette.*

Variations:

Half ground veal and half ground beef can be used for a meat loaf lower in calories.

Leftover cold meat loaf is a favorite lunch sandwich with ketchup on dark rye bread.

Make-It-Easy Tips:

√ Chop the onion, garlic, parsley, and green pepper or celery together in food processor.

√ A new gadget called a "fat-free meat loaf pan" is currently available. It consists of two pans, one fitting inside the other. The inner pan has holes in it to allow fat to drip off into the other pan. *See* Appendix A.

Low-fat meat loaf pan

Chinese Ground Beef Loaf

SERVES: 6
Preparation time: 15 minutes
Cooking time: 45 minutes

This oriental-flavored loaf can be served as a main course or chilled and served as a pâté.

The Ingredients:

1 pound ground beef
1 tablespoon peanut oil
1 tablespoon oriental sesame oil
¼ teaspoon sugar
2 tablespoons soy sauce
1 tablespoon dry sherry
2 scallions (white and green included), finely minced
¼ teaspoon minced garlic
2 eggs, lightly beaten
½–¾ cup Hoisin sauce (available at oriental grocery stores and by mail order, *see* Appendix A)

The Steps:

1. Preheat oven to 350°. Lightly oil, or spray with non-aerosol vegetable shortening, an 8″ x 4″ x 2″ loaf pan or glass pie plate.
2. Combine all ingredients, except Hoisin sauce, using hands or pulsating in a food processor.
3. Form into a loaf and place in pan, or into a circular mound in glass pie plate. Generously "frost" with a layer of Hoisin sauce.
4. Bake for 45 minutes.
5. Discard accumulated fat and serve hot or at room temperature with additional Hoisin sauce.

Accompaniments:

Fried Rice, Chinese Asparagus Salad with Spicy Dressing.

Variations:

For a fluffier loaf, add ½ cup cooked rice to the loaf.
Pork can be substituted for the beef. If using pork, increase cook-

ing time to 1 hour, and decrease the amount of oil since ground
pork often has a higher fat content.

Serve the loaf cold the next day as a pâté or in a Pita bread sandwich with additional Hoisin sauce.

Make-It-Easy Tip:

√ Prepare the Chinese Beef Loaf in muffin tins, cook only 30–40
minutes, and serve as a first course.

FISH AND SEAFOOD

Fish is adaptable to almost any form of cooking. It can be grilled,
sautéed, pan-fried, baked, braised or even stir-fried in a matter of minutes for a quick and easy entrée.

When buying fish for a particular recipe note the length of cooking time. Thicker, fleshy fish, such as haddock, halibut, or bass, are
more adaptable to baking or broiling, and thin fillets of flounder or sole
are best suited for sautéing.

Try to buy fish or seafood at a fish store rather than at a supermarket. You can be a little more certain of freshness. Get to know the
people who sell at your fish market since they can advise you on the
freshest local fish to buy. They will also provide information about the
ideal seasons for shrimp, clams, mussels, scallops, or other seafood,
thus reducing your costs.

Freshness is of the utmost importance when purchasing fish. Use
odor as the main criterion. If there is an unpleasant or "fishy" smell,
the fish is not fresh. Whole fish should have bright and clear bulging
eyes. The flesh should be firm and resilient to the touch, and the gills
should be reddish and intact. Freezing masks most of these criteria so,
if possible, buy fresh fish. If you freeze fresh fish yourself, thaw well
wrapped for 12–24 hours in the refrigerator.

Fish is low in calories and low in cholesterol, a perfect dietetic
main course. It can be grilled with fresh lemon juice and herbs for a
simple, easy entrée to please family and friends, who all seem to be
conscious of burgeoning waistlines. For another low-calorie variation,
try cooking fish *en papillote* (wrapped in parchment paper), to steam
in fresh juices and flavor, avoiding the often dried-out taste of many
low-calorie fish recipes.

Baked Whole Salmon

SERVES: 6
Preparation time: 15 minutes
Cooking time: 45–60 minutes
Chilling time: 4–6 hours or overnight

This Make-It-Easy recipe enables you to cook a whole salmon when you don't own a large poacher and you wish to avoid tying up the fish in cheesecloth. The salmon is baked in foil, steaming in flavor and juices.

The Ingredients:

    1 whole salmon, 6–7 pounds, cleaned and scaled
    2 large lemons, thinly sliced
    1 medium onion, thinly sliced
  ½ cup dry white wine or dry vermouth
    2 tablespoons freshly chopped parsley
  ½ teaspoon freshly ground pepper
      Garnish: Watercress, lemon wedges, and *Cucumber Dill Sauce* or *Spinach Mayonnaise*

The Steps:

1. Preheat oven to 350°.
2. Place salmon on large sheet of *heavy-duty* foil.
3. Layer lemon and onion slices over fish; add wine, sprinkle with parsley and pepper. Seal well.
4. Bake for 45–60 minutes or until fish is flaky and tender.
5. Remove from oven, open foil package, arrange salmon on platter, cover, and chill for 4–6 hours or overnight.
6. Serve salmon chilled, garnished with watercress and lemon wedges and *Cucumber Dill Sauce* or *Spinach Mayonnaise*.

Accompaniments:

Rice Salad Niçoise, and *Broccoli Florets Vinaigrette*.

Variations:

Poached fish is low in calories but the *Cucumber Dill Sauce* or *Spinach Mayonnaise* is not. If concerned about calories, substitute *Yogurt Dill Sauce* or Cucumber Dressing and serve the salmon with tomatoes with *Spicy Tomato Dressing with No Oil.*

Additional fresh herbs such as dill or chives can be added to the salmon before baking.

Salmon can also be served hot with a hollandaise sauce or sprinkled with melted butter.

Leftover salmon makes a wonderful salad with mayonnaise, herbs, and lemon juice.

Make-It-Easy Tip:
√ To transfer salmon easily from foil package to platter, roll carefully, gently pulling the foil away.

Haddock "Blacksmith Shop"

SERVES: 4
Preparation time: 15 minutes
Cooking time: 20 minutes

This recipe comes from The Blacksmith Shop, a restaurant on Cape Cod.

The Ingredients:
- 2 tablespoons Dijon mustard
- 2 tablespoons lemon juice
- 2 teaspoons Worcestershire sauce
- 2 pounds haddock or similar filleted fish such as scrod
- 1 large onion, thinly sliced
- 1½ pints dairy sour cream
- Garnish: Watercress sprigs, lemon slices

The Steps:
1. Preheat oven to 400°.
2. Combine mustard, lemon juice, Worcestershire, and spread completely over fish in a baking dish.
3. Cover with onion and top with a thick blanket of sour cream.

4. Bake for 20 minutes or until fish is flaky and top is golden at edges.
5. Serve hot, garnished with sprigs of watercress and lemon slices.

Accompaniments:
Lemon Rice, and *String Bean Salad.*

Make-It-Easy Tips:
√ The fish can be prepared earlier in the day by marinating in refrigerator in mustard, Worcestershire, and lemon juice.
√ To avoid "fishy" smells while cooking, boil a separate pot of water with 3 or 4 whole cloves for a pleasant aroma.

Marinated Grilled Swordfish Steaks

SERVES: 4
Preparation time: 10 minutes
Cooking time: 14–18 minutes

The Ingredients:
   4 swordfish steaks
   2 tablespoons unsalted butter, melted
   2 tablespoons olive oil
   ¼ teaspoon salt, or to taste
   ¼ teaspoon freshly ground white pepper
   Pinch of paprika
Sauce:
   2 tablespoons olive oil
   1 tablespoon lemon juice
   2 teaspoons freshly chopped parsley
   ¼ teaspoon finely minced garlic

The Steps:
1. Place fish in dish. Combine butter and oil and pour over fish; sprinkle with salt, pepper, and paprika and allow to marinate for ½ hour at room temperature, turning once or twice.
2. Preheat broiler or outdoor grill.

3. Broil fish for 6–9 minutes per side or until just flaky, basting occasionally. (Do not overcook or the fish will dry out.)
4. While fish is broiling, combine sauce ingredients in bowl.
5. Place fish on platter, pour a little sauce over each piece, and serve immediately.

Accompaniments:

August Pasta, and *Caesar Salad.*

Variations:

Other firm fleshy fish or fish steaks such as halibut or salmon can be substituted.

Mash leftover fish with mayonnaise, a little lemon juice, chives or scallions, and seasoning to use as a fish salad the next day.

Make-It-Easy Tip:

√ If cooking outdoors, it is easier to turn fish if it is placed in a flat-grid hamburger or hot dog grill.

Herb Broiled Fish Fillets

SERVES: 4
Preparation time: 10–15 minutes
Cooking time: 8–10 minutes

It is not necessary to use the specific herbs I have listed in the ingredients. Select one herb, or make up a combination of fresh herbs that you prefer equal to one tablespoon.

The Ingredients:

½ cup mayonnaise
1 tablespoon lemon juice
1 teaspoon freshly snipped dill
1 teaspoon freshly chopped chives (or scallion stalks)
1 teaspoon freshly chopped parsley
½ teaspoon salt, or to taste
¼ teaspoon freshly ground pepper

2 pounds fish fillets or fish sticks (e.g., flounder, halibut, haddock, bass, red snapper, swordfish)
Garnish: Freshly grated lemon peel

The Steps:
1. Preheat broiler.
2. Combine mayonnaise, lemon juice, and herbs and mix until smooth.
3. Sprinkle salt and pepper over both sides of fish and place on broiling pan.
4. Spread ½ mayonnaise-herb mixture on fish and broil for 3–5 minutes a side, depending on thickness of fish.
5. Turn fish, spread on remaining mayonnaise-herb mixture, and continue to broil until fish is flaky.
6. Serve fish hot, garnished with freshly grated lemon peel.

Accompaniments:
Stir-Fried Straw and Hay Summer Squash, and crusty French bread.

Variation:
Leftover Tip: Any remaining fish can be eaten cold as a fish salad the next day.

Make-It-Easy Tips:
√ Chop fresh herbs in food processor or blender and keep extra fresh herbs frozen in small containers or plastic bags.
√ If using dried herbs, remember that 1 teaspoon of dried herbs = 1 tablespoon of fresh herbs.

Fish with Butter and Capers en Papillote

SERVES: 2
Preparation time: 15 minutes
Cooking time: 10–15 minutes

Cooking in parchment paper (available at cookware shops and department stores) steams in flavors and keeps very thin fish from drying out while baking.

The Ingredients:

- 2 pieces of parchment paper (about 18″ in length)
- 2 fish fillets, ½ pound each (e.g., sole, flounder, snapper, or sand dabs)
- 2 tablespoons unsalted butter, melted
- 2 teaspoons fresh lemon juice
- 2 tablespoons capers
- 1 tablespoon freshly chopped parsley
- ½ teaspoon salt, or to taste
- ¼ teaspoon freshly ground pepper
- 1 lemon, thinly sliced
- Garnish: Lemon slices, freshly chopped parsley, capers

The Steps:

1. Preheat oven to 350°
2. Prepare parchment and fish according to instructions in the figures.
3. Brush fish with a little melted butter, and then drizzle a teaspoon of lemon juice on each. Distribute capers and parsley evenly over fish and season with salt and pepper.
4. Finally, place a few thin slices of lemon on each portion. Fold paper over and seal by crimping edges all around (see figure).
5. Place packet on a baking sheet and bake for 10–15 minutes or until fish is tender and flaky. (Timing depends on thickness of the fish.)
6. Serve fish garnished with additional lemon slices, chopped parsley, and capers.

Accompaniments:

Rice Pilaf with Pine Nuts, and *Snow Pea Salad.*

Variations:

For a low-calorie steamed fish, omit butter and garnish with lots of lemon juice and some grated lemon rind.

For another low-calorie version, top 2 pounds fish fillets with one 10-ounce package frozen chopped spinach, 4 mushrooms sliced, 2 tablespoons lemon juice, 2 scallion stalks, salt and pepper to taste, and a sliced lemon, and proceed as above.

Make-It-Easy Tips:

√ Lemons will yield more juice if they are at room temperature when squeezed.

1. To cook en papillote, cut a large rectangular piece of parchment paper. Fold the rectangle in half.

2. Using scissors or a knife, start cutting from the folded side, following an imaginary line that resembles a heart.

3. Place the fish fillet on top and add seasonings.

4. Cover the fish with the other half of the paper.

5. Seal edges of paper by folding the edges over and crimping them all the way around from the fold. If the edges aren't tightly sealed, the paper won't puff.

6. An individual papillote after baking.

√ Foil can be used in place of parchment paper, but the paper produces a better result.

√ Parchment paper is a useful kitchen tool for baking, too. Line cookie sheets with it and cookies will slide off easily.

Chinese Baked Fish

SERVES: 3–4
Preparation time: 15 minutes
Cooking time: 20 minutes

Rather than setting up a steamer basket, use this recipe to make cooking fish easy by simply baking it with Chinese herbs.

The Ingredients:

Peanut oil

1½ pounds thick, firm, fleshy fish (sea bass, snapper, halibut), cut 1″–1¼″ thick

3 tablespoons soy sauce

3 tablespoons dry sherry

3 scallion stalks, cut into ¼″ pieces

½ teaspoon freshly minced ginger root (or ¼ teaspoon powdered)

½ teaspoon freshly minced garlic

¼ teaspoon sugar

2 teaspoons oriental sesame oil

The Steps:

1. Preheat oven to 350°. Lightly oil a baking dish with peanut oil.
2. Arrange fish in dish. Sprinkle evenly with soy sauce, sherry, scallions, ginger, garlic, and sugar.
3. Bake for 20 minutes or until flaky, basting occasionally. (The cooking time depends on the thickness of the fish, so adjust accordingly.)
4. Drizzle sesame oil over fish and serve immediately.

Oil slick

Accompaniments:
 Plain White Rice, the Chinese Way, and *Oriental Zucchini Salad.*

Variation:
 Leftover fish can be served cold as a fish salad the next day, sprinkled with a few teaspoons of Japanese rice vinegar.

Make-It-Easy Tips:
 √ An "oil slick," the small gadget that keeps a brush soaked and ready in oil, can be conveniently used to oil the pan.
 √ Sea bass, snapper, and halibut are all lean fish that work better than mackerel or striped bass, which are fat fish.
 √ Do not substitute sweet sherry. If necessary, use sake (Japanese wine).

Fish Fillets Véronique

SERVES: 4–6
Preparation time: 15 minutes
Cooking time: 6–7 minutes

No butter is necessary on the Fish Fillets Véronique, making this a low-calorie main course.

The Ingredients:
- 1 cup seedless grapes, sliced in half
- 2 tablespoons dry white wine or vermouth
- 2 pounds fish fillets (sole, flounder, snapper, sand dabs)
- 1 teaspoon grated lemon peel
- 2 tablespoons lemon juice
- ½ teaspoon salt, or to taste
- ¼ teaspoon freshly ground pepper, or to taste
  - Garnish: Lemon slices, parsley sprigs

The Steps:
1. Preheat broiler.
2. Combine grapes and wine in bowl and toss.
3. Place fish in foil-lined broiling pan; sprinkle with lemon peel and juice. Season with salt and pepper.
4. Broil fish 3"–4" from heat until golden, about 5 minutes.
5. Arrange grapes, cut side down, over top of fish and broil 1–2 minutes longer.
6. Taste, and adjust seasoning to taste. Serve fish hot, garnished with lemon slices and parsley sprigs.

Accompaniments:
Perfect Baked Potatoes, and a mixed green salad with *Low-Calorie Buttermilk Thousand Island Dressing.*

Variations:
Tiny julienne strips of sweet red pepper, thin slices of fresh ginger, and freshly chopped parsley can be sprinkled over fish in Step 3 for an attractive confetti-like appearance.

If desired, 1–2 tablespoons butter can be added in Step 3, but then the calorie content is increased.

Make-It-Easy Tip:
√ The grapes can be marinated earlier in the day, if desired.

Braised Fish in Wine and Dill Sauce

SERVES: 4–6
Preparation time: 15 minutes
Cooking time: 15–20 minutes

The Ingredients:

1½ tablespoons unsalted butter
1 small onion, finely chopped
½ cup dry vermouth or dry white wine
¼ cup Madeira (Marsala or port can be substituted)
1 cup chicken broth
2 tablespoons tomato paste
1 teaspoon Dijon mustard
1 teaspoon freshly snipped dill or ⅓ teaspoon dried dill
2 pounds flaky fish fillets (e.g., halibut, snapper, sea bass)
Garnish: Freshly snipped dill, freshly chopped parsley

The Steps:

1. In large skillet melt butter; sauté onions over medium heat until soft, about 5 minutes.
2. Add vermouth and Madeira and allow to boil a minute or two, stirring well.
3. Add broth, tomato paste, mustard, and dill; stir until mixed.
4. Add fish, season to taste with salt and pepper. Bring to boil; then reduce heat and simmer, partially covered, for 10–15 minutes or until fish is flaky and tender.
5. Adjust seasoning if necessary, and serve hot in deep soup bowls, garnished with freshly snipped dill and/or freshly chopped parsley.

Accompaniments:

Crusty French bread, and a mixed green salad with *Laurie's Basic Vinaigrette* dressing.

Variation:

Fish can be cut up into small chunks, broth increased to 2 cups, and the recipe turned into a fish stew.

Make-It-Easy Tip:
√ The new Italian tomato paste available in tubes is a convenient way to obtain a small amount without opening a large can.

Quick and Easy Cioppino

SERVES: 6
Preparation time: 25 minutes
Cooking time: 20–25 minutes

Cioppino is an Italian shellfish stew that can be served as a complete meal in deep soup plates with lots of Italian bread for dunking. Use any variety of fresh shellfish or fish that is in season and reasonably priced. As a one-pot supper, it is low in calories yet very filling.

The Ingredients:
- 1 tablespoon olive oil
- 1 medium onion, finely chopped
- ¾ cup dry vermouth
- 2 cups marinara sauce (*see* Chapter 2 for fresh, or use prepared sauce)
- 2 8-ounce bottles clam juice
- ½ teaspoon salt, or to taste
- ¼ teaspoon freshly ground pepper
- 16 small cherrystone clams, scrubbed clean
- 1 pound raw, medium shrimp, shelled and cleaned
- 1 pound fresh, firm, fleshy fish [i.g., monk fish (*lotte*), halibut, haddock, bass, or snapper]
- ½ pound sea scallops, cut in half
  Garnish: One loaf Italian, French, or sourdough bread, toasted; freshly chopped parsley

The Steps:
1. In a Dutch oven or deep skillet, heat olive oil; sauté onion over medium heat until soft and golden, 10 minutes.
2. Add wine, stir well, then add marinara sauce and clam juice until consistency is soupy but still thick.

3. Add salt and pepper to taste, and bring to a boil.
4. Add clams, cover, and cook 5 minutes.
5. Add shrimp, fish, and scallops, cover again and cook for 5–6 minutes longer or until clam shells open.
6. Place a slice of toasted bread in a deep soup bowl, pour hot soup over, and garnish with lots of freshly chopped parsley.

Accompaniment:

Mixed green salad including artichoke hearts, red onions, black olives, and Parmesan cheese, with *Laurie's Basic Vinaigrette* dressing.

Variations:

Mussels can be added with clams. They, too, must be washed and scrubbed thoroughly. If you're lucky and lobsters are in season, use a small, cut up lobster and cook with the clams in Step 4.

If buying prepared marinara sauce, read the list of ingredients carefully. There are many available without chemicals, preservatives, salt, or sugar.

For a less expensive version, use only local, seasonal fresh fish.

Red wine can be substituted for dry vermouth.

Make-It-Easy Tips:

√ Have the fishman clean the shrimp for you or it will add an extra 15–20 minutes to preparation time. If this is not possible, substitute extra fish.

√ The stock and sauce may be assembled through Step 4 and reheated when adding the seafood.

√ When selecting clams or mussels at the market, pick out only ones that are completely closed, which indicates they are alive. After cooking and before serving, discard any clams that fail to open.

√ To clean clams easily, soak in cold water with a tablespoon of oatmeal. The clams will take in the oatmeal and spit it out along with the sand. Scrub well with a vegetable brush or strong wire brush.

Super-Easy Shrimp Soufflé

SERVES: 4–6
Preparation time: 20 minutes
Cooking time: 45 minutes to 1 hour

This is one soufflé that will not fall. It can be served as a lunch dish, light supper main course, or even as a spectacular first course.

The Ingredients:
- ½ cup mayonnaise (not salad dressing)
- ¼ cup all-purpose flour
- 2 teaspoons curry powder (or more to taste) dissolved in
- 1 tablespoon lemon juice
- ½ teaspoon salt, or to taste
- ¼ teaspoon freshly ground pepper
- ¼ cup half-and-half
- 1 pound cooked tiny bay shrimps
- 4 egg whites

The Steps:
1. Preheat oven to 350°. Generously butter a 1½-quart soufflé dish or straight-sided casserole.
2. Mix together the mayonnaise, flour, curry powder dissolved in lemon juice, salt, and pepper.
3. Gradually add the cream and whisk until smooth.
4. Stir in the shrimp and toss well.
5. Beat the egg whites until stiff with an electric beater or by hand and gently fold into mixture.
6. Pour batter in prepared soufflé dish and bake for 45 minutes to 1 hour until puffed up and golden brown on top.
7. Serve the soufflé immediately.

Accompaniments:
Serve as a first course by itself, or for a luncheon or supper with *Tabbouleh*.

Variation:
Flaked crabmeat can be substituted for the bay shrimp.

Make-It-Easy Tips:

√ Egg yolks can be reserved for *Zabaglione* or *Quick Chocolate Mousse*. To keep yolks, cover with water and refrigerate for 1–2 days.

√ For greater volume, allow egg whites to come to room temperature before whipping.

√ Do not whip egg whites in an aluminum bowl; it will tint them slightly grey. Use copper, glass, china, or stainless steel. Plastic tends to retain moisture and the water will prevent the egg whites from whipping properly. To increase volume add ¼ teaspoon cream of tartar after egg whites are foamy and begin to stiffen.

√ If egg whites overbeat try saving them by adding another white and beating again.

Shrimp al Pesto

SERVES: 4
Preparation time: 10 minutes
Cooking time: 5 minutes

The Ingredients:

    2 tablespoons unsalted butter
    2 tablespoons olive oil
    1½ pounds raw medium shrimp, cleaned and shelled
    2 tablespoons fresh lemon juice
    3–4 tablespoons Pesto (*see* Chapter 2)
    ¼ teaspoon freshly ground white pepper
    Garnish: White rice, Parmesan cheese

The Steps:

1. In large skillet, heat butter and oil together; sauté the shrimp, stirring constantly, until they just begin to turn pink.
2. Add lemon juice, stir to combine, cover, and cook for 2 minutes or until shrimp are tender.
3. Add Pesto and stir to coat shrimp.
4. Taste, and adjust seasoning if necessary. Serve shrimp hot, with sauce, over white rice. Serve Parmesan cheese on the side.

Accompaniments:
White rice, and sliced tomatoes with *Laurie's Basic Vinaigrette dressing*, and *Garlic Bread*.

Variations:
Substitute sea scallops, cut in half, or bay scallops, if available, and cook for only 1 minute, in Step 1.

Curried Scallops

SERVES: 3–4
Preparation time: 10 minutes
Cooking time: 5 minutes

The Ingredients:
2 tablespoons unsalted butter
1 tablespoon olive oil
1 pound sea scallops, cut in half, or 1 pound bay scallops
2 teaspoons curry powder, or to taste
¼ cup dry white wine or dry vermouth
1 tablespoon lemon juice
½ teaspoon salt, or to taste
½ teaspoon freshly ground pepper
Garnish: Freshly chopped parsley

The Steps:
1. In large skillet, heat butter and oil; sauté scallops over medium heat, stirring constantly, for 2 minutes.
2. Sprinkle curry powder over scallops, toss well, and cook for an additional 2 minutes, stirring constantly.
3. Deglaze with wine and lemon juice by scraping up browned particles from bottom of pan into sauce.
4. Season to taste with salt and pepper and serve hot, garnished with freshly chopped parsley.

Accompaniments:
White rice, and *Spinach Salad with Creamy Dressing*.

Variation:

Fish fillets cut in strips can be substituted for the scallops for a less expensive version of the dish.

Make-It-Easy Tips:

√ Curried Scallops can be easily cooked in a wok.

√ When selecting scallops, choose ones that are translucent and shiny in appearance and have a sweetish aroma.

Oriental Flavor Ceviche

SERVES: 2–3
Preparation time: 15 minutes
Chilling time: 6 hours or overnight

Ceviche is raw fish or seafood that is prepared by marinating. Ceviche is traditionally a South American or Mexican specialty but in this recipe it has an oriental flavor. Serve it as a main course on a hot night or as an appetizer served on little plates with toothpicks.

The Ingredients:

1 pound bay scallops or sea scallops, cut in bite-size pieces
½ cup fresh lime juice
2 teaspoons soy sauce
1 teaspoon sugar
¼ teaspoon salt, or to taste
1 tablespoon minced scallions
½ teaspoon freshly grated ginger
Salt and pepper to taste
Garnish: Lettuce leaves, coriander or parsley, thin lime slices

The Steps:

1. Place scallops in a small, deep bowl. Combine lime juice, soy sauce, sugar, and salt, and pour over scallops. Cover and chill in refrigerator 6 hours or overnight.
2. Drain scallops and discard lime juice; combine with scallions, ginger, salt, and pepper to taste.

3. Place scallops on a lettuce-lined platter garnished with coriander or parsley and slices of lime.

Accompaniment:
Oriental Noodle Salad.

Variations:
For a less expensive meal, any firm fleshy fish can be substituted for the scallops. Be sure the fish is non-parasite bearing.

Ceviche can be part of a luncheon menu served with a hot quiche and *Spinach Salad.*

Make-It-Easy Tips:
√ Scallops can be prepared through Step 2 and chilled for several hours before serving.

√ Red leaf lettuce, Boston, or Romaine are particularly attractive as liners for platters.

STIR-FRIED ENTREES

Chinese cooking appears to be complicated, involving lots of chopping, slicing, stirring, mixing, and other tedious work. What takes longest in cooking a Chinese meal is the preparation—the cutting and chopping that must go on before the meal can be cooked. But this cutting and chopping can be done ahead of time so that, when it comes time to cook the dish, it's a simple, fast procedure.

The meat, poultry, or fish can be purchased fresh, cut into family-size portions and frozen. Just before a meal, a portion can be removed from the freezer, thawed for 20 minutes to half an hour, and easily sliced in that semi-frozen state.

Canned beef or chicken broth can be kept on hand. Minced fresh garlic can be kept in a jar covered with peanut oil, and minced fresh ginger can be kept in a jar covered with dry sherry.

In order to make stir-frying easy, you must be well organized. The 15–20 minute preparation time should be spent getting all the ingredients in small dishes or bowls around the stove. Once this preparation is done, completing the recipe takes only a few minutes.

Remember to have *all* ingredients assembled because, once you've started stir-frying, it's impossible to stop and chop some garlic.

By all means, use a food processor or hand chopping gadgets to simplify these chores.

When adding cornstarch paste (cornstarch mixed with a liquid), make sure to stir it again just before adding because the paste tends to thicken and gum up when standing.

Chinese stir-frying does not have to be a mysterious gourmet skill. It can be an easy way to prepare fabulous meals in a few minutes. It is an economical, healthful way to cook, and the finished product looks appealing because the vegetables retain their brilliant colors. And, it tastes wonderful because the textures, flavors, and nutrients of the foods are retained.

The Equipment and Its Preparation

If I had to choose only one pot to do all my cooking in, I would definitely select a wok.

1. A wok can be used for all kinds of cooking from French to American—it's not just for Chinese cooking!

2. A wok is so versatile it can be used for all types of kitchen chores; deep-frying, steaming (on a rack or with a bamboo steamer), boiling, sautéing, poaching, braising, parboiling, simmering and, of course, stir-frying.

3. A wok is an inexpensive investment—you need only one pot.

4. A wok is durable; if cared for properly, it will last forever.

5. A wok is easily cleaned; once "seasoned," it needs only a rinsing, brushing, drying, and light coating with oil.

6. A wok is perfect for low-calorie cooking; it needs only a little oil, a little poultry, and lots of fresh vegetables for a perfect dietetic meal.

7. A wok allows the true flavors of foods to come out because foods are seared in hot oil, keeping natural juices and favors within.

Woks come in iron, aluminum, copper, brass, and stainless steel. You can also purchase an electric version. The wok I recommend is made of rolled, tempered steel. This type retains heat well, is easy to care for, and is low in price. I find that the heat in electric woks cannot be controlled well enough to accommodate the quick changes necessary for Chinese cooking. You just can't remove an electric wok from the heat!

Woks range in sizes from 12" to 26". I prefer a 14" wok, which will allow a large amount of food to be cooked and still retain a high heat level. Conventional cooktops cannot handle the heat necessary for an oversized wok.

There are a few utensils that make wok cooking easy:

Bamboo scrubber (or stiff brush): For easy clean-ups without scratching the surface of the wok.

Flat lifter: Spatula shaped for stir-frying.

Ladle: For stir-frying, braising, soups, and serving.

Chopsticks: For stir-frying, scrambling, and to use as tongs.

Mesh strainer: For deep frying.

Dok (or ring) on which to set the wok: Originally, the wok was designed for wood-burning and charcoal-style Chinese stoves. The dok helps to adapt the wok's round bottom to the American stove. Use upright on gas stoves

and upside down on electric stoves.

Cleaver: For chopping.

Bamboo steamer (or steaming rack): To convert the wok into a steamer.

Seasoning a Wok

Seasoning a wok used to be a lengthy procedure involving lots of steps (and lots of snob appeal). You can make the seasoning of a wok a very easy procedure, taking only a few simple steps. Once seasoned, you need only rinse it, scrub with a stiff brush, dry well, and rub with a light coating of vegetable oil to keep it in great condition and keep food from adhering to it.

Remember to follow the manufacturer's instructions and remove the tough layer of machine oil in which the wok is packaged.

1. Wash the new wok well in hot, soapy water, and rinse. (This is the one time you will use soap—to remove the tough layer of machine oil.)
2. Grease the inside of the wok with vegetable oil.
3. Heat the oiled wok over high heat in the ring for a minute and then rinse well.
4. Repeat the procedure.
5. Rinse the wok carefully, with hot water only.

Stir-frying is the cooking technique most associated with Chinese wok cookery. The secret to successful stir-frying is to cook quickly at maximum heat. That way, meat juices are sealed in and vegetables retain their color, vitamins, and crispness. Stir-fried main dishes are usually a combination of complementary meats and vegetables.

Chicken with Hoisin and Nuts

SERVES: 6
Preparation time: 15 minutes
Cooking time: 10 minutes

This recipe was taught to me by the noted Chinese cooking expert and teacher, Madame Grace Zia Chu.

The Ingredients:

6 large Chinese or Japanese (dried) mushrooms
1 small green pepper or 1 small sweet red pepper (or a combination of both)
1 8-ounce can water chestnuts, drained and sliced (or use pre-sliced water chestnuts, which are now available in cans)
1 tablespoon cornstarch
2 tablespoons dry sherry
2 large, whole chicken breasts, skinned, boned, and cut into 1″ pieces
1 tablespoon peanut or vegetable oil
½ teaspoon salt, or to taste
3 tablespoons peanut or vegetable oil
1 tablespoon granulated sugar
3 tablespoons Hoisin sauce (available at some supermarkets, oriental groceries, or by mail, *see* Appendix A)
¼ cup split unsalted raw cashew nuts (or use unsalted, natural almonds, pecans, or peanuts)
Garnish: Coriander sprigs (Chinese parsley) or regular parsley sprigs

The Steps:

1. Soak mushrooms in water for 20 minutes; drain, squeeze dry, cut away hard stem ends, and slice into quarters.
2. Cut pepper in similar-size wedges, add to water chestnuts, and set aside.
3. Combine cornstarch and sherry and add to chicken cubes; stir and set aside.
4. Heat the wok or large heavy skillet until very hot; add 1 table-

spoon oil and stir-fry mushrooms for 1 minute; add peppers and water chestnuts and continue to stir-fry another minute.

5. Add salt, mix, and remove vegetables; set aside.
6. Heat the wok again; add 3 tablespoons additional oil and stir-fry chicken pieces for about 3 minutes or until the chicken turns opaque.
7. Add sugar and Hoisin sauce, toss well, return the cooked vegetables, and continue to mix.
8. Add nuts and serve immediately with white rice garnished with coriander sprigs (Chinese parsley) or regular parsley sprigs.

Accompaniments:
Plain White Rice, the Chinese Way, and *Eggplant Szechwan-Style.*

Variation:
Bamboo shoots, cut in strips, can be added to the dish.

Make-It-Easy Tips:
√ Although it may lose a slight amount of texture, I prepare the chicken earlier in the day and reheat it when ready to serve.
√ Hoisin sauce is now available at many supermarkets along with a wide variety of oriental groceries. Opened jars will keep for quite a while stored in the refrigerator.

Stir-Fried Beef and Black Bean Sauce

SERVES: 4
Preparation time: 20 minutes
Cooking time: 5–6 minutes

This is a non-spicy Chinese dish flavored with the distinctive taste of Chinese fermented black beans.

The Ingredients:
½ pound flank steak, sirloin, or other tender cut of beef
1 tablespoon fermented black beans (available at some supermarkets, most oriental grocery stores, or by mail order, *see* Appendix A)

    1 large red pepper (or, if not in season, use green pepper),
      roughly chopped
    1 onion, roughly chopped
    1 slice ginger, minced
    1 clove garlic, minced
    1 tablespoon sherry
    1 tablespoon water
    1 tablespoon cornstarch
    ½ cup beef broth
    3 tablespoons peanut oil

The Steps:

1. Slice beef across the grain into thin slices, about 2″ square.
2. Soak black beans for 10 minutes in warm water; drain and mash with side of cleaver or knife.
3. Place peppers and onions in a bowl near cooking area.
4. Combine ginger and garlic in bowl near cooking area.
5. Mix sherry, water, and cornstarch together until it forms a paste. Set near range along with beef broth.
6. Heat a wok or large heavy skillet; add 2 tablespoons of oil and, when hot, stir-fry ginger and garlic for 30 seconds; add beef and continue to stir-fry for about 2 minutes. Remove and set aside.
7. Add remaining 1 tablespoon oil and, when hot, stir-fry pepper and onions for 2 minutes.
8. Add black beans and stir-fry 30 seconds; stir and add sherry/water/cornstarch paste, and broth.
9. Return beef, stir until smooth and slightly thickened; serve over white rice.

Accompaniment:

Snow Pea Salad.

Variations:

Boneless chicken, cut into dice, shrimp, or even pork can be substituted for the beef in this recipe.

Make-It-Easy Tips:

√ It is easier to cut the beef when it's in a semi-frozen state. Cut on the bias into strips.

√ Chop onions, garlic, ginger, and pepper in food processor, pulsating until just barely chopped. Do not over-process!

√ Remember to stir the sherry/water/cornstarch mixture just before adding in Step 8.

√ Use old margarine tubs or paper plates as containers for ingredients for less clean-up afterwards.

√ Fresh ginger can be peeled, placed in a jar, covered with dry sherry, and stored in refrigerator for several months.

Lamb with Scallions
(Ts'ung Pao Yang Jou)

SERVES: 4
Preparation time: 15 minutes
Cooking time: 5 minutes

The Ingredients:

1½ pounds boneless lean lamb, cut into 2" x 2" x ⅛" slices

6 scallion stalks, cut into ½" slices
1 clove garlic, finely minced

3 tablespoons peanut oil

Marinade:
2 tablespoons soy sauce
2 tablespoons cold water
4 teaspoons cornstarch
1 teaspoon sugar

Sauce:
2 tablespoons soy sauce
2 tablespoons dry sherry
2 teaspoons rice vinegar (or white wine vinegar)
1 tablespoon sesame oil

The Steps:

1. Combine marinade ingredients in medium bowl; add lamb and set near cooking area to marinate for 10–15 minutes while preparing rest of ingredients.
2. Place scallions and garlic near cooking area; mix sauce ingredients together and set near range.
3. Heat wok or large heavy skillet, add peanut oil and, when hot,

stir-fry garlic for 30 seconds; add lamb and continue to stir-fry until lamb loses its pink color.
4. Add scallions and stir-fry; add sauce and continue to stir until smooth.
5. Serve lamb hot over white rice.

Accompaniment:
Bean Sprout Salad.

Variations:
Beef (flank steak or sirloin or other tender cut of meat) can be substituted for the lamb in this recipe.

Make-It-Easy Tip:
√ It is easier to cut the lamb when it's in a semi-frozen state.

Ground Pork with Cellophane Noodles, Szechwan-Style

SERVES: 4
Preparation time: 15 minutes
Cooking time: 5–7 minutes

The spiciness of this Szechwan pork dish can be altered to taste.

The Ingredients:
2 ounces (1 package) oriental dry cellophane noodles (available in oriental grocery stores or by mail order, *see* Appendix A)
1 pound lean ground pork
2 scallion stalks, minced
8 water chestnuts, minced
2 tablespoons dry sherry
2 tablespoons soy sauce
½ teaspoon salt, or to taste
½ teaspoon sugar
1 teaspoon chili paste with garlic, or more to taste (available at oriental groceries or by mail order, *see* Appendix A)
1 cup beef broth
2 tablespoons peanut oil

The Steps:

1. Soak cellophane noodles in warm water for 20 minutes to soften; drain and snip with kitchen shears, chef's knife, or Chinese cleaver, into 2" sections.
2. Assemble noodles, ground pork, scallions, and water chestnuts in separate containers near the range; mix sherry, soy sauce, salt, sugar, and chili paste together and set near stove; place beef broth near cooking area.
3. Heat wok or large heavy skillet, add oil and, when hot, stir-fry scallions for 30 seconds.
4. Add half the ground pork and break up until crumbly; push cooked pork to the sides of wok, add the remaining pork and continue to stir-fry until all pork is separated and crumbly.
5. Add water chestnuts and sherry mixture and stir to combine.
6. Add noodles and broth; cover and cook over medium heat until much of liquid has been absorbed.
7. Serve pork hot over white rice.

Accompaniments:

Chinese Asparagus Salad with Spicy Dressing.

Variation:

If you prefer beef to pork, substitute ground round for the pork and increase the peanut oil to 3 tablespoons.

Make-It-Easy Tip:

√ Pork with Cellophane Noodles can be cooked a few hours earlier and reheated.

Stir-Fried Shrimp

SERVES: 4
Preparation time: 15 minutes
Cooking time: 5 minutes

Serve the shrimp hot or cold as a first course or cold as hors d'oeuvres before a Chinese or American dinner.

The Ingredients:
    1 pound raw, cleaned shrimp
    2 scallion stalks cut into 1" pieces
    2 slices fresh ginger
    1 large clove garlic
    2 tablespoons soy sauce
    1 tablespoon dry sherry
    2 tablespoons ketchup
    1 teaspoon sugar
    3 shakes Tabasco
    3 tablespoons peanut oil

The Steps:
1. Rinse shrimp and pat dry on paper towels.
2. Place scallions in a small container; mash ginger and garlic together and place in another container; put both containers near cooking area.
3. Combine soy sauce, sherry, ketchup, sugar, and Tabasco together and set near range.
4. Heat a wok or heavy skillet, add oil and, when hot, add ginger/garlic; stir-fry for 30 seconds.
5. Add shrimp and stir-fry for 3 minutes or until pink.
6. Add scallions, stir-fry 30 seconds; add soy sauce mixture, stir, and continue to cook.
7. Taste, and adjust seasoning if necessary. Serve immediately with rice, or refrigerate if you plan to serve shrimp cold.

Accompaniments:
Oriental Roast Pork and Snow Pea Salad.

Make-It-Easy Tips:
√ Shrimp can be cooked in advance, which is a great help when more than one stir-fried dish is to be prepared.
√ Ask the fishman to clean the shrimp for you—it saves a lot of time.
√ Tabasco should be added at the end of cooking. If cooked too long, it can become bitter tasting.

CHAPTER SIX

PASTA, RICE AND THEIR MORE EXOTIC RELATIVES

August Pasta
Fettuccine Carbonara
Linguini with Smoked Salmon
Pasta al Pesto
Linguini con Piselli (Pasta
  with Peas)
Pasta with Broccoli
Chicken Pasta Alfredo
Broad Noodles with Spinach
Noodle Pudding
Plain White Rice—
  The Chinese Way
Plain Brown Rice
Rice Pilaf with Pine Nuts
Lemon Rice
Curried Rice
Apricot Rice
Fried Rice
Green Rice
Bulgur Baked with Onions
  and Mushrooms
Kasha
Barley Casserole
Southern Style Cheese Grits
Orzo with Mushrooms and
  Onions
Couscous

QUICK & EASY PASTA DISHES

Quick and easy pasta dishes are the answer to what to serve to unexpected company. If ingredients are kept on hand, the meal can be assembled in just a few minutes.

Pasta is lower in calories than people think. If you cut down on rich sauces, you can have a fabulous low-calorie pasta feast. Pasta dishes are also inexpensive, especially when garnished with simple sauces.

Leftover hot pasta makes a splendid salad when served cold the next day. Add a sprinkling of vinegar or lemon juice for extra flavor or toss in some leftover cooked, chopped vegetables.

The general rules for cooking dried pasta are:

1. Bring a large pot of water with a teaspoon of salt to a boil.
2. Add 1 teaspoon vegetable oil to keep the pasta from sticking.
3. Cook according to package directions but test periodically so the pasta does not overcook. It should be *al dente*, just tender, a phrase translated from the Italian meaning "to the teeth."
4. Drain the pasta and toss immediately with the sauce. There are those who maintain that it is necessary to rinse the pasta with cold water after draining to remove excess starch and stop the cooking immediately. I find this an unnecessary step and prefer the pasta to be as hot as possible before mixing with the sauce.

Fresh pasta is now available at many specialty stores in large cities throughout the country. It can be used fresh or can be frozen successfully. When preparing fresh pasta, cook it for only 2–3 minutes, depending on the thickness of the noodle. It overcooks easily, so watch carefully. If cooking frozen fresh pasta, do not defrost it. Simply drop it frozen into the water and cook for 3–4 minutes, or until *al dente*.

A spaghetti pot filled with a built-in colander is a helpful Make-It-Easy tool for cooking pasta—cook the pasta, lift up, drain, and serve. Pasta measures are now available, designed to calculate perfect portions of uncooked spaghetti. Remember to consider the richness of the sauce before deciding the amount of pasta to cook. In general, one pound of pasta will serve three ravenous or four moderate diners as a main course.

If available, purchase imported Italian brands of dried pasta, such as de Cecco, Mennucci, Carmine Russo or del Verde. By law, Italian dried pasta has less water than the American brands and is made of the heart of durum wheat. Italian dried pasta holds its shape better and cooks up *al dente*, tender and firm. The American brands use a different flour and, because they have a higher water content, tend to become gummy and soft if not properly cooked.

If dinner is postponed and pasta must be reheated, place in a colander over a pot of simmering water. Cover the pot and the pasta will keep for a short while. Or, drain the pasta, toss it with oil, cover, and refrigerate. Before serving, plunge into boiling water, drain, and toss with sauce.

Pasta measure

Pasta pot

August Pasta

SERVES: 6
Preparation time: 15 minutes
Cooking time: 10–12 minutes

August Pasta is so named because the tomatoes used in the sauce are at their ripest and juiciest, and basil is at its most plentiful, in the month of August.

The Ingredients:

    4 large or 6 medium very ripe, juicy tomatoes, cut into small chunks

    2 zucchini, cut in thin julienne strips (matchstick shape)

    2 tablespoons olive oil

    1 tablespoon freshly chopped parsley

1 tablespoon freshly chopped basil (or 1 teaspoon dried basil, crumbled)
1 teaspoon freshly minced garlic (or more to taste)
½ teaspoon salt, or to taste
½ teaspoon freshly ground pepper
1 pound fusilli or similar-size spaghetti twists
2–3 tablespoons freshly grated Parmesan cheese

The Steps:

1. In large serving bowl, combine tomatoes, zucchini, oil, parsley, basil, garlic, salt and pepper to taste.
2. Cook pasta in salted boiling water until just tender, *al dente.*
3. Drain in colander and immediately toss drained pasta with sauce.
4. Sprinkle with grated Parmesan cheese, taste, adjust seasoning if necessary, and serve immediately.

Accompaniments:

Cheese-Garlic Bread (*see* Garlic Bread, Variations), and *Raw Mushroom Salad.*

Variations:

Substitute linguini or spaghetti for the fusilli.
Serve as a cold pasta salad the next day by adding a tablespoon of red wine vinegar plus extra salt and pepper to taste after chilling.

Tomato corer

Make-It-Easy Tips:

√ A tomato corer will lift the core out of the tomato making it easier to cut the tomato into small chunks with a serrated tomato knife.
√ Since fresh basil is available only in the summer months, chop it in large bunches and freeze in small containers or plastic bags for use year 'round.

√ In the off-season, when ripe tomatoes are very expensive, substitute canned Italian tomatoes, drained, with the addition of a pinch of sugar to cut acidity.

Fettuccine Carbonara

SERVES: 4–6
Preparation time: 20 minutes
Cooking time: 15–20 minutes

Fettuccine Carbonara is a super-rich dish—so rich that it only needs a light Italian salad to make a whole meal.

The Ingredients:
    1 tablespoon unsalted butter
    1 teaspoon olive oil
    4 large shallots, minced, or 4 scallions, white part only, minced
    6 strips bacon, sliced crosswise into julienne strips
    1 pound fettuccine noodles
    3 egg yolks, at room temperature
    ¼ cup heavy cream
    ½ cup freshly grated Parmesan cheese
    ½ teaspoon salt, or to taste
    ½ teaspoon freshly ground white pepper
    Garnish: Freshly grated Parmesan cheese, freshly ground white pepper

The Steps:
1. In saucepan, heat butter and oil together; sauté shallots over medium heat until soft, about 5 minutes. Add bacon and continue to cook over medium heat for an additional 10 minutes or until bacon begins to brown; set aside.
2. Drop pasta into pot of boiling salted water and cook until *al dente,* just tender.
3. In the meantime, beat egg yolks with cream until smooth with a wire whisk; add cheese.
4. Drain pasta in colander; return to warm pot.

5. Pour bacon sauce over noodles, then add egg mixture, tossing well so that hot pasta "cooks" the other ingredients.
6. Add salt and pepper to taste, and serve with extra cheese and a pepper mill on the side.

Accompaniment:
Italian salad (*see* Greek Salad, Variations).

Variations:
Leftover cubed ham or prosciutto can be added to the sauce.
Spinach fettuccine is a nice variation in color and taste.
Spaghetti or other thin noodles can be substituted for fettuccine.

Make-It-Easy Tips:
√ The preparation of Fettuccine Carbonara is similar to that of Chinese dishes because all ingredients should be assembled in advance near cooking area ready for last-minute cooking.
√ To set up in advance, cook bacon sauce and ready eggs and cheese mixture. When ready to cook, boil pasta, and toss.
√ Use kitchen scissors to julienne bacon easily. Cut width-wise across package of uncooked bacon.

Linguini with Smoked Salmon

SERVES: 4
Preparation time: 15 minutes
Cooking time: 10–12 minutes

This is an unusual and very rich pasta dish that should be served with light accompaniments.

The Ingredients:
1 pound linguini
3 tablespoons unsalted butter
¼ pound thinly sliced smoked salmon, cut into julienne strips
½ cup heavy cream
2 tablespoons cream cheese, cut into bits
Salt and freshly ground white pepper to taste

½ cup freshly grated Parmesan cheese
Garnish: Freshly chopped parsley

The Steps:

1. Drop pasta into boiling salted water and cook until *al dente*, just tender. Drain in colander.
2. In the meantime, melt butter in saucepan; add salmon and toss to warm, but do not sauté.
3. Add cream and cream cheese and cook until boiling and smooth, stirring often.
4. Season to taste with salt and pepper, taking into account the saltiness of salmon.
5. Mix pasta with sauce; stir in Parmesan cheese and serve immediately, garnished with freshly chopped parsley.

Accompaniment:

Raw Mushroom Salad.

Variations:

A 10-ounce package of frozen tiny peas, thawed, can be added to pasta with sauce in Step 5.

Cappellini, very, very thin spaghetti, also called "Angel's Hair," can be substituted for linguini.

Pasta al Pesto

SERVES: 4
Preparation time: 10 minutes
Cooking time: 12 minutes

The Ingredients:

1 pound linguini, spaghetti, or spaghettini
4–5 tablespoons Pesto sauce (*see* Chapter 2)
½ cup freshly grated Parmesan cheese
¼ teaspoon freshly ground white pepper, or to taste
Garnish: Extra Parmesan cheese

The Steps:
1. Drop pasta into salted boiling water and cook until *al dente*, just tender.
2. Drain pasta in colander. Toss with Pesto, cheese, and pepper to taste.
3. Serve hot with extra Parmesan cheese on the side.

Accompaniments:
    Marinated Butterflied Leg of Lamb, and a mixed green salad with *Laurie's Basic Vinaigrette* dressing.

Variation:
    Two tablespoons of heavy cream can be added for a richer sauce.

Make-It-Easy Tip:
    √ Toss drained pasta with 1 tablespoon butter first to keep noodles from sticking.

Linguini con Piselli
(Pasta with Peas)

SERVES: 4–6
Preparation time: 20 minutes
Cooking time: 12 minutes

Linguini con Piselli is a wonderful accompaniment to veal or chicken dishes, or can stand on its own as a vegetarian main dish, or can even be served as a first course.

The Ingredients:
    2 tablespoons unsalted butter
    1 tablespoon olive oil
    1 large onion, finely chopped
    ½ pound prosciutto, cut into thin julienne strips (if prosciutto is unavailable, use 2 slices minced bacon and eliminate the butter and oil)

    2 tablespoons freshly chopped parsley
    2 tablespoons freshly chopped basil or 2 teaspoons dried
       basil, crumbled
       Pinch of nutmeg
    ½ teaspoon salt, or to taste
    ½ teaspoon freshly ground white pepper
    1 cup strong chicken broth
    1 cup heavy cream
    1 pound linguini, or spaghetti, or vermicelli
    20 ounces frozen tiny peas, thawed and drained (or use 20
       ounces regular green peas, cooked 2 minutes)
    ¾–1 cup freshly grated Parmesan cheese

The Steps:
1. In large skillet, heat butter and oil together; add onion and prosciutto and cook over medium heat until soft, 5–7 minutes.
2. Add parsley, basil, nutmeg, salt, and pepper; stir to coat with butter.
3. Add broth and cook until smooth; add cream and continue to cook until slightly thickened.
4. In the meantime, cook linguini in boiling salted water until just tender, *al dente*. Drain in colander.
5. Toss pasta with peas; sprinkle with Parmesan cheese and serve piping hot.

Accompaniments:
Basic Vertically Roasted Chicken, and *Garlic Bread*.

Variations:
Linguini con Piselli can be transformed into an easy *pasta primavera* (pasta with vegetables in a creamy sauce) with the addition of frozen broccoli florets, cooked until just tender, some cooked zucchini, carrots, asparagus, or whatever other crunchy, but cooked, vegetables are available.

Cappellini, the very fine "Angel's Hair" pasta, makes a good substitute for linguini.

Pasta with Broccoli

SERVES: 4
Preparation time: 10–15 minutes
Cooking time: 12 minutes

Pasta with Broccoli is brimming with garlic flavor; it is recommended for a non-romantic dinner or one where you're sure everybody will have some!

The Ingredients:

1 large head fresh broccoli, about 2 pounds, broken into small florets, stalks reserved for another use
2 tablespoons unsalted butter
3 tablespoons olive oil
2 cloves garlic, finely minced
¼–½ teaspoon hot red pepper flakes, or to taste
1 pound spaghetti or linguini
½ teaspoon salt, or to taste
¼ teaspoon freshly ground pepper
3–4 tablespoons freshly grated Parmesan cheese
Garnish: Freshly grated Parmesan cheese

The Steps:

1. Drop broccoli into boiling salted water and cook uncovered 2–3 minutes or until just tender, *al dente*; drain in colander and run under cold water.
2. In saucepan, heat butter and oil together; add garlic and cook for 2 minutes. Add hot pepper flakes and set aside.
3. In the meantime, cook pasta in boiling salted water until just tender, *al dente*, and drain in colander.
4. In large bowl, toss spaghetti with garlic-butter sauce.
5. Add broccoli, salt, pepper, and cheese; toss to coat spaghetti well.
6. Serve hot, with additional Parmesan cheese on the side.

Accompaniments:

Can be served as a vegetarian main course by itself, or as an accompaniment to plain broiled chicken or fish, with *Tomato and Onion Salad* and crusty Italian bread.

Variations:

Sliced zucchini or asparagus tips can be substituted for the broccoli, and fettuccine can be used in place of the linguini.

Make-It-Easy Tips:

√ Broccoli is cooked in boiling water and then drained with cold water to maintain the bright green color.

√ Base of stalk closest to florets can be peeled with a sharp paring knife, thinly sliced, and cooked as a vegetable. Tough, woody base of stem should be discarded.

Chicken Pasta Alfredo

SERVES: 4–6
Preparation time: 20 minutes
Cooking time: 12 minutes

The addition of chicken to the traditional Alfredo cream sauce makes this pasta a full main course.

The Ingredients:

⅛ pound (½ stick) unsalted butter
⅔ cup heavy cream
⅔ cup freshly grated Parmesan cheese
1 pound spinach fettuccine (if unavailable, use plain fettuccine)
1 whole skinned and boned chicken breast, poached and shredded
⅓ cup freshly grated Parmesan cheese
  Pinch of ground nutmeg
½ teaspoon salt, or to taste
½ teaspoon freshly ground white pepper, or to taste
  Garnish: Additional grated Parmesan cheese, and ground white pepper

The Steps:

1. In large skillet, melt butter over medium heat, and stir in cream; as sauce begins to thicken, add ⅔ cup Parmesan cheese; stir and set aside.

2. In the meantime, cook the fettuccine in boiling salted water until just tender, *al dente*, and drain in colander.
3. In large bowl, immediately toss noodles with the butter/cream cheese mixture.
4. Add chicken, additional ⅓ cup Parmesan cheese, nutmeg, salt and pepper to taste.
5. Serve immediately with additional cheese on the side and a generous sprinkling of ground white pepper.

Accompaniment:
Snow Pea Salad.

Variation:
Diced baked ham can be substituted for the chicken.

Make-It-Easy Tips:
√ Poach chicken in broth to cover for 20 minutes at a simmer or until just tender. Baked chicken can be substituted but it is not as juicy or flavorful as poached chicken. For an easy method to poach chicken, *see Madame Chu's Szechwan Peppercorn Chicken Salad.*

Broad Noodles with Spinach

SERVES: 4
Preparation time: 10 minutes
Cooking time: 10 minutes

The Ingredients:
1 10-ounce package frozen chopped spinach, thawed and squeezed dry
1 8-ounce package broad noodles
1 cup dairy sour cream
2 tablespoons unsalted butter
1 teaspoon lemon juice
Fat pinch of ground nutmeg

½ teaspoon salt, or to taste
¼ teaspoon freshly ground white pepper, or to taste

The Steps:

1. In large pot of boiling salted water, cook noodles until just tender; drain in colander and return noodles to hot pot.
2. Immediately toss noodles with sour cream, spinach, butter, lemon juice, nutmeg, salt and pepper to taste; pour into a serving bowl and serve immediately.

Accompaniments:

Marinated Flank Steak or any other grilled meat or poultry dishes.

Variation:

One 10-ounce package frozen chopped broccoli can be substituted for spinach.

Make-It-Easy Tip:

√ Spinach does not have to be cooked, just thaw well, squeeze dry, and toss with hot noodles.

Noodle Pudding

SERVES: 6–8
Preparation time: 5–10 minutes
Cooking time: 60 minutes

This sweet noodle pudding, sometimes called a Kugel, is a perfect accompaniment for *Brisket Like My Mother Makes* or *Basic Vertically Roasted Chicken*. It can be served hot, at room temperature, or cold.

The Ingredients:

1 8-ounce package medium-wide egg noodles
1 cup whole milk
1 cup (8 ounces) dairy sour cream
1 cup (8 ounces) cottage cheese
2 eggs

½ cup granulated sugar
1 teaspoon vanilla
¾ cup golden seedless raisins
1–2 teaspoons cinnamon
⅔ tablespoon butter

The Steps:

1. Preheat oven to 350°. Generously grease a 9″ x 12″ baking dish.
2. Cook noodles according to package directions. Drain and rinse with cold water in colander.
3. While noodles are cooking, place milk, sour cream, cottage cheese, eggs, sugar, and vanilla in the blender or food processor. Blend for 10–15 seconds.
4. Pour blended ingredients into prepared baking dish.
5. Add raisins and noodles, spreading evenly.
6. Dust top generously with cinnamon, dot with small pieces of butter, and bake for 60 minutes.
7. Allow Kugel to cool for 15 minutes and serve hot, or cool longer and serve at room temperature.

Accompaniments:

Roast poultry or potted beef dishes.

Variations:

Substitute 1 cup of drained, canned, juice-packed pineapple cut in small pieces for the raisins.
Low-fat cottage cheese and low-fat milk can be substituted for the cottage cheese and whole milk.

Make-It-Easy Tip:

√ Substitute 2 smaller baking dishes for large one and freeze one of the puddings for a family dinner.

RICE

Rice is a staple of Make-It-Easy cooking. White rice takes only 20 minutes to cook, can be reheated and, once cooked, can be used in a variety of dishes.

For plain white rice, I use the Chinese method of cooking rice (*see Plain White Rice, the Chinese Way*). I find this to be the easiest way to produce perfect, separated grains.

For rice dishes that include sautéed vegetables, the easiest and most successful method of cooking is to sauté the onions or other vegetables in 3–4 tablespoons of butter. Add the rice, coating the grains well with the butter, which will keep the grains separate when cooked. Finally, add hot broth in the ratio of 2 cups broth to 1 cup rice. Cover, reduce to a simmer, and cook over very low heat for 20–25 minutes or until liquid is absorbed and rice is tender.

There are many varieties of rice but, to simplify, they divide into two categories—long grain and short grain. Long grain is best for plain white rice or for use in casseroles, whereas short grain cooks down to a softer consistency that's better for puddings.

Brown rice is unpolished rice in which only the husks have been removed. Brown rice is nutritionally superior to white rice, richer in vitamins, minerals, and fiber.

Wild rice is really not rice at all. It is the seed of a wild plant called water grass. It is high in nutrition and fiber content but is expensive.

Plain White Rice, the Chinese Way

YIELD: 3 cups

This is the easiest and most successful method for preparing plain white rice.

The Ingredients:
    1 cup long-grain rice
    1¾ cups cold water

The Steps:
1. Put rice in a 2-quart saucepan with a tight-fitting lid, add water, bring to a boil, cover, reduce to a simmer, and cook very slowly for 20 minutes.
2. Turn off heat and allow rice to sit, covered and undisturbed, for an additional 20 minutes.
3. Fluff up with a fork or chop sticks and serve hot.

The term "converted rice," also called "parboiled," "pre-cooked," or "pre-fluffed" is rice that has been steam-treated so that the grains become tender without gumming up. "Quick-cooking" or "minute rice" is tasteless and should be avoided. All of the rice recipes in this section can be prepared with nutritionally higher brown rice. When substituting brown rice for white rice, increase the cooking time by 30 minutes.

Raw Rice	Water	Saucepan Size
1½ cups rice	2⅝ cups water	3-quart pan
2 cups rice	3¼ cups water	3-quart pan
3 cups rice	4 cups water	4-quart pan
4 cups rice	5 cups water	6-quart pan
10 cups rice	11 cups water	large stock pot

Note: The proportion of water to rice decreases as the amount of rice increases.

Regardless of the amount of rice cooked, once the rice comes to a boil, the 20 minutes' simmering time and the 20 minutes' sitting time remain the same.

Make-It-Easy Tips:

√ *Reheating Instructions:* Cook rice the regular length of time or a little less. When ready to reheat, fluff up rice and place in a colander. Bring 2–3 inches of water to a boil in a large pot and place colander in pot so that colander is above the water. Steam for only 10–15 minutes. Mix once during that time.

Plain Brown Rice

SERVES: 6–8
Preparation time: 5 minutes
Cooking time: 35–45 minutes

The Ingredients:

4 cups water
2 cups brown rice

½ teaspoon salt, or to taste
Garnish: Freshly chopped parsley

The Steps:

1. In large saucepan, bring water to boil; add rice but do not stir.
2. Sprinkle with salt, cover; reduce heat to simmer and cook slowly for 35–40 minutes, or until liquid is absorbed and grains are tender.
3. Fluff rice and serve garnished with freshly chopped parsley.

Variations:

Substitute boiling chicken, beef, or vegetable broth for water; eliminate salt.

Make-It-Easy Tip:

√ 1 cup raw brown rice yields about 3 cups cooked brown rice.

Rice Pilaf with Pine Nuts

SERVES: 4–6
Preparation time: 15 minutes
Cooking time: 25 minutes

This is the basic recipe I use for a side dish of rice flavored with broth.

The Ingredients:

3 tablespoons unsalted butter
1 medium onion, finely minced
1 small clove garlic, finely minced
1¼ cups long-grain rice
⅓ cup pine nuts (*pignoli*) or slivered almonds
2½ cups chicken or beef broth
½ teaspoon salt, or to taste
¼ teaspoon freshly ground pepper
Garnish: Freshly chopped parsley

The Steps:

1. In small, heavy saucepan, melt butter over medium heat, add onion and garlic, and sauté until soft, about 5 minutes.

2. Add rice and pine nuts and stir until all grains are coated.
3. Add broth, salt, and pepper; bring to boil, cover, lower heat, and simmer slowly without lifting lid for 25 minutes.
4. Allow to rest 5 minutes; fluff with 2 forks and serve garnished with freshly chopped parsley.

Variations:
Use beef or chicken broth, depending on the main course.

Make-It-Easy Tip:
√ The rice should be coated well with butter so that the grains remain separate and tender.

Lemon Rice

SERVES: 4
Preparation time: 15 minutes
Cooking time: 25–30 minutes

The Ingredients:
2 tablespoons unsalted butter
1 tablespoon olive oil
1 small onion, finely chopped
1 cup long-grain rice
1¾ cups chicken broth
¼ cup fresh lemon juice
1½ teaspoons freshly grated lemon rind
½ teaspoon salt, or to taste
¼ teaspoon freshly ground pepper, or to taste
Garnish: Freshly chopped parsley, freshly grated lemon peel

The Steps:
1. Preheat oven to 350°.
2. Heat butter and oil together in small casserole; add onion, and sauté over medium heat until soft, about 5 minutes.
3. Add rice and stir to coat with butter and oil.

4. Add broth, lemon juice, lemon rind, salt and pepper to taste; bring to a boil, cover, and bake for 25–30 minutes or until liquid is absorbed and grains are tender.
5. Serve rice hot, garnished with freshly chopped parsley and freshly grated lemon peel.

Variations:

This rice can be cooked successfully on top of range at a slow simmer if oven is in use.

Orange juice and orange rind can be substituted for lemon juice and rind, and mixed with a teaspoon of curry powder and some raisins for a curried orange rice variation.

Make-It-Easy Tip:

√ Grate lemon rind first, and then squeeze lemon at room temperature to obtain the optimum amount of juice.

Curried Rice

SERVES: 4–6
Preparation time: 10 minutes
Cooking time: 25 minutes

Curried Rice goes very well with roast lamb, poultry, or pork dishes.

The Ingredients:

3 tablespoons unsalted butter
1 small onion, finely chopped
1 cup long-grain rice
2 cups hot chicken or beef broth
¼ cup golden seedless raisins
1 teaspoon curry powder
Garnish: Dairy sour cream, chutney (optional)

The Steps:

1. In heavy saucepan, melt butter; sauté onion over medium heat until soft, 5–7 minutes.
2. Add rice, and stir to coat grains with butter.
3. Add broth, raisins, and curry powder; bring to a boil, cover,

and cook for 25 minutes or until rice is tender and liquid absorbed.
4. Serve rice hot with sour cream, and chutney, if desired.

Variations:

Toasted slivered almonds can be added during last few minutes of cooking.

The rice can also be baked in a 325° oven for 25 minutes.

Apricot Rice

SERVES: 6
Preparation time: 15 minutes
Cooking time: 20–25 minutes

Apricot Rice makes a great accompaniment to roast pork or roast turkey.

The Ingredients:

3 tablespoons unsalted butter
1 small onion, finely chopped
½ cup chopped celery
½ teaspoon freshly minced ginger (or ¼ teaspoon powdered ginger added with broth)
1 cup long-grain rice
2 cups chicken broth
1 cup diced dried apricots
¼ cup chopped chutney
½ cup toasted slivered almonds
Garnish: Freshly chopped parsley

The Steps:

1. In a deep saucepan, melt butter; sauté the onions, celery, and ginger over medium heat until soft, about 5 minutes.
2. Add rice, and continue to sauté until grains are coated.
3. Add broth, apricots, and chutney; bring to a boil, reduce heat, cover, and simmer slowly for 20–25 minutes or until rice is tender.
4. Add nuts and serve hot, garnished with freshly chopped parsley.

Variations:

⅓ cup golden seedless or dark raisins can be substituted for the chutney.

Dried peaches, pineapple, apples, or other dried fruits can be substituted for the apricots.

Make-It-Easy Tip:

√ Toast nuts easily in a toaster-oven or under the broiler for 1–2 minutes, turning once with a spatula and watching carefully.

Fried Rice

SERVES: 6–8
Preparation time: 20–25 minutes
Cooking time: 5–7 minutes

Fried Rice is a great way to use up leftover rice and . . . leftover poultry, meat, fish, or vegetables.

The Ingredients:

3 eggs, lightly beaten
⅓ cup chopped scallion stalks
½ teaspoon minced fresh ginger
½ teaspoon minced garlic
3 cups cold cooked rice
¼ teaspoon salt, or to taste
¼ teaspoon sugar
1½ tablespoons dark soy sauce
⅓ pound baked ham, finely diced
½ cup frozen tiny peas, thawed
3 tablespoons peanut oil
1 teaspoon oriental sesame oil

The Steps:

1. Place the eggs, scallions, ginger, garlic, rice, salt, sugar, soy sauce, ham, and peas in small containers or on paper plates near the cooking area.

2. Heat wok or large heavy skillet; add 1 tablespoon of peanut oil and, when hot, scramble eggs very loosely; remove from pan and set aside.
3. Heat remaining 2 tablespoons peanut oil and, when hot, stir-fry scallions, ginger, and garlic for 30 seconds.
4. Add rice, stir-fry until tossed with ingredients.
5. Add salt, sugar, soy sauce, and ham and stir-fry to combine.
6. Add reserved scrambled eggs, breaking them up to distribute evenly.
7. Gently fold in peas, glaze with sesame oil, and serve immediately.

Variations:

Dark soy sauce is available at oriental grocery stores (*see* Appendix A) but regular, light soy sauce, the kind found in supermarkets, can be substituted.

Any leftover meats or vegetables can be added to fried rice: bacon bits, cooked chicken strips, roast pork, roast beef, bean sprouts, water chestnuts, bamboo shoots, button mushrooms, or any cooked vegetable desired.

Leftover Fried Rice can be refrigerated and reheated. It can even be frozen.

Make-It-Easy Tips:

√ This is fast Chinese wok cookery, so remember to have all ingredients assembled and ready to go.

√ The rice must be cold before stir-frying in order to obtain the best texture and taste.

Green Rice

SERVES: 8–10
Preparation time: 15–20 minutes
Cooking time: 45 minutes

This Green Rice casserole dish is a great way to use up leftover cooked rice. The addition of cheese, mentioned in the Variations, and the eggs make this dish substantial enough to serve as a main dish for lunch.

The Ingredients:

6 cups cooked white rice (2 cups raw rice)
4 eggs
2 cups half-and-half
1 10-ounce package frozen chopped spinach, thawed and squeezed dry
½ cup freshly chopped parsley
½ cup freshly grated Parmesan cheese
¼ cup finely chopped onion
3 tablespoons unsalted butter, melted
1 tablespoon Worcestershire sauce
½ teaspoon salt, or to taste
½ teaspoon freshly ground pepper, or to taste
Garnish: Freshly chopped parsley

The Steps:

1. Preheat oven to 325°. Generously butter 2-quart casserole or soufflé dish.
2. In large bowl, combine the cooked rice, eggs, half-and-half, spinach, parsley, Parmesan cheese, onion, butter, Worcestershire, salt, and pepper; mix well, and pour into prepared casserole.
3. Bake for 45 minutes or until hot and bubbly.
4. Serve rice dish hot, garnished with additional freshly chopped parsley.

Variations:

Add ½ cup grated Swiss Gruyère or Monterey Jack cheese to transform Green Rice into a vegetarian main course.
Brown rice can be substituted for white rice.

Make-It-Easy Tip:

√ Green Rice can be assembled well in advance, refrigerated, and baked just before serving.

ALTERNATIVES TO RICE

Innovative and healthy alternatives to the routine white rice/noodles side-dish slump are available, only their names aren't as familiar: bulgur, couscous, barley, kasha, grits, orzo. All of these offer the chance to mix tastes and cuisines creatively; try Armenian bulgur with *Cuban Chicken*. Your meal will be anything but dull.

Bulgur Baked with Onions and Mushrooms

SERVES: 4–6
Preparation time: 15 minutes
Cooking time: 50 minutes

Bulgur (Bulghur, Burghul, Bulgar), the staple of Middle Eastern cooking, is cracked wheat that has been hulled and parboiled, a process that makes the grain easier to cook and gives it a pronounced flavor and lighter texture. Serve as a side dish in place of rice or use in the Lebanese salad *Tabbouleh* in which bulgur is mixed with mint, onions, and parsley. Bulgur Baked with Onions and Mushrooms goes well with brisket and other pot roasts.

The Ingredients:
  2 tablespoons unsalted butter
  1 small onion, finely chopped
  6 mushrooms, finely chopped
  1 cup bulgur
  2 cups hot chicken or beef broth
  ½ cup toasted pine nuts (or toasted almonds)
     Salt and freshly ground pepper to taste
     Garnish: Freshly chopped parsley

The Steps:
  1. Preheat oven to 350°.
  2. In small oven-proof casserole, melt butter; sauté the onions and mushrooms over medium heat until soft and golden, about 5 minutes.
  3. Add bulgur to casserole, toss to coat grains with butter and vegetables. Add hot broth, bring to a boil, reduce heat, cover, and bake for 40 minutes.
  4. Remove from oven, top with pine nuts, and return to oven for an additional 10 minutes.
  5. Taste, adjust seasoning with salt and pepper, and serve bulgur hot, garnished with freshly chopped parsley.

Variation:
The use of chicken or beef broth should depend on the main dish.

Make-It-Easy Tip:
   √ It is easy to toast nuts; brown in a toaster-oven or under the broiler for 1–2 minutes, turning once with a spatula and watching carefully.

Kasha

SERVES: 4
Preparation time: 15 minutes
Cooking time: 15 minutes

Kasha is a dish of braised buckwheat groats that is served as a side dish or used in soups.

The Ingredients:
   2 tablespoons unsalted butter
   1 small onion, chopped
   1 egg
   ½ teaspoon salt, or to taste
   ¼ teaspoon freshly ground pepper
   1 cup kasha
   2 cups hot chicken or beef broth, depending on main course
   1 8-ounce can water chestnuts, drained and chopped
      Garnish: Freshly chopped parsley

The Steps:
   1. Melt butter in saucepan; sauté onion over medium heat until translucent, 5–7 minutes.
   2. In a small bowl, beat egg with salt and pepper, add kasha, stir with a fork until combined, pour into saucepan, and stir well.
   3. Add broth and bring to boil, reduce heat, cover, and simmer for 10 minutes.
   4. Add water chestnuts, cover again, and cook for 5 minutes longer.
   5. Taste for seasoning, adjust if necessary, and serve hot, garnished with freshly chopped parsley.

Variations:
   Rendered chicken fat can be substituted for butter.
   Chopped celery can be sautéed with onions.

Cashews, pine nuts, or almonds can be added with water chestnuts for additional crunchiness.

Barley Casserole

SERVES: 6–8
Preparation time: 15 minutes
Cooking time: 1¼ hours

The Ingredients:
 4 tablespoons unsalted butter
 2 medium onions, finely chopped
 ½ pound mushrooms, sliced
 1½ cups pearl barley
 3 cups chicken or beef broth, depending on the main course
 1 4-ounce jar pimientos, drained and coarsely chopped
 ¼ teaspoon salt, or to taste
 ¼ teaspoon freshly ground pepper, or to taste
 Garnish: Freshly chopped parsley

The Steps:
1. Preheat oven to 350°.
2. Melt butter in a large casserole; sauté onions for 2 minutes over medium heat, add mushrooms and continue to sauté until soft, 5–7 minutes.
3. Add barley and cook until lightly browned. Add 2 cups of the broth, pimientos, salt, pepper, and stir; bring to a boil, cover, reduce heat, and bake for 45 minutes.
4. Add remaining 1 cup broth, return to oven and cook 30 minutes longer.
5. Serve hot, garnished with freshly chopped parsley.

Variations:
Toasted egg barley, called *farfel*, can be substituted for pearl barley.

Drained roasted Italian red peppers in jars or cans are a nice substitute for pimientos.

Make-It-Easy Tip:
√ If oven is in use, barley can be cooked on top of range at a very slow simmer.

Southern-Style Cheese Grits

SERVES: 6
Preparation time: 15 minutes
Cooking time: 30–40 minutes

Grits, also called hominy grits or corn grits, are coarsely ground corn-meal. In the southern United States, grits are popular served either as a breakfast cereal or as a substitute for potatoes.

This recipe adapts grits for use as an alternative to rice, a side dish flavored with garlic-cheese that is great with barbecued spareribs or chicken.

The Ingredients:

1 cup quick-cooking grits, cooked according to package directions
1 4-ounce package garlic-and-herb cheese (Boursin, Rondele, or Alouette)
1 egg, lightly beaten
4 tablespoons (½ stick) unsalted butter
¼ cup whole milk

The Steps:

1. Preheat oven to 375°. Lightly butter a 1½-quart baking dish.
2. In large bowl, combine grits, cheese, egg, butter, and milk and stir well until combined.
3. Pour into prepared baking dish and bake 35–45 minutes or until golden brown on top and center is set.
4. Serve grits piping hot.

Variation:

One cup grated Cheddar, Swiss, or Jack cheese can be substituted for the garlic cheese.

Make-It-Easy Tip:

√ The easiest way to cook quick grits is to stir 1 cup grits into 4 cups boiling salted water, reduce heat to a simmer, cover, and cook 4–5 minutes, stirring occasionally. This recipe yields 4 cups of cooked grits.

Orzo with Mushrooms and Onions

SERVES: 6–8
Preparation time: 15 minutes
Cooking time: 10–15 minutes

Orzo is rice-shaped pasta. It's available in Greek or Armenian grocery stores.

The Ingredients:
    4 tablespoons unsalted butter
    1 large onion, finely chopped
    8 mushrooms, thinly sliced
    1 16-ounce box orzo
    ½ cup freshly grated Parmesan cheese
    ½ teaspoon salt, or to taste
    ¼ teaspoon freshly ground pepper
    Garnish: Freshly chopped parsley

The Steps:
1. In large skillet, melt the butter; sauté onions over medium heat until soft, about 5 minutes.
2. Add mushrooms and continue to cook for an additional 5 minutes or until golden.
3. Cook orzo in boiling salted water, according to directions on box; drain in colander.
4. Toss orzo with onion/mushroom mixture; sprinkle cheese on top. Season to taste with salt and pepper and serve hot, sprinkled with freshly chopped parsley.

Variations:
Tiny Italian noodles can be substituted for orzo.
Chopped water chestnuts can be added with the orzo for a crunchy texture.

Couscous

SERVES: 6–8
Preparation time: 5 minutes
Cooking time: 5 minutes

Couscous is a traditional Moroccan dish made with steamed grains of semolina. It can be served as the basis for a main course, accompanied by soups, sauces, stews, or vegetables, or served alone as a side dish.

The Ingredients:

1 16-ounce package couscous, pre-cooked medium grain (Near East brand is good)
2 cups boiling broth, beef or chicken (or water)
2 tablespoons unsalted butter (or oil), or to taste
Garnish: Freshly chopped coriander or parsley

The Steps:

1. Combine couscous with boiling broth or water (if using less than 16 ounces, combine equal amounts of couscous, by volume, and boiling broth or water); cover, and allow to stand for 5 minutes.
2. Add 2 tablespoons butter, or to taste, stir well, and fluff with a fork.
3. Place couscous in a serving dish, garnish with freshly chopped coriander or parsley, and serve hot.

Variations:

Use chicken or beef broth, depending on the main course.

Couscous is traditionally cooked in a Couscousier, a double boiler-like pot with a steamer attachment. To simulate a Couscousier, complete preparation through Step 1 and place couscous in strainer or colander over pot of boiling broth. Do not let broth come in direct contact with the strainer. Allow the steam to penetrate the couscous for 5 minutes and then complete Step 2 as above.

CHAPTER SEVEN

VEGETABLES

Crisp Fresh Asparagus

Baked Asparagus

Carrots and Parsnips
Combined

Carrot Purée in Artichoke
Bottoms

Sautéed Chayote with
Tomatoes

Braised Daikon

Eggplant Szechwan-Style

Baby Lima Beans and
Prosciutto

Petite Peas Française

Potatoes Boiled in Jackets

Perfect Baked Potatoes

Baked Potato Skins

Stir-Fried Spinach

Baked Spinach with Cheese

Stir-Fried Straw and Hay
Summer Squash

Baked Acorn Squash

Banana Squash Purée

Baked Spaghetti Squash

Sweet Potato Soufflé

Cherry Tomatoes Flavored
with Dill

Tomatoes Filled with Peas

Tomato Pie

Dilled Zucchini

Italian Zucchini Bake

Once thought of as an unimportant side dish, vegetables are now considered an important part of any meal. In fact, they are occasionally the main course. We appreciate their taste, their versatility, and especially their nutritional benefits. Color, texture, and flavor are all being taken into consideration in modern vegetable cookery.

Steaming and boiling are the simplest methods of preparing fresh vegetables. Steaming is the most advantageous, preserving vitamins, minerals, and other nutrients. The only drawback to steaming is the loss of the vibrant green color. Boiling vegetables uncovered retains the bright color, but some nutrients are lost in the water.

Several years ago it was popular to add baking soda to the cooking water to retain the bright color of vegetables. We now realize that, although the color is retained, many of the vitamins are destroyed and the vegetables become mushy.

Fresh vegetables are definitely preferable to canned. Canned vegetables, high in salt content and often filled with preservatives, are a poor substitute for fresh, no matter how much time they save. It takes only a few minutes to steam or boil a fresh vegetable. Frozen vegetables are the next best thing to fresh and several types, such as chopped spinach and broccoli, can be tremendous time-savers.

Ask the produce person at your market to advise you on the freshness of specific vegetables. Be wary of chemicals, waxes, food colors, and sprays. Scrub vegetables with a brush before using and try to steam or bake in the natural skin to preserve nutrients.

Sautéing the cut-up vegetables for a few minutes in butter or oil is another easy method of preparation. Add water or broth plus a few spices and seasonings, cover, and continue to cook until crunchy. Serve with the liquid to retain important nutrients.

Stir-frying is yet another easy and quick way to cook vegetables. The shape and roominess of a wok make it a perfect vehicle. You brown the vegetables quickly in hot oil, turning them around and around over very high heat and, in so doing, preserve their crunchy texture, vibrant colors, natural flavors, and nutrients. The hot oil seals in the vegetables' juices, while at the same time extracting their flavors. All ingredients should be readied in advance and placed in the area near the wok so that the final cooking is truly Make-It-Easy.

Baked vegetables—cooked alone or combined with noodles, rice, cheese, or other staple ingredients—share a similar Make-It-Easy advantage. They can be prepared well in advance, cooked, and reheated at serving time.

Stuffed vegetables are an especially attractive side dish but often appear too complicated to prepare. The stuffed vegetable recipes in this chapter show how, with a few hints, tips, and shortcuts, it is easy to cook *Tomatoes Filled with Peas,* or prepare stuffed artichoke bottoms, or patty pan squash. In addition, stuffed vegetables can be assembled in advance and reheated just before serving, while maintaining optimum flavor and texture.

You may also find some close encounters with vegetables of an unfamiliar kind. Spaghetti squash, chayote, and daikon are the kinds of exotic arrivals you're bound to find in your supermarket produce section or at the green grocer's. So some Make-It-Easy recipes are included to bring them down to earth.

In general, cut vegetables right before cooking to avoid vitamin loss and, whenever possible, cook them at the last minute to preserve crispness, bright color, and great flavor.

Crisp Fresh Asparagus

SERVES: 4
Preparation time: 10 minutes
Cooking time: 8–10 minutes

I find boiling asparagus in an uncovered skillet (yes, a large frying pan) is the easiest way to prepare them. It ensures a bright green color and even cooking. Peeling the base of the asparagus is optional, but it makes them very attractive and the stalks tender and totally edible. The hollandaise can be prepared in advance and kept warm in a Thermos jar that has been rinsed with hot water.

The Ingredients:
2 pounds fresh spring asparagus
Water
Salt
Garnish: Hollandaise Sauce (*see* Hollandaise with Ease, Chapter 2), or 3–4 tablespoons unsalted butter, melted

The Steps:
1. Wash asparagus in cold water and break off tough ends. If desired, peel asparagus 2–3 inches up the stalk. (An asparagus peeler or vegetable peeler can be used.)
2. Bring large skillet of salted water to a boil and drop in asparagus. Cook uncovered 8–10 minutes depending on thickness of the vegetable. Do not overcook! The tips and stalks should be *al dente*, crunchy but tender.
3. Drain at once and serve immediately with Hollandaise with Ease or melted butter.

Variations:
Serve asparagus with a light sprinkling of fresh lemon juice instead of hollandaise or butter to reduce calories.

Buttered bread crumbs can be used as an alternate topping for asparagus. Place 4 tablespoons (½ stick) unsalted butter in a small saucepan with ¼ cup dry bread crumbs and toss until lightly brown. Sprinkle over hot asparagus.

Leftover asparagus, although a rare occurrence at today's prices, make a wonderful cold salad tossed with *Laurie's Basic Vinaigrette* dressing.

Make-It-Easy Tips:
√ An asparagus steamer can be used instead of a skillet. Asparagus should be tied together, placed upright in enough boiling water to cover stalks but not tips, covered, and steamed until just tender. The timing of steamed asparagus should be about 15 minutes but color will not be as green since they are cooked covered.

Baked Asparagus

SERVES: 4
Preparation time: 15 minutes
Cooking time: 13 minutes

Here's a great, easy way to prepare fresh asparagus in advance while still preserving the texture and flavor of steamed or boiled asparagus.

Thin asparagus work best in this dish. Prepare in the spring when they are in season.

The Ingredients:

    1½ pounds very thin, fresh asparagus
     3 tablespoons unsalted butter, melted
     1 tablespoon lemon juice
    ¼ teaspoon freshly ground white pepper
    ½ cup freshly grated Parmesan cheese

The Steps:

1. Wash asparagus and break off tough ends.
2. Place asparagus in large skillet; add lightly salted, boiling water to cover, bring to a boil again, and cook uncovered for 3 minutes or until almost crisp. Drain asparagus and run under cold water to refresh. Drain again on paper towels.
3. Brush an oven-proof dish with 1 tablespoon melted butter and lay asparagus in dish.
4. Top asparagus with remaining 2 tablespoons melted butter, lemon juice, pepper, and, finally, Parmesan cheese. (The saltiness of the cheese precludes the need for any added salt.) At this point, the dish can be covered with plastic wrap and refrigerated until ready to use.
5. At serving time, bring casserole to room temperature, if possible. Preheat oven to 400° and bake asparagus, uncovered, for 5–10 minutes until hot and bubbling.

Variation:

Buttered bread crumbs can be baked atop asparagus.

Carrots and Parsnips Combined

SERVES: 4
Preparation time: 15 minutes
Cooking time: 6 minutes

This vegetable combination is quick to prepare with a food processor or blender, and makes an especially colorful side dish.

The Ingredients:

    4 medium carrots, peeled
    4 medium parsnips, peeled
  2–3 tablespoons unsalted butter
  ½ teaspoon salt
  ¼ teaspoon freshly ground white pepper
  ½ teaspoon dried tarragon, crumbled (optional)

The Steps:

1. Shred or grate carrots and parsnips in food processor, blender, or by hand.
2. Drop into a large pot of salted water and allow to cook for 2 minutes or until barely tender. Drain and run under cold water. Drain again. (Can be prepared up to this point and refrigerated until ready to use.)
3. At serving time, heat butter in a large skillet. Quickly sauté vegetables in hot butter and season to taste with salt and pepper, and tarragon, if desired.

Variations:

Other shredded vegetables can be substituted for carrots and parsnips according to taste preference, color appeal, and accompanying main dish: For example, zucchini and carrots with veal, or turnips and carrots with turkey.

Make-It-Easy Tips:

√ When selecting parsnips, choose small- to medium-size ones that are solid and have an even surface.

√ To prepare vegetables in blender, cut them coarsely and fill jar half full; cover with water, replace top of jar, and place hand lightly on cover top. Blend on "high" until just chopped. (Watch carefully!) Drain thoroughly in a colander.

Carrot Purée in Artichoke Bottoms

SERVES: 8
Preparation time: 1 minute
Cooking time: 20 minutes

A simple Carrot Purée can be served plain in a bowl garnished with parsley or piled into artichoke bottoms, patty pan squash, or small zucchini boats for an especially attractive presentation. The Carrot Purée is so sweet and creamy tasting, guests often mistake it for mashed sweet potatoes—yet the calorie count is low since only a tablespoon of butter is used in the preparation.

The Ingredients:

2 cans artichoke bottoms, drained
1 pound carrots, peeled and thickly sliced
½ teaspoon salt, or to taste
¼ teaspoon freshly ground white pepper
1 tablespoon unsalted butter

The Steps:

1. Bring large pot of salted water to boil. Drop carrots into water and boil, covered, for 15–20 minutes or until tender.
2. Drain carrots and purée in food processor or blender.
3. Season with salt and pepper; add butter and continue to purée until very smooth.
4. Taste, adjust seasoning if necessary, and pile into artichoke bottoms.
5. Serve immediately, or reheat in a 325° oven for 10 minutes.

Variations:

For a lower calorie vegetable dish, omit the butter.
For an extra-fancy presentation, pipe carrot purée through a cake decorating bag.

Make-It-Easy Tip:

√ Do not store carrots with apples. Apples release a gas that gives carrots a bitter taste.

Chayote squash

Sautéed Chayote with Tomatoes

SERVES: 4–6
Preparation time: 15 minutes
Cooking time: 25 minutes

Chayote, also called Mango Squash and Vegetable Pear, is a squash cultivated in tropical regions. Originally from Mexico and South America, it is now grown in Florida and some other regions of the United States. It can be used interchangeably with zucchini in recipes. To prepare to serve alone, cut in half; remove the pulp and mash it; season well and add butter to taste. Pile into scooped-out shells, and bake.

The Ingredients:
    2 chayotes, scrubbed clean with a brush
    2 tablespoons unsalted butter
    1 medium onion, minced
    1 16-ounce can tomatoes, drained and roughly chopped
    1 tablespoon freshly chopped parsley
      Pinch of sugar
      Pinch of thyme
    1 tablespoon freshly chopped parsley
    ½ teaspoon salt, or to taste
    ¼ teaspoon freshly ground pepper, or to taste

The Steps:

1. Cut scrubbed chayotes into 1″ cubes, discarding center seed.
2. In large skillet, melt butter; sauté onions over medium-low heat until soft but not brown, 5–7 minutes.
3. Add chayotes, stir to coat with the onions; add tomatoes, parsley, sugar, thyme, salt and pepper to taste; bring to a boil, cover, reduce heat, and slowly simmer for 20 minutes or until tender.
4. Taste, adjust seasoning if necessary, and serve garnished with freshly chopped parsley.

Variation:

For a spicier version, add chopped green chilies in Step 3, according to taste.

Make-It-Easy Tip:

√ Select hard, firm, smooth chayotes, without blemishes.

Braised Daikon

SERVES: 4
Preparation time: 10 minutes
Cooking time: 10 minutes

Long, white, tapered, and hotter in taste than a regular radish, daikon is often used as decoration since it's easily carved. This Japanese radish can also be shredded for salad, or thinly sliced and braised like a turnip.

The Ingredients:

  1½ pounds daikon, peeled
    Chicken broth
  2 tablespoons unsalted butter
  ¼ teaspoon salt, or to taste
    Freshly ground white pepper

The Steps:

1. Thinly slice daikon by hand or in food processor.
2. Place in saucepan, cover with chicken broth, bring to boil. Cover, reduce heat, and simmer slowly for 8–10 minutes or until vegetable softens.
3. Drain off all broth, place in bowl, top with butter, salt and pepper, and serve immediately.

Variations:

For a lower calorie version, use only 1 teaspoon butter for flavoring.

For an Oriental Salad, slice daikon and marinate overnight in a dressing of 1 cup water, ¾ cup Japanese or white vinegar, ⅓ cup brown sugar, and 2 teaspoons salt or to taste, stirred together.

Make-It-Easy Tips:

√ Peel daikon with a vegetable peeler as if peeling a carrot.
√ Store daikon in the refrigerator as you would store a red radish.

Eggplant Szechwan-Style

SERVES: 4–6
Preparation time: 15 minutes
Cooking time: 8–10 minutes

Eggplant Szechwan-Style can be served hot as a side vegetable, or cold as a salad or hors d'oeuvre.

The Ingredients:

  1 medium eggplant (about 1 pound), unpeeled and cut into 1½″ cubes

    1 large clove garlic, finely minced
    1 slice ginger, finely minced
  ¼ cup chicken broth
    1 tablespoon soy sauce
    1 teaspoon sugar
    1 teaspoon chili paste with garlic, or more to taste (available at oriental groceries or by mail order, *see* Appendix A)
    2 teaspoons Japanese vinegar or white wine vinegar
    1 tablespoon oriental sesame oil
4–5 tablespoons peanut oil

The Steps:

1. Place eggplant and garlic and ginger near cooking area; combine broth, soy sauce, sugar, and chili paste in small bowl and place near cooking area; place vinegar and sesame oil within reach.
2. Heat wok or large skillet, add oil, and stir-fry eggplant over medium heat until softened, 4–5 minutes; remove with slotted spoon.
3. Turn heat to high, add additional tablespoon oil if necessary, and stir-fry garlic and ginger for 30 seconds.
4. Add broth mixture, bring to boil, return eggplant to wok and cook, stirring, for 2 minutes.
5. Add vinegar and sesame oil, stir to combine, and serve hot as a vegetable side dish, or cold as a salad or hors d'oeuvre.

Variation:

If a spicier flavor is desired, increase the amount of chili paste, at your own risk!

Make-It-Easy Tips:

√ Both garlic and ginger can be smashed together with the side of a cleaver and then peeled and chopped easily.

√ Four to five tablespoons of oil are needed because eggplant tends to absorb oil readily and will begin sticking to wok or skillet if there is not enough oil.

√ When selecting an eggplant, check bottom end (without the stem). The shape of the greyish "scar" or indentation on this end is an indicator of the number of seeds. If the scar is oval or oblong, there will be many seeds and the eggplant will be bitter. Select the one with the round scar, about the size of a dime, which will have fewer seeds and thus be less bitter.

Baby Lima Beans and Prosciutto

SERVES: 6
Preparation time: 10 minutes
Cooking time: 15 minutes

The Ingredients:
- 3 slices prosciutto, diced
- 1 tablespoon unsalted butter
- ¼ cup finely minced onion
- 2 10-ounce packages frozen baby lima beans, thawed and drained
- ½ cup chicken broth
- ¼ teaspoon salt, or to taste
- ¼ teaspoon freshly ground pepper

The Steps:
1. In a small skillet, sauté prosciutto over medium heat until it releases its fat.
2. Add butter to pan and sauté onions until soft but not brown, about 5 minutes.
3. Add lima beans, broth, salt, and pepper; cover, and simmer for 8–10 minutes or until beans are tender.
4. Taste, adjust seasoning if necessary, and serve hot.

Variations:
If baby lima beans are unavailable, substitute regular lima beans and cook until tender.

If prosciutto is unavailable, substitute Westphalian ham or use 2 slices diced bacon. (If using bacon, omit butter.)

Make-It-Easy Tip:
√ Dice prosciutto easily with kitchen shears.

Petit Pois Française

SERVES: 4
Preparation time: 10 minutes
Cooking time: 4–5 minutes

This dish utilizes the traditional French approach to cooking peas with lettuce. The lettuce releases its moisture to braise the peas.

The Ingredients:

1½ cups shredded lettuce
2 10-ounce packages frozen tiny peas, thawed
¼ cup minced scallions (green and white included)
1 teaspoon sugar
¼ teaspoon salt, or to taste
⅛ teaspoon freshly ground white pepper
2 tablespoons unsalted butter, cut into bits

The Steps:

1. In a small saucepan, place ¾ cup shredded lettuce.
2. Top with peas and scallions, sprinkle with sugar, salt, and pepper; dot with butter.
3. Top with remaining lettuce, cover tightly, and cook over medium low heat for 3–4 minutes or until peas are tender.
4. Adjust seasoning to taste, and serve hot.

Variations:

Chopped shallots can be substituted for scallions.
Substitute regular green peas and cook for 5–10 minutes or until tender.
Garnish peas with freshly chopped mint for a refreshing taste.

Potatoes Boiled in Jackets

SERVES: 4
Preparation time: 5 minutes
Cooking time: 15–20 minutes

This recipe is for the small, round, red potatoes that look more attractive and are better nutritionally when cooked in their vitamin-rich jackets. New potatoes in thin skins can also be used and cooked until tender.

The Ingredients:
8 small, round, red or other boiling potatoes
1 teaspoon salt
½ teaspoon salt, or to taste
¼ teaspoon freshly ground pepper, or to taste
2–3 tablespoons unsalted butter, melted
1 tablespoon freshly chopped parsley

The Steps:
1. Scrub potatoes clean with a stiff brush.
2. In large pot, put enough water to cover the potatoes, plus 1 teaspoon salt, and bring to a boil.
3. Add potatoes and cook covered in boiling water until just tender, 15–20 minutes. (Do not allow to overcook or they will be mushy.)
4. Drain potatoes and toss in bowl with ½ teaspoon salt, pepper, melted butter, and parsley.
5. Serve immediately, piping hot.

Variations:
For a low-calorie version, potatoes can be served plain without butter or seasonings. They are delicious as is.

Leftover cooked potatoes can be chopped and sautéed in butter with onions the next day as hash browns. They can also be used in roast beef salad, potato salad, corned beef hash, or sautéed in omelets.

Make-It-Easy Tips:
√ A clean, stiff toothbrush makes a great vegetable brush.

√ Do not store potatoes in the refrigerator. The starch will convert to sugar and an unpleasant sweetish taste will result. If you have already done this, simply remove from refrigerator, store at room temperature, and the starch will be converted back. Also, do not store potatoes with onions. Onions release a gas that hastens the spoilage of potatoes.

Perfect Baked Potatoes

Preparation time: 5 minutes
Cooking time: 1 hour

The Ingredients:
Baking potatoes, 1 per person (Idaho potatoes, also called Russets, are best for baking)

Garnishes: Butter, sour cream, grated cheese, chives, bacon

The Steps:
1. Preheat oven to 400°.
2. Scrub potatoes well, prick with a fork to allow steam to escape, and bake on center rack for 1–1¼ hours, depending on size.
3. Remove from oven; hold each potato with pot holder and gently squeeze to test for doneness, and also to make them fluffy.
4. Cut a cross in top to allow steam to escape and to avoid soggy potatoes.
5. Serve hot with butter or sour cream and assorted garnishes, such as chopped chives, bacon bits, or grated cheese.

Variation:
For a low-calorie potato, top with pepper, yogurt, and fresh herbs such as chives, parsley, or dill.

Make-It-Easy Tips:
√ On hot nights when you don't want to heat the oven, bake potatoes in the toaster-oven at 375° for 1½–2 hours. The outside will be crispy and the inside powdery soft.

√ A Potato Party can be an inexpensive way to entertain. Just bake lots of potatoes and have an assortment of condiments on hand, like chili, guacamole, cheese, chopped onions, shredded lettuce, chilies, bacon, salsa, etc.

√ For a softer skin, rub with oil prior to baking.

√ A metal prong or baking nail speeds up cooking time 10–15 minutes by acting as a heat conductor on the inside of the potato.

√ Do not use foil to wrap potatoes. The results will be soggy skins and lumpy, hard interiors.

Baked Potato Skins

SERVES: 6–8
Preparation time: 10 minutes
Cooking time: 5 minutes

The Ingredients:
6 Idaho potatoes, baked
⅓ cup unsalted butter, melted
½ teaspoon salt, or to taste
¼ teaspoon freshly ground white pepper
Garnish: Sour cream and chives (optional)

The Steps:
1. Preheat broiler.
2. Cut potatoes in half and scoop out all the potato inside (reserve for mashed potatoes or other recipe).
3. Cut skins in half again, generously paint with melted butter, and sprinkle to taste with salt and pepper.
4. Brown under the broiler, 5–6 inches from heat, until crisp, about 3 minutes, watching carefully.
5. Serve skins hot, garnished with sour cream and chives if desired.

Accompaniments:
A variety of fillings and toppings can be used on potato skins, such as bacon, chives, grated Cheddar or Swiss cheese, Guacamole, or even sour cream and caviar.

Variations:

Cut the skins in strips and serve as a cocktail party canapé, plain or filled with sour cream and caviar.

Make-It-Easy Tips:

√ Prepare the potatoes early in the day, cut skins, and then butter, season, and broil at the last minute.

√ Potato skins can also be baked in a 475°–500° oven for 8–10 minutes or until crisp.

Stir-Fried Spinach

SERVES: 3–4
Preparation time: 5 minutes
Cooking time: 3 minutes

The Ingredients:

1 pound fresh spinach leaves, washed, with tough stems removed
2 tablespoons peanut oil
½ teaspoon salt, or to taste
Pinch sugar

The Steps:

1. Heat wok or large, heavy skillet, add oil and, when hot, stir-fry spinach for 1 minute.
2. Add salt and sugar and continue to stir-fry for 1 minute.
3. Taste, adjust seasoning if necessary, and serve immediately.

Make-It-Easy Tips:

√ Select fresh bunches of spinach with dark green leaves without blemishes. If fresh bunches are unavailable, the cellophane-wrapped packages are the next best choice.

√ One pound of fresh spinach equals approximately 1 cup of cooked spinach.

Baked Spinach with Cheese

SERVES: 4
Preparation time: 15 minutes
Cooking time: 30 minutes

The Ingredients:
2 10-ounce packages frozen chopped spinach, thawed and thoroughly squeezed dry
2 eggs, lightly beaten
⅓ cup grated Monterey Jack or Muenster cheese
1 tablespoon grated onion
½ teaspoon salt, or to taste
¼ teaspoon freshly ground pepper
¼ teaspoon nutmeg
1½ tablespoons unsalted butter, diced
2 tablespoons freshly grated Parmesan cheese

The Steps:
1. Preheat oven to 325°. Generously butter small casserole or au gratin dish.
2. In bowl, combine spinach, eggs, cheese, onion, salt, pepper, and nutmeg and spoon into casserole.
3. Bake for 15 minutes; dot with butter and Parmesan cheese and bake for an additional 15 minutes. Serve hot and bubbly.

Make-It-Easy Tips:
√ Baked Spinach with Cheese can be assembled through Step 2 and refrigerated until ready to bake. Bring to room temperature before baking.

Stir-Fried Straw and Hay Summer Squash

SERVES: 6
Preparation time: 10 minutes
Cooking time: 3–4 minutes

Although this dish does not have oriental ingredients, it benefits from the stir-frying technique. The zucchini and yellow squash maintain their crunchy textures, vibrant colors and juicy flavors. The dish gets its name from the pasta dish called Straw and Hay or *Paglia e Fieno*, referring to its green and white colors.

The Ingredients:
    2 tablespoons olive oil
    3 scallions, finely chopped (green and white parts included)
    3 medium crookneck squash (yellow summer squash), cut into ½" slices
    3 medium zucchini, cut into ½" slices
    ¼ cup chicken broth
       Pinch of salt
    ¼ teaspoon freshly ground white pepper
       Garnish: Freshly chopped parsley

The Steps:
1. Heat wok or large heavy skillet until very hot; add oil and heat 30 seconds.
2. Add scallions and stir-fry 1 minute, stirring constantly.
3. Add crookneck and zucchini and continue to stir-fry until squash begins to turn lightly golden.
4. Add broth, cover, and cook over low heat for 2 minutes, until just tender.
5. Season to taste with salt and pepper and serve immediately, sprinkled with freshly chopped parsley.

Variations:
If vegetable is to accompany beef dish, substitute beef broth.
The new hybrid, yellow "gold rush" squash, can be substituted for the crookneck.

Make-It-Easy Tip:
√ When selecting summer squash, choose small- to medium-size ones with a rind tender enough to be punctured by a fingernail.

Baked Acorn Squash

SERVES: 4
Preparation time: 15 minutes
Cooking time: 1 hour

Acorn squash has a variety of names including Table Queen, Danish, or Des Moines.

The Ingredients:
       2 acorn squash, cut in half lengthwise
    ¼ cup dark brown sugar
    ¼ cup (½ stick) unsalted butter, melted
    ¼ cup unsweetened applesauce
       4 teaspoons grated onion
    ½ teaspoon cinnamon
    ¼ teaspoon nutmeg
    ⅛ teaspoon ground ginger
       1 tablespoon dark rum
    ½ teaspoon salt, or to taste
    ¼ teaspoon freshly ground white pepper, or to taste

The Steps:
1. Preheat oven to 350°.
2. Remove seeds and fibers from cut squash and place cut side down in a shallow baking pan. Pour ½" of hot water in bottom of pan and bake for 25 minutes; drain off water and turn squash upright.
3. In small bowl, combine brown sugar, butter, applesauce, onion, cinnamon, nutmeg, ginger, rum, salt, and pepper and stir well.
4. Spoon mixture into squash shells, dividing it evenly among the 4 halves.

5. Return to oven and bake an additional 35–40 minutes or until golden brown, basting once or twice.
6. Serve squash hot, or reheat for 2–3 minutes under a broiler until golden, watching carefully.

Make-It-Easy Tips:
√ Squash can be assembled through Step 2 and refrigerated until ready to use.
√ Acorn squash can be found in either a dark-green color, meaning it was recently picked, or an orangy color, indicating longer storage. Both are good to use.
√ Place aluminum foil in pan before proceeding with Step 4 to avoid messy clean-ups.

Banana Squash Purée

SERVES: 4
Preparation time: 10 minutes
Cooking time: 10 minutes

The oversize banana squash is generally cut up into usable sections in the grocery store since it runs a staggering, tapering 18″ to 24″ long and 5″ to 6″ wide. A pale olive gray at first, it becomes creamy pink upon storage, with bright orange flesh. Since it is often sold cut, it will not keep more than a week under refrigeration, but if purchased whole it will last about four weeks in a dry place.

The Ingredients:
1 1-pound section banana squash
3 tablespoons unsalted butter
2 tablespoons light brown sugar
1 tablespoon Curaçao or other orange-flavored liqueur
½ teaspoon cinnamon
½ teaspoon salt
¼ teaspoon nutmeg
Pinch mace
Garnish: Grated lemon rind or grated orange rind

The Steps:

1. Peel hard outer shell from squash and cut flesh into 2″ squares.
2. Drop the squash into pot of boiling salted water and, when water returns to a boil, cook covered over medium heat for 8–10 minutes, or until tender; drain.
3. Purée in food processor, blender, or through a food mill until just smooth. (Do not over-process or it will become too pasty in texture.)
4. Remove to a mixing bowl, add the butter, brown sugar, liqueur, cinnamon, salt, nutmeg, and mace; stir until smooth.
5. Taste, adjust seasoning if necessary, and serve hot, garnished with grated lemon or orange rind.

Make-It-Easy Tips:

√ The squash purée can be reheated in a double boiler.
√ When selecting pre-cut banana squash, choose crisp, clean flesh. Avoid discolored, blemished, or bruised pieces, which indicate age.

Baked Spaghetti Squash

SERVES: 4–6
Preparation time: 10 minutes
Cooking time: 1½ hours

Spaghetti Squash, also called Vegetable Spaghetti, Diet Spaghetti, Manchurian Squash (owing to its oriental origin), Cucuzzi or Suzza Melon, is actually an edible gourd. A large oval-shaped yellow vegetable, it owes its name to the stringy texture of its flesh which, when cooked, turns into spaghetti-like strands ready for anything from meat sauce to an Alfredo treatment.

The Ingredients:

2 pounds spaghetti squash
3–4 tablespoons unsalted butter
3–4 tablespoons freshly grated Parmesan cheese
½ teaspoon salt, or to taste

Spaghetti squash

½ teaspoon freshly ground white pepper, or to taste
Garnish: Freshly grated Parmesan cheese

The Steps:
1. Preheat oven to 350°.
2. Prick squash all over with a fork; place on rack in oven and bake for 1½ hours, turning once during cooking.
3. Split in half horizontally, scoop out seeds and discard.
4. With a fork, string fibers out of each half into a large serving bowl and toss with butter, cheese, salt, and pepper.
5. Serve in bowl, or return to shell halves to serve with additional cheese on the side.

Variation:
Use limited amounts of butter and cheese for a low-calorie "spaghetti" dish.

Make-It-Easy Tips:
√ Store unblemished squash in a cool, dry place for up to 4 weeks.
√ Spaghetti squash often contains a sticker explaining how to cut and steam it. I have yet to find anyone who can cut through this gourd with anything less than a hacksaw. Baking or boiling whole softens the skin and makes cutting easy.

Sweet Potato Soufflé

SERVES: 8
Preparation time: 15 minutes
Cooking time: Potatoes–40 minutes
Casserole–45 minutes

Sweet Potato Soufflé is the perfect Thanksgiving accompaniment but can be used year 'round with any poultry or baked ham dish. It is called a soufflé but that doesn't mean it has to be watched carefully. It can be assembled a day in advance and refrigerated until ready to use. The easiest way to prepare the dish is in an electric mixer. A food processor or blender will overmix the potatoes, causing them to become gluey and pasty.

The Ingredients:
    6 large sweet potatoes
    5 tablespoons unsalted butter
    1 cup heavy cream
    ⅓ cup granulated sugar
    ⅓ cup dark brown sugar
    3 large eggs, lightly beaten
    1 teaspoon grated orange rind
    ½ teaspoon nutmeg
    ½ teaspoon salt, or to taste

The Steps:
1. Bring large pot of salted water to a boil; add potatoes, bring to boil and cook, covered, about 40 minutes or until very tender. Drain and allow to cool slightly. Peel.
2. Preheat oven to 350°. Generously butter a large, round 2-quart casserole or rectangular baking dish.
3. Place hot potatoes in bowl of electric mixer (or use hand mixer) and beat in butter; add cream, white and brown sugars, eggs, orange rind, nutmeg, and salt and continue to beat until smooth.
4. Pour mixture into prepared casserole and bake for 40 minutes.
5. Serve immediately.

Variations:

Yams can be substituted for sweet potatoes.

And . . . for those who nostalgically connect sweet potatoes with a marshmallow topping—place 2 cups of tiny marshmallows on top of the baked casserole and return to the oven for just 3–4 minutes or until melted, watching very carefully.

Cherry Tomatoes Flavored with Dill

SERVES: 6
Preparation time: 10 minutes
Cooking time: 4–5 minutes

The Ingredients:

3 tablespoons unsalted butter
2 pints cherry tomatoes, washed and stems removed
¼ cup freshly snipped dill or 2 teaspoons dried dill
½ teaspoon salt, or to taste
½ teaspoon freshly ground pepper, or to taste

The Steps:

1. In large saucepan, melt butter; when hot and foamy add cherry tomatoes, dill, salt, and pepper.
2. Cover, reduce heat, and cook slowly for 4–5 minutes until the tomatoes are just cooked but not bursting open.
3. Taste, adjust seasoning if necessary, and serve immediately.

Variations:

Heavy cream can be added with the seasonings for a rich vegetable dish.

Freshly chopped chives or freshly chopped basil, when in season, can be substituted for the dill.

Make-It-Easy Tip:

√ Wash tomatoes first and then remove stem ends to prevent loss of juice.

Tomatoes Filled with Peas

SERVES: 4
Preparation time: 10–15 minutes
Cooking time: 10–15 minutes

The Ingredients:
4 medium-size tomatoes
1 tablespoon unsalted butter
2 tablespoons finely minced onion
1 10-ounce package frozen tiny peas, thawed
½ teaspoon salt, or to taste
¼ teaspoon freshly ground pepper, or to taste

The Steps:
1. Preheat oven to 325°.
2. Cut tops off tomatoes, scoop out centers with a grapefruit spoon or similar tool; discard the seeds and pulp and allow to drain upside down for 5 minutes on paper towels.
3. Place tomatoes in a baking pan and bake for 10 minutes, until just softened.
4. While tomatoes are baking, heat butter in small saucepan; sauté onion over medium heat until soft but not brown, about 5 minutes. Add peas and stir to coat with onion-butter mixture; cover, and cook for 2 minutes or until just warmed through.
5. Season to taste with salt and pepper, fill baked tomatoes with peas, and serve hot.

Variations:
Tomatoes can also be filled with chopped spinach, which has been sautéed with onion and butter and enriched with sour cream; or filled with chopped broccoli, sautéed with butter and garlic and enriched with Parmesan cheese.

Make-It-Easy Tips:
√ Place tomatoes in a muffin tin to keep them from falling over.
√ To prepare in advance, cook the shells only 7 minutes, fill with peas and, when ready, reheat in a moderate 350° oven for 3–4

minutes. Do not overcook or tomatoes will become too soft and may fall apart.

√ Select tomatoes by color, lack of blemishes, and especially odor. Local, vine-ripened tomatoes have a distinct, flavorful aroma as opposed to the ones that are ripened during shipping, which have little or no aroma. And vine-ripened tomatoes contain almost twice the amount of vitamin C.

Tomato Pie

SERVES: 6
Preparation time: 15 minutes
Cooking time: 40 minutes

This Tomato Pie makes an attractive side dish, but can also be served as a lunch or brunch dish.

The Ingredients:
    1 frozen pastry shell (9")
    4 medium, ripe tomatoes, sliced, and slices cut in half
    ¼ cup chopped chives or scallion stalks
    ¾ teaspoon freshly chopped basil or ¼ teaspoon dried basil, crumbled
    ¼ teaspoon dried oregano, crumbled
    ¼ teaspoon salt, or to taste
    ¼ teaspoon freshly ground pepper, or to taste
    1 cup grated Swiss Gruyère cheese
    ¼ cup mayonnaise

The Steps:
    1. Preheat oven to 425°.
    2. Bake pie crust for 5 minutes. Remove from oven. Reduce heat to 400°.
    3. Place tomato pieces on bottom of pie shell.
    4. Sprinkle tomatoes with chives or scallions, basil, oregano, salt, and pepper.
    5. Combine cheese and mayonnaise and carefully spread mixture

evenly over tomatoes, making sure it reaches edges of pie crust and seals in tomatoes completely.

6. Bake for 35 minutes or until hot and bubbly.
7. Allow to sit for 5–10 minutes, cut in wedges, and serve hot.

Variations:

Grated Cheddar or Monterey Jack can be substituted for Swiss cheese.

Make-It-Easy Tips:

√ Pie can be frozen successfully for future use. Double the recipe to save extra work.

√ The pie crust is pre-baked for 5 minutes to prevent it from becoming soggy.

√ Ripen tomatoes to full maturity in a brown paper bag that has been pierced with a few holes, or in one of the new Lucite fruit ripeners, checking daily. Do *not* ripen in direct sunlight. Warmth, not light, ripens tomatoes.

Fruit ripener

Dilled Zucchini

SERVES: 4
Preparation time: 10 minutes
Cooking time: 7–8 minutes

Dilled Zucchini is low in calories.

The Ingredients:
1 tablespoon unsalted butter
1 teaspoon olive oil
1 pound zucchini, cut in ¼″ slices (thick julienne strips)
¼ cup chicken broth
1–2 tablespoons freshly snipped dill, or 1 teaspoon dried dill, to taste
½ teaspoon salt, or to taste
¼ teaspoon freshly ground pepper, or to taste

The Steps:
1. In large saucepan, melt butter and oil together; add zucchini and sauté for 1 minute over medium heat.
2. Add broth and dill, stir to combine; cover pot and cook over medium heat for 4–5 minutes or until zucchini is cooked but still crunchy.
3. Season to taste with salt and pepper and serve immediately.

Variation:
Serve leftovers with *Laurie's Basic Vinaigrette* dressing to make a cold zucchini salad.

Zucchini

Italian Zucchini Bake

SERVES: 8
Preparation time: 15 minutes
Cooking time: 30–35 minutes

The Ingredients:
3–4 tablespoons unsalted butter
2 large onions, sliced
3 pounds zucchini, washed and cut into ¼" slices
3 tablespoons tomato paste
2 tablespoons freshly grated Parmesan cheese
½ teaspoon salt, or to taste
¼ teaspoon freshly ground pepper
¼ teaspoon freshly minced garlic
3 tablespoons freshly grated Parmesan cheese

The Steps:
1. Preheat oven to 350°. Generously butter a 9" x 12" x 2" baking dish.
2. Melt butter in large skillet; add onions and zucchini; sauté over medium heat until golden brown, 5–7 minutes.
3. Remove from heat and add tomato paste, 2 tablespoons cheese, salt, pepper, and garlic and toss well.
4. Pour into baking dish, sprinkle 3 tablespoons remaining cheese on top, and bake for 25–30 minutes or until golden brown on top; serve hot.

Make-It-Easy Tips:
√ A wok is a handy pot to use when sautéing zucchini. This large amount of vegetables can be tossed around in a wok without falling out.
√ Zucchini Bake can be assembled through Step 3, poured into baking dish, and refrigerated until ready to bake. Bring to room temperature and proceed with recipe.

CHAPTER EIGHT

SALADS

Flavored Vinegar

Raspberry Vinegar

Raspberry Vinaigrette Dressing

French Dressing

Laurie's Basic Vinaigrette and Variations

Basic Blender Mayonnaise

Mustard Mayonnaise

Thousand Island Dressing

Curry Mayonnaise

Dill Mayonnaise

Lemon-Caper Mayonnaise

Spinach Mayonnaise

Green Goddess Salad Dressing

Low-Calorie Buttermilk Dill Dressing

Yogurt Dressing

Spicy Tomato Dressing with No Oil

Low-Calorie Buttermilk Thousand Island Dressing

Greek Salad

Romaine Salad with Litchi Nuts

Caesar Salad

Spinach Salad

Spinach Salad with Creamy Dressing

Tossed Salad with Red Onions

Cabbage Salad with Caraway Seeds

Chinese Asparagus Salad with Spicy Dressing

Bean Sprout Salad

Broccoli Florets Vinaigrette

Dilled Cucumber Salad

Middle Eastern Salad

Raw Mushroom Salad

Snow Pea Salad

String Bean Salad

Tomato and Onion Salad

Oriental Zucchini Salad

Pasta Salad with Chicken and Vegetables

Oriental Noodle Salad

Rice Salad Niçoise

Curried Brown Rice Salad with Fruit

Tabbouleh

Roast Beef Salad

Marinated Oriental Beef and Pepper Salad

Oriental Roast Pork and Snow Pea Salad

Chinese Seafood Salad

Madame Chu's Szechwan Peppercorn Chicken Salad

Curried Chicken Salad

Chinese Chicken and Cucumber Salad

Salads have been around since ancient times. As early as 1390, a recipe for "sallet" from *The Forme of Cury*, a cookbook compiled by the cooks of Richard II, listed lettuce and vegetables prescribing they be washed, torn with the hands, and well dressed with oil, vinegar, and salt.

The first published literary work on Salads was *Acetaria, a Discourse of Sallets*, written by John Evelyn in 1699, who states that "we are by Sallets to understand a particular Composition of certain Crude and Fresh Herbs, such as usually are, or may safely be eaten with some Acetous Juice, Oyl, Salt, etc. to give them a grateful Gust and Vehicle."

Today's salads are no longer lost as a side dish. They are used as first courses, either hot or cold, and flavored with exotic ingredients such as *Raspberry Vinegar* or even sea urchins. Salads can be used as main courses, composed of meat, lettuce, vegetables, and even fruits. Main-course salads are often Make-It-Easy summer dinners.

The important points to remember in salad preparation are:

1. Purchase first-quality ingredients. A salad is only as good as the sum of its parts. Buy *green* lettuce, no brown or yellow or wilted leaves. Buy good-quality oils and vinegars—the taste will tell the difference.

2. Make the salad attractive. Presentation is important no matter how simple the recipe. Place the ingredients in an attractive manner in the bowl, selecting them on the basis of color, eye appeal, and taste.

3. Be imaginative, be creative and, above all—have fun! This is the time to be inventive and also the time to use up some precious leftovers. Why not try *Romaine Salad with Litchi Nuts*, or how about *Oriental Roast Pork and Snow Pea Salad*?

PROCEDURE FOR MAKING SALADS

1. Wash, and then dry the salad greens in a colander, salad spinner, salad basket or between paper towels. Salad greens must be thoroughly dried or the dressing won't cling to the leaves and it will be diluted.

2. Wrap dried lettuce in absorbent towels and place in a plastic bag in the refrigerator to chill for about an hour before serving. This chore can be done in the morning and the greens will remain crisp for dinner.

3. Additional salad vegetables should be shredded, chopped, or sliced and placed, covered, in the refrigerator until ready to use.
4. When ready to serve the salad, break the larger lettuce leaves into the bowl. Do *not* use a knife—it may bruise the greens. The smaller leaves can remain whole.
5. Once the greens are prepared in the bowl, pour on the dressing, toss, and serve immediately with lots of freshly ground pepper.

SALAD DRESSINGS

Most of the prepared, bottled salad dressings on the market, besides tasting awful, are full of chemicals, salt, and preservatives. It's easy to prepare fresh salad dressings that are flavorful.

The following dressings offer a wide range of choice to enhance any type of greens. Beginning with a basic vinaigrette and a quick blender mayonnaise, and concluding with several unusual low-calorie dressings, there is something for everyone—and every green.

OIL

A good-quality oil is essential to a great salad. Olive oil is the traditional salad oil but its prohibitive cost makes it a luxury. Olive oil in combination with a lighter vegetable oil such as corn, peanut, soy, sunflower, or safflower saves on cost and gives a lighter more delicate flavor than the heavier olive oil alone. Exotic oils such as walnut or hazelnut are interesting taste additions to salads but are extremely costly.

Flavored oils are easy to prepare and add an extra zing to the salad. Oil can be flavored with fresh herbs, such as basil, dill, or rosemary. A peeled clove of garlic or a peeled shallot impaled on a bamboo skewer inserted in a bottle of olive oil will add something extra to the salad. These flavored oils and the flavored vinegars make excellent gifts year 'round.

VINEGAR

A good French wine vinegar is important to a great salad. Either red or white, it adds a subtle flavoring to the salad dressing.

Spanish sherry vinegar imparts a slightly sweet taste, which complements fruit or cheese salads. Cider vinegar is best used in limited amounts in sweet fruit salads, for pickling, or as a basis for mayonnaise.

Japanese rice vinegar is so delicate in flavor that it can be used in larger quantities than most other vinegars.

The newest vinegar on the market is called Balsamico which, loosely translated, means "that which is good for the health." Balsimic vinegar is prepared from special sweet grapes and aged for many years, resulting in a dark brown vinegar that is intensely aromatic and so flavorful that it can stand on its own as a salad dressing, especially on slices of ripe tomatoes.

The flavored vinegars are my favorites. They are simple to prepare, make excellent gifts, and the subtle flavors contribute to the success of a salad.

Flavored Vinegar

YIELD: As desired
Preparation time: 5 minutes
Marinating time: 2 weeks

The Ingredients:
Old bottle (the cruets with stoppers make the herb-vinegar a beautiful gift)
Few sprigs fresh herbs (dill, basil, rosemary, tarragon, oregano, etc.)
Red or white wine vinegar

The Steps:
1. Wash bottle.
2. Place fresh herbs in bottle and fill with wine vinegar. Cover and allow to steep for two weeks before using.
3. Herbs can remain in jar or they can be removed, if desired, after the two weeks of steeping time.

Herb-Flavored Vinegar will keep for at least 1 year, tightly sealed.

Raspberry Vinegar

YIELD: 3 quarts
Preparation time: 5–10 minutes
Marinating time: 12 hours
Cooking time: 2–3 minutes

Raspberry vinegar has been made popular by the school of *Nouvelle Cuisine* where the French chefs use this sweet vinegar in warm, first-course salads. They also use Raspberry Vinegar like a wine to deglaze a pan after sautéing poultry or fish, resulting in an amazing sauce.

The Ingredients:
    1 10-ounce package frozen, unsweetened raspberries, thawed
    3 quarts red wine vinegar
      Glass jars

The Steps:
    1. Place raspberries in colander and wash under cold running water. Drain, and place in large enamel or stainless steel pot covered with the vinegar for 12 hours or overnight.
    2. The next day, heat raspberries and vinegar and bring to a boil; then turn off heat and allow to cool.
    3. Strain vinegar into bottles, cover tightly, and label.

Raspberry Vinaigrette Dressing

YIELD: ¾ cup
Preparation time: 5 minutes

This dressing is especially delicious on a salad of crisp greens topped with toasted walnut halves.

The Ingredients:
        8 tablespoons olive oil (or 2 tablespoons walnut oil and 6 tablespoons olive oil)

1½–2 tablespoons raspberry vinegar
1 teaspoon Dijon mustard
½ teaspoon salt
¼ teaspoon freshly ground pepper
1 teaspoon freshly snipped chives (optional)

The Steps:

1. Combine oil, vinegar, mustard, salt, and pepper in a screw-top jar, cover, and shake well.
2. Add chives, if desired, and toss with crisp greens.

Variations:

Add minced garlic, minced dill, or minced parsley, and a few tablespoons of sour cream or *Crème Fraîche* (*see* Chapter 2).

FRENCH DRESSING

"French" dressing is a misnomer, like "Danish" pastry, "Russian" dressing or "English" muffins. The classic French salad dressing is the versatile vinaigrette, basically composed of oil, vinegar, salt, and pepper. Variations come in the proportions, the methods of mixing, and the additional ingredients added to it.

My general preference is 3 parts oil to 1 part vinegar, but this pattern varies slightly, depending on the heaviness of the oil and the acidity of the vinegar. I also add a small amount of lemon juice to certain vinaigrettes for added flavor.

I try to make the preparation as easy as possible, so I shake the dressing in a jar or I use the food processor to do the mixing for me, especially when minced garlic is included.

My basic recipe (*Laurie's Basic Vinaigrette*) makes about 1½ cups of dressing. I make it a practice to add only a few tablespoons at a time to the salad bowl. A little vinaigrette travels far. As a rule, I use only ¼–⅓ cup of dressing for four people but I always perform the taste test on a few greens before serving.

The cardinal rule in serving green salads that are not marinated is to toss at the very last minute. I keep my greens chilled and my dressing at room temperature (unless it contains egg or cream) and toss just before serving.

Laurie's Basic Vinaigrette (and Variations)

YIELD: 1½ cups
Preparation time: 5 minutes

The Ingredients:
¾ cup olive oil (or ¼ cup olive oil, ½ cup corn, safflower, or soy oil)
¼ cup wine vinegar
1 teaspoon Dijon mustard
½ teaspoon dry mustard
¼ teaspoon granulated sugar
½ teaspoon salt, or to taste
½ teaspoon freshly ground white or black pepper, or to taste

The Step:
1. Combine oil, vinegar, Dijon mustard, dry mustard, sugar, salt, and pepper in a screw-top jar and shake to combine.

Variations:
Add 1 tablespoon lemon juice, especially if mushrooms are used. I toss the mushrooms in the lemon juice to marinate them and then add both to the salad.

Add 1 teaspoon crushed garlic or shallots: a more subtle way of adding garlic is to crush a clove and allow it to sit, whole, in the oil for several days to release the garlic flavor.

Fresh herbs: 2 tablespoons minced chives, parsley, tarragon, basil, dill (one, or all).

Worcestershire sauce: ½ teaspoon for spiciness.

Capers: 1 teaspoon chopped capers.

Curry powder: ½ teaspoon curry powder.

Egg yolk: 1 egg yolk adds body and lemony color.

Chopped, hard-cooked egg: 1 chopped, hard-cooked egg adds texture.

Cheese: 2 tablespoons freshly grated Parmesan cheese or 2 tablespoons crumbled Roquefort or Bleu cheese.

Make-It-Easy Tip:
    √ Any unused Vinaigrette dressing can be refrigerated until ready to
    use. If possible, bring to room temperature before serving.

Basic Blender Mayonnaise

YIELD: 1¾ cups
Preparation time: 10 minutes

Preparing your own mayonnaise may not appear to be a Make-It-Easy
recipe, but the blender or food processor really does make it a simple
chore. The taste is wonderful, the cost is less, and it can be prepared
without salt and sugar for those on restricted diets.

The Ingredients:
    1   whole egg
    1   tablespoon fresh lemon juice or 1 tablespoon cider vinegar
    ½   teaspoon dry mustard
    ½   teaspoon salt, or to taste
    ¼   teaspoon freshly ground white pepper
        Pinch of cayenne pepper
    ¼   cup olive oil
    1   cup corn, safflower, or soy oil, or any other vegetable oil de-
        sired

The Steps:
    1. Place egg, lemon juice, mustard, salt, white pepper, and
       cayenne in blender or food processor and process quickly for 5
       seconds, just to blend.
    2. Start machine again and, while machine is running, gradually
       pour olive and vegetable oils into container until the mixture
       becomes thickened. (Do not overprocess.)
    3. With a rubber spatula, remove mayonnaise from work bowl,
       place in a jar or plastic container, and refrigerate until ready to
       use.

Variation:
    Two egg yolks can be substituted for 1 egg.

Make-It-Easy Tips:
   √ Because there are no preservatives, the mayonnaise will keep for
      only 8–10 days in the refrigerator.
   √ To avoid splatters, loosely cover top of blender container with a
      towel when adding oil in Step 2.
   √ If mayonnaise does not thicken as it should, do not despair. Pour
      mixture into another bowl and rinse out blender jar or work
      bowl. Place another egg in cleaned bowl, start machine, gradu-
      ally pour mixture back into bowl, and process until the mayon-
      naise thickens.

MAYONNAISE VARIATIONS

Mustard Mayonnaise

YIELD: 1½ cups
Preparation time: 5 minutes

The Ingredients:
   1 cup mayonnaise
   4 teaspoons Dijon mustard
   1 teaspoon lemon juice
   ½ teaspoon freshly ground white pepper
   2 tablespoons minced *cornichons* (sour pickles), optional
   2 tablespoons minced fresh parsley (optional)

The Steps:
   1. Combine mayonnaise, mustard, lemon juice, and pepper in a
      bowl and mix until smooth.
   2. Add *cornichons* and parsley, if desired, and serve immediately,
      or chill until ready to use.

Thousand Island Dressing
(for Cold Seafood or Salads)

YIELD: 2 cups
Preparation time: 5 minutes

The Ingredients:
- 1 cup mayonnaise
- ½ cup chili sauce
- 2 tablespoons India Relish
- 1 hard-cooked egg, chopped
- 1 tablespoon minced onion or scallion
- Pinch of paprika

The Steps:
1. Combine all ingredients in a bowl and mix until smooth.
2. Serve immediately, or chill until ready to use.

Curry Mayonnaise
(for Dips)

YIELD: 1 cup
Preparation time: 2 minutes

The Ingredients:
- 1 cup mayonnaise
- 1½–2 teaspoons curry powder, dissolved in
- 2 teaspoons lemon juice

The Steps:
1. Combine in a bowl and mix until smooth.
2. Serve immediately, or chill until ready to use.

Dill Mayonnaise
(for Seafood or Salads)

YIELD: 1 cup
Preparation time: 5 minutes

The Ingredients:
   1 cup mayonnaise
   1–2 tablespoons snipped fresh dill or 1 teaspoon dried dill

The Steps:
   1. Combine in a bowl and mix until smooth.
   2. Serve immediately, or chill until ready to use.

Make-It-Easy Tip:
   √ Dill is easily snipped with kitchen shears.

Lemon–Caper Mayonnaise
(for Dips or Seafood)

YIELD: 1½ cups
Preparation time: 5 minutes

The Ingredients:
   1 cup mayonnaise
   3 tablespoons lemon juice
   2 tablespoons capers, drained and minced
   2 tablespoons freshly minced parsley

The Steps:
   1. Combine all ingredients in a bowl and mix until smooth.
   2. Serve immediately, or chill until ready to use.

Spinach Mayonnaise

YIELD: 3 cups
Preparation time: 15 minutes
Chilling time: 4–6 hours or overnight

Spinach Mayonnaise accompanies poached fish dishes and steamed vegetables, or can be used by itself as a dip for crudités.

The Ingredients:

2 10-ounce packages frozen chopped spinach, thawed and squeezed dry
4 scallions, finely minced (green and white included)
½ cup chopped parsley
1 tablespoon freshly snipped dill or 1 teaspoon dried dill
2 cups mayonnaise
1 tablespoon lemon juice
½ teaspoon salt, or to taste
¼ teaspoon freshly ground pepper

The Steps:

1. In food processor or blender, chop spinach with scallions, parsley, and dill, pulsating until finely chopped.
2. Add the mayonnaise and lemon juice and continue to process until smooth.
3. Season to taste with salt and pepper; mix again, and chill for 4–6 hours or overnight.
4. Serve sauce chilled with cold fish, vegetables, or as a dip.

Make-It-Easy Tips:

√ Sauce can be kept for several weeks in a jar in refrigerator.
√ Squeeze spinach dry by placing in a sieve and pressing down on it. Place ball of spinach in your fist and squeeze out any remaining liquid.

Green Goddess Salad Dressing

YIELD: 2 cups
Preparation time: 10–15 minutes

This dressing was created in California by a chef honoring George Arliss, the actor, who was opening in William Archer's play, *The Green Goddess*. It is best served over very crisp romaine lettuce with watercress and sliced endive added. The dressing can be prepared easily in a food processor or blender and used for a salad, or refrigerated and used as a dip with crudités.

The Ingredients:

    4 anchovy fillets, drained
    ¼ cup parsley, coarsely chopped
    ¼ cup snipped chives
    3 tablespoons tarragon vinegar
    1 scallion, diced (green and white included)
    1 clove garlic, smashed and peeled
    ½ teaspoon dry mustard
    ½ teaspoon Worcestershire sauce
    ½ teaspoon dried tarragon, crumbled, or ½ tablespoon freshly chopped tarragon
    ½ teaspoon chili powder
    ½ teaspoon salt, or to taste
    ¼ teaspoon freshly ground pepper
    1 cup mayonnaise
    1 cup dairy sour cream

The Steps:

1. Place all ingredients, except mayonnaise and sour cream, in food processor or blender. Process until smooth.
2. Add mayonnaise and sour cream and process just until blended.
3. Taste, adjust seasoning if necessary with salt and pepper, and chill in tightly covered jar in refrigerator until ready to use.
4. Serve over crisp romaine, leaf lettuce, or spinach leaves.

Variation:

If chives are unavailable, increase the amount of scallions to 2.

Make-It-Easy Tip:

√ The dressing should keep for a week to 10 days in the refrigerator.

Low-Calorie Buttermilk Dill Dressing

SERVES: 4
Preparation time: 10 minutes

The Ingredients:

2 teaspoons finely minced parsley
2 scallions, finely minced (green and white included)
½ cup low-fat buttermilk
1½ tablespoons mayonnaise
½ teaspoon freshly snipped dill or ¼ teaspoon dried dill
¼ teaspoon freshly ground white pepper
Pinch of salt

The Steps:

1. Mince parsley and scallions together in food processor or blender, add remaining ingredients, and process until smooth dressing is formed.
2. Serve immediately, or chill until ready to use.
3. Serve over crisp greens with cherry tomatoes.

Variation:

Leftover dressing can be used as a low-calorie dip for vegetable crudités.

Make-It-Easy Tips:

√ It is difficult to prepare any less than the dressing amount indicated, so refrigerate any leftover for future salads.
√ This dressing has only about 12 calories per tablespoon. To further reduce, check the calorie listings on several buttermilks and choose the lowest.

Yogurt Dressing

SERVES: 4
Preparation time: 15 minutes
Chilling time: 2 hours

The spicy seasonings in this low-calorie salad dressing make a delicious addition to green or leafless salads. I use it as a dressing when I combine bean sprouts, radishes, mushrooms, cucumbers, and scallions. It's a refreshing accompaniment for spicy lamb or Szechwan stir-fried dishes, and is only about 20 calories per serving.

The Ingredients:
  6 ounces plain yogurt, low-fat or whole milk
  1 tablespoon soy sauce
  1 teaspoon lemon juice
  ¼ teaspoon ground coriander
  ¼ teaspoon ground cumin
  ½ teaspoon salt, or to taste
  ¼ teaspoon freshly ground white pepper

The Steps:
  1. Combine all ingredients in a bowl and whisk or stir until smooth.
  2. Serve immediately, or chill until ready to use.

Variation:
  For a low-salt version, substitute the new, milder, salt-restricted soy sauce, and eliminate the ½ teaspoon salt.

Spicy Tomato Dressing with No Oil

YIELD: 1½ cups
Preparation time: 10 minutes
Chilling time: 2–3 hours

This dressing has only five calories per tablespoon!

The Ingredients:
    1 cup tomato juice or vegetable juice
    ¼ cup chopped green pepper
    ¼ cup chopped scallions (green and white included)
    3 tablespoons red wine vinegar
    2 teaspoons Worcestershire sauce
    1 teaspoon Dijon mustard
    ½ teaspoon freshly minced garlic
    ½ teaspoon salt, or to taste
    ½ teaspoon freshly ground black pepper
    Pinch of sugar or a few drops of honey

The Steps:
1. In a food processor or blender, combine all ingredients and process until smooth.
2. Chill for 2–3 hours or until ready to use.
3. Serve dressing over tossed greens, sprouts, sliced radishes, and sliced carrots.

Variation:
For a creamier-style dressing, ½ cup low-fat cottage cheese can be pureed with the dressing until smooth.

Low-Calorie
Buttermilk Thousand Island Dressing

YIELD: 1½ cups
Preparation time: 10 minutes
Chilling time: 2–3 hours

This dressing has only 13 calories per tablespoon.

The Ingredients:
⅓ cucumber, peeled, seeded, cut into chunks
1 scallion, cut into 2" sections (green and white included)
⅓ cup buttermilk
¼ cup tomato sauce
3 tablespoons cider vinegar
2 tablespoons vegetable oil
½ teaspoon Dijon mustard
½ teaspoon salt, or to taste
¼ teaspoon freshly ground pepper

The Steps:
1. Place cucumber and onion in food processor or blender and chop fine.
2. Add remaining ingredients, process until smooth, and chill for 2–3 hours or until ready to use.
3. Serve over tossed greens and tomatoes.

Make-It-Easy Tip:
√ The dressing can be prepared by hand and whisked until smooth, but vegetables must then be finely chopped.

SALADS WITH GREENS AND LEAFLESS SALADS
Choosing from the variety of greens available, we can create quick and easy salads that can no longer be labeled "plain green salad."

As a change from the usual tossed green salads, leafless salads add variety and creativity to the meal. By using vegetables in the salad, you've combined two courses in one, saving on kitchen chores. Vegetable haters may actually be inspired to like vegetables when they're combined in international salads such as *Chinese Asparagus Salad with Spicy Dressing* or *Middle-Eastern Salad.* Remember to taste marinated salads just before serving. Chilling diminishes flavors and an adjustment of seasoning is often necessary.

Greek Salad

SERVES: 4
Preparation time: 15 minutes

The Ingredients:
   1 large head Boston lettuce, torn in pieces
   1 cucumber, peeled and cut into ¼" slices
   3 ripe tomatoes, cut into small chunks
   12 Greek olives, or black olives
   1 small red onion, thinly sliced into rings
   ¼ pound Feta cheese (¾ cup), crumbled

Dressing:
   ½ cup olive oil (Greek or Italian)
   2 tablespoons red wine vinegar
   ½ teaspoon minced garlic
   ½ teaspoon salt, or to taste
   ¼ teaspoon freshly ground black pepper
   ¼ teaspoon dried oregano, crumbled
   ¼ teaspoon dried basil, crumbled
   Garnish: Freshly chopped parsley, capers, chopped pimientos

   Optional Additional Ingredients: Drained marinated mushrooms, drained marinated artichoke hearts, red or green pepper strips, pimiento-stuffed olives, drained marinated stuffed eggplants.

The Steps:
   1. Place lettuce, cucumbers, tomatoes, olives, and onions in a bowl and chill (covered with paper towel and plastic wrap until ready to use).
   2. When ready to serve, crumble Feta cheese over greens.
   3. Combine dressing ingredients in a screw-top jar and shake to combine well.

4. Pour dressing over salad, toss well, and serve immediately, garnished with chopped parsley, capers, and chopped pimientos (optional). Additional vegetables can be added if desired.

Variations:

Greek Salad can be transformed into a main course by adding one 7-ounce can tuna, drained and chunked. It can be served as a supper or lunch dish with buttered, toasted pita bread.

To transform the Greek Salad into an Italian Salad, omit the Feta cheese and Greek olives and add Parmesan cheese and pimiento-stuffed olives, pimientos, cubes of Mozzarella cheese and, for a main course, add chopped salami and ham.

Romaine Salad with Litchi Nuts

SERVES: 4–6
Preparation time: 10 minutes

This is an unusual combination of crisp greens and sweet litchi nuts. It can be especially effective as a side dish to accompany curries or oriental dishes.

The Ingredients:
1 large head romaine lettuce, washed and dried
1 11-ounce can litchi nuts, thoroughly drained
½ cup chopped walnuts
Dressing:
½ cup olive oil or vegetable oil
2 tablespoons white wine vinegar
2 tablespoons chili sauce
1 tablespoon lemon juice
½ teaspoon sugar
½ teaspoon salt, or to taste
¼ teaspoon freshly ground black pepper, or to taste
¼ teaspoon dry mustard
  Pinch of paprika

The Steps:
1. Break up pieces of lettuce into salad bowl.
2. Add litchi nuts and sprinkle with walnuts.
3. Combine dressing ingredients in a screw-top jar and shake to combine; pour over salad, toss, and serve immediately.

Caesar Salad

SERVES: 4
Preparation time: 10 minutes

A traditional Caesar Salad should be prepared in a wooden bowl at the last minute at the table. Romaine lettuce, garlic, Parmesan cheese, lemon juice, anchovies, and an egg are all essential to a Caesar Salad.

The Ingredients:
- 1 head romaine lettuce, washed and dried
- 1 clove garlic, pressed or finely chopped
- 1 2-ounce can anchovy fillets, drained and mashed
- ¼ teaspoon salt, or to taste
- ½ teaspoon freshly ground black pepper, or to taste
- ½ cup olive oil
- 1 teaspoon Dijon mustard
- 3 tablespoons lemon juice
- 1 egg
- ¼ cup freshly grated Parmesan cheese
- 1 cup toasted croutons

  Garnish: Freshly cracked black pepper

The Steps:
1. Wash and dry lettuce, break into small pieces, and set aside or chill until ready to use.
2. In wooden salad bowl, place garlic and anchovies. Add salt and pepper and mash together.
3. Add oil, mustard, and lemon juice and stir to combine.
4. Add crisp romaine lettuce pieces and toss with dressing.
5. Carefully lower an egg (in shell) into boiling water, allow to sit

for 1 minute, and crack over salad; toss until lettuce is well-coated.

6. Sprinkle with Parmesan cheese and croutons, toss again, and serve immediately with additional freshly cracked pepper.

Variation:

If you're not fond of anchovies, by all means omit them, but increase the salt to ½ teaspoon, or to taste.

Make-It-Easy Tip:

√ Croutons without preservatives are now available at the market. If you prefer to make them yourself, you can bake them easily in the oven without the messy job of frying. Brush both sides of bread with melted butter (or garlic-flavored butter, if desired), cut into cubes, spread on an ungreased baking sheet and bake, uncovered, for 15–20 minutes, turning occasionally.

Spinach Salad

SERVES: 6
Preparation time: 10 minutes

The Ingredients:

1½ pounds fresh spinach leaves, washed and dried
4 scallions, sliced into ¼" pieces (green and white included)

Dressing:

½ cup corn oil
3 tablespoons white wine vinegar
2 teaspoons Dijon mustard
1 teaspoon soy sauce
½ teaspoon curry powder
½ teaspoon sugar
½ teaspoon salt, or to taste
¼ teaspoon freshly ground white pepper, or to taste
Garnish: One tablespoon toasted sesame seeds

The Steps:

1. Remove tough stems from spinach; tear leaves into small pieces and place in a salad bowl along with scallions.

2. Combine all dressing ingredients in a screw-top jar and shake until smooth.
3. Pour dressing over spinach leaves, toss well, and serve immediately, garnished with toasted sesame seeds.

Variations:

Peanut, safflower, soy or any other light oil can be substituted for corn oil.

One peeled, chopped Pippin, Granny Smith or other tart apple can be added together with ⅓ cup roasted Spanish peanuts.

Make-It-Easy Tips:

√ An easy way to dry spinach is to wrap up leaves in layers of paper towels or tea towels, place in plastic bag, tie up, and refrigerate for several hours. The spinach will be dry and crisp.

√ To prepare ahead of time, prepare greens as above, make salad dressing, chop scallions, and refrigerate all until ready to use. (If time permits, allow dressing to come to room temperature before using.)

Spinach Salad with Creamy Dressing

SERVES: 4
Preparation time: 10 minutes

The Ingredients:

1 pound fresh spinach, stems removed
2 hard-cooked eggs, finely chopped
2 scallions (green and white included), minced

Dressing:

¼ cup dairy sour cream
2 tablespoons mayonnaise
1 tablespoon lemon juice
Pinch of sugar
¼ teaspoon minced garlic
½ teaspoon salt, or to taste
¼ teaspoon freshly ground pepper, or to taste
Garnish: Freshly chopped parsley

The Steps:

1. Place spinach in salad bowl, grate egg over top, sprinkle on scallions.
2. In small bowl, combine remaining ingredients and whisk until smooth.
3. Toss dressing with spinach/egg/scallion combination and serve immediately, garnished with freshly chopped parsley.

Variation:

Crisp bacon bits can be added for extra flavor and texture.

Make-It-Easy Tip:

√ Dressing can be prepared in advance, in a food processor to save time, and chilled for up to a week. Dressing can also be used as a dip for fresh vegetables.

Tossed Salad with Red Onions

SERVES: 4
Preparation time: 10 minutes

The Ingredients:

1 head Boston lettuce, broken into pieces
1 bunch watercress
3 slices red onions, broken into rings
Dressing:
6 tablespoons olive oil
2 tablespoons red wine vinegar
½ teaspoon Dijon mustard
¼ teaspoon dried oregano, crumbled
½ teaspoon salt, or to taste
¼ teaspoon freshly ground white pepper

The Steps:

1. Place lettuce, watercress, and onion rings in a salad bowl and chill, covered with paper towels and plastic wrap, in the refrigerator.

2. Combine dressing ingredients in screw-top jar and shake to combine.
3. When ready to serve, toss greens with dressing and serve immediately.

Variations:

Corn, peanut, safflower or soy oil can be substituted for olive oil.

Cabbage Salad with Caraway Seeds

SERVES: 4
Preparation time: 15 minutes
Chilling time: 2–4 hours or overnight

The Ingredients:
1 large head cabbage, shredded
1 small onion, finely minced by hand or in food processor
2 tablespoons lemon juice
½ teaspoon salt, or to taste
½ teaspoon freshly ground white pepper, or to taste
⅔ cup mayonnaise
1 tablespoon caraway seeds
Garnish: Tomatoes, parsley sprigs

The Steps:
1. Place cabbage in bowl; add onion, lemon juice, salt, and pepper.
2. Add mayonnaise and caraway seeds, toss well, and chill for 2–4 hours or overnight.
3. Serve in bowl garnished with cherry tomatoes, or with tomato wedge in center and parsley sprigs around the edges.

Make-It-Easy Tip:
√ The easiest way to shred cabbage in a food processor is with the *slicing* blade, not the shredding blade.

Chinese Asparagus Salad with Spicy Dressing

SERVES: 4–6
Preparation time: 15 minutes

Prepare this salad during the spring when asparagus is in season, or year 'round using frozen asparagus.

The Ingredients:
1 pound fresh asparagus or two 10-ounce packages frozen asparagus spears

Dressing:
3 tablespoons soy sauce
3 tablespoons oriental sesame oil
1 teaspoon sugar
2–3 shakes Tabasco, or to taste

The Steps:
1. Break off tough, rubbery stalk ends of asparagus and discard. Cut asparagus on the diagonal into 1″ pieces. (If using frozen asparagus, thaw slightly and cut as above.)
2. Drop fresh asparagus pieces into pot of boiling salted water and cook for 2–3 minutes or until barely tender. Drain, run under cold water, and drain again. (If using frozen asparagus, place in a strainer or colander and rinse with boiling water to cook slightly without actually parboiling; drain.)
3. Combine dressing ingredients in small bowl, whisk to combine, and toss over asparagus spears.
4. Serve at room temperature or chilled.

Variations:
The Chinese serve this salad garnished with red preserved ginger cut into strips. Pimientos, cut into strips, can be substituted as a colorful garnish.

Make-It-Easy Tips:
√ When selecting asparagus, choose firm, bright green spears with tips that are compact.

√ Break off tough stem ends easily by allowing them to snap off where they will.

Bean Sprout Salad

SERVES: 4–6
Preparation time: 10 minutes

Sprouts can be grown indoors in a jar in no time, which makes this salad possible to prepare at any time of the year.

The Ingredients:
    4 cups fresh bean sprouts (the popular mung or soy bean sprouts are best to use)
    ¾ cup shredded green pepper (can be done in food processor)
Dressing:
    ¼ cup soy sauce
    3 tablespoons wine vinegar (Chinese or Japanese are preferable, if available)
    4 teaspoons peanut oil
    4 teaspoons oriental sesame oil
    ½ teaspoon salt, or to taste
    ¼ teaspoon freshly ground pepper, or to taste
    Garnish: Red preserved ginger, optional (available at oriental grocery stores or by mail order, *see* Appendix A), 3 tablespoons sesame seeds (toasted in toaster-oven or in a hot skillet)

The Steps:
1. Place bean sprouts and green pepper in salad bowl.
2. Combine dressing ingredients in screw-top jar and shake until smooth.
3. Toss sprouts and green pepper with dressing, garnish with optional red preserved ginger and toasted sesame seeds, and serve immediately.

Variations:

Other vegetables can be used as alternatives or with the sprouts: Snow peas; broccoli, partially cooked; asparagus, partially cooked; sliced water chestnuts; zucchini slices, partially cooked.

Sliced pimiento strips can be substituted for the red preserved ginger.

Make-It-Easy Tip:

√ If fresh sprouts are unavailable, substitute canned sprouts that have been drained and soaked overnight in cold water. The next day, drain them, place in boiling water, drain again, and use for salad.

Broccoli Florets Vinaigrette

SERVES: 6
Preparation time: 15 minutes
Chilling time: 2–3 hours or overnight

Parboiled vegetables marinated in a zesty vinaigrette dressing can be a great change of pace from the typical tossed green salad. Broccoli, with its bright green color, can be used, or try cauliflower, zucchini, string beans, or whatever seasonal vegetable you prefer.

The Ingredients:

4 cups broccoli florets, about 2 pounds (reserve the stems for another use)

Vinaigrette Dressing:

6 tablespoons olive oil
2 tablespoons red wine vinegar
¼ teaspoon salt, or to taste
¼ teaspoon freshly ground white pepper
⅛ teaspoon dried oregano, crumbled
⅛ teaspoon dried basil, crumbled
Pinch of dry mustard
Pinch of sugar

Mimosa Topping:
1 teaspoon freshly chopped parsley
2 hard-cooked egg yolks, grated

The Steps:

1. Drop broccoli florets into large pot of boiling salted water and, when water returns to boil, cook, uncovered, for 2–3 minutes, or until just tender but still crunchy. Drain in colander and rinse under cold running water.
2. Combine vinaigrette ingredients in screw-top jar and shake until smooth.
3. Toss florets with vinaigrette dressing and chill for 2–3 hours or overnight.
4. When ready to serve, prepare Mimosa Topping: Combine chopped parsley and grated egg and sprinkle over salad. Serve chilled or at room temperature.

Variation:

The amount of olive oil can be reduced to save on calories; use 3 tablespoons oil and 1½ tablespoons vinegar.

Make-It-Easy Tip:

√ The florets are immediately rinsed with cold water after parboiling to stop the cooking process at once and to preserve the intense green color.

Dilled Cucumber Salad

SERVES: 4
Preparation time: 15 minutes
Chilling time: 30 minutes plus 2 hours or overnight

The Ingredients:

4 medium cucumbers
½ teaspoon salt
1 cup dairy sour cream
2 tablespoons lemon juice
2 tablespoons freshly snipped dill or 2 teaspoons dried dill

1 tablespoon minced chives or scallion stalks
¼ teaspoon paprika
½ teaspoon salt, or to taste
¼ teaspoon freshly ground white pepper, or to taste
Garnish: Sprigs of dill or watercress

The Steps:

1. Peel cucumbers and thinly slice into bowl of ice water. Add ½ teaspoon salt and allow cucumbers to sit for ½ hour, covered, in refrigerator.
2. In the meantime, combine sour cream, lemon juice, dill, chives or scallions, paprika, salt, and pepper.
3. Drain cucumbers and blot dry on paper towels. Pour dressing over cucumbers and mix well. Chill again for 2 hours or overnight.
4. Taste, and adjust seasoning if necessary. Serve the cucumbers chilled, garnished with sprigs of dill or watercress.

Variations:

Two European hothouse hydroponic cucumbers can be substituted. They are especially easy to use since they need no salting.

Make-It-Easy Tip:

√ The cucumbers are salted to extract the excess water.

Middle-Eastern Salad

SERVES: 4
Preparation time: 15 minutes
Chilling time: 30 minutes

The combined flavors of cracked wheat, mint, tomatoes, and onions create a Middle-Eastern treat that can be served as a salad, side dish, or appetizer.

The Ingredients:

1 large ripe tomato, cubed
1 small white onion, coarsely chopped

1 slice cracked-wheat toast, cut into small cubes
1 cup freshly chopped parsley

Dressing:

3 tablespoons olive oil
2 tablespoons red wine vinegar
1 tablespoon chopped fresh mint leaves or 1 teaspoon dried
  mint leaves, crumbled
½ teaspoon ground allspice
½ teaspoon salt, or to taste
¼ teaspoon freshly ground pepper, or to taste
  Garnish: Coriander or parsley

The Steps:

1. Combine tomato, onion, toast cubes, and parsley in bowl and gently toss to combine.
2. Combine dressing ingredients in screw-top jar and shake until smooth.
3. Half an hour before serving, gently toss salad ingredients with dressing, chill for ½ hour, and serve garnished with sprigs of coriander or parsley.

Variation:

If cracked-wheat bread is unavailable, use any other whole grain bread, toasted.

Make-It-Easy Tip:

√ Store extra chopped parsley in a sealed jar in the refrigerator. Store fresh parsley sprigs wrapped in a towel and placed in a large jar or plastic bag, tightly closed.

Raw Mushroom Salad

SERVES: 4
Preparation time: 10 minutes
Chilling time: 1 hour

Mushroom Salad is a light and refreshing salad served with the meal or as a first course, California-style. The mushrooms should be tossed with dressing immediately after they are sliced, so prepare the dressing first.

The Ingredients:
 1 pound fresh mushrooms, sliced
Dressing:
 5 tablespoons olive oil
 2 tablespoons lemon juice
 ½ teaspoon salt, or to taste
 ¼ teaspoon freshly ground black pepper
 2 tablespoons capers, drained
 Garnish: Freshly chopped parsley, freshly ground black pepper

The Steps:
 1. Combine dressing ingredients in screw-top jar and shake to combine.
 2. Immediately toss sliced mushrooms with dressing to keep from discoloring.
 3. Add capers, and chill for 1 hour or until ready to serve.
 4. Serve on chilled salad plates topped with freshly chopped parsley and freshly ground black pepper.

Make-It-Easy Tips:
 √ A mushroom brush, or similar style soft brush, dipped in lemon juice is a handy tool for cleaning mushrooms without soaking them.
 √ The mushrooms should not be sliced until the dressing is ready or they may discolor on standing.
 √ Store mushrooms most successfully in a brown paper bag, which absorbs excess moisture.

Snow Pea Salad

SERVES: 4
Preparation time: 15 minutes

Crisp Chinese snow peas are becoming more and more popular as a stir-fried vegetable or as a salad ingredient, either with a Chinese flavor or as here with a French vinaigrette dressing.

The Ingredients:

    1 pound fresh Chinese snow peas, stringed

Vinaigrette Dressing:

    ½ cup olive oil (or vegetable oil)
    2 shallots or scallions (white part only), finely chopped
    2 tablespoons lemon juice
    1 tablespoon white wine vinegar
    ½ teaspoon Dijon mustard
    ½ teaspoon salt, or to taste
    ¼ teaspoon freshly ground white pepper, or to taste
    Pinch of sugar

The Steps:

1. Drop peas into pot of boiling salted water and, when water returns to boil, drain peas into colander. Place colander under cold running water.
2. Combine dressing ingredients in a food processor, blender, or screw-top jar.
3. Toss dressing with snow peas in salad bowl and serve at room temperature or chilled.

Variation:

Substitute sugar snap peas, the new vegetable on the market that is an ingenious cross between the Chinese snow pea and the standard pea. They are prepared and eaten shell and all. Cook sugar snap peas 1 minute longer than snow peas.

Make-It-Easy Tips:

√ The snow peas are immediately rinsed with cold water after the parboiling to stop the cooking at once and to preserve the intense green color.

√ Frozen snow peas cannot be substituted in a salad because they turn soggy immediately after thawing. If stringing and parboiling the snow peas requires too much work, try using bean sprouts in combination with thinly sliced zucchini or cucumber.

String Bean Salad

SERVES: 4
Preparation time: 15 minutes

The Ingredients:
1 pound fresh string beans, washed
Vinaigrette Dressing:
6 tablespoons olive oil
2 tablespoons red wine vinegar
¼ teaspoon freshly minced garlic or ⅛ teaspoon garlic powder
¼ teaspoon salt, or to taste
¼ teaspoon freshly ground pepper, or to taste
⅛ teaspoon dried oregano, crumbled
⅛ teaspoon dried basil, crumbled
⅛ teaspoon paprika
Pinch of sugar

The Steps:
1. Break tip ends off string beans, drop into pot of salted boiling water; bring to boil again and cook until just tender but still crunchy, 7–9 minutes. Drain in colander, rinse under cold running water, and drain again.
2. Combine the vinaigrette ingredients in screw-top jar and shake to combine.
3. Combine drained string beans with vinaigrette dressing, toss well to combine, and serve at room temperature or chilled.

Variations:
Haricots Verts, the new, delicate, tiny French green beans, can be substituted for large green beans but should be cooked only 5–6 minutes, or until tender.

Raspberry vinegar can be substituted for the red wine vinegar. In this case, omit the sugar.

If beans are very large, cut on diagonal into 1½" pieces and parboil only 5–6 minutes, or until tender.

Frozen whole green beans, thawed, can be substituted if time is limited but they will not be as crisp in texture.

Make-It-Easy Tip:
√ Green beans are immediately rinsed with cold water to stop cooking process at once and preserve intense green color.

Tomato and Onion Salad

SERVES: 4
Preparation time: 10 minutes

Serve this salad during the summer months when tomatoes and Spanish onions are in season. It makes a wonderful side dish or even a first course for an outdoor barbecue.

The Ingredients:
3 large beefsteak tomatoes
1 large white Spanish onion (or red onion), cut into ½" cubes
½ cup olive oil (Italian is preferable)
2 tablespoons red wine vinegar
½ teaspoon salt, or to taste
¼ teaspoon freshly ground black pepper, or to taste
Pinch of sugar
Garnish: Freshly chopped parsley

The Steps:
1. Cut tomatoes in half horizontally and remove excess water and seeds by gently squeezing. Then cut tomatoes into ½" cubes and place in bowl.
2. Add onions to tomatoes.
3. Combine oil, vinegar, salt, pepper, and sugar in screw-top jar and shake together until smooth.
4. Pour dressing over salad and chill for 1 hour or serve immediately, garnished with freshly chopped parsley.

Variations:
For an Italian flavor, dried, crumbled oregano and basil can be added to the dressing and allowed to marinate for 10 minutes to soften.

To reduce calories, prepare the dressing with a substitution of 3 tablespoons oil and 3 tablespoons vinegar.

Make-It-Easy Tip:
√ A serrated tomato or bread knife is an invaluable tool to use when cutting tomatoes.

Oriental Zucchini Salad

SERVES: 6
Preparation time: 10 minutes
Cooking time: 3 minutes

Oriental Zucchini Salad is a spicy, refreshing, crisp salad that is low in calories.

The Ingredients:
6 medium zucchini, cut into 2" julienne strips
Dressing:
2 tablespoons soy sauce
2 tablespoons oriental sesame oil
2 tablespoons Japanese rice vinegar or white vinegar
1 tablespoon sugar
2 teaspoons sake (Japanese wine) or dry sherry
½ teaspoon salt, or to taste
Garnish: Chopped scallion stalks

The Steps:
1. Bring pot of salted water to boil, add zucchini and, when water returns to boil, cook for 2–3 minutes or until just fork tender. Drain, rinse under cold running water, and drain again. Place zucchini in salad bowl.
2. Combine dressing ingredients in a screw-top jar and shake until smooth.
3. Pour dressing over zucchini and toss.
4. Serve at room temperature or slightly chilled, garnished with chopped scallion stalks.

Variation:
> For a low-salt version, substitute the new milder salt-restricted soy sauce and eliminate the ½ teaspoon salt.

Make-It-Easy Tip:
> √ Drained zucchini are placed under cold running water to stop the cooking process immediately and to preserve the bright green color.

PASTA AND RICE SALADS

Spaghetti was not made just for a tumble with tomato sauce; fettuccine was meant for more than a treatment Alfredo; rice needn't be served only alongside chicken—any one of these staple starches can also be used as a salad. And, I'm not just talking about mundane macaroni salad. The following recipes are designed to show the adaptability of pasta and rice to the salad course.

Pasta Salad with Chicken and Vegetables

SERVES: 6–8
Preparation time: 15 minutes
Cooking time: 12 minutes

This Pasta Salad can be served chilled or at room temperature.

The Ingredients:
- 1 pound linguini, perciatelli, or spaghetti
- 2 teaspoons vegetable oil
- ½ cup *Laurie's Basic Vinaigrette* dressing (*see* page 246) including 1 teaspoon capers and 1 tablespoon chopped parsley
- ½ cup mayonnaise
- 1 teaspoon paprika, or to taste
- 1 large, whole chicken-breast, poached and shredded
- 1 7-ounce jar roasted Italian peppers cut into strips (if unavailable, use pimientos)
- 1 medium zucchini, cut into thin julienne strips
- ½ teaspoon salt, or to taste

½ teaspoon freshly ground pepper to taste
Garnish: Freshly chopped parsley and chopped chives or scallion stalks

The Steps:

1. Cook linguini in boiling salted water until just tender, *al dente*, and drain in colander. Run under cold water and drain again. Toss with vegetable oil and set aside.
2. In the meantime, mix vinaigrette dressing with mayonnaise and paprika and whisk until smooth.
3. Toss pasta with vinaigrette mixture, coating thoroughly.
4. Add chicken, roasted peppers, and zucchini; toss again until well mixed.
5. Cool, and then chill in refrigerator.
6. Taste, and adjust seasoning with salt and freshly ground pepper. Serve cold or at room temperature, garnished with freshly chopped parsley and chopped chives.

Accompaniment:

Crunchy French bread.

Variations:

White meat turkey breast can be substituted for chicken.
Additional vegetables can be added for color or texture, as desired.

Make-It-Easy Tips:

√ Place zucchini in boiling water for 2 minutes, run under cold water to give it an *al dente* texture like the pasta, and drain thoroughly.
√ For an easy method to poach chicken, *see Madame Chu's Szechwan Peppercorn Chicken Salad.*
√ If possible, use imported Italian pasta which is easier to cook to *al dente* perfection than the American varieties.

Oriental Noodle Salad

SERVES: 4–6
Preparation time: 20 minutes
Cooking time: 8–10 minutes
Chilling time: 2 hours

Cold Oriental Noodle Salad can be used as a side dish or as an appetizer for an oriental or American dinner.

The Ingredients:
½ pound thin egg noodles or linguini
2 tablespoons peanut oil
1 cup fresh bean sprouts
¼ cup chopped radishes
2 cups shredded lettuce (Iceberg is preferable)

Dressing:
2 tablespoons peanut butter
2 tablespoons water
2 tablespoons soy sauce
2 tablespoons rice vinegar, or white wine vinegar
2 tablespoons peanut oil
2 tablespoons oriental sesame oil
2 tablespoons minced scallion stalks
2 teaspoons sugar
½ teaspoon minced garlic
½ teaspoon minced fresh ginger
½ teaspoon salt, or to taste
Dash hot chili oil, optional (available at oriental groceries or by mail order, *see* Appendix A)
Garnish: Toasted sesame seeds

The Steps:
1. Cook noodles in boiling salted water until *al dente*, just tender; drain, and toss with 2 tablespoons peanut oil to keep from sticking.
2. Place bean sprouts, radishes, and lettuce in a large bowl and chill until ready to use.

3. Combine dressing ingredients in food processor, blender, or bowl and process or whisk until smooth.
4. Toss dressing with the cooked noodles and chill until ready to use.
5. When ready to serve, toss the dressed noodles with the vegetables, garnish with toasted sesame seeds, and serve.

Variation:
Serve the Oriental Noodle Salad as an appetizer.

Make-It-Easy Tips:
√ Toast sesame seeds easily in a toaster-oven, on top brown, tossing lightly once and watch carefully.
√ Fresh sprouts can be grown in only a few days indoors in a sprouting jar available at oriental groceries or health food stores.

Rice Salad Niçoise

SERVES: 8
Preparation time: 15–20 minutes
Chilling time: 2 hours or overnight

Any leftover rice, either brown or white, can be put to good use in this salad.

The Ingredients:
   1 3-ounce can solid packed tuna, drained (water- or oil-packed)
  ½ small red onion, chopped
  8 small pitted ripe olives
  2 teaspoons capers, drained
4½ cups cooked rice (1½ cups raw rice)
Vinaigrette:
  ½ cup olive oil
  2 tablespoons red wine vinegar
  1 tablespoon lemon juice
  2 teaspoons freshly chopped parsley

½ teaspoon Dijon mustard
½ teaspoon salt, or to taste
¼ teaspoon freshly ground black pepper, or to taste
    Garnish: Two hard-cooked eggs, cut in wedges; four anchovy
    fillets, drained; 4 thin strips pimiento

The Steps:

1. Crumble the tuna in a large bowl; add the red onion, olives, and capers.
2. Combine vinaigrette ingredients in screw-top jar and shake until smooth.
3. Pour dressing over the tuna and vegetables; toss to combine.
4. Add rice, continue to toss, coating all grains well. Cover, and chill for 2 hours or overnight.
5. When ready to serve, adjust seasonings to taste with salt and pepper; serve garnished with hard-cooked egg wedges, drained anchovy fillets, and strips of pimiento attractively laid on top.

Variations:

Thawed frozen peas or string beans, or additional cooked vegetables can be added to taste.

Make-It-Easy Tips:

√ Rice Salad will keep for several days, covered, in the refrigerator.
√ Pimientos can be frozen individually. Shave into thin pieces easily while semi-frozen.
√ For the best way to cook rice for salads, *see Plain White Rice, the Chinese Way.*

Curried Brown Rice Salad with Fruit

SERVES: 6–8
Preparation time: 20 minutes
Chilling time: 2 hours or overnight

Add cut-up chicken or roast pork to this salad and it can be served as a main course.

The Ingredients:
- ½ cup mayonnaise
- ½ cup heavy cream
- 1 tablespoon curry powder
- 1 tablespoon lemon juice
- 4½ cups cold cooked brown rice (about 1½ cups raw brown rice)
- 1 cup finely chopped carrots
- 1 11-ounce can Mandarin-orange segments, drained
- 1 8-ounce can juice-packed crushed pineapple, drained
- ½ cup seedless golden raisins
- 2 ounces chopped walnuts
- ¼ cup toasted pine nuts (*pignoli*) or toasted almonds
- 2 tablespoons chopped chutney
- ¼ teaspoon salt, or to taste
- ¼ teaspoon freshly ground white pepper, or to taste
  Garnish: Toasted pine nuts or slivered almonds

The Steps:
1. In large bowl, prepare dressing by whisking mayonnaise with cream until smooth.
2. Make a paste of the curry powder and lemon juice and add to mayonnaise mixture.
3. Add rice to dressing, and stir to coat all the grains.
4. Add carrots, oranges, pineapple, raisins, walnuts, pine nuts, chutney, salt and pepper to taste; cover, and chill for 2 hours or overnight.
5. Taste, adjust seasoning with salt and pepper to taste, and serve garnished with toasted pine nuts.

Variations:
Additional chopped fresh fruits and nuts can be added or substituted to taste.

The salad can be prepared with white rice but is more flavorful and healthier with brown rice.

For the best way to cook brown rice, *see Plain Brown Rice.*

Curry powder is actually a blend of many spices. Taste varies with different brands so try out several to find the one you like best. Curry powder should be dissolved in liquid before adding to recipes.

Tabbouleh, or Tabbouli
(Wheat Pilaf Salad)

SERVES: 4–6
Preparation time: 15–20 minutes
Marinating time: 1–2 hours
Chilling time: 2 hours or overnight

Tabbouleh is a salad made with the Middle-Eastern grain called bulgur, a cracked wheat, which is marinated in olive oil with lemon juice, scallions, and fresh mint. Tabbouleh is low in calories, high in fiber, and is a refreshing complement to spicy dishes. Fresh mint is essential to the preparation of Tabbouleh. For best results, use a fine-grained bulgur.

The Ingredients:
1   cup fine-grain bulgur (cracked wheat)
2   cups boiling water
1   cup seeded and coarsely chopped tomato
1   small onion, minced
2   scallions (green and white included), finely chopped
¾   cup freshly chopped parsley
¼   cup lemon juice
¼   cup olive oil
3   tablespoons chopped fresh mint
½   teaspoon salt, or to taste
¼   teaspoon freshly ground black pepper, or to taste
    Garnish: Halved cherry tomatoes, fresh mint sprigs

The Steps:
1. Pour boiling water over bulgur to cover, and allow to stand 1–2 hours or until wheat is light and fluffy. Drain through a fine mesh strainer, pushing out excess water.
2. Combine remaining ingredients, toss with bulgur, and mix well; chill, covered, in refrigerator for 2 hours or overnight.
3. Taste, adjust seasoning with salt and pepper to taste, and serve Tabbouleh chilled, garnished with halved cherry tomatoes and fresh mint sprigs.

Variations:

Lime juice can be substituted for the lemon juice.
Chopped pecans can be added, to taste.

Make-It-Easy Tips:

√ To seed a tomato quickly, slice in half and, using your hand, gently squeeze until seeds have fallen out. Remove any remaining seeds with a spoon.

MAIN-COURSE SALADS

A hot summer night is not the only time when a soothingly cool, main-course salad is appealing. There are plenty of long, hectic days when a light, cold supper can actually help you to unwind. These salads are easy to prepare and can often serve as one-dish suppers, with bread and wine.

No more banal chef's salads; no more marshmallows, Miracle Whip, or maraschinos, either. Main-Course Salads have progressed beyond this familiar territory to include wild game, pâté, and exotic seafood. Even an old standby like seafood salad takes on new life with the addition of curry and water chestnuts.

Roast Beef Salad

SERVES: 4
Preparation time: 15 minutes
Chilling time: 2–3 hours

The Ingredients:

½ pound rare roast beef, cut into julienne strips (matchstick)
1 large or 2 small cooked potatoes, peeled and diced
½ cup thinly sliced red or white onion
1 hard-cooked egg, chopped
Vinaigrette:
½ cup olive oil
3 tablespoons red wine vinegar
2 tablespoons freshly chopped parsley

    1 tablespoon chopped sour pickles (*cornichons*)
    1 tablespoon finely chopped chives or scallion stalks
    1 teaspoon lemon juice
    1 teaspoon Dijon mustard
    ½ teaspoon salt, or to taste
    ¼ teaspoon freshly ground pepper
    ¼ teaspoon Worcestershire sauce
    Garnish: Freshly chopped parsley

The Steps:

1. Place beef, potato, and onion in bowl; top with chopped egg.
2. Combine vinaigrette ingredients in screw-top jar and shake until smooth (for an extra-smooth dressing, prepare in food processor or blender).
3. Toss dressing with beef and potatoes and allow to marinate, covered, in refrigerator for 2–3 hours.
4. Adjust seasonings to taste and serve salad chilled or at room temperature, garnished with chopped parsley.

Accompaniment:

Mustard Herb Toast.

Variations:

Any kind of cooked beef will work in this salad—pot roast, steak, London broil, or whatever is available. Rare roast beef is often available at a delicatessen. Ask for the very rare, unsliced portion.

Make-It-Easy Tips:

√ A leftover baked potato can be used, or 2 small new potatoes, boiled for 20–40 minutes, depending on size. *See* page 221, *Potatoes Boiled in Jackets.*

√ An easy way to hard-cook eggs is to pierce them with a thumbtack or egg piercer and place in cold salted water; bring to a boil, cover, turn off heat entirely, and allow to sit undisturbed for 20 minutes.

√ An easy way to chop a hard-cooked egg fine is to grate it on the medium side of a kitchen grater.

Marinated Oriental Beef and Pepper Salad

SERVES: 6
Preparation time: 20 minutes
Marinating time: 3 hours

This salad is a great way to use up leftover meat—roast beef, steak, or even pot roast.

The Ingredients:
    3 cups rare roast beef, steak, or other cooked beef, cut into 2" x 1" strips
    1 green pepper, cut into thin strips (julienned)
    2 tomatoes, cut into small wedges
    3 scallions, minced (green and white parts included)
    ½ cup mushrooms, sliced (optional)
    ½ cup jicama (a Mexican vegetable) cut in julienne strips, or substitute
    ½ cup sliced water chestnuts (optional)
    4 cups mixed greens: leaf lettuce, red lettuce, or romaine

Marinade:
    ½ cup teriyaki sauce
    ⅓ cup dry sherry
    3 tablespoons peanut oil
    3 tablespoons Japanese rice vinegar or white wine vinegar
    2 tablespoons oriental sesame oil
    1½ teaspoons freshly grated ginger (or 1 teaspoon ground ginger)

The Steps:
1. In large bowl, place beef, green pepper, tomatoes, scallions, mushrooms, and jicama.
2. Combine marinade ingredients in screw-top jar and shake until smooth.
3. Pour marinade over meat and vegetables and toss well.
4. Cover, and refrigerate for 3 hours.
5. At serving time, drain off excess marinade; line a large salad bowl with the lettuce, place marinated meat and vegetables on top, and serve immediately.

Accompaniment:
   Pita Toast.

Make-It-Easy Tips:
   √ Rare roast beef is generally available at delicatessens. Ask for about a pound of the rarest meat and slice into strips at home.
   √ A serrated tomato or bread knife is an invaluable tool to use for cutting tomatoes.

Oriental Roast Pork and Snow Pea Salad

SERVES: 4–6
Preparation time: 15–20 minutes
Cooking time: 2 minutes

This dish requires Chinese roast pork, which can be purchased at a Chinese restaurant the day before or the day on which the dish is to be served. Leftover glazed pork loin can be substituted, sliced into strips, and tossed in this unusual and fabulous salad.

The Ingredients:
   1 pound Chinese roast pork, thinly sliced
   ½ pound snow peas, stringed
   2 large carrots, shaved with a vegetable peeler into curls
   2 scallions, finely minced (green and white parts included)
Dressing:
   2 tablespoons soy sauce
   2 tablespoons oriental sesame oil
   2 tablespoons Japanese rice vinegar or white wine vinegar
   1 tablespoon dry sherry or sake (Japanese wine)
   1 tablespoon sugar
   ½ teaspoon salt
   Garnish: Coriander, parsley, or watercress

The Steps:
   1. Slice pork and place in bowl.
   2. Drop snow peas into pot of boiling salted water, stir once and,

when water returns to boil, drain peas into colander. Run under cold water and, when drained, place atop pork.

3. Shave carrots with a vegetable peeler to form curls. (Curls can be made in advance and placed in bowl of water in refrigerator to chill.) Place curls in salad bowl.
4. Top pork and vegetables with minced scallions.
5. Combine dressing ingredients in screw-top jar and shake to combine.
6. Pour dressing over salad, toss, and serve at room temperature, garnished with coriander, parsley, or watercress.

Accompaniments:
Stir-Fried Shrimp, and white rice for a complete oriental dinner.

Variations:
Oriental (dried) mushrooms, soaked in water and then cut into strips, are another good addition to this salad.
Sliced, drained water chestnuts can be added for color and texture.

Make-It-Easy Tip:
√ Carrot curls don't take as long to make, but carrots julienned into matchstick strips and boiled with the snow peas are a wonderful addition.

Chinese Seafood Salad

SERVES: 4
Preparation time: 15 minutes
Chilling time: 2–3 hours

Chinese Seafood Salad should be eaten the same day it is prepared (the next day at the latest). Any combination of cooked seafood can be used.

The Ingredients:
1 pound cooked medium or large shrimp
½ pound cooked crab, flaked

½ pound cooked sea scallops, cut in half (or bay scallops whole)
1 8-ounce can water chestnuts, drained and cut in half (or use can of pre-sliced water chestnuts)
4 scallion stalks, cut in ½" slices

Oriental Dressing:
3 tablespoons peanut oil
3 tablespoons soy sauce
1 tablespoon oriental sesame oil
2 teaspoons sugar
1 teaspoon grated fresh ginger
½ teaspoon salt, or to taste
¼ teaspoon freshly ground white pepper
Garnish: Coriander or parsley sprigs

The Steps:

1. Mix seafood together in a bowl, add water chestnuts and scallions; toss.
2. Combine oriental dressing ingredients in screw-top jar and shake until smooth.
3. Toss seafood with dressing and allow to marinate for 2–3 hours, covered, in refrigerator.
4. Serve salad chilled, garnished with sprigs of coriander or parsley.

Accompaniment:

Pita Toast.

Variation:

Cold poached fish can be substituted for some of the seafood for a less expensive version of the salad.

Make-It-Easy Tip:

√ Store peeled ginger, covered with sherry, in a jar in the refrigerator.

Madame Chu's Szechwan Peppercorn Chicken Salad

SERVES: 6
Preparation time: 20 minutes
Cooking time: 35 minutes

This recipe was taught to me many years ago by Madame Grace Zia Chu, who helped introduce Chinese cooking to Americans with her participatory classes in New York City. This dish is amazingly easy to prepare and most unusual. The chicken is cooked "white-cut" style, which is a perfect way to poach chicken to a velvety texture.

The Ingredients:
2 whole chicken breasts
2 slices fresh ginger root
1 scallion stalk
3 cups shredded Iceberg lettuce

Sauce One:
3 tablespoons peanut oil
3 tablespoons chopped scallion stalks
1 tablespoon minced ginger root
1 teaspoon Szechwan peppercorns, crushed (available in oriental groceries or by mail order, *see* Appendix A)
¼ teaspoon crushed chili pepper

Sauce Two:
2 tablespoons soy sauce
2 cloves garlic, minced
1 tablespoon dark Karo syrup
1 tablespoon Hoisin sauce (available in oriental groceries or by mail order, *see* Appendix A)
Garnish: Sprigs of coriander or parsley

The Steps:
1. Bring 2 quarts of water or chicken broth to a boil in a pot large enough to hold the chicken breasts comfortably; add chicken breasts, ginger slices, and scallion stalk; bring to boil again, cover tightly, reduce heat to medium, and cook without peeking for 15 minutes.

2. Turn flame off entirely and allow to cool in cooking liquid in covered pot for 20 minutes.
3. Skin and bone the chicken and pull the meat apart into shreds.
4. Place lettuce in a bowl and top with chicken.
5. Place ingredients for Sauce One in small pot and heat until boiling.
6. Combine ingredients for Sauce Two in small bowl and mix until smooth.
7. Combine the two sauces and mix well. Toss well with chicken and lettuce.
8. Serve immediately, garnished with sprigs of coriander or parsley.

Accompaniments:
Oriental rice crackers or sesame crackers.

Make-It-Easy Tips:
√ Crush the peppercorns between sheets of waxed paper with the side of a cleaver.
√ If poaching a whole chicken "white-cut" style, follow directions for chicken breasts but simmer for 30 minutes. Allow chicken to cool in cooking liquid in covered pot.

Curried Chicken Salad

SERVES: 6
Preparation time: 15 minutes

The Ingredients:
    4 cups cooked chicken, cubed or shredded
    ½ cup drained, chopped water chestnuts
    2 tablespoons chopped scallions, white part only (save the greens for garnish)
Dressing:
    ¾ cup dairy sour cream
    ¼ cup mayonnaise
    1 tablespoon chopped chives or scallion stalks

    1 teaspoon Dijon mustard
   ½ teaspoon salt, or to taste
 ½–1 teaspoon curry powder, or more to taste
   ¼ teaspoon freshly ground white pepper
      Pinch of paprika
      Garnish: Toasted slivered almonds
      Additional Garniture: Chopped scallion stalks, cold asparagus, sliced black olives, capers, or sliced tomatoes

The Steps:

1. Place the chicken in large bowl. Top with water chestnuts and scallions; chill until ready to serve.
2. In separate bowl, combine dressing ingredients until smooth, and chill until ready to serve.
3. When ready to serve, combine chicken with dressing and toss to combine. Serve garnished with toasted slivered almonds and additional garniture of scallion stalks, cold asparagus, sliced black olives, capers, or tomato slices.

Accompaniment:

Sliced rye bread.

Variations:

Leftovers can be blended into a smooth paste in a food processor. Serve the paste with sesame crackers as an hors d'oeuvre.

Turkey breast meat can be substituted for chicken, but it will be slightly drier.

A few teaspoons of mango chutney can be added, to taste.

Make-It-Easy Tips:

√ Prepare chicken "white-cut" method. *See Madame Chu's Szechwan Peppercorn Chicken Salad.*

√ The salad can be assembled earlier in the day or even the night before and refrigerated until ready to serve. Garnish at the last minute.

Chinese Chicken and Cucumber Salad

SERVES: 4–6
Preparation time: 15 minutes

Chinese Chicken and Cucumber Salad can be served as a main course for lunch or dinner, as a brunch dish, or as an appetizer.

The Ingredients:

 2 cups cooked chicken, cut into julienne strips
 1 large European hothouse hydroponic cucumber or 2 regular cucumbers, peeled and cut into julienne strips
 ¼ cup chopped scallion greens

Dressing:

 2 tablespoons soy sauce
 2 tablespoons Japanese rice vinegar or white wine vinegar
 2 tablespoons oriental sesame oil
 1 tablespoon sugar
 2 teaspoons sake (Japanese wine) or dry sherry
 ½ teaspoon salt, or to taste
 2 shakes Tabasco, or to taste
 Garnishes: Four tablespoons toasted sesame seeds and coriander or parsley sprigs. (Pre-roasted sesame seeds are available at oriental groceries or by mail order, *see* Appendix A)

The Steps:

1. Put chicken, cucumber, and scallions in salad bowl and toss.
2. Combine all ingredients for dressing in a screw-top jar and shake until smooth.
3. Pour dressing over salad, toss, and serve immediately on a platter garnished with toasted sesame seeds and coriander or parsley sprigs.

Accompaniment:

Sesame seed or oriental rice crackers.

Variation:

Shredded turkey breast meat can be substituted for the chicken.

Make-It-Easy Tips:
√ The chicken, cucumber, and scallions can be prepared in advance
and refrigerated. The dressing can be combined and set aside,
and all that is left to do is a quick tossing.

√ Prepare chicken "white-cut" method. *See Madame Chu's Szechwan Peppercorn Chicken Salad.*

CHAPTER NINE
BREADS

Pita Toast
Mustard Herb Toast
Pumpernickel Cheese Crisps
Garlic Bread and Variations
Quick Popovers
Light Beer Bread
Custardy Corn Bread
Banana Nut Bread
Blueberry-Orange Bread
Spicy Pumpkin Bread

Long-rising yeast breads cannot be considered Make-It-Easy, so in this chapter I have included only "quick" breads that all take 20 minutes or less to prepare. There are also some clever ways of improving bread that you buy, such as pita, so that it has an herb-toasted homemade quality.

Quick breads and muffins depend on the leavening power of baking powder, baking soda, or a combination of both rather than long-rising yeast. Quick breads require no extensive kneading. Simply combine the dry and wet ingredients, pour into pans, and bake. Quick breads should be made in advance and allowed to cool before cutting. They are easier to cut and taste better if allowed to cool thoroughly.

The following hints and tips will help in the preparation of quick breads or muffins.

Bake in mini-loaf pans for shorter baking time.

For dusting flour on buttered pans, use a powdered-sugar shaker or even a powder puff to sprinkle evenly.

For the height of luxury, indulge in one of those battery-operated, cordless sifters, especially when doubling recipes that require much sifting.

If you've forgotten to soften the butter, don't fret; just grate it and it will soften quickly.

Do not overbake breads. They will be moist and flavorful if slightly underbaked.

Mix dry ingredients together first, to distribute evenly throughout the batter.

Fill pans only two-thirds full to avoid overflows and oven mess.

To prevent sogginess, allow bread to cool in pans for five minutes and then remove and place on a rack to cool thoroughly.

Quick bread recipes can be baked in muffin pans as cupcakes. Bake them for approximately one-third the amount of the cooking time.

Double recipes for quick breads, bake them in mini-loaf pans, wrap tightly in plastic wrap or foil, and freeze for future use. It's nice to have them available if company arrives, and they make excellent house gifts.

Pita Toast

SERVES: 8–10
Preparation time: 10 minutes
Cooking time: 2–3 minutes

Pita Toast accompanies soups or stews and can also be served as a canapé.

The Ingredients:
    8 large Pita breads (plain, whole-wheat, or sesame)
    6 ounces (1½ sticks) unsalted butter, softened to room temperature
    2 tablespoons freshly chopped parsley
    1 tablespoon freshly chopped chives
    1 tablespoon lemon juice
    1 clove garlic, minced
    ½ teaspoon salt, or to taste
    ¼ teaspoon freshly ground pepper

The Steps:
1. Preheat broiler.
2. Cut Pita bread in half so there are four wedges from each Pita bread.
3. In food processor, blender, or by hand, blend butter with herbs, lemon juice, garlic, and seasonings until smooth.
4. Arrange Pita pieces on cookie sheet; generously spread interiors with herb butter and broil until butter is bubbly and tops begin to brown.
5. Serve toast hot and crisp.

Variations:
Toast can be spread with softened butter, sprinkled with Parmesan cheese and herbs, and broiled until golden.

Toast can be baked in the top third of a 450° oven for 5 minutes instead of broiling.

Make-It-Easy Tip:
√ If made in advance, keep the cooked toast in a tightly sealed jar or plastic bag to keep fresh. Warm again before serving.

Mustard Herb Toast

SERVES: 8–10
Preparation time: 15 minutes
Cooking time: 20 minutes

Crisp Mustard Herb Toast accompanies hot soups or stews.

The Ingredients:

4 ounces (1 stick) unsalted butter, softened
¼ cup freshly chopped parsley
2 tablespoons minced scallions
2 tablespoons Dijon mustard
1 tablespoon toasted sesame seeds
1 teaspoon lemon juice
1 loaf French, Italian, or sourdough bread, cut into 1″ slices

The Steps:

1. Preheat oven to 350°.
2. In a food processor or blender, process butter, parsley, scallions, mustard, sesame seeds, and lemon juice until smooth. (This butter mixture can be prepared in advance, refrigerated for several days, and brought to room temperature before spreading.)
3. Lightly spread the butter on both sides of bread; arrange on a cookie sheet and bake for 10 minutes on each side or until crisp.
4. Serve toast hot with soups or stews.

Variations:

Slice bread almost all the way through; spread each cut surface with butter mixture, wrap in foil, and bake in a 400° oven for 15–20 minutes. Serve in a long breadbasket.

Make-It-Easy Tip:

√ Toasted sesame seeds are available in supermarkets and at oriental grocery stores, or by mail order, *see* Appendix A.

Pumpernickel Cheese Crisps

SERVES: 4
Preparation time: 10 minutes
Cooking time: 5 minutes

Pumpernickel Cheese Crisps can be served as an appetizer, or with soups or salads.

The Ingredients:
    8 slices hors d'oeuvre bread, such as Westphalian Pumpernickel
    ½ stick unsalted butter, softened
    ¼ cup freshly grated Parmesan cheese

The Steps:
1. Preheat broiler.
2. Lay slices of bread on cookie sheet and broil on one side for 1–2 minutes to lightly toast.
3. Remove from broiler; turn bread, spread with butter and sprinkle with cheese, and return to broiler to cook for a minute or two until the cheese is hot and bubbly.
4. Serve warm, or keep in airtight container until ready to use. Heat again before serving, if desired.

Variation:
    Melba toast crackers can be substituted for pumpernickel.

Garlic Bread
(and Variations)

SERVES: 8–10
Preparation time: 5 minutes
Cooking time: 15–20 minutes

The Ingredients:
    ¼ pound (1 stick) unsalted butter, softened

1 clove garlic, peeled and minced
1 loaf French, Italian, or sourdough bread, about 18" long

The Steps:
1. Preheat oven to 400°.
2. Blend butter and garlic until smooth.
3. Slice bread 1" thick, cutting almost through to bottom crust but leaving it attached.
4. Spread both sides of each slice with garlic butter; wrap in aluminum foil leaving a small portion unwrapped at the top.
5. Bake in preheated oven for 15–20 minutes or until golden brown.

Variations:
Herb-Garlic Bread: Add 2 tablespoons freshly chopped parsley, ¼ teaspoon dried crumbled oregano, and ¼ teaspoon dried crumbled basil to the softened butter.

Cheese-Garlic Bread: Add 2–3 tablespoons freshly grated Parmesan cheese to the butter. The bread will be extra-golden brown.

Herbed Italian Bread: Mix basil, oregano, and a pinch of thyme to taste with softened butter and Parmesan cheese.

Bread can be split horizontally, spread on both cut sides with butter and broiled open-faced until golden. Slice and serve hot.

Make-It-Easy Tip:
√ Bread can be assembled through Step 4, wrapped well in foil, and refrigerated. When ready to serve, leave a small portion unwrapped at the top and proceed with the recipe.

Quick Popovers

SERVES: 6–8
Preparation time: 10 minutes
Cooking time: 30–35 minutes

The Ingredients:
1 cup sifted flour
1 cup whole milk

2 eggs
½ teaspoon salt

The Steps:
1. Preheat oven to 425°. Lightly butter 6 large metal, or 8 small metal or glass, muffin molds.
2. Combine flour, milk, eggs, and salt in blender, food processor, electric mixer, or by hand, mixing until smooth.
3. Place greased pans on a cookie sheet in the oven to preheat for 2 minutes.
4. Pour batter into preheated cups, filling two-thirds full; return to oven and bake in top third of oven for 30–35 minutes or until puffy and golden brown.
5. Serve immediately with whipped sweet butter.

Make-It-Easy Tips:
√ The large metal popover tins, which are deeper and fuller than regular muffin tins, are best to use since they can be preheated and turn out larger, lighter, and airier popovers.
√ The best volume is achieved if ingredients are at room temperature when combined.

Light Beer Bread

YIELD: One 9″ x 5″ x 3″ loaf
Preparation time: 10 minutes
Rising time: 1–1½ hours
Cooking time: 1 hour

This recipe was passed on to me by the actor Pat Rooney, who promised it would work, and it certainly did! The beer and the self-rising flour act to make the bread rise in only 1 hour. Serve this bread warm or toasted, with whipped sweet butter.

The Ingredients:
3¼ cups self-rising flour
3 tablespoons granulated sugar
1 12-ounce bottle of light beer, at room temperature

The Steps:
1. Lightly butter a large loaf pan or spray it with nonaerosol vege-table shortening.
2. Mix flour and sugar together in large bowl; pour in beer and stir together until sticky dough is formed.
3. Place dough in prepared pan, shape into a loaf and allow dough to rise covered with a dampened dish towel for 1–1½ hours.
4. Preheat oven to 350°.
5. Bake for 1 hour or until lightly browned on top.
6. Serve bread warm with whipped sweet butter.

Variations:
Sesame seeds can be sprinkled on top before baking.
Herbs can be added to the dough for a flavorful herb bread.
Regular beer may be substituted for light beer.

Make-It-Easy Tips:
√ It's easiest to mix the dough with your hands and much more fun!
√ One of the new, superstrength paper towels can be dampened and used to cover the rising bread dough.
√ If dough is too sticky to the touch, add a few tablespoons of flour.

Custardy Corn Bread

SERVES: 6–8
Preparation time: 15 minutes
Cooking time: 30 minutes

I use this corn bread in place of rice or potatoes as a side dish since it is so creamy and rich.

The Ingredients:
1 cup stone-ground yellow cornmeal
¼ cup all-purpose flour
2 teaspoons sugar
1 teaspoon baking powder

½ teaspoon salt
1½ cups whole milk
1 egg, lightly beaten
2 tablespoons unsalted butter
Garnish: Whipped sweet butter

The Steps:

1. Preheat oven to 400°.
2. In mixing bowl, combine cornmeal, flour, sugar, baking powder, and salt.
3. Add 1 cup of the milk and stir to combine; then add egg and stir until well mixed.
4. Melt butter in 8" square baking pan in oven.
5. When butter is melted and hot, pour prepared batter in pan.
6. Pour remaining ½ cup milk over the top but do *not* stir.
7. Bake for 30 minutes or until golden on top but still custardy on the inside.
8. Serve hot, with whipped sweet butter.

Variations:

White cornmeal can be substituted for yellow.

Chopped pimientos or diced green chilies can be added for a spicy variation.

Banana-Nut Bread

YIELD: **Three 8" x 4" x 2" loaves or eight 6" x 3½" x 2" mini-loaves**
Preparation time: 20 minutes
Cooking time: 45 minutes–1 hour

This bread can be served as a bread with lunch or dinner, as a sweet for dessert, certainly as a tea bread, and even as a sweet bread for breakfast!

The Ingredients:

2½ cups all-purpose flour
2 teaspoons cornstarch
2 teaspoons baking soda

1 teaspoon salt
1 cup (2 sticks) unsalted butter, softened
2 cups granulated sugar
5 medium ripe bananas, mashed (about 3 cups)
4 eggs, lightly beaten
½ cup sour cream
1¼ cups chopped walnuts

The Steps:

1. Preheat oven to 350°. Lightly butter 3 large loaf pans or 8 mini-loaf pans and dust with flour.
2. Sift flour, cornstarch, baking soda, and salt together.
3. Cream butter and sugar together with electric beater until light and lemon-colored, about 3 minutes.
4. Add bananas, eggs, and sour cream and continue to beat until smooth.
5. Combine flour mixture with banana mixture but do not over-beat. Stir in walnuts.
6. Pour into prepared pans and bake for 45 minutes for mini-loaves, 55 minutes for larger loaves, or until firm in the center and the edges begin to separate from the pan.
7. Let rest on rack for 10 minutes; remove from pans, allow to cool slightly, and serve.

Variations:

Omit nuts and replace with raisins or chopped dates.

Make-It-Easy Tips:

√ Quick breads are easier to slice, and the flavors will mellow, if given 2–3 hours to sit after removing from pans.
√ Cornstarch is added to the flour to make it more crumbly in texture, reminiscent of cake flour.
√ Soften butter in its paper wrapper, place butter in mixing bowl, and use wrapper to butter the pans without getting fingers greasy.

Blueberry-Orange Bread

YIELD: One 9" x 5" x 3" loaf or four 6" x 3½" x 2" mini-loaves
Preparation time: 15–20 minutes
Cooking time: 40–60 minutes

The Ingredients:

½ cup orange juice
¼ cup hot water
2 tablespoons unsalted butter, melted
1½ teaspoons grated orange rind
1 egg, lightly beaten
⅓ cup dairy sour cream
2 cups all-purpose flour
1 cup granulated sugar
1 teaspoon baking powder
½ teaspoon salt
¼ teaspoon baking soda
1 cup fresh blueberries (or frozen, thawed; or canned, well drained)
2 tablespoons all-purpose flour

The Steps:

1. Preheat oven to 350°. Grease and dust with flour 1 large or 4 mini-loaf pans.
2. Combine orange juice, water, butter, and orange rind in a bowl; add egg and sour cream and mix well.
3. Combine 2 cups flour, sugar, baking powder, salt, and baking soda in a bowl; add these dry ingredients to juice mixture and mix until smooth.
4. Sprinkle blueberries with 2 tablespoons flour, toss lightly, and gently fold into batter.
5. Pour in pans and bake large loaf for 55–60 minutes; mini-loaves for 40–45 minutes or until an inserted knife comes out clean.
6. Let rest in pan for 10 minutes; remove from pan and allow to cool for 10–15 minutes before slicing.

Variations:

Chopped walnuts or pecans can be added in Step 4; stir them in before adding blueberries.

Make-It-Easy Tips:
√ The blueberries are dusted with flour to keep them from sinking in the batter.
√ The egg should be at room temperature to avoid curdling when adding to the warm liquid.
√ When grating orange rind, grate extra and freeze in small containers for future use.

Spicy Pumpkin Bread

YIELD: **Three 8″ x 4″ x 2″ loaves or seven 6″ x 3½″ x 2″ mini-loaves**
Preparation time: 20 minutes
Cooking time: 45–60 minutes

Spicy Pumpkin Bread can be eaten as a breakfast or lunch bread with sweet butter, or as a dessert, or as a snack by itself.

The Ingredients:
3½ cups all-purpose flour
2 teaspoons baking soda
1 teaspoon baking powder
1 teaspoon salt
1 teaspoon ground cinnamon
1 teaspoon ground nutmeg
1 teaspoon ground allspice
½ teaspoon ground cloves
2½ cups granulated white sugar
1 cup light brown sugar
1 cup corn oil
3 eggs
1 16-ounce can cooked pumpkin
1 cup buttermilk
1 cup diced pecans (two 2¼-ounce packages)
Garnish: Sweet butter

The Steps:
1. Preheat oven to 350°. Generously butter 3 large loaf pans or 7 mini-loaf pans and lightly dust with flour.

2. Sift flour, baking soda, baking powder, salt, cinnamon, nutmeg, allspice, and cloves and set aside.
3. In a large bowl with an electric beater, beat sugars and oil until smooth.
4. Add eggs and beat well; add pumpkin, continuing to beat until smooth.
5. Add dry ingredients, alternating with the buttermilk, beating until batter is smooth.
6. Fold in pecans; pour into prepared loaf pans and bake for 45 minutes for mini-loaf pans and 55 minutes–1 hour for larger loaves or until a knife inserted comes out clean.
7. Let rest for 10 minutes in pans, then turn out onto a wire rack to cool. Serve warm or at room temperature with sweet butter or by itself.

Variation:

Half whole-wheat flour and half white flour can be substituted for white.

Make-It-Easy Tips:

√ If diced nuts are not available, chop whole shelled nuts in blender or food processor.

√ If buttermilk is unavailable, add 1 tablespoon vinegar or 1 tablespoon lemon juice to 1 cup whole milk and allow to stand and thicken for 5 minutes.

CHAPTER TEN

DESSERTS

Ice Cream Cookie Freakout

Cassis Froth

Instant Ice Cream

Instant Sorbet

Hazelnut Topped Ice Cream
  plus Variations

Zabaglione

Crème aux Fruits

Apple Crumble

Blueberry Pudding

Blackberry Cobbler

Strawberries with Almond
  Cream

Poached Pears

Apricot Apples

Quick Chocolate Mousse

Bar Cookies

Pecan-Butterscotch Squares

Lemon Squares

Raspberry Tea Squares

World's Tastiest Brownies

Double Fudge Chip Cake

Short Shortbread

Chocolate Meringue Pie

Mud Pie

Frozen Lime Pie

Raisin Pie

Unless sweets are your "thing," you probably want dessert to be the simplest part of the meal to prepare. At least, that's how I feel about it. So I have selected recipes, many of which appear to be very elegant, but are a snap.

You will find a number that involve ice cream—just about everybody's favorite. It can be used in cakes, pie fillings, or whips and is always a major hit. Try the *Ice Cream Cookie Freakout*, which is simply crushed Oreos mixed with vanilla ice cream to form a "cookie ice cream," or combine chocolate wafers with coffee ice cream to form a "mocha freakout."

The ultimate Make-It-Easy dessert is a bowl of fresh fruits accompanied by assorted cheeses. In the summer, berries, especially, provide a base for whipped cream, ice cream, sour cream, or crème fraîche. In the winter months, pears and apples can be baked or served fresh with cheese for quick, easy, and refreshing finishes to dinner. If fresh fruit is unavailable, substitute frozen, unsweetened fruits—they work well in baked dishes, sauces, or puddings.

Baking cakes, pies, cookies, on the other hand, requires care, patience, and an exactness that only time will allow. The measuring, sifting, mixing, greasing, flouring, creaming, whipping, preheating, first rising, second rising, cooling, and frosting are time-consuming activities befitting the Sunday afternoon pastry chef who loves to concoct extravaganzas.

There's definitely nothing wrong with the activity. It can be totally relaxing and, best of all, can satisfy a craving for that picture on the front of the current *Bon Appétit* magazine, the one with the dripping chocolate sauce over the coffee mousse with the whipped cream and shaved chocolate curls and. . . .

I'm talking fun! But when there's no time for such fun, and a dessert is called for, I have a few hints that will make baking quicker and easier. For example, cakes can be assembled by using crumbled cookies and layering them with ice cream or whipped cream and garnishing with chips, chocolate, or even crushed candy bars (I have a "thing" for crushed Heath Bars!)

Bar cookies are the easiest form of cookie to bake. They can be blended together, poured into a large pan, baked, cooled, and cut into dozens of cookies.

Pies are made Make-It-Easy with crumb crusts. Although prepared crusts are available, whipping up a cookie crust in the blender or food processor requires no more than five minutes. Besides, you can vary the taste by using graham crackers, gingersnaps, chocolate wafers, vanilla wafers, macaroons, or Amaretti cookies.

Pies can be prepared in Pyrex or metal pie pans, or in springform pans with a sprinkling of crumbs on the edges to save preparing a crust. The usual procedure for a crumb crust is to mix 1–1⅓ cups crumbs with 2 tablespoons sugar (or less, according to the sweetness of the crumbs). Add ½ stick of softened or melted butter, and combine in blender or food processor until crumbly. Variations can be made by adding grated lemon or orange rind, cinnamon, shredded coconut, cereal crumbs, or chopped nuts.

Whether it's ice cream, fruit, cakes, or cookies for dessert, remember to serve it attractively. It takes no time to pour an ice cream dessert into long-stemmed glasses, or arrange cookies on a paper-lace doily on a pretty plate. This extra special touch will make even the simplest dessert look elegant.

What's best about the desserts in this section, besides the taste, is that you can make most of them in 15 minutes or less.

Ice Cream Cookie Freakout!

SERVES: 3–4
Preparation time: 5 minutes

This is my family's favorite recipe to test. We must test it two or three times a week just to make sure we get it right! The best part about it is that an Ice Cream Cookie Freakout can be made on the spur of the moment. Just keep gobs of vanilla ice cream and Oreo cookies around—just in case. . . .

The Ingredients:
5 Oreo cookies
1 pint vanilla ice cream, softened for 3–4 minutes at room temperature

The Steps:
1. In food processor or blender, crush cookies slightly.
2. Add ice cream in scoops and process until smooth.
3. Pour into goblets or sherbet glasses and serve immediately.

Variations:

Variations on the Freakout are innumerable. Try gingersnaps and vanilla ice cream, Oreos and coffee ice cream for a Mocha Freakout, oatmeal cookies and chocolate ice cream, peanut butter cookies and vanilla ice cream, or the totally sinful Oreos and chocolate fudge ice cream for a Double Fudge Freakout! By all means, improvise and come up with your own Freakout!

Make-It-Easy Tips:

√ Use regular Oreo cookies, *not* the "double" ones, which will be too sweet. Hydrox cookies are also good. Test the Oreos versus the Hydrox to determine your personal preference.

√ Ice Cream Cookie Freakout can be frozen for future use but the best part of it is the soft texture reminiscent of those times as a child when you mashed your cookies and ice cream together.

√ If using a blender, it may be necessary to prepare the Freakout in 2 batches.

Cassis Froth

SERVES: 6–8
Preparation time: 5 minutes

Any flavor liqueur or ice cream can be used to make a Froth. Try Crème de Cacao or Kahlua with coffee ice cream, Crème de Menthe with chocolate ice cream, apricot brandy with peach ice cream or Cherry Herring with cherry-vanilla ice cream. Improvise and come up with your own Froth.

The Ingredients:

2 pints vanilla ice cream, softened 3–4 minutes at room temperature

6–8 tablespoons Crème de Cassis

Garnish: Fresh berries (optional)

The Steps:

1. Just before serving, place ice cream in food processor or blender container.

2. Add liqueur and blend until smooth. The consistency should be thick, like a double-thick milk shake.
3. Pour into stemmed goblets or sherbet glasses and serve immediately, garnished with fresh berries if desired.

Make-It-Easy Tips:
√ If using a blender, do in 2 or 3 batches.
√ The Cassis Froth can be frozen again for future use, but it is best served immediately, when it has a soft, creamy texture.

Instant Ice Cream

SERVES: 3–4
Preparation time: 5 minutes

A food processor or very strong blender is necessary to prepare this dish. Just drop the frozen fruit into the cream, and presto! Instant Ice Cream! I find it the perfect dessert to serve to unexpected guests, or to my family, who likes to watch it being prepared.

The Ingredients:
 1 cup heavy cream
 ⅓ cup granulated sugar
 1 20-ounce package (loosely packed) unsweetened frozen fruit (strawberries, raspberries, blueberries, cherries, or peaches)

The Steps:
1. Place cream and sugar in food processor bowl (fitted with steel knife) and blend for 1 minute.
2. Through the feed tube, add frozen fruit, a few pieces at a time, and process until smooth (an ice cream will form).
3. Serve immediately, garnished with cookies or fresh fruit.

Make-It-Easy Tip:
√ The dessert can be frozen, but it's best when served immediately.

Instant Sorbet

SERVES: 4
Preparation time: 5 minutes
Freezing time: 4–6 hours

The food processor transforms fresh frozen fruit into Sorbet (French sherbet) in a matter of minutes. Freeze any fruit desired, mix with sugar to taste, and brandy or liqueur, process, and *voilà!* Sorbet!

The Ingredients:

3–4 large ripe bananas
1 teaspoon lemon juice
4–6 tablespoons apricot brandy (or Crème de Banana)
1 tablespoon confectioners' sugar or to taste (optional)
Garnish: Sprigs of fresh mint (optional)

The Steps:

1. Peel bananas, wrap tightly in plastic wrap and freeze for 4–6 hours or overnight.
2. Unwrap bananas, cut into 1″ slices, place in food processor with lemon juice; pulsate on and off to combine.
3. Add liqueur and continue to process until smooth.
4. Add confectioners' sugar, if desired, and serve in a goblet or attractive dish garnished with mint sprigs, if desired. (The Sorbet can be placed in small freezer-proof dishes, covered, and frozen for future use.)

Variations:

Be creative and make up your own variations. The fruit selected should be fleshy without a lot of peel. Grapes and blueberries should be avoided. Remember to peel the fruit and seal it in plastic wrap before freezing to keep from browning. Don't forget to cut it in small pieces before processing. Here are a few variations on which to start: Melon with Grand Marnier; peaches with peach brandy; pear with apple brandy; kiwi with apple brandy.

Make-It-Easy Tips:
   √ Frozen, unsweetened fruit such as peaches can be used and placed right in food processor, bypassing Step 1.
   √ The lemon juice is added to fruit to prevent it from turning brown.

Hazelnut-Topped Ice Cream (plus Variations)

SERVES: 6
Preparation time: 5 minutes

The easiest dessert to whip up at the last minute is ice cream with a special topping or liqueur. Select a favorite ice cream or sherbet, some unusual toppings or liqueurs, and an instant and always pleasing dessert is created.

The Ingredients:
   1 5-ounce hazelnut chocolate bar (Cadbury or other good brand)
   2 pints coffee ice cream or "rainbow" sherbet (or use whatever flavor desired)

The Steps:
   1. Break chocolate bar into small pieces and crumble in food processor or blender. (Chocolate bar can be frozen, placed in a strong plastic bag, and pounded with a hammer until crumbly.)
   2. Place scoops of ice cream or sherbet in tall goblets or sherbet glasses, top with chocolate crumbs, and serve immediately.

Variations:
   Chocolate ice cream topped with crushed peppermint candies.
   Butter-pecan ice cream topped with crushed Amaretti or macaroon cookies.
   Mocha ice cream topped with Amaretto liqueur and toasted slivered almonds.

Coffee ice cream topped with coffee liqueur, whipped cream, and crushed toffee candy.

Vanilla ice cream topped with sliced, ripe pears and Crème de Menthe liqueur.

Vanilla ice cream topped with a mixture of 1 thawed, 12-ounce package frozen raspberries pureed, and berry-flavored liqueur.

Vanilla ice cream topped with candied chestnuts (*marrons glacés*).

Vanilla ice cream topped with warmed apricot jam thinned with Kirsch.

Orange sherbet and vanilla ice cream topped with Grand Marnier and mandarin orange segments.

Orange sherbet topped with warmed ginger marmalade thinned with brandy.

Pineapple sherbet topped with crushed pineapple and chopped fresh mint.

Raspberry sherbet topped with Crème de Cassis.

Zabaglione

SERVES: 6–8
Preparation time: 10 minutes
Cooking time: 5–10 minutes

A small double boiler is essential to the successful preparation of Zabaglione.

The Ingredients:
 4 egg yolks, at room temperature
 ¼ cup granulated sugar
 2½ tablespoons dry Marsala
 1 tablespoon grated lemon rind
 2 pints fresh strawberries, blueberries, raspberries, or other fruit

The Steps:
 1. In top of double boiler, combine egg yolks, sugar, Marsala, and lemon rind; whip with a whisk until smooth.

2. Place the double boiler top over simmering water on high heat and whisk vigorously until the mixture becomes foamy and begins to thicken.
3. Spoon immediately over fresh berries or fruit, or cake.

Variation:
Zabaglione can also be served chilled.

Make-It-Easy Tips:
√ If not using the Zabaglione immediately, it can be kept warm in the top of the double boiler with the heat turned off for 10 minutes.
√ Freeze egg whites individually in ice-cube trays. Once frozen, remove from tray and store in a sealed plastic bag to be used as needed.
√ If using a large double boiler, double the recipe so that you can whisk the ingredients easily.

Crème aux Fruits

SERVES: 6
Preparation time: 20 minutes
Cooking time: 50–60 minutes
Chilling time: 4–6 hours or overnight

The custard of this dessert is the traditional base for crème brulée, the sinfully rich French concoction. Instead of the time-consuming caramelizing procedure, I've substituted berries as the topping. Serve it on the Fourth of July for a red, white, and blue dessert.

The Ingredients:
2 cups heavy cream
4 egg yolks, at room temperature
¼ cup granulated sugar
Pinch of salt
1 teaspoon vanilla extract
1½ pints washed blueberries or halved strawberries (or a combination of both)

The Steps:
1. Preheat oven to 350°.
2. In a small saucepan, scald cream by heating until bubbles just begin to appear around the edges; allow to cool for 5 minutes.
3. In the meantime, beat yolks until thickened and a light lemon color; gradually beat in sugar and salt until smooth.
4. Slowly pour cream into egg-yolk mixture, whisking constantly; flavor with vanilla and pour into a shallow, one-quart baking dish.
5. Place dish in a larger pan. Add hot water to larger pan until it reaches 1" up the sides of the baking dish. Bake for 50–60 minutes or until a knife inserted comes out clean; cool for 30 minutes.
6. Chill in refrigerator for 4–6 hours or overnight.
7. Just before serving, garnish with berries.

Variations:
Dessert can be baked in 6 individual ramekins or Pyrex cups.

Other varieties of fruit can be used as a garnish, such as sliced kiwi, sliced grapes, or poached peaches or apricots.

For a more authentic variation, slice a vanilla bean and add to the cream while scalding (discard bean). Omit vanilla extract from recipe.

Make-It-Easy Tips:
√ The scalded cream must be cooled slightly before adding to egg yolks to prevent curdling.

√ Hot water bath in Step 5 prevents the custard from curdling or overcooking.

√ The dessert is best when prepared a day in advance and allowed to chill thoroughly overnight.

√ For a glazed effect, dip the blueberries and halved strawberries into ¼ cup currant jelly that has been melted and glaze each before garnishing in Step 7.

Apple Crumble

SERVES: 4–6
Preparation time: 15 minutes
Cooking time: 45–50 minutes

Apple Crumble is a combination of apple pie and apple brown betty, but can be prepared in only 15 minutes. It can be made in a 9″ pie plate, in 4 small, individual quiche pans, or in flat oven-proof dishes.

The Ingredients:
    4 tart apples
    2 tablespoons lemon juice
Streusel Topping:
    ⅓ cup all-purpose flour
    ½ cup brown sugar
    ½ teaspoon ground cinnamon
    ¼ teaspoon freshly grated nutmeg
    4 tablespoons unsalted butter, softened
       Garnish: Vanilla ice cream or whipped cream

The Steps:
1. Preheat oven to 375°. Generously butter a 9″ pie plate or 4 individual dishes.
2. Peel and core apples and cut each into 8 wedges.
3. Place sliced apples in prepared dish and sprinkle with lemon juice.
4. Prepare streusel topping in food processor or blender or by hand by blending flour, brown sugar, cinnamon, nutmeg, and butter together until just crumbly but not overprocessed.
5. Sprinkle streusel topping atop apples and bake in preheated 375° oven for 45–50 minutes or until tip is golden and apples are tender (smaller dishes should be done in 45 minutes).
6. Serve Apple Crumble warm, garnished with vanilla ice cream or whipped cream.

Variations:
Sliced peaches or berries can be substituted for the apples.

Apple corer

Make-It-Easy Tips:
- √ A gadget called an apple slicer cores and slices apples in one swift motion.
- √ Crumble may be prepared earlier in the day and reheated before serving.
- √ The lemon juice is sprinkled on the apples to keep them from discoloring.
- √ Streusel topping can also be used on coffee cakes or similar fruit bakes.

Blueberry Pudding

SERVES: 6–8
Preparation time: 15 minutes
Cooking time: 30–35 minutes

The Ingredients:
- 1 quart fresh blueberries, washed, or two 12-ounce boxes frozen blueberries, thawed
- 2 tablespoons granulated sugar
- 1 tablespoon flour
- 1 teaspoon grated orange rind
- 24 coconut or almond macaroon cookies (one 13-ounce package)
- 2 eggs, lightly beaten
- ¼ cup light brown sugar
- 1 teaspoon grated lemon or orange rind
- 2 tablespoons unsalted butter, diced
  Garnish: Vanilla or lemon ice cream, or *Crème Fraîche* (*see* Chapter 2)

The Steps:
1. Preheat oven to 350°.
2. Place berries in bottom of 7" x 11" x 2" baking dish or similar-size oven-proof dish and gently toss with 2 tablespoons sugar, flour, and 1 teaspoon rind.
3. Crumble cookies and place in a bowl.
4. Add eggs, brown sugar, 1 teaspoon rind and stir well.
5. Spread mixture evenly over blueberries, dot with butter bits, and bake for 30–35 minutes or until top is lightly golden.
6. Serve warm with vanilla or lemon ice cream, or *Crème Fraîche*.

Variations:

Other berries, such as raspberries, blackberries, boysenberries, or strawberries, can be similarly baked, varying the sweetener to taste and substituting lemon for the orange rind if desired.

Make-It-Easy Tips:
√ Cookies can be crumbled easily in a food processor or blender.
√ Blueberry pudding can be cooked and frozen for future use.
√ Orange and lemon rind can be grated in large quantities and kept frozen for future use.
√ When buying fresh berries, look on the underside of the container to be sure there are no decaying berries. If you find some after you get home, remove them before the mold spreads.

Blackberry Cobbler

SERVES: 6–8
Preparation time: 15 minutes
Cooking time: 45 minutes–1 hour

A cobbler is a deep-dish pie with no bottom crust and a top crust of streusel or biscuit dough. It is derived from the early American expression "to cobble up," meaning to put together quickly. This dish is put together in even less time with the help of a food processor.

The Ingredients:

- 4 cups fresh blackberries, or frozen unsweetened blackberries, thawed
- ½ cup granulated sugar
- ¼ pound (1 stick) unsalted butter, broken into bits, at room temperature
- 1 cup all-purpose flour
- ½ cup granulated sugar
  Pinch of cinnamon
  Pinch of nutmeg
  Garnish: Vanilla ice cream, or whipped cream or *Crème Fraîche* (*see* Chapter 2).

The Steps:

1. Preheat oven to 350°.
2. Place the blackberries in bottom of a deep-dish pie plate or a rectangular oven-proof baking dish.
3. Sprinkle with ½ cup granulated sugar and gently toss.
4. In bowl of food processor (or in a mixing bowl) combine butter, flour, ½ cup granulated sugar, cinnamon, and nutmeg; pulsate with several on-off turns of the processor until butter/sugar mixture is crumbly. Or use fork, or your fingers, and crumble by hand.
5. Sprinkle topping over sweetened berries and bake until lightly browned, 45 minutes–1 hour.
6. Serve hot, with vanilla ice cream, whipped cream, or *Crème Fraîche*.

Variations:

Blueberries, raspberries, or peaches can be used in a cobbler.

Make-It-Easy Tips:

√ The cobbler can be cooked and frozen for future use.

√ Cinnamon and nutmeg, as well as many other spices, are now available in disposable grinders at supermarkets. The grinders produce a fresh-ground taste and aroma, and extend the shelf-life of the spices, which remain constantly sealed.

Strawberries with Almond Cream

SERVES: 4–6
Preparation time: 10 minutes
Chilling time: 1 hour

The Ingredients:
Sauce:
   1 cup (8 ounces) dairy sour cream
   3 tablespoons confectioners' sugar
1½ tablespoons almond liqueur (I use Amaretto)
   1 teaspoon almond extract
   2 pints fresh strawberries, washed, hulled and split in half

The Steps:
1. In small bowl combine sour cream, sugar, liqueur, and almond extract; stir until smooth. Cover, and chill for 1 hour or until ready to use.
2. Serve almond cream over hulled and split berries.

Variations:
A combination of berries (strawberries, raspberries, and blueberries) can be used.
Crème Fraîche (*see* Chapter 2) can be substituted for sour cream.

Make-It-Easy Tips:
√ Cream can be prepared a day or two in advance and chilled until ready to use.
√ Wash strawberries before hulling to prevent loss of juice.
√ A strawberry huller, an inexpensive gadget shaped like a fat tweezer, is a wonderful tool for hulling strawberries. It is available at gourmet specialty shops. If unavailable, use a beer can opener to pick out the hull.

Strawberry huller

Poached Pears

SERVES: 3–4
Preparation time: 10 minutes
Cooking time: 20 minutes

This is a light, low-calorie dessert.

The Ingredients:
2 pears, medium ripe
1 cup unsweetened apple juice
1 teaspoon lemon juice
1 stick cinnamon
1 whole clove
Pinch of nutmeg
Garnish: *Reduced-Calorie Sour Cream*

The Steps:
1. Preheat oven to 350°.
2. Peel pears, slice in half lengthwise, and remove the cores and seeds.
3. Place pears, cut side down, in a small casserole.
4. In small bowl, combine apple juice, lemon juice, cinnamon stick, clove, and nutmeg. Stir and pour over the pears.
5. Cover pan and bake for about 20 minutes or until tender. (Do not overcook or they will be mushy.)
6. Remove pan from oven and allow to cool in liquid for 10 minutes.
7. Discard cinnamon stick and serve warm with *Reduced-Calorie Sour Cream*, if desired.

Variations:
For a higher calorie version, top pears with vanilla ice cream or sweetened whipped cream.
Poached Pears can also be served cold.

Make-It-Easy Tips:
√ Pears can be cooked earlier in the day for 5 minutes. When ready to serve, heat for an additional 15 minutes and serve.
√ Anjou or Bosc pears are excellent for baking.

Apricot Apples

SERVES: 4
Preparation time: 10 minutes
Cooking time: 40–50 minutes

Baked apples do not need gobs of syrup and sugar to taste good. Try these apples covered with juice and reduced-sugar preserves.

The Ingredients:

   4 baking apples (Rome Beauty, Pippin, or Granny Smiths can be used)
   4 teaspoons lemon juice
½–¾ cup low-calorie (reduced sugar) apricot jam
   1 cup unsweetened apple juice
   1 teaspoon cinnamon
   ½ teaspoon grated nutmeg

The Steps:

1. Preheat oven to 350°.
2. Wash apples, remove cores with an apple corer or knife, and immediately sprinkle open cores with lemon juice.
3. Arrange apples in baking dish and fill cavities with apricot jam.
4. Pour juice into pan, sprinkle cavities with cinnamon and nutmeg, and bake for 40–50 minutes or until apples are tender, basting occasionally with pan juices.
5. Serve apples hot, at room temperature, or chilled.

Variations:

Other low-calorie preserves, such as strawberry or grape, can be substituted for apricot.

Make-It-Easy Tip:

√ Lemon juice is sprinkled over openings in apples to prevent discoloration.

Quick Chocolate Mousse

SERVES: 6–8
Preparation time: 10 minutes
Chilling time: 6 hours or overnight

This is a super-fast mousse to prepare on a moment's notice. Keep the chips and liqueur on hand and you're ready to go.

The Ingredients:
    1 6-ounce package semisweet chocolate chips
    2 eggs
    3 tablespoons very strong, hot coffee
    2 tablespoons coffee liqueur (I use Kahlua)
    ¾ cup scalded milk
      Garnish: Sweetened whipped cream or *Crème Frâiche* (*see* Chapter 2)

The Steps:
1. In container of food processor or blender, place chocolate chips, eggs, hot coffee, Kahlua, and scalded milk and process until very smooth.
2. Pour into 6 ramekins, or 8 *pots de crème* dishes, or 1 large, 1½-quart dish, and chill 6 hours or overnight.
3. Serve chilled with sweetened whipped cream or *Crème Frâiche*.

Make-It-Easy Tips:
√ Instant coffee can be used, with or without caffeine, for the strong, hot coffee.
√ To scald milk, heat until milk just begins to bubble around the edge of the pan.

BAR COOKIES
No, bar cookies are not the sweet-tooth equivalent of pretzels and peanuts, something to be wedged between the mixed drinks and the bartender at holiday get-togethers. They are, in fact, a cross between a traditional cookie and a cake and are baked in sheets, cooled, and then cut into squares, triangles, or whatever shape you prefer. They can be

frozen in small batches and defrosted whenever the spirit moves you—a totally Make-It-Easy cookie!

Before you begin baking your bar cookies, here are a few tips to keep in mind:

1. Always use real (as opposed to artificial) ingredients. Even though they're more expensive, you'll taste the difference.
2. Soften the butter or cream cheese ahead of time.
3. Use a large (9″ x 13″) baking pan; for thicker cookies, use a 7″ x 11″ or an 8″ or 9″ square pan. Adjust cooking time accordingly.
4. Generously grease baking pans before pouring in the batter. Dusting with flour after greasing often makes removing the bars easier.
5. Use an electric mixer or hand beater to make the batter. Do not use a food processor or blender (unless specified), which can overprocess the dough and hence toughen the cookies.
6. Bake the bars on the middle rack of the oven.
7. If you like chewy, fudgy squares, underbake them slightly. The top should be dull, not shiny, and, when you press your finger on the top, a slight imprint should remain. If you prefer cakey squares, bake them until the top springs back to the touch or an inserted toothpick comes out clean.
8. And . . . if you've forgotten to soften the butter, grate it and it will soften in minutes.

Pecan-Butterscotch Squares

YIELD: 4 dozen
Preparation time: 15–20 minutes
Cooking time: 40 minutes

These pecan squares are very popular around my house. If coconut is not your favorite, by all means omit it—they will still be a knockout.

The Ingredients:

¼ pound (1 stick) unsalted butter, softened
½ cup dark brown sugar

1 cup all-purpose flour
2 eggs, lightly beaten
1 cup dark brown sugar
1 teaspoon vanilla extract
1 cup pecans, chopped
1 cup (4 ounces) flaked or shredded coconut
1 6-ounce package butterscotch chips
2 tablespoons flour
Pinch of salt

The Steps:

1. Preheat oven to 375°. Generously butter a 7″ x 11″ baking pan and lightly dust with flour.
2. To prepare crust, cream butter and ½ cup brown sugar together until smooth; gradually add flour; mix until crumbly. Press into prepared pan and bake for 15–20 minutes or until golden.
3. In the meantime, combine eggs, 1 cup brown sugar, pecans, coconut, butterscotch chips, 2 tablespoons flour, vanilla, and salt. Spread mixture over baked crust and return to oven for an additional 20 minutes.
4. Let cool thoroughly and cut into squares.

Make-It-Easy Tips:

√ Freeze squares uncut and later slice into squares while semi-frozen for easier cutting.
√ Prepare crust easily with an electric beater.
√ Nut meats keep indefinitely in the freezer.

Lemon Squares

YIELD: 16 cookies
Preparation time: 20 minutes
Cooking time: 45 minutes

The Ingredients:

1 cup all-purpose flour
6 tablespoons (¾ stick) unsalted butter, softened

¼ cup confectioners' sugar
1½ ounces cream cheese, softened
1 cup granulated sugar
2 tablespoons all-purpose flour
2 eggs, lightly beaten
3 tablespoons lemon juice
1 teaspoon finely minced lemon rind
½ teaspoon baking powder
　Garnish: Confectioners' sugar

The Steps:

1. Preheat oven to 350°. Generously butter an 8″ square baking pan and lightly dust with flour.
2. In large mixing bowl with an electric mixer, combine 1 cup flour, butter, ¼ cup confectioners' sugar, and cream cheese and beat until crumbly.
3. Press dough into prepared baking pan and bake for 20 minutes.
4. In the meantime, combine granulated sugar, 2 tablespoons flour, eggs, lemon juice, lemon rind, and baking powder; beat until smooth.
5. Spread mixture over baked layer; bake for additional 25 minutes.
6. Remove from oven, cool in pan for 10 minutes; while still warm, run a knife around outer edge, cut into bars, and sprinkle with confectioners' sugar.

Make-It-Easy Tip:

√ Since this recipe requires a longer preparation time, why not double the recipe and bake in two 8″ square pans or one 9″ x 13″ x 2″ pan, baking for the same amount of time. Freeze extra squares without sprinkling with garnish of confectioners' sugar.

Raspberry Tea Squares

YIELD: 20–24 cookies
Preparation time: 15–20 minutes
Cooking time: 35 minutes

The Ingredients:
  6 ounces (1½ sticks) unsalted butter, softened
  1 cup granulated sugar
  1 egg, lightly beaten
  1 teaspoon vanilla extract
  2 cups all-purpose flour
  Pinch of allspice
  1 cup chopped almonds
  ¾ cup raspberry preserves
  Garnish: Confectioners' sugar (optional)

The Steps:
  1. Preheat oven to 350°. Generously butter a 9″ square baking pan and lightly dust with flour.
  2. In large mixing bowl with an electric mixer, cream butter and sugar until light and fluffy; add egg and vanilla and continue to beat until smooth. Add flour, allspice, and nuts, mixing until well combined.
  3. Place half the batter in bottom of prepared baking pan; gently and carefully spread preserves over mixture and top with remaining batter.
  4. Bake for 30–35 minutes or until lightly golden.
  5. Remove from oven and sprinkle with confectioners' sugar, if desired. Allow to cool 15–20 minutes and cut into squares.

Variations:
  Both jam and nuts can be varied to suit your taste. Try apricot with pecans; strawberry with filberts; or peach with walnuts.

Make-It-Easy Tip:
  √ Freeze squares uncut and later slice into squares while semi-frozen for easier cutting.

World's Tastiest Brownies

YIELD: 32 brownies
Preparation time: 20 minutes
Cooking time: 20–25 minutes

These brownies require a little extra time, but they are worth every minute of it. They are sensational!

The Ingredients:
    1 12-ounce package real chocolate bits
    ½ pound unsalted butter (2 sticks) or margarine
    4 eggs
    1 cup sugar
    1 teaspoon vanilla extract
    1 cup all-purpose flour

The Steps:
1. Preheat oven to 350°. Generously butter two 8″ square baking pans or one 9″ x 13″ x 2″ pan.
2. Melt chocolate bits and butter together in the top of a double boiler, or over low heat in a heavy-bottomed saucepan. Stir until smooth. Allow to cool slightly.
3. In large bowl, beat eggs with an electric beater or by hand. Add sugar and vanilla and continue to beat for 2–3 minutes until smooth.
4. Add chocolate mixture to eggs; add flour and stir well.
5. Pour batter into prepared pans and bake for 20–25 minutes, according to whether you prefer them soft or cakey.
6. Allow to cool slightly, cut into squares, and serve.

Variation:
    1 cup chopped walnuts can be added.

Make-It-Easy Tips:
√ Baked brownies can be turned out onto a sheet of aluminum foil, wrapped, and chilled or frozen. Brownies can then be easily cut, cold or semi-frozen, and brought to room temperature before serving.

√ Never cover a pot in which chocolate is melting. Any excess moisture or condensation will "stiffen" the chocolate and prevent it from combining easily with the rest of the ingredients.

Double-Fudge Chip Cake

YIELD: Two 8" x 4" x 2" loaf pans or five 6" x 3½" x 2" mini-loaf pans
Preparation time: 10–15 minutes
Cooking time: 40–55 minutes

The shortening and eggs for this cake are in the unusual form of mayonnaise. It is a very rich and fudgy dessert.

The Ingredients:
  2 cups all-purpose flour
  1⅓ cups granulated sugar
  ½ cup unsweetened cocoa
  1½ teaspoons baking soda
  1½ cups buttermilk
  1 cup mayonnaise (not salad dressing)
  1 teaspoon vanilla extract
  1 12-ounce package semisweet chocolate bits

The Steps:
  1. Preheat oven to 350°. Generously butter 2 large or 5 or 6 mini-loaf pans and lightly dust with flour.
  2. Combine flour, sugar, cocoa, and baking soda in a large bowl and stir well.
  3. Add buttermilk, mayonnaise, and vanilla and beat until smooth.
  4. Stir in chips; pour batter in prepared pans.
  5. Bake for 40–45 minutes for mini-loaves, or 50–55 minutes for larger loaves.

Variation:
Buttered pans can be dusted with cocoa instead of flour.

Make-It-Easy Tips:

    √ Prepare cake in a double batch and bake in mini-loaf pans; freeze. Use loaves as desserts for family, company, or as wonderful house gifts.

    √ If buttermilk is unavailable, add 1 tablespoon vinegar or lemon juice to 1 cup fresh milk and allow to stand 5 minutes.

Short Shortbread

SERVES: 8–10
Preparation time: 10–15 minutes
Cooking time: 1 hour

Shortbread, a Scottish delicacy also called shortcake, is a very rich dough made of butter, flour, and sugar that, when baked in a 9″ round pan, comes out like an oversize cookie. It is served broken into wedges.

    The shortbread can be split horizontally, filled with preserves or fruit, and used as a cake. A clay shortbread mold carved with designs can be used for an attractive presentation, or a 9″ pie plate can be used. The dough can be prepared in 30 seconds in the food processor.

The Ingredients:

    2 cups sifted all-purpose flour
    ¾ cup confectioners' sugar
    Pinch of salt
    ½ pound (2 sticks) unsalted butter, softened

Shortbread mold

The Steps:
1. Preheat oven to 325°. Lightly spray a clay shortbread mold with vegetable shortening or line a 9″ pie plate with parchment paper or waxed paper.
2. In food processor, with electric mixer, or by hand, combine ingredients until a smooth dough is formed.
3. Press dough firmly into mold or pie pan, making sure dough fits into all crevices of mold or lies flat in pan.
4. Bake filled mold or pan for 50 minutes to 1 hour or until pale in color but not brown.
5. Remove from oven, allow to cool 10–15 minutes, break into pieces, and serve.

Make-It-Easy Tip:
√ Do not overprocess in food processor. Just blend until a dough forms. If too sticky, add additional flour.

Chocolate Meringue Pie

SERVES: 8–10
Preparation time: 15 minutes
Cooking time: 35 minutes
Chilling time: 2–3 hours or overnight

The texture of the meringue-cookie base, topped with the sweetened whipped cream, makes this an unusual and terrific dessert. The whipped cream topping is important because the cold meringue needs an attractive topping.

The Ingredients:
20 chocolate wafers
½ cup chopped walnuts
3 egg whites, at room temperature
½ cup granulated sugar
1 teaspoon baking powder
    Pinch of salt
1 teaspoon vanilla extract

Topping:
1 cup heavy cream
1 tablespoon confectioners' sugar
1 teaspoon vanilla extract

The Steps:
1. Preheat oven to 325°. Generously butter a 9″ pie plate.
2. In food processor or blender, chop wafers and nuts briefly. (Do not make them too fine.)
3. Beat egg whites until stiff. Gradually add granulated sugar, baking powder, salt, and vanilla; continue to beat until stiff peaks form.
4. Gently fold in wafer/nut mixture; pour mixture into buttered pie plate and bake for 35 minutes. Cool, and then chill in refrigerator for 2–3 hours or overnight.
5. Whip cream until almost stiff, add confectioners' sugar and vanilla, and continue to whip until stiff.
6. Serve chilled pie topped with the sweetened whipped cream.

Variations:
For an unusual variation, substitute 20 Ritz crackers for the chocolate wafers and increase the granulated sugar to 1 cup.
Pecans can be substituted for walnuts.

Make-It-Easy Tips:
√ Egg whites must be at room temperature before beating to achieve proper volume. To warm chilled egg whites quickly, place in a metal bowl. (Do not use aluminum, which will give whites a greyish tint.) Set bowl in a basin of warm water; stir to remove the chill. To increase volume, add ¼ teaspoon cream of tartar after egg whites are foamy and begin to stiffen.

Mud Pie

SERVES: 8
Preparation time: 20 minutes
Freezing time: ½ hour plus 3–4 hours

The Ingredients:

Crust:
18 Oreo cookies, crushed
⅓ cup unsalted butter, melted
Filling:
1 quart coffee ice cream (or desired flavor), slightly softened
Topping:
2 squares unsweetened chocolate
1 small (5⅓-ounce) can evaporated milk
½ cup granulated sugar
1 tablespoon unsalted butter

The Steps:

1. Crush cookies in blender or food processor. Combine with butter and press into buttered 9" springform pan or 9" pie plate.
2. Soften ice cream and place in shell. Freeze for ½ hour.
3. In small saucepan, melt chocolate with milk, sugar, and butter. Cook over low heat or in double boiler until syrupy and smooth, 5–10 minutes.
4. While still warm, pour topping over filling; freeze pie for 3–4 hours. Remove from freezer, allow to stand at room temperature for 10 minutes, and serve in slices.

Variation:

Use mint chocolate chip ice cream for filling and top with crushed toffee candy.

Make-It-Easy Tips:

√ If desired, pie can be prepared up through Step 2 and served in slices with hot sauce on top.
√ Mud Pie can be prepared in advance and frozen for several weeks.

Frozen Lime Pie

SERVES: 8
Preparation time: 20 minutes
Freezing time: ½ hour + 3 hours + ½ hour

The chocolate crust makes this Frozen Lime Pie special, but if time is a problem use a prepared graham cracker crust.

The Ingredients:
Crust:
⅓ cup unsalted butter, softened
1¼ cups chocolate wafer crumbs (20–22 wafers)
3 tablespoons granulated sugar
Filling:
1 14-ounce can sweetened condensed milk
4 eggs
1 tablespoon grated lime rind
½ cup fresh lime juice
Topping:
1 cup vanilla ice cream, slightly softened
1–2 tablespoons grated lime rind

The Steps:
1. Generously butter a 9″ pie pan, or spray with non-aerosol vegetable shortening.
2. Blend butter, crumbs, and sugar. Pat mixture firmly into prepared pie pan and freeze for ½ hour.
3. In food processor, blender, or electric mixer, combine condensed milk, eggs, lime rind, and lime juice and process until smooth.
4. Pour mixture into prepared crust and freeze until firm, about 3 hours.
5. When pie is set, spread softened ice cream over top and freeze until firm, about ½ hour.
6. Just before serving, sprinkle top with grated lime rind.

Make-It-Easy Tips:
√ After ice cream is set, you can cover pie with plastic wrap and keep in freezer for up to two weeks.

√ Remember to grate lime rind first for filling and topping, and then juice peeled limes easily. Limes will release more juice if at room temperature.

Raisin Pie

SERVES: 8
Preparation time: 20 minutes
Cooking time: 35 minutes

The Ingredients:
1¼ cups seedless raisins
⅔ cup chopped pecans (or walnuts)
1 teaspoon grated lemon rind
2 tablespoons lemon juice
4 ounces (1 stick) unsalted butter, softened
⅔ cup granulated sugar
⅓ cup dark brown sugar (firmly packed)
1 teaspoon cinnamon
¼ teaspoon salt
3 eggs
1 9″ frozen unbaked pie shell, thawed
Garnish: Whipped cream, or vanilla ice cream, or *Crème Fraîche* (*see* Chapter 2).

The Steps:
1. Preheat oven to 400°.
2. In a mixing bowl, combine raisins, nuts, lemon rind, and lemon juice; set aside.
3. With electric mixer, food processor, or by hand beat butter until light and fluffy.
4. Add granulated sugar, brown sugar, cinnamon, and salt and continue to beat until well mixed.
5. Add eggs, one at a time, beating well after each addition. Stir in raisin mixture, spoon into pie shell, and bake in 400° oven for 15 minutes.

6. Reduce heat to 350° and continue to bake for an additional 20 minutes or until set.
7. Serve warm or at room temperature, garnished with whipped cream, or vanilla ice cream, or *Crème Fraîche*.

Make-It-Easy Tips:
√ If raisins are dry, place in a strainer and steam over simmering water. They can also be plumped and softened by blanching in boiling water and then draining.

√ To prevent a soggy crust, brush unbaked crust with beaten egg white and then lightly dust with a mixture of flour and sugar.

√ To keep pie crusts from browning too fast, cover edges with foil.

PART TWO

MAKE IT EASY
ENTERTAINING

INTRODUCTION

The fun of Make-It-Easy entertaining is getting into the spirit of each party, using the theme as inspiration for invitations, music, or unique table settings. One of the first steps is setting the scene. You will find real variety in this book's suggestions, ranging from a breakfast in bed for two to the most elegant sit-down dinner using your best china and crystal. In between there are casual and formal menus for almost any occasion.

The next step is one of the trickiest elements in successful party giving—selection and seating of guests. I try to be adventurous. I combine married couples and single men and women freely. I also mix people from varying occupations and of various ages. I intermingle them at the table—inspiring cross conversation for more stimulating and less "business"-oriented parties.

Unless parties are large, such as an open house or cocktail party, I generally telephone my guests to invite them. That way I get an instant response and don't have to follow up with calls. Once your party reaches 15 to 20 guests, however, I suggest sending out invitations. If I feel creative and have some time, I make my own invitations with marker pens on heavy white card stock. If not, I buy the simplest invitations available and fill in as necessary. I also send one to myself to make sure the mail gets through properly.

I find organization the key to successful entertaining. I write out a daily schedule of chores—those done ahead of time and those left for the last minute. I even keep a record of party menus so that repeat guests don't get repeat meals. I go through each recipe carefully, listing the necessary ingredients—including all the extras. I check the bar supplies and I freeze or purchase extra ice. I check on flowers or arrange to invade a neighbor's garden. I check my staples to be sure there is enough oil, vinegar, broth, coffee, tea, seasonings, and other necessities in the cupboard. I check the house for repairs and special cleaning jobs. (Now is the time to tackle those washing and dusting chores you keep putting off!) I freeze the dessert or any part of the meal that can be prepared earlier. I try to do as much in advance so I leave myself time to relax for a few hours just before the party.

After I've gotten organized, I can begin to set the scene. I clear out space in my living room, dining room, or bedroom. I move furniture back against the walls to make the floor space larger, especially for large buffets. I get rid of odd clutter and old magazines so that guests can have surfaces on which to set their plates or drinks. If seating space is limited, I place large pillows on the floor. If table space is short, I clear off dressers and bureaus, protect them with padding and cloths, and transform them into tables or bars.

Once the space is clear, I try to make the house as festive as possible by using plants or fresh flowers. In large cities, you can take advantage of inexpensive flower markets which open *very* early in the morning. I always enjoy the trip to the flower mart, and I have a good time creating my own arrangements by simply combining odd groups of flowers in vases, bowls, or even an old coffee urn. I own a few "frogs"—those wonderful porcupine-like devices that easily hold flowers at the base of a bowl. You can also lay a fresh flower at each guest's place or garnish all types of dishes with one rose, tulip, or whatever. When fresh flowers are unavailable, I substitute dried flowers, such as a big bowl of baby's breath or even brightly colored paper flowers. Silk flowers are another alternative, though typically more expensive.

When setting up any centerpiece, my rule of thumb is *Keep it low!* Guests shouldn't have to crane their necks to talk across the table. If you are using a centerpiece on a buffet, it should be low enough so that guests don't knock it over in their enthusiasm to get to the food. Centerpieces can be as simple as a bowl of apples combined with walnuts, a basket of vegetables, a collection of toys, or a bunch of balloons. The important thing is to make it pretty and colorful, yet not so massive that it distracts from the food. As another option, I lay fresh greens down the center of the table and reserve a few to garnish large platters and serving dishes.

The next step is setting the table. What I don't own myself I can generally borrow from my friends or neighbors. A solid white cloth always makes a table look elegant. I own a permanent-press one that saves time and money. I mix and match colorful plates. You don't need a perfect set of china, flatware, or glassware. I intermingle place mats, tie up glasses with napkins, or wrap silver with colorful ribbons to disguise mismatched sets. I prefer extra large napkins—actually I like to use colorful bandanas, especially for buffets. If the occasion is formal, I tie up the cutlery in the bandana and wrap it with white ribbon topped off with a sprig of baby's breath. For an informal party, I tie up the napkins with colorful yarn.

Party-style paper plates may appear to be both cheap and convenient but are actually expensive and ungainly. They're fine to use on a picnic, but when used in a buffet they become soggy, unattractive, and unmanageable for guests. Keep paper plates for outdoors, where they serve a great function.

Place mats are useful but large napkins, opened and laid flat, can substitute. They are especially eye-arresting if set down in an interesting geometric pattern over a tablecloth. This idea is particularly practical if you have an old cloth that you love which shows wear or tear from previous parties. I find baskets also extremely useful. I line them with foil, plastic, or napkins and fill them with breads, appetizers, or bowls of salads. The wicker ones are inexpensive, light, and decorative.

CHAPTER ELEVEN

BIG SPLASHES

1. **Carbo-Loading Pasta Party**
   Spaghetti all'Amatriciana
   Fusilli with Spinach and Cream
   Insalata di Mare con Farfalle
   *Toasted Sourdough Bread
   Biscuit Tortoni

2. **Open House Championship**
   Chili Party
   LBG's Salsa
   Easiest Championship Chili
   Sour Cream Corn Bread
   Spicy Tomato Salad
   Heavenly Caramel-Pecan Squares
   Cookie Crunch

3. **Pitch-In Paella Dinner**
   White Sangria
   Sour Cream-Avocado Dip
   Paella
   Green Salad with Lime Dressing
   Make-It-Easy Flan

4. **Guess Who's Coming to**
   Dinner
   Tossed Salad with Pine Nuts and
   Mushrooms
   Scallops of Veal in Madeira Sauce
   Brown Rice Primavera
   Cheesecake Pie

* Not a recipe

I CONSIDER A BIG SPLASH to be any major occasion—that special time when I want to toss a party to celebrate a birthday, a bridal shower, an open house, the night before a big race, or even a wonderfully special intimate dinner for four. We all know that holidays are big splashes, but other events equally deserve special festivities. The last section of this book is devoted to these important and unique occasions.

Each of the Make-It-Easy menus in this chapter is presented with a combination of food, music, decor, and ambience—all tied together with a theme.

The *Carbo-Loading Pasta Party* stresses carbohydrates in an effort to fuel the runners for the upcoming race. It offers three pasta dishes—two hot and one cold. The pasta suggests an Italian motif; red, green, and white, the colors of the Italian flag, set the decor to create an evening that becomes a perfect excuse to gorge on pasta in a casual setting.

The *Open House Championship Chili Party* is a splash prepared beforehand. When I expect a large group, I cook as much as possible in advance. Buffet-style is the easiest to handle, and I stick to one-fork recipes, chili, salad, and corn bread, so guests don't have to balance plates in their laps.

The *Pitch-in Paella Dinner* is an "in-the-kitchen participation party." Guests are invited to work and eat. A number of dishes lend themselves to this kind of warm and special evening; I've chosen Paella for the book since many can help while sipping refreshing White Sangria and nibbling on a little avocado dip. Everyone feels satisfied with his or her contribution—and the results.

Whether your big splash is an all-out party for a crowd or an elegant dinner for four to impress the boss, it requires advance thought and careful planning. Prepare lists for shopping, preparation chores, and table settings. Accomplish as much as possible in advance. Once carefully planned, these Make-It-Easy splashes become celebrations to remember.

Carbo-Loading Pasta Party

SERVES: 6–8
Spaghetti all'Amatriciana
Fusilli with Spinach
Insalata di Mare con Farfalle (Pasta Seafood Salad)
*Toasted Sourdough Bread
Biscuit Tortoni

A race soon to follow is a great excuse for a pasta party. Runners need lots of carbohydrates before any race, whether it's a marathon or only a run around the park. So here are three different pasta dishes and a sweet dessert. (A tossed green salad with vinaigrette dressing can be offered as well for nonrunners who don't need a high-carbohydrate meal.) Pasta and Italy go hand in hand; the Italian theme makes this an easy, enjoyable, and colorful send-off even for those who only plan to watch the race.

Echo the three colors of the Italian flag with an amusing centerpiece made of bundles of dried white or green spaghetti tied with red ribbons. Place the bundles in glass jars, bottles, canisters, vases, boxes, decorated tomato cans, or any attractive containers. Arrange them in the center of the table bunched together, with a few of the bunches at different heights. For a variation, you might mix different-colored dried pastas, such as carrot, beet, pumpkin, tomato, or herb, in these "spaghetti bouquets," or tie them up with brand-new colored sneaker laces instead of ribbons.

Sneaker laces can also tie up your napkins in place of napkin rings. Or, to accent the Italian theme, roll up the napkins and slip them through manicotti shells (uncooked, of course!).

Continue the tricolor Italian theme by serving the red Spaghetti and the green Fusilli in white bowls. Pile the Sourdough Bread in a basket lined with a red or green napkin—or two napkins, one in each color. Or use any red and white checkered or patterned cloth, even a colorful clean dish towel.

Supportive handmade banners, running posters, racing T-shirts, or old racing numbers are great ways to liven up the walls. And if people already have their numbers for the race, why not use them on place cards, too? Energize the atmosphere with some upbeat background music, like the theme from *Rocky*, and organize a quick stretch class before dinner.

Serve the two hot pastas at the last minute. The sauces can be assembled easily in advance. Then all you have to do is boil the pasta, top with the steamy hot sauces, and serve alongside the chilled seafood-and-pasta salad.

Spaghetti all'Amatriciana

SERVES: 6–8
Preparation time: 10–15 minutes
Cooking time: 35–40 minutes

This Italian specialty takes it name from the town of Amatrice, in the Sabine Hills near Rome. It is traditionally prepared in Italy with *pancetta*, Italian bacon. My version uses regular bacon, but if the salt-cured pancetta found in Italian grocery stores is available, use it for an authentic Italian taste.

The Ingredients:

    12 thin slices bacon, diced (or 8 thick slices bacon)
     1 large onion, finely chopped

  1 28-ounce can crushed tomatoes packed in puree (I use
Progresso brand)
½–1 teaspoon red pepper flakes
Salt to taste
1½ pounds spaghetti
Garnish: Freshly grated Parmesan cheese

The Steps:
1. In large skillet, sauté bacon over medium-high heat until it just begins to brown; drain off all but 2 tablespoons fat.
2. Add onion, and continue to sauté until bacon and onion turn lightly golden, stirring occasionally.
3. Add tomatoes, red pepper flakes, and salt; cook uncovered over medium-low heat for 20–25 minutes, stirring often.
4. Meanwhile, bring large pot of salted water to a boil and cook pasta just until *al dente*; drain.
5. Place cooked pasta in large bowl and immediately toss with sauce; sprinkle with cheese and serve at once, with extra grated cheese on the side.

Variations:
Parmesan and Romano cheese can be used, as a garnish alone or in combination.

Fettucine or other thick long noodles can be substituted for spaghetti.

If tomatoes packed in puree are unavailable, use regular whole juice-packed tomatoes; chop, drain off most of the liquid. Return tomatoes to can, and fill to the top with canned tomato puree.

Make-It-Easy Tip:
√ To freeze bacon easily, lay strips flat, slice after slice, on waxed or freezer paper; roll up, place in a plastic bag, and store in freezer. When ready to use, unroll, peel off slices, and cut easily by making a pile of frozen bacon slices; then dice with sharp knife or even kitchen scissors.

Fusilli with Spinach and Cream

SERVES: 6–8
Preparation Time: 10 minutes
Cooking Time: 10–15 minutes

Any type of short tubular or twisted pasta such as *penne*, small shells, or even *ziti* can be used for this pasta dish.

The Ingredients:

       4 tablespoons (½ stick) unsalted butter
       ½ cup finely chopped scallions (green and white parts included)
       2 10-ounce packages frozen chopped spinach, thawed and
          thoroughly squeezed dry
       1 cup whole-milk ricotta cheese
    1¾ cups heavy cream
       ½ teaspoon nutmeg
          Salt and freshly ground pepper to taste
    1½ pounds fusilli or similarly shaped pasta
       1 cup freshly grated Parmesan cheese
          Garnish: Toasted pine nuts, freshly grated Parmesan cheese

The Steps:

1. Heat butter in large nonaluminum saucepan and sauté scallions over medium heat until just soft, but not brown.
2. Add spinach and toss well; add ricotta and stir to combine.
3. Add cream, nutmeg, salt, and pepper and continue to cook over medium heat until sauce thickens.
4. Meanwhile, cook pasta in salted boiling water until *al dente*; drain.
5. Toss hot pasta with sauce and cheese; serve immediately, garnished with pine nuts and extra cheese.

Variation:

1 cup chopped mushrooms can be added with scallions, but increase butter to 5–6 tablespoons since mushrooms will absorb the fat.

Make-It-Easy Tips:
√ The cheese is added at the end to avoid a stringy texture.
√ A nonaluminum saucepan is advised because when cooking spinach in aluminum pots, a chemical reaction occurs that results in a slightly metallic taste.

Insalata di Mare con Farfalle (Seafood Salad with Bow-Tie-Shaped Pasta)

SERVES: 6–8
Preparation time: 20 minutes
Cooking time: 8–10 minutes or until pasta is tender
Chilling time: 2–3 hours

This pasta salad should be served the same day it is prepared, or possibly the next day, since the cooked seafood will not keep long.

The Ingredients:
 1 pound small spaghetti twists (*farfalle* or *farfallette*)
 2 tablespoons olive oil
6–8 ounces fresh crabmeat or one 6-ounce package frozen crabmeat, thawed and flaked
 1 pound tiny bay shrimp
 6 scallions (green and white parts included), finely minced
 4 stalks celery, finely chopped

Dressing:
 1½ cups mayonnaise
 ¼ cup chili sauce
 1 tablespoon fresh lemon juice
 1 teaspoon celery seed
 Salt and freshly ground white pepper to taste

 Garnish: Freshly chopped chives or scallion stalks

The Steps:

1. Cook pasta in boiling salted water, drain, and toss with olive oil to prevent sticking.
2. Place seafood in large bowl; top with scallions and celery.
3. Combine dressing ingredients in small bowl; whisk until smooth and toss with seafood.
4. Add cooked pasta, continue to toss; cover and chill for 2–3 hours.
5. Taste for seasonings, adjust with salt and pepper, and garnish with chopped chives or scallions.

Variations:

Serve the salad as an appetizer or main course salad.

If fresh or frozen crabmeat is unavailable, substitute canned crab-meat soaked in very cold water to remove any trace of tinny taste.

Cold cooked fish, such as flounder, snapper, or even the new, popular orange roughy can be substituted for the more expensive crabmeat.

Make-It-Easy Tips:

√ Pasta salad must be tasted after chilling since cold diminishes the intensity of the seasoning.

√ Even if crabmeat is frozen or canned, always pick through to detect pieces of shell before serving.

Biscuit Tortoni

SERVES: 8
Preparation time: 10–15 minutes
Chilling time: 1 hour or until ready to use.

A cooling, refreshing finish to a pasta dinner.

The Ingredients:

1 cup crushed almond macaroons (I use the Italian Ameretti di Saronna)
⅓ cup chopped almonds, toasted
3 tablespoons unsalted butter, melted
1 teaspoon almond extract
3 pints vanilla ice cream, slightly softened
1 12-ounce jar apricot preserves.

The Steps:

1. Line an 8″-square pan with aluminum foil, with overlapping edges.
2. Mix together macaroons, almonds, butter, and extract. Reserve ¼ cup mixture for topping. Sprinkle half of remaining mixture on bottom of pan.
3. Spoon half of ice cream over crumbs; drizzle with half the preserves; sprinkle with remaining half of crumb mixture.
4. Repeat ice cream and preserve layers; top with reserved ¼ cup crumbs. Freeze 1 hour, or until ready to use.
5. When ready to serve, pull out foil, cut into squares, and serve immediately.

Make-It-Easy Tips:

√ To quickly toast almonds, brown in toaster-oven or broil 4″–6″ from heat source, watching carefully.
√ For longer storage, place the finished Tortoni in a large food storage bag, tie closed, and freeze.

Open House Championship Chili Party

SERVES: 20
LBG's Salsa
Easiest Championship Chili
Sour Cream Corn Bread
Spicy Tomato Salad
Heavenly Caramel-Pecan Squares
Cookie Crunch

Housewarmings, celebrations, or holidays of any kind can mean a day full of guests dropping in. Surprise them with this hearty buffet menu that has a Southwestern flair.

To decorate, create a centerpiece of colorful paper Mexican flowers, or even fresh flowers, in a bowl or on a tray surrounded by clusters of small clay or earthenware pots of cactus plants. Ceramic tiles used as trivets add a dash of the Spanish-mission look. For the cowboy connection, a multi-color assortment of bright bandanas makes unusual napkins.

First on the buffet come napkins and cutlery. Fold the bandanas into triangles and lay them overlapping in a circle, like a big pinwheel. Slip a fork into the fold of each. Or roll up the forks in the bandanas, securing them with twine or rope tied like miniature lariats. Better yet, combine both styles—with a basket or clay pot full of bandana-wrapped forks, and extra napkins in a circle around it.

Since this is a large party, invitations are necessary. Have them reflect the party theme by drawing brightly colored Mexican flowers with marker pens on heavy white card stock. Or, for a great idea for a housewarming party, take Polaroids of your house, attach them to white card stock, and send them as postcard invitations!

Start your party off with piquant spicy salsa. It keeps for weeks in the refrigerator, so don't worry about making too much. Served with chips or even raw, cut-up vegetables, it makes great, easy hors d'oeuvres.

The main dish is thick, red chili. Serve it from an electric crockery cooker (crock-pot) to keep it steamy, or use an earthenware bean pot or casserole to retain heat. Cups or mugs for the chili balance easily on a plate. Arrange them in a pretty, geometric pattern on the table next to the pot. This chili freezes well—either in advance for your party, or as leftovers when the party's over.

The Spicy Tomato Salad adds even more color. It's one of those salads that's made to marinate, so don't worry about it sitting for hours as guests come and go.

The smooth, subtle taste of the Sour Cream Corn Bread complements the spicy chili and salad. This is a rich variation on an all-American tradition, equally delicious whether baked in muffin tins or in baking pans and cut into chunky squares. A crock of whipped butter, served at room temperature for easy spreading, is the perfect accompaniment for the bread. Serve the Corn Bread squares in an easy-to-make napkin basket. Open two stiffly-starched large napkins and place one on top of the other. Fold into a triangle. Fold the two end corners in, tucking the second one securely into the folds envelope style. Fold back the top flaps and place the napkin basket inside a wicker basket. (See illustration.)

The Heavenly Caramel-Pecan Squares can be frozen in advance, and the Cookie Crunch can be prepared a day or two ahead and kept fresh in a sealed container or plastic bag. Dessert is strictly finger food, so make sure to have lots of extra napkins on hand.

LBG's Salsa

YIELD: 3 cups
Preparation time: 10 minutes

This version of a spicy Mexican salsa is made easy with the use of canned tomatoes and tomato paste. Use the salsa with chips, on omelettes, or as a vegetable topping—wherever spiciness and flavor are needed.

The Ingredients:
  3 tablespoons chopped onions
  3 tablespoons chopped coriander (cilantro)
  2 cloves garlic, minced
  2 long green mild chili peppers, seeded
  2 16-ounce cans whole tomatoes, drained and roughly chopped
  3 tablespoons tomato paste

Salt and freshly ground pepper to taste
Accompaniments: Tortilla chips or raw cut-up vegetables
(carrots, celery, or zucchini sticks)

The Steps:
1. In food processor or blender, chop onion, cilantro, garlic, and chili, pulsating on and off, until just chopped. (DO NOT OVERPROCESS.)
2. Add tomatoes, tomato paste, and salt and pepper to taste; continue to chop just until combined.
3. Serve immediately with chips or raw vegetables, or chill for future use.

Variation:
For hotter version, add spicy chili peppers to taste.

Make-It-Easy Tips:
√ Cilantro, occasionally called Chinese or Mexican parsley, is actually the leaf of the coriander plant. The parsley-like leaves, which have a zesty taste, should be used in moderation, or to taste.
√ Salsa will keep for several weeks in a jar in the refrigerator.
√ Tomato paste is now available in handy tube containers. Simply squeeze out what you need, cap the tube, and store it in the refrigerator for future use.

Easiest Championship Chili

SERVES: 20
Preparation time: 20–25 minutes
Cooking time: 2 hours

My favorite chili is Texas-style—without beans. It can be prepared way in advance and frozen until ready to use.

The Ingredients:
8 tablespoons (1 stick) unsalted butter
4 tablespoons olive oil

8 medium onions, finely chopped
4 large green peppers, finely chopped
8 pounds lean ground beef
2½ cups beer
2 28-ounce cans crushed tomatoes packed in puree
4 cups beef broth
8 cloves garlic, finely chopped
7 tablespoons chili powder
5 teaspoons ground cumin
1½ teaspoons paprika
1½ teaspoons dried oregano, crumbled
1½ teaspoons dried basil, crumbled
1½ teaspoons cayenne pepper, or to taste
1 teaspoon crushed red peppers, or to taste
Salt to taste
Garnish: Sour cream, grated cheddar, chopped onions

The Steps:

1. In large deep skillet or Dutch oven, heat butter and oil; when hot, sauté onion and green pepper over medium heat until golden. Add meat and brown over high heat, stirring until crumbly; drain off fat.
2. Add beer and allow to boil; add remaining ingredients and stir to combine.
3. Bring to a boil, reduce heat, cover, and simmer for 1½–2 hours.
4. Adjust seasonings to taste, adding more hot pepper if desired, and serve hot with garnishes.

Variation:

2–3 cans drained kidney or pinto beans can be added if desired.

If tomatoes packed in puree are unavailable, use regular whole juice-packed tomatoes; chop, drain off most of the liquid. Return tomatoes to can, and fill to the top with canned tomato puree.

Make-It-Easy Tips:

√ It may be necessary to sauté the meat in batches, draining off the excess fat as it accumulates. Once the beer is added, the chili can be transferred to a large stock pot or soup kettle for easy cooking.
√ Ask butcher to grind meat coarsely for chili.
√ The food processor speeds up the chopping process for chili. Just

keep chopping the ingredients without cleaning the work bowl, since it all goes into the same pot.
√ Garlic can be crushed in large amounts with a food processor or blender, covered with a few tablespoons of oil, then stored for several weeks in the refrigerator in a small, tightly capped jar.

Sour Cream Corn Bread

SERVES: 20
Preparation time: 10–15 minutes
Cooking time: 25–30 minutes

The Ingredients:

    3 cups yellow cornmeal
    3 cups all-purpose flour
    6 tablespoons sugar
    3 tablespoons baking powder
 1½ teaspoons salt
 2¼ cups dairy sour cream
 1½ cups whole milk
    6 eggs
  18 tablespoons (2¼ sticks) unsalted butter, melted
      Accompaniment: Whipped sweet butter

The Steps:

1. Preheat oven to 350°. Butter one 9″ x 13″ x 2″ rectangular and one 9″-square baking pan.
2. In large mixing bowl, combine cornmeal, flour, sugar, baking powder, and salt.
3. In separate bowl, whisk together sour cream, milk, and eggs. Gradually add butter and continue to whisk until smooth.
4. Combine dry ingredients with sour cream mixture; pour into prepared pans and bake for 25–30 minutes, or until knife inserted comes out clean.
5. Remove from oven, cut into squares, and serve with whipped sweet butter.

Variation:
Bake batter in muffin tins for 20–25 minutes, or until done.

Make-It-Easy Tip:
√ Stone- or water-ground cornmeal is more nutritious than the processed granulated variety. Since stone-ground only remains fresh a short time, purchase in small quantities.

Spicy Tomato Salad

SERVES: 20
Preparation time: 10–15 minutes
Chilling time: 1–2 hours

The Ingredients:
  12 large tomatoes, stems removed and sliced
   4 medium onions, thinly sliced (sweet Bermuda or sweet red onions are best to use)
   1 large can (6 ounces net weight) pitted black olives (about 40), drained
  ⅓ cup freshly chopped parsley

Dressing:
  ¾ cup olive oil
  ½ cup fresh lemon juice
  2 teaspoons sugar
1½ teaspoons ground cumin
  ¼ teaspoon turmeric
    Salt and freshly ground pepper to taste
    Garnish: Parsley sprigs

The Steps:
1. Place sliced tomatoes on deep platter and intersperse slices of onions. Top with olives and sprinkling of parsley.
2. Combine dressing ingredients in screw-top jar and shake until smooth.
3. Pour dressing over vegetables, cover, and marinate for 1–2 hours in refrigerator.
4. Serve chilled, garnished with parsley sprigs.

Variation:

Pitted ripe green olives can be substituted for black olives, or a combination of both can be used.

Make-It-Easy Tips:

√ Slice raw tomatoes vertically so that the inner pulp holds its shape for salads.

√ Select firm and plump-looking tomatoes with good color. Most tomatoes require further ripening at home. Place away from direct sunlight in a plastic bag with a few holes to allow air to circulate. Once ripened, refrigerate and use within a few days.

Heavenly Caramel-Pecan Squares

YIELD: 48 squares
Preparation time: 20 minutes
Cooking time: 20 minutes

The Ingredients:

2 cups all-purpose flour
1 cup dark brown sugar, firmly packed
4 ounces (1 stick) unsalted butter, softened
1 cup pecan halves
6 ounces (1½ sticks) unsalted butter
⅔ cup dark brown sugar, firmly packed
6 ounces (1 package) semisweet chocolate bits

The Steps:

1. Preheat oven to 350°. Lightly butter a 9" x 13" x 2" baking dish.
2. In food processor or in mixing bowl, combine flour with 1 cup brown sugar and 4 ounces butter; mix until well combined and place in prepared pan.
3. Pat firmly and evenly to form crust, and distribute pecan halves over it evenly.
4. In small saucepan, combine 6 ounces butter with ⅔ cup brown sugar. Cook over medium heat, stirring constantly until entire surface of mixture begins to boil; stir and boil for 1 minute.

5. Spoon hot mixture evenly over pecans and crust and bake for 20 minutes, or until top is bubbly and crust is golden brown.
6. In the meantime, melt chocolate in small saucepan. When cookie dough is baked, drizzle melted chocolate over it; then cool completely before cutting into 1½" squares.

Variation:
Walnut halves can be substituted for pecan halves.

Make-It-Easy Tip:
√ When melting chocolate, never cover the pot; moisture makes the chocolate stiffen.

Cookie Crunch

YIELD: about 24 cookies
Preparation time: 10 minutes
Cooking time: 10–15 minutes

This recipe is bequeathed to me by a friend, Susan Grode. Although graham crackers are associated with children, this recipe changes a child food into wonderful, tasty, crunchy dessert treats.

The Ingredients:
2 packages graham crackers (22 whole crackers), broken up into various sizes
8 ounces (2 sticks) unsalted butter, melted
1 cup sugar mixed with 1 tablespoon cinnamon
1 cup (3¾-ounce package) sliced almonds

The Steps:
1. Preheat oven to 275°.
2. On large cookie sheet or jelly roll pan with sides, place cookie pieces, allowing cookies to touch but not overlap.
3. Drizzle half of melted butter over crackers and sprinkle with half of cinnamon-sugar mixture. Top with half of almonds.
4. Drizzle with remaining butter; then top with remaining cinnamon-sugar and finally almonds.

5. Bake for 10–15 minutes, just until crackers appear soft. Remove from oven; cool 10 minutes before removing from cookie sheet.
6. Break apart and serve.

Variation:

Crumble cookies and use as a topping for ice cream.

Make-It-Easy Tip:

√ Cookies are baked at a low temperature to avoid burning. If your oven temperature tends to be erratic, watch cookies carefully while baking.

Pitch-In Paella Dinner

SERVES: 8
White Sangria
Sour Cream–Avocado Dip
Paella
Green Salad with Lime Dressing
Make-It-Easy Flan

One of the easiest and most enjoyable ways to toss a big splash is to get everyone into the act. This informal dinner takes place right in the kitchen, where the guests play a role in the preparation of the meal.

Everyone has a good time and feels a great sense of accomplishment. The idea is to provide a very relaxed atmosphere for everyone.

An informally set table is ideal for this casual splash. Decorate with brightly colored paper flowers, or assorted fruits or vegetables such as avocados, oranges, and lemons, or even a wreath of red chili peppers to emphasize the Spanish theme. A cream-colored or white cloth can also be used, accented with colorful napkins laid out in a diamond pattern. In the summer, move the Paella party outdoors on a casually set picnic table.

A large pitcher fitted with a long-handled wooden spoon is perfect for the White Sangria. Prepare this and the Sour Cream-Avocado Dip in advance, ready to take the edge off the thirst and appetites of your helpful guests.

Paella is the perfect dish for participatory cooking because the chopping and "prepping" chores can be divided up and then the final assembly completed at the last minute. The chicken should be started first while another group can be dicing the ham. Still another few can be cleaning the seafood and vegetables. The Paella can be served in a traditional Paella pan, a large deep skillet, or even a wok.

The Green Salad can be prepared in a glass or ceramic bowl and tossed at the last minute. Place the salad, bowl and all, in a large glazed terracotta plant saucer for a Latin presentation. Little terra-cotta saucers can also be used as ashtrays or even liners for the individual desserts.

The Flan is best prepared a day in advance and allowed to chill. Unmold an hour or so before guests arrive and continue to chill. Orange segments make an attractive garnish for this cooling dessert.

This is a casual and fun splash to be enjoyed by adults or even teenagers. For the younger set, substitute a fruit punch for the Sangria.

White Sangria

SERVES: 8
Preparation time: 15 minutes
Chilling time: 4–6 hours or overnight

White Sangria is a light and refreshing drink to serve in the summer or year round for those who prefer white wine.

The Ingredients:
    2 bottles dry white wine
    ¼ cup Grand Marnier (or brandy)
    ¼ cup superfine sugar
    10 strawberries, hulled and halved
    1 navel orange, unpeeled and sliced
    1 lemon, unpeeled and sliced
    1 ripe pear, cored and sliced
    1 peach, peeled and sliced
    ½ cup seedless grapes
    2–3 cups chilled sparkling water
    Ice
    Garnish: Mint sprigs

The Steps:

1. Combine wine, Grand Marnier (or brandy), and sugar in a very tall pitcher and stir with long wooden spoon.
2. Add cut-up fruits, cover with plastic wrap, and allow to marinate in refrigerator for 4–6 hours or overnight.
3. At serving time, add chilled sparkling water and ice; serve in large goblets, topping each serving with sprig of mint.

Variation:

Add sparkling water to taste. I prefer the Sangria without the bubbles, but many prefer it with them.

Make-It-Easy Tips:

√ Superfine sugar is used because it dissolves faster in cold liquid. Regular sugar may be used if superfine is unobtainable.

√ To peel a peach easily, drop into boiling water for 1 minute, remove, and the peel will slide off easily. A few frozen unsweetened peaches may be substituted.

√ Ice cubes, frozen with a slice of lemon peel, make an attractive addition to the Sangria.

Sour Cream–Avocado Dip

YIELD: 3 cups
Preparation time: 10 minutes
Chilling time: 1 hour

The Ingredients:

2 ripe avocados
1¾ cup dairy sour cream
2 ripe tomatoes, roughly chopped
4 scallions, roughly chopped (green and white parts included)
4 teaspoons lemon or lime juice
4–5 shakes Tabasco, or to taste
   Accompaniments: Nacho Chips or vegetable crudités (raw vegetables for dipping).

The Steps:

1. In food processor or blender, combine avocado with sour cream, tomato, scallions, lemon juice, and Tabasco and blend until smooth. Chill for 1 hour.
2. Serve chilled sauce with nacho chips or vegetable crudités.

Variations:

The sauce may be used as a topping for pita bread that has been stuffed with chopped tomatoes, cheese, chicken, and lettuce for a lunch or supper dish.

It can also be used on tacos or tostados as a substitute for guacamole.

Make-It-Easy Tips:

√ The sauce should be prepared the same day it is to be served.

√ Avocados will ripen in a brown paper bag or dark place in a few days. Once ripe, refrigerate until ready to use.

Paella

SERVES: 8
Preparation time: 20–25 minutes
Cooking time: 25–35 minutes

Paella, a saffron-flavored rice dish from Spain, is a mixture of many in-gredients—chicken, meat, seafood, and vegetables. This Make-It-Easy version can be varied with additional seafood, sausages, and vegetables, as you like, since there is no one traditional Paella. Each region in Spain emphasizes the ingredients that are most readily available.

The Ingredients:

4–5 tablespoons good olive oil
1 large onion, roughly chopped
1 green or red pepper, sliced thinly into julienne strips
1 teaspoon freshly minced garlic
8–10 chicken thighs (or combination of thighs and breasts, cut into pieces)
2 cups raw rice

½ cup dry white wine or dry vermouth
1 cup cubed baked ham (or 2 broiled and sliced *chorizos*—
    Spanish sausages; or 2 broiled and sliced sweet or hot
    Italian sausages)
½–1 teaspoon saffron flowers (or a healthy pinch of saffron
    powder), to taste
3½ cups chicken broth, hot
½ teaspoon paprika
Pinch of thyme
Pinch of ground coriander seed (optional)
1 dozen cherrystone clams, scrubbed
8–10 medium shrimp, shelled and deveined
8–10 frozen artichokes, thawed
1 cup frozen peas, thawed
Garnish: Freshly chopped parsley, pimiento strips

The Steps:

1. Heat 3 tablespoons of olive oil in very large deep skillet and sauté onions and peppers over medium heat, until soft. Add garlic, stir well, and remove to platter with slotted spoon.
2. Add 1–2 tablespoons olive oil and sauté the chicken over medium-high heat until golden. Remove and set aside with cooked vegetables.
3. Remove skillet from heat; add rice and stir well to coat grains with oil.
4. Return skillet to high heat, immediately add wine, and stir well to deglaze pan, incorporating browned particles from bottom of pan into sauce.
5. Return chicken and vegetables to pan and add ham or sausages. Dissolve saffron in hot broth and pour into pan. Bring to boil, add paprika, thyme, and optional coriander; cover and simmer for 10 minutes.
6. Add clams; recover and cook an additional 10 minutes.
7. Add shrimp, artichokes, and peas, and continue to cook until shrimp are pink, clams are totally open, and rice is tender.
8. Taste for seasonings, adjust as necessary, and serve Paella immediately, garnished with freshly chopped parsley and strips of pimientos.

Variations:

Additional seafood such as scallops, lobsters, snails, or mussels may be added to the Paella, depending on cost factors. Add seafood gradually, timing accordingly.

Sautéed pork, bacon, or other ethnic sausages (such as Polish *kielbasa* or Portuguese *linguica*) may be substituted for the ham.

Peas may be omitted if desired or replaced by other green vegetables.

Saffron, the world's most expensive herb, is made from dried orangered stigmas of autumn crocuses. To avoid bitterness, leaf saffron is first dissolved in liquid. Less expensive powdered saffron may be substituted. Mexican saffron, *achiote*, can be used as a substitute for color but not for flavor. The saffron available at local East Indian groceries is more economical than the kind available in spice departments of markets.

Make-It-Easy Tips:

√ The garlic is not sautéed to avoid the bitter taste that often accompanies browned garlic.

√ If using sausages, prick all over and boil or broil them to release excess grease; then slice.

√ To easily clean clams, place in a bowl of cold water with a sprinkling of oatmeal. The clams will eat the oatmeal and spit it out along with any accumulated sand and dirt.

√ Remember, do not eat unopened clams since it is likely that they were not alive before cooking and therefore might be spoiled.

Green Salad with Lime Dressing

SERVES: 8
Preparation time: 10 minutes

The Ingredients:

2 large heads romaine lettuce, washed and dried
½ pound piece jicama, peeled and cut into matchstick strips

Dressing:

¾ cup olive oil
¼ cup fresh lime juice
2 tablespoons sugar

¼ teaspoon ground ginger
Pinch of cayenne
Salt and freshly ground pepper to taste

The Steps:
1. Break lettuce into small pieces and place in salad bowl; top with jicama.
2. Combine dressing ingredients together in screw-top jar and shake.
3. Pour dressing over greens, toss well, and serve immediately.

Variations:
Substitute sliced water chestnuts or shredded Jerusalem artichokes (sunchokes) for jicama
Substitute lemons and lemon juice for limes and lime juice.

Make-It-Easy Tips:
√ Store limes away from direct light. If yellowing, use as quickly as possible; the juice will still be good.
√ Jicama is a Mexican root vegetable that resembles a potato yet tastes like a sweet water chestnut. Recently it has become popular as a *crudité*, a raw vegetable used with dips.

Make-It-Easy Flan

SERVES: 8
Preparation time: 15 minutes
Cooking time: 35 minutes
Chilling time: 4–6 hours or overnight

A traditional flan has a caramelized top. Here there is a sprinkling of brown sugar, which melts into the creamy and delicious finished dessert.

The Ingredients:
8 teaspoons brown sugar
2 cups whole milk
2 cups half-and-half
6 eggs

½ cup sugar
½ teaspoon salt
2 teaspoons vanilla extract

The Steps:

1. Preheat oven to 350°. Lightly butter 8 oven-proof custard cups.
2. Place 1 teaspoon brown sugar in the bottom of each custard cup.
3. In medium saucepan, heat milk and half-and-half together just until bubbles form around edges of pan.
4. In large bowl, beat eggs slightly with whisk or electric beater. Add sugar, salt, and vanilla.
5. Add small amount of hot milk to eggs, whisking constantly; gradually add remaining milk and whisk until smooth.
6. Pour into prepared dishes, set them in larger roasting pan, pour boiling water to ½″ in bottom of pan, and bake for 30–35 minutes, or until inserted knife comes out clean.
7. Remove from pan, allow to cool, and then chill for 4–6 hours or overnight.
8. To serve, run small knife around edge of dishes to loosen. Invert on small plates, and shake gently to loosen, allowing brown sugar to cover top and sides.

Variations:

Flan can be served as is from the cups, without inverting.

A real caramel topping can be prepared by heating 1 cup brown sugar in a heavy saucepan over medium-high heat stirring constantly until a syrup is formed. Quickly pour the syrup into little dishes, using pot holders to hold them and protect your hands from the hot syrup. Proceed with custard.

Flan can also be prepared in a 9″ pie plate or round baking dish; cook for 5–10 minutes longer, or until set.

Make-It-Easy Tips:

√ A few tablespoons of the hot milk must be added to the egg mixture in Step #5 to prevent curdling of the eggs. Once they are warmed, the rest of the hot milk can be safely added.

√ The water bath in Step #6, also called a *bain marie*, promotes even cooking.

√ Time baking carefully. Too long a time and the custard will be curdled; too short, and the custard will not set.

Guess Who's Coming to Dinner

SERVES: 4
Tossed Salad with Pine Nuts and Mushrooms
Scallops of Veal in Madeira Sauce
Brown Rice Primavera
Cheesecake Pie

"Elegant and understated" is the theme for this dinner. It's an occasion for bringing out the good china and silverware, finest tablecloth and napkins, and sparkling glassware. A simple and lovely floral arrangement makes a fitting centerpiece, especially when placed atop a mirror to reflect its color.

Napkins may be folded simply, but napkin rings are an elegant touch. As a pretty and quick alternative, fold both ends of the napkins into the center, leaving a ½″ opening. Accordian-pleat from left side in 1½″ fold. Secure them in the center with a decorative clip, ring, or festive colored ribbon, and then flare into a flower shape. (See illustration.)

The cheesecake for dessert is made well ahead of time, and the first steps for the salad can also be completed in advance. Assembling the ingredients for the veal and rice early will allow you to prepare them quickly and easily. Only the salad should be wilted in this menu, not the cook!

Flower
1. Fold both ends in toward the center leaving a ½″ opening.   **2.** Crease, accordion-style from left in 1½″ pleats.   **3.** Secure in center with decorative clip or ribbon; flare into a circle.

The veal is pounded, seasoned, and floured before dinner. The salad is served as a first course while the rice finishes simmering. After the salad, let people know you're about to prepare something special—which you are—and will be back in just a few minutes—which you will. Guests and your spouse or dinner companion will have a little time to chat. At this time, add the broccoli to the rice. While it cooks, continue preparing the veal through Step #4. Toss the final ingredients into the rice, and finish cooking the veal while the rice sets. In 5 minutes or less, the rice and veal are ready for the serving dish and platter. Arrange them attractively, and prepare for your guests to be thoroughly delighted.

Tossed Salad with Pine Nuts and Mushrooms

SERVES: 4–6
Preparation time: 15 minutes
Cooking time: 5–10 minutes

The unique flavor of raspberry vinegar makes this "warm" or "wilted" salad a wonderful first course as well as a side dish.

The Ingredients:
   2 heads Boston lettuce
   ½ cup sliced water chestnuts
   ⅓ cup walnut oil
   ½ pound mushrooms, thinly sliced
   ¼ pound pine nuts
   ⅓ cup raspberry vinegar
   Salt and freshly ground pepper to taste

The Steps:
   1. Wash and dry lettuce and break into small pieces. Slice water chestnuts and place in salad bowl atop lettuce.
   2. In skillet, heat 2 tablespoons oil and sauté mushrooms for 2 minutes or until lightly golden.
   3. Add pine nuts and continue to sauté until golden brown.

4. Remove from heat; add remaining oil and raspberry vinegar, stirring constantly.
5. Season to taste with salt and pepper; pour over lettuce and serve immediately.

Variations:
As substitutions: for Boston lettuce, use romaine or leaf lettuce; for water chestnuts, use jicama or Jerusalem artichokes (sunchokes); for walnut oil, use almond, hazelnut, or olive oil; for pine nuts, use slivered almonds.

Make-It-Easy Tips:
√ To prepare in advance: Chill lettuce in the morning. Sauté nuts and mushrooms an hour before, and reheat before deglazing with vinegar.
√ Select mushrooms with closed caps and no exposed gills. Brush them or wipe them clean with acidulated water (water plus lemon juice). Dry thoroughly before sautéing.

Scallops of Veal in Madeira Sauce

SERVES: 4
Preparation time: 10 minutes
Cooking time: 7–10 minutes

The high cost of veal reserves this elegant dinner for very special occasions. Pounded chicken breasts are a wonderful and less expensive alternative. Remember that this is a last-minute recipe. Assemble all ingredients in advance and be ready to serve immediately.

The Ingredients:
1½ pounds veal scallopine, sliced ⅜" thick
    Salt and freshly ground pepper to taste
½ cup all-purpose flour
2 tablespoons unsalted butter
2 tablespoons olive oil
½ cup Madeira wine

¼ cup chicken or beef broth
2 tablespoons unsalted butter
1 teaspoon lemon juice
Garnish: Freshly chopped parsley

The Steps:

1. Place veal between layers of waxed paper and pound with mallet, meat pounder, or side of cleaver until ¼" thick.
2. Sprinkle with salt and pepper; lightly dip into flour, shaking off excess.
3. In large skillet, melt 2 tablespoons butter and oil together. When butter is hot and beginning to lightly brown, sauté single layer of veal scaloppine; brown 2–3 minutes on each side; remove to platter and brown remaining veal.
4. When all veal has been browned and removed, pour off all but a light film of fat and add Madeira, stirring and scraping up browned particles from bottom of skillet. Add broth and continue to cook over high heat for 1–2 minutes, or until sauce thickens.
5. Return veal to skillet, reduce heat to low and cook 1–2 minutes, just to warm scallopine, basting with sauce.
6. Remove scaloppine to platter with slotted spatula and arrange attractively. Add 2 tablespoons butter and lemon juice to sauce remaining in skillet, stir well to combine, and adjust with salt and pepper to taste. Serve immediately, garnished with freshly chopped parsley.

Variations:

Sautéed sliced mushrooms can be added to taste.
Dry Marsala or even port wine can be substituted for Madeira.

Make-It-Easy Tips:

√ The butcher will often agree to pound the veal for you. Make sure it has been pounded to ¼" so that it needs only a short amount of cooking to keep it tender.
√ When browning veal, watch it carefully, regulating heat so that the veal browns without burning.

Brown Rice Primavera

SERVES: 4–6
Preparation time: 15–20 minutes
Cooking time: 50 minutes

The Ingredients:

1 tablespoon unsalted butter
1 tablespoon olive or vegetable oil
1 clove garlic, minced
1⅓ cups chicken broth
1 cup water
¼ teaspoon nutmeg
Salt and freshly ground pepper to taste
1 cup raw brown rice
2 cups tiny broccoli florets
1 cup cherry tomatoes, sliced in half
Garnish: Freshly grated Parmesan cheese

The Steps:

1. In large saucepan, heat butter and oil together; add garlic and sauté over low heat for only 1–2 minutes, until just soft.
2. Add broth, water, nutmeg, salt, and pepper. Bring to a boil, add rice, cover tightly, reduce heat, and cook over low heat for 40 minutes.
3. Place broccoli on top, cover, and continue to cook until all liquid has been absorbed, about 10 minutes.
4. Stir in tomatoes, cover to heat through, and serve hot, garnished with Parmesan cheese.

Variations:

Sliced mushrooms, grated carrots, julienned zucchini, minced scallions, or other chopped vegetables can be added to taste.
Beef or vegetable broth can be substituted for chicken broth.
Grated Monterey Jack cheese, Cheddar cheese, or even Swiss cheese can be used as alternative garnishes.

Make-It-Easy Tips:
√ Brown rice requires more liquid during the cooking process because of the longer cooking time.

√ Buy brown rice in small quantities since its shelf life is shorter than white rice's, due to the oxidation of the bran layer that covers the grain. For long storage, refrigerate.

Cheesecake Pie

YIELD: One 9″ pie
Preparation time: 10–12 minutes
Cooking time: 35 minutes
Chilling time: 5 hours or overnight

This recipe comes from an acquaintance, Judy Selzer, who finds it easier to bake cheesecake in a pie plate rather than a springform pan.

The Ingredients:

Crust:
    1 cup vanilla wafer crumbs (about 25)
    2 tablespoons unsalted butter, melted
    1 tablespoon sugar

Filling:
    12 ounces cream cheese
    ½ cup sugar
    ½ teaspoon vanilla
    2 eggs

Topping:
    1 cup dairy sour cream
    ¼ cup sugar
    ½ teaspoon vanilla

The Steps:
1. Preheat oven to 350°. Generously butter 9″ pie plate.
2. Combine crust ingredients in small bowl, mix well, and press into bottom and sides of pie plate.

3. With elecric beater or by hand, beat cream cheese with sugar and vanilla. Add eggs, one at a time, beating well after each addition. Pour into prepared crust and bake for 25 minutes or until firm. Cool 5 minutes.
4. Combine topping ingredients and mix well until smooth and creamy; place atop baked cheesecake and bake 10 minutes longer.
5. Remove from oven, cool, and chill at least 5 hours or overnight.
6. Serve cut in wedges.

Variation:

Crumb crust can be varied to taste. Substitute zwiebacks, graham crackers, gingersnaps, or even chocolate wafer crumbs.

Make-It-Easy Tips:

√ Cream cheesecake freezes successfully, wrapped securely.
√ The easiest method of slicing cheesecake is with dental floss. Take a long strand of tautly held waxed or unwaxed floss (not mint-flavored) and press it through the cake; pull it out without pulling it up again.

CHAPTER TWELVE

INEXPENSIVE FEASTS

1. **Hearty Winter Soup Supper**
   Zuppa Salsiccie
   Potage Crécy (Cream of Carrot Soup)
   Cheese Wafers
   *Crusty French Bread
   Old-Fashioned Gingerbread
   Whipped Apple Cream

2. **Leftovers for the Connoisseur**
   Leftover Vegetable Soup
   Curried Chicken
   Apricot Chutney
   *Plain White Rice
   Cucumbers in Sour Cream
   Banana Mousse

3. **Far Eastern Delights**
   Kung Pao Chicken
   *White Rice
   Spicy Chilled Chinese Noodles
   Stir-Fried Zucchini and Water
     Chestnuts
   (It Doesn't Matter That It Isn't
     Chinese) Strawberry Fool

4. **Limited-Funds Feast**
   The Ultimate Casserole
   Radish, Cucumber, and Fennel
     Salad
   Onion Bread
   Make Your Own Sundaes
   Hot Fudge Sauce/Hot Butterscotch
     Sauce

   * Not a recipe

5. **Country Fare**
   Tortilla Baskets
   Addy's Chicken
   Green Bean and Onion Salad
   *Bread
   Light Lemon Pie

THE MENUS IN THIS SECTION are designed to utilize economical ingredients, transforming them into festive events. Memorable parties need not be expensive affairs.

The *Hearty Winter Soup Supper* features a whole meal in your most attractive soup bowls or mugs—easy, inexpensive, and, best of all, comforting on a cold winter's night. Soup is a great filler-upper. I offer three in the other menus in this section, allowing for smaller main-course portions. Remember, if you prepare soup ahead and leave it in the refrigerator for any length of time, simmer it for at least 5 minutes every 2 or 3 days to keep it fresh. Soups freeze beautifully as well, so double quantities to save on extra chores.

There are other ways to economize without sacrificing quality. For ex-.mple, *Leftovers for the Connoisseur* revitalizes cooked vegetables in soup, poultry in curry, and an abundance of bananas in Banana Mousse. *The Limited-Funds Feast* capitalizes on one of my favorite inexpensive ingredients—pasta. Pasta is so versatile it can stretch the smallest amount of meat into a nutritious main course.

There are many tried-and-true tips on how to save money at the supermarket, but they are worth repeating because they work. Try to consolidate marketing trips to save on gas and avoid impulse purchases. Buy "on special" but investigate prices in the weekly food section of your local newspapers to save costly trips and Make-It-Easy on your shopping chores. Also remember to shop after eating rather than before. It's obviously easier to give in to temptation if you're hungry.

When purchasing produce, look for locally grown vegetables and fruits, which are fresher, tastier, and less expensive than the shipped varieties. Buy produce in season and ask the greengrocer for advice about what's best. If, for example, green beans are unavailable for the *Country Fare* dinner, by all means substitute broccoli, asparagus, or whatever is in season and freshest. When preparing salads, always make your own dressing. It has the advantages of being both less expensive and free of additives. Made properly, it always tastes infinitely better!

Fortunately, just about everybody likes chicken, and it is the least expensive meat you can use. In this inflation-fighting section, I emphasize its versatility. You will find it in *Far Eastern Delights* as Kung Pao Chicken, as Curried Chicken in *Leftovers for the Connoisseur* and in a one-pot recipe called Addy's Chicken in *Country Fare*. If time and energy permit, buy whole, uncut chickens and chop them yourself. It's quite a money-saver.

When purchasing beef, buy on special and select the leaner meats, which are less expensive and better for your health. Tenderize them in marinades or by long and slow cooking. Slab bacon is much more economical than the sliced variety and can be frozen for future use.

The most important tip in purchasing meats, poultry, or fish at the market is to make friends with the butcher. Very often he or she will be more than happy to cut up a chicken, bone a leg of lamb, or even fillet a fish for no charge at all.

There are some excellent, inexpensive jug wines available. Again, your local wine merchant is the person to turn to for advice. For an extra-special presentation, decant red wine into a carafe a few hours before serving to allow it to "breathe." Chill white wine in a carafe or decanter to keep it icy cold.

Inflation-fighting parties require some easy table-setting tips and clever handiwork to create attractive presentations. Perrier bottles as individual bud vases, tiered plates of desserts, or an edible bread centerpiece are all wonderful ideas to make these menus appealing.

Don't be shy about sharing or borrowing coffee pots, platters, serving pieces, tables, chairs, flowers from a garden, or other necessities. Friends and neighbors are usually delighted to oblige, especially if you offer to reciprocate.

Hearty Winter Soup Supper

SERVES: 8
Zuppa Salsiccie
Potage Crécy
Cheese Wafers
*Crusty French Bread
Old-Fashioned Gingerbread
Whipped Apple Cream

Whether you're warming up winter travelers or skiers, hot soup is a great way to chase away the cold. It's also an economical way to feed a crowd, especially when the budget has been stretched thin by holiday expenses.

Here two hearty and savory soups are served: one meaty, the other creamy vegetable—both rich enough to fill up and warm a large group. The Cheese Wafers and Crusty French Bread lend the perfect crunchy texture to accompany the soups.

You can accent the peasant theme by draping a shawl across the table-cloth. Flowers—fresh, dried, or cloth—will look country-pretty clustered

*Not a recipe

in a pitcher, or here and there in jars or tumblers. Or set candles on a tray or plate and surround them with pinecones.

The Cheese Wafers and sliced Crusty Bread piled in a basket lined with napkins and two tureens full of steamy soup complete the table setting. A crock-pot or bean pot makes a nice substitute for a tureen.

This meal is ideal for buffet serving, since each person needs only a soup spoon for dinner and a teaspoon for dessert. The soup spoons can be rolled up in napkins and tied with yarn, macrame cord, or even burlap twine for a rustic effect. Place them in a basket or a flowerpot to finish off the country look. Serve the soup in mugs on plates large enough to hold the bread. Have extra mugs handy, since people will very likely want to try both soups. And, if your kitchen is large enough, try serving the soup in an attractive pot, kept warming on the range. All the accessories and mugs can be placed alongside or arranged decoratively on a kitchen counter or table.

The Whipped Apple Cream can be prepared an hour or two ahead and chilled. The Zuppa Salsiccie can be made a day earlier and refrigerated or even frozen well in advance. Then simply reheat it while the Potage Crécy simmers, the gingerbread bakes, the French bread toasts, and your whole house fills with the most incredible homemade aromas.

Zuppa Salsiccie

SERVES: 8
Preparation Time: 15 minutes
Cooking time: 1½ hours

This hearty Italian sausage soup has a wonderful spiciness.

The Ingredients:
2 tablespoons olive oil
1 pound hot Italian sausage, sliced in ½" circles
1 pound sweet Italian sausage, sliced in ½" circles
2 large onions, chopped
1 green pepper, chopped
2 cups red wine
1 28-ounce can crushed tomatoes packed in puree

    5 cups canned beef broth
    2 tablespoons freshly chopped parsley
    1 teaspoon finely minced garlic
    ½ teaspoon dried basil, crumbled
    ½ teaspoon dried oregano, crumbled
      Salt and freshly ground pepper to taste
    1 7-ounce package bow-tie noodles
      Garnish: 1–1½ cups freshly grated Parmesan cheese

The Steps:

1. In large deep saucepan or Dutch oven, heat oil and sauté sausages until lightly browned over high heat. Discard excess grease, leaving 2 tablespoons in pan.
2. Add onions and green pepper and sauté until soft, about 5–7 minutes. Add wine and allow to boil for two minutes.
3. Add tomatoes, broth, parsley, garlic basil, oregano, salt, and pepper. Bring to a boil, reduce heat, cover, and simmer slowly for 1 hour.
4. Add noodles, cover, and continue to simmer for 20 minutes or until noodles are tender.
5. Serve in deep soup plates garnished with Parmesan cheese.

Variations:

All hot or all sweet Italian sausages can be substituted for the combination. Polish *kielbasa*, Mexican *chorizo*, or Portuguese *linguiça* can be substituted as well.

If fresh herbs are in season, substitute 1 tablespoon fresh herbs for 1 teaspoon of the dried.

Additional vegetables such as diced celery or carrots can be added with the onions in Step #2.

Diced potatoes or kidney or white beans can be substituted for the pasta.

If a thinner soup is desired, add an additional cup of beef broth.

If tomatoes packed in puree are unavailable, use regular whole juice-packed tomatoes; chop, drain off most of the liquid. Return tomatoes to can, and fill to the top with canned tomato puree.

Make-It-Easy Tips:

√ To further reduce the fat level, parboil the sausages for 15 minutes before sautéing.

√ Prepare the soup a day in advance and refrigerate so that excess grease can be easily removed the next day.

√ Refrigerate canned stocks so that when they are opened, any excess fat can be easily removed.

Potage Crécy (Cream of Carrot Soup)

SERVES: 8–10
Preparation time: 15–20 minutes
Cooking time: 1 hour

This recipe is an adaptation of one taught to me by cooking teacher Ann Roe Robbins. The French call this soup Crécy because their best carrots grow in the town of this name.

The Ingredients:

  4 tablespoons (½ stick) unsalted butter
10 medium carrots, peeled and thinly sliced
  1 large onion, thinly sliced
  2 leeks, white part only, carefully washed and thinly sliced
10 cups chicken broth
¼ pound whole slab bacon, cut into large chunks
  1 teaspoon sugar
    Salt and freshly ground pepper to taste
⅓ cup raw rice
  1 cup heavy cream
    Garnish: Freshly chopped parsley

The Steps:

1. In large saucepan, heat butter; when melted, sauté carrots, onion, and leeks over medium-low heat, until soft, about 10–15 minutes.
2. Add broth, bacon, sugar, salt, and pepper. Bring to boil, cover, and simmer slowly for 20 minutes, or until carrots are tender.
3. Add rice and continue to cook an additional 20 minutes.
4. Purée in food processor or blender until smooth.
5. Return to saucepan, add cream, and heat just until warmed through. Adjust seasonings to taste and serve hot, garnished with freshly chopped parsley.

Variations:

Bacon can be omitted if desired.

Two large scallions can be substituted for leeks.

Beef broth can be substituted for chicken broth.

Make-It-Easy Tips:

√ Store unwashed leeks with roots attached in paper towels to keep dry. If wet, they rot quickly.

√ Leeks' wide flat leaves pick up dirt and grit easily, so they must be carefully washed before use. Cut off roots, leaving a thin layer of the vegetable's base intact. Cut off tops just above junction with the white stem.

√ Do not store carrots with apples. Apples release a gas that gives carrots a bitter taste.

If desired, the chunks of bacon can be boiled for 3–5 minutes, drained, and then added in Step #2 to reduce excess fat.

Cheese Wafers

YIELD: 36–40
Preparation time: 15–20 minutes
Cooking time: 14–16 minutes

The Ingredients:

6 ounces (1½ sticks) unsalted butter, softened

1¼ cups grated Swiss cheese

¼ cup grated Parmesan cheese

1 teaspoon Dijon mustard

1 cup all-purpose flour

The Steps:

1. In food processor, electric mixer, or by hand, combine butter with Swiss cheese, Parmesan cheese, and mustard. Add flour and continue to process until well blended.

2. Shape dough into a large circle, wrap in plastic wrap, and refrigerate for 1 hour.

3. Preheat oven to 350°. Lightly butter a cookie sheet.

4. Pinch small pieces of dough, roll into ½″ balls, and place on cookie sheet. Flatten with palm of hand and bake for 14–16 minutes or until golden brown.
5. Remove from spatula, allow to cool, and serve.

Variation:

1½ cups Cheddar cheese can be substituted for Swiss and Parmesan.

Make-It-Easy Tips:

√ If you've forgotten to soften the butter, grate it and it will soften quickly and easily.

√ Store baked wafers in sealed containers and they will keep for several days. Wafers can also be frozen successfully.

Old-Fashioned Gingerbread

YIELD: 4 mini-loaves or 1 large loaf
Preparation time: 15–20 minutes
Cooking time: 35–55 minutes

This traditionally spicy cake is especially wonderful served warm, topped with Whipped Apple Cream or even vanilla ice cream.

The Ingredients:

¾ cup molasses
1 cup light brown sugar, firmly packed
¼ pound (1 stick) unsalted butter, melted
2 eggs
2½ cups all-purpose flour
2 teaspoons ginger
1 teaspoon cinnamon
1 teaspoon ground nutmeg
½ teaspoon ground cloves
½ teaspoon mace
½ teaspoon baking powder
½ teaspoon salt
2 teaspoon baking soda

1 cup boiling water
Accompaniments: Whipped Apple Cream (recipe follows) or
vanilla ice cream

The Steps:

1. Preheat oven to 350°. Generously butter one 9" x 5" x 3" or four
   6" x 3½" x 2" mini-loaf pans and lightly dust with flour.
2. Combine molasses and brown sugar in bowl of food processor,
   strong blender, electric mixer, or by hand in mixing bowl.
3. Add butter and process for a few seconds; add eggs and mix well.
4. Combine flour, ginger, cinnamon, nutmeg, cloves, mace, baking powder, and salt; stir and add to molasses mixture.
5. Dissolve baking soda in boiling water, stir, and add, continuing
   to beat until smooth.
6. Pour into prepared pans and bake for 50–55 minutes for large
   loaf or 35–40 minutes for mini-loaves.
7. Allow to cool slightly. Serve warm, accompanied by Whipped
   Apple Cream or vanilla ice cream.

Variation:

½ cup chopped walnuts or pecans can be added to the batter after
Step 5.

Make-It-Easy Tips:

√ To avoid residue when measuring sticky liquids such as molasses,
  rinse the measuring cup in very hot water first.
√ Baking powder's potency diminishes with age and thus loses its effectiveness as a leavening agent. To test to see if your supply is still
  good, place ½ teaspoon of powder in ¼ cup of hot water. If active, bubbles will appear; if no bubbles appear, it's time to buy a
  new supply.

Whipped Apple Cream

SERVES: 8
Preparation time: 10 minutes

Serve this chilled cream with the squares of gingerbread.

The Ingredients:
    2 cups unsweetened applesauce, well-chilled
      Sugar to taste
    2 cups heavy cream, well chilled
    1 teaspoon vanilla extract
      Garnish: Cinnamon

The Steps:
    1. Sweeten applesauce with sugar to taste.
    2. Whip cream until it begins to thicken. Add vanilla and continue
       to whip until soft peaks form. Gently fold into applesauce, sprin-
       kle with cinnamon, and serve immediately, or chill for 1–2
       hours before serving.

Variation:
    Homemade applesauce, easy to prepare, can be substituted. Simply
    core, slice, but do not peel 4–6 large, tart Pippin, Granny Smith,
    or even McIntosh apples. Simmer with a few tablespoons apple
    juice until soft, strain through food strainer, discard peels, and
    fresh sauce is ready to use.

Make-It-Easy Tips:
    √ Applesauce is sweetened to taste rather than the presweetened apple-
      sauce available at the market which is loaded with sugar.
    √ When whipping cream, chill bowl and beater so that cream will not
      turn while beating. The applesauce must also be cold so that the
      cream can hold its stiffness.

Leftovers for the Connoisseur

SERVES: 4
Leftover Vegetable Soup
Curried Chicken
Apricot Chutney
* White Rice
Cucumbers in Sour Cream
Banana Mousse

Leftovers for company? Why not? Just serve them up with that extra something special—in this case a sprinkling of curry powder. You might even find yourself cooking extra meat, rice, and vegetables just so you can cook this meal anytime.

Select a colorful tablecloth or an assortment of brightly colored place mats as the basis for the table setting. A bouquet of wildflowers will brighten the table further. Daisies and asters last longer than many wildflowers and are extremely economical. They don't even need a fancy vase—leftover jars and bottles will do fine. Or place a few potted plants in a basket for an easy table decoration.

A variety of small candles, perhaps of different colors, give a pretty light. Tiny candles that come in colored glass holders are inexpensive and easy to find at supermarkets. Just be sure they're unscented so they don't interfere with the taste of the food.

The chutney can be prepared weeks in advance and refrigerated until serving time. Both the Leftover Vegetable Soup and the Cucumbers in Sour Cream can also be made ahead of time and chilled. On a cold night, the soup can be warmed and served piping hot. And if you want to skip the first course, feel free to omit the soup.

For a lighter and lower-calorie accompaniment to curry, substitute plain yogurt for the sour cream, seasoned with a touch of cumin. Either way, the cucumbers provide that cooling taste in contrast to the hot curry. The banana mousse supplies an additional creamy, cool, and smooth taste after a spicy meal.

* Not a recipe

Leftover Vegetable Soup

SERVES: 4
Preparation time: 10 minutes
Chilling time: 2 hours or overnight

This calls for cooked vegetables and turns them into a wonderfully flavorful chilled or hot soup. I serve this chilled in summer, hot in winter. The best vegetables to use are carrots, broccoli, zucchini, asparagus, squash, or even potatoes. The vegetables should be well cooked. If not, cook them for a few minutes longer in the broth and process, liquid and all.

The Ingredients:
2 cups leftover vegetables, cooked until soft
1 cup chicken broth
1 cup half-and-half
1–2 tablespoons fresh herbs (chives, parsley, basil, dill)
Salt and freshly ground pepper to taste
Garnish: Dairy sour cream or yogurt and freshly chopped parsley

The Steps:
1. In food processor or blender, process vegetables with broth until just combined.
2. Add half-and-half and continue to process until smooth.
3. Season to taste with herbs, salt, and pepper and chill for 2 hours or overnight.
4. Just before serving, adjust seasonings and serve garnished with dollop of sour cream or yogurt and freshly chopped parsley.

Variations:
Be creative with seasonings. Here are some suggestions:
Carrots—ground ginger, ground nutmeg, and chopped parsley
Broccoli—chopped chives and chopped parsley
Zucchini—chopped basil, chopped parsley, and chopped chives
Asparagus—chopped chives and chopped parsley
Squash—ground nutmeg, chopped chives, and chopped parsley
Potatoes—heavy cream instead of half-and-half for a richer vichyssoise; 3 tablespoons chopped chives, with extra chopped chives for garnish.
Beef broth can be substituted for chicken broth.

Make-It-Easy Tips:
√ Cook the vegetables in broth for increased flavor.
√ Remember to add more seasonings after chilling, since cold diminishes the intensity of the flavors.

Curried Chicken

SERVES: 4
Preparation time: 15 minutes
Cooking time: 8–9 minutes

I suggest chicken curry only because it tends to be the most reasonable in price. However, this basic recipe will rejuvenate just about any type of leftover available. Cooked meat, fish, or seafood in the same amount can be turned into a fabulously easy main course. Vary the amount of curry powder for spiciness as desired. I suggest using chicken broth with poultry, fish, or shellfish and beef broth with meat.

The Ingredients:
3–4 tablespoons unsalted butter
  1 cup peeled and finely chopped tart apple (1 large)
  2 cloves garlic, finely minced
4–5 teaspoons curry powder dissolved in 2 tablespoons broth plus
    1 teaspoon lemon juice
    Salt to taste
  2 tablespoons all-purpose flour
1⅓ cups chicken broth
1½ pounds (about 2 cups) cooked chicken, cut in bite-size pieces

Condiment Garnishes: Chopped scallions, chopped hard-cooked eggs, chopped bacon, chopped peanuts, chopped coconut, raisins, and Apricot Chutney (recipe follows)
Accompaniment: White rice

The Steps:
1. In large skillet, heat butter and sauté apple, onion, and garlic over medium heat until just soft, about 5 minutes.
2. Add curry powder (dissolved in liquid), and salt to taste. Stir until smooth. Add flour, stir, and cook 2 minutes longer.

3. Add broth and chicken, stir well, heating to warm through.
4. Serve hot over white rice with several condiment garnishes.

Variation:

½–1 cup whipping cream can be added to the finished curry and warmed through for a creamier version.

Make-It-Easy Tips:

√ Curry powder is not a spice by itself. It is a blend of herbs and spices that varies in intensity and strength. Try several brands to find one that best suits your taste.

√ If you prefer a milder curry, begin with a paste of 2 tablespoons curry powder plus 2 tablespoons broth mixed with 1 teaspoon lemon juice. Taste sauce and continue to add a paste of curry mixed with broth until desired taste is achieved.

Apricot Chutney

YIELD: 1 quart
Preparation time: 15 minutes
Cooking time: 1½ hours

A food processor allows you to easily prepare this wonderful preserved fruit accompaniment. Seal the chutney in glass jars and give it as a thoughtful house gift.

The Ingredients:

12 ounces (2 cups) coarsely cut dried apricots
1 cup golden raisins
1 large onion, finely chopped
1 cup dark brown sugar, firmly packed
1½ cups cider vinegar
½ cup orange juice
¼ cup minced candied ginger
1 tablespoon grated lemon rind
1 tablespoon grated orange rind
1 teaspoon minced garlic
½ teaspoon crushed dried red pepper flakes

¼ teaspoon ground allspice
Salt to taste

The Steps:

1. In large saucepan, combine ingredients and bring to boil; reduce heat, cover, and simmer 1 hour.
2. Uncover and continue to simmer 30 minutes longer, or until thickened.
3. Cool, then chill until ready to use.
4. Serve at room temperature as a side dish for curry.

Variations:

Chutney can also be served as an accompaniment to poultry or meat, used as a glaze for roasting poultry or meats, or added to a salad as a flavoring.

Chopped apples, pineapple, mangoes, pears, peaches, and other fruits can be added to the chutney as desired.

Make-It-Easy Tip:

√ Chutney will keep in the refrigerator for several weeks or can be frozen for future use. To preserve in jars, pour hot chutney into sterilized jars, adjust caps according to manufacturer's directions; process in a hot water bath 10 minutes, and store on the shelf.

Cucumbers in Sour Cream

SERVES: 4
Preparation time: 15 minutes
Chilling time: 1 hour

The Ingredients:

2 medium cucumbers, peeled and thinly sliced
½ teaspoon salt

Dressing

½ cup sour cream
1 tablespoon freshly snipped dill or 1 teaspoon dried dill
2 teaspoons lemon juice

Pinch of sugar
Salt and freshly ground white pepper to taste

The Steps:

1. Place cucumber slices in bowl, sprinkle with salt, and refrigerate 30 minutes. Drain well and pat dry on paper towels.
2. In small bowl, combine dressing ingredients; whisk until smooth.
3. Add cucumbers to sour cream mixture, toss gently, and chill 1 hour before serving.

Variations:

A pinch of cayenne pepper can be added to taste.
Yogurt can be substituted for sour cream.

Make-It-Easy Tips:

√ Cucumbers are sprinkled with salt to extract excess moisture and make them crisper.
√ If using a hothouse cucumber, eliminate salting and refrigerating step. Slice, pat dry on towels, and proceed.

Banana Mousse

SERVES: 4
Preparation time: 15–20 minutes
Chilling time: 6 hours or overnight

I've included a banana mousse in this menu because I always seem to have a surplus of ripe bananas. It is an unusual dessert. Prepare it the morning it is to be served, or the night before, but not any earlier.

The Ingredients:

2 teaspoons unflavored gelatin
3 tablespoons cold water
1⅛ cups heavy cream
3 large, ripe bananas
1 tablespoon lemon juice

¼ cup granulated sugar
1 teaspoon vanilla extract
Garnish: Whipped cream and/or sliced strawberries, raspberries, or blueberries

The Steps:

1. Soften gelatin in water in Pyrex cup for 5 minutes.
2. Meanwhile, whip cream until stiff with electric beater and place in covered bowl in refrigerator.
3. Without cleaning beaters, mash bananas and beat with lemon juice until smooth. Add sugar and vanilla and continue to beat until smooth.
4. Place Pyrex cup of softened gelatin in small pan of simmering water and heat, stirring until gelatin is dissolved.
5. Add dissolved gelatin to banana puree; fold in whipped cream and pour into 2-quart soufflé dish or 8 little ramekins or custard dishes; chill for 6 hours or overnight.
6. Serve mousse chilled, garnished with additional whipped cream and sliced strawberries, raspberries, or blueberries.

Make-It-Easy Tips:

√ Lemon juice is added to keep banana from discoloring.
√ To get the foamiest whipped cream, chill bowl and beaters before beating. Use a deep and narrow bowl to prevent splatters. Whip slowly at first and then speed up until foamy.
√ Ultra-pasteurized cream has a longer storage life than regular pasteurized cream, but it has a poorer whipping quality and is a less effective sauce thickener.
√ If powdered gelatin is added to hot water directly, some of the granules will lump and not properly dissolve, thereby reducing the gelatin's thickening power. Once softened in cold water, the moistened crystals can easily dissolve.
√ Make sure that gelatin is thoroughly dissolved in Step #4, with no graininess, before adding remaining ingredients.

Far Eastern Delights

SERVES: 4
Kung Pao Chicken
*White Rice
Spicy Chilled Chinese Noodles
Stir-Fried Zucchini and Water Chestnuts
(It Doesn't Matter That It Isn't Chinese) Strawberry Fool

Chinese cooking is a lifesaver when it comes to saving time *and* saving money. So when you're busy and on a budget, it's time to whip out the nearest wok and whip up some Oriental delights.

Chinese presentation is as uncomplicated as the cooking is speedy. Loaded with bright, glossy vegetables, the dishes look pretty in themselves and don't need a lot of extra fuss.

But a few extra touches can be inexpensive and fun. For instance, chopsticks add authenticity, and smiles, at low cost. Don't omit the forks, though—most Westerners will break down and use them before the meal is over.

Red is the traditional Chinese good-fortune color. If you have red napkins left over from Christmas or Valentine's Day, now is the time to use them. Fold like fans to enhance the Oriental mood, then stand them in goblets or tea cups.

Fan in a Goblet
1. Fold the napkin in half.   2. Pleat in 1-inch accordion pleats all the way to the top.   3. Slip one end into a glass and allow the other to open up.

* Not a recipe

Chrysanthemums symbolize immortality to the Chinese—usually they are inexpensive, so they'll leave some life in your budget, too. You can bunch them in a bouquet, or arrange three blossoms floating in a recycled fish or punch bowl to liven up your table.

For serving dishes, any bowls, platters, or plates are fine. Footed bowls, if you have them, accent the Chinese look, but plain oval platters follow the custom of most Chinese restaurants. A vividly colored bowl sets off white rice with a striking contrast.

Chili peppers brighten both the color and the flavor of the zippy Kung Pao Chicken. Season it as you like, cutting down on the peppers for people who prefer a milder taste. You can even use a bunch of dried red peppers as part of the table decor. By all means be flexible with the Stir-Fried Zucchini and Water Chestnuts. Substitute other seasonal vegetables as desired.

Was it the Chinese who taught pasta to the Italians, or vice versa? Either way, the Spicy Chilled Chinese Noodles combine chewy and crunchy textures with a classic Chinese blend of flavors. Punctuate this dish with an easy garnish of scallion brushes.

It's doubtful, anyway, that the Europeans learned Strawberry Fool from the Chinese. Nevertheless, it's so cool and refreshing after a spicy meal that no one will waste time arguing about its origins.

Because these recipes cook so quickly and should reach the table shortly after they leave the stove, organizing ingredients is a must. Do all the chopping and measuring ahead of time and line up the ingredients in the order in which you will need them.

Have the noodles and their sauce ready to assemble. Cook the chicken dish first, then slip it into a warm oven for a few moments while you stir-fry the zucchini dish. Since the zucchini sits covered for a few moments, you'll have the perfect opportunity to assemble the noodle dish. And in minutes dinner is ready for the table.

Kung Pao Chicken

SERVES: 4
Preparation time: 20 minutes
Cooking time: 5–6 minutes

This spicy hot chicken dish can be toned down easily by limiting the amount of hot peppers.

The Ingredients:

½ cup raw peanuts
2 cups boneless chicken (approximately 2 breasts cut into 1¼ inch cubes)
1 tablespoon soy sauce
1 tablespoon cornstarch
6 whole dried red chili peppers, or to taste
3 scallions, cut into ¼" slices (green part only)
1 clove garlic, finely minced
1 teaspoon finely minced ginger

Seasoning Sauce:
2 tablespoons soy sauce
1 tablespoon dry sherry
2 teaspoons sugar
1 teaspoon white vinegar
1 teaspoon toasted sesame oil
¼ cup peanut oil

The Steps:

1. While readying other ingredients, roast nuts in a 400° oven for 15 minutes or until golden.
2. In small bowl, combine chicken with soy sauce and cornstarch; mix well and set aside.
3. Wipe chili peppers with dampened towel, remove tips, and set on plate. Place scallions, garlic, and ginger on separate plate near cooking area; place roasted peanuts alongside other ingredients.
4. Combine soy sauce, sherry, sugar, vinegar, and sesame oil and stir to form seasoning sauce.
5. Heat wok, add peanut oil, and when hot, stir-fry red peppers until they turn dark red; add chicken and continue to stir-fry over high heat for 3 minutes or until chicken turns opaque. Remove chicken with slotted spoon, leaving excess oil in pan.

6. Add scallions, ginger, and garlic; stir-fry for 1 minute. Return chicken, add seasoning sauce, and stir-fry for 1 minute to combine flavors.
7. Add peanuts, stir, and serve immediately over white rice.

Variations:

Soaked Chinese mushrooms can be squeezed dry, cut into small triangles, and added with scallions.

Stir-fried noodles can be added in Step #7 and served instead of rice.

Nuts can be used untoasted to save time.

Make-It-Easy Tips:

√ Any type of chicken, dark or light meat, can be used.

√ Make sure to assemble all ingredients around the cooking area before heating the wok.

√ The dried red chili peppers used in this recipe can be found in Chinese, Italian, Greek, and Mexican stores. They are very hot, so proceed with caution. Store in a tightly covered jar at room temperature.

Spicy Chilled Chinese Noodles

SERVES: 4–6
Preparation time: 15–20 minutes
Cooking time: 10–15 minutes

The Ingredients:

1 pound spaghetti, spaghettini, or capellini
1½ tablespoons toasted sesame oil
¼ pound baked ham, shredded
1 8-ounce can water chestnuts, drained and diced
4 scallions, cut into ¼ inch pieces (green part only)

Sauce:

¼ cup soy sauce
¼ cup beef or chicken broth
3 tablespoons sesame seed paste or peanut butter
3 tablespoons Japanese rice or white wine vinegar

2 tablespoons toasted sesame oil
1 tablespoon sugar
1 teaspoon grated ginger
  Tabasco to taste
  Garnish: 2 tablespoons toasted sesame seeds

The Steps:

1. Drop noodles in boiling salted water, and cook until just tender, *al dente*. (Cook fresh noodles for 1–2 minutes, and dry according to package directions.) Drain well and sprinkle with 1½ tablespoons toasted sesame oil.
2. Place cooked noodles in serving bowl and garnish with ham, water chestnuts, and scallions.
3. In food processor, blender, or electric mixer, combine sauce ingredients until smooth.
4. Pour over noodles, top with sesame seeds, toss, and serve immediately, garnished with scallion brushes.

Variation:

Hot chili oil can be added to sauce for spiciness with Tabasco omitted.

Make-It-Easy Tips:

√ Do not assemble salad until just before serving or noodles may become gummy. Sauce and noodles can be readied in advance and assembled at last minute.

√ Tiny cooked shrimp, shredded chicken, diced pork, or whatever fish, poultry, or meat desired can be added to salad.

√ If substituting fresh pasta, either Italian or Chinese, cook no longer than 1–2 minutes or it will become gummy and pasty. If fresh pasta is frozen, cook without thawing.

√ Chinese sesame seed paste, prepared from toasted sesame seeds, has a nuttier and more pronounced flavor than the Middle Eastern tahini, which is prepared with untoasted sesame seeds.

√ Sesame seeds can turn rancid if stored at room temperature. For long storage, keep in refrigerator or freezer; thaw, toast, and proceed with recipe.

√ To make a scallion brush easily, cut off root end of onion and top part; leave piece 2½"–3" long. With sharp paring knife make many crisscross incisions in each end. Soak in cold water for several hours and they will "flower." (See illustration.)

Scallion Brushes

Stir-Fried Zucchini and Water Chestnuts

SERVES: 4
Preparation time: 10–15 minutes
Cooking time: 5 minutes

The Ingredients:

    1 pound zucchini, sliced in ¼" thick rounds
    1 8-ounce can sliced water chestnuts, drained (or use one
       5-ounce can whole water chestnuts, drained and sliced in
       half vertically)
  ¼ cup chicken broth
    1 tablespoon soy sauce
  ½ teaspoon sugar
    3 scallions, cut in ¼" pieces (green part only)
2–3 tablespoons peanut oil
     Salt to taste

The Steps:

1. Assemble zucchini and water chestnuts in bowls near cooking area; mix broth, soy sauce, and sugar together and also set near cooking area.
2. Heat wok and add oil; when hot, add scallions and stir-fry for 30 seconds; add salt and stir.
3. Add zucchini and stir-fry for 1–2 minutes, coating well with the oil; add water chestnuts.
4. Add soy sauce mixture, stir, cover, reduce heat to medium-low and cook 2–3 minutes, or until zucchini is tender but still crunchy in texture.
5. Taste for seasonings, adjust to taste, and serve zucchini hot.

Variations:

Substitute parboiled broccoli or asparagus for the zucchini.

Substitute shredded Jerusalem artichokes (sunchokes) or the Mexican root vegetable jicama for the crunchy texture of water chestnuts.

Low sodium soy sauce may be substituted for those who wish to restrict their salt intake.

Make-It-Easy Tip:

√ Select fresh, firm, young zucchini. Avoid limp ones with blemishes. Zucchini are quite perishable. Keep in refrigerator in a plastic bag for only 1–2 days before using.

(It Doesn't Matter That It Isn't Chinese) Strawberry Fool

SERVES: 4
Preparation time: 20 minutes
Chilling time: 2–3 hours or overnight

The name "fool" originated from the French word "foulé," meaning crushed. It is a dessert made of any cooked fruit and cream.

The Ingredients:

½ pound fresh strawberries, hulled, or equivalent amount frozen strawberries, thawed

¼ cup granulated sugar
1½ cup heavy cream
¼ cup confectioner's sugar, or to taste

The Steps:

1. In small saucepan, heat berries with granulated sugar until boiling. Reduce heat and simmer slowly, stirring often, for 8–10 minutes.
2. Remove from heat and puree in food processor, blender, or through food mill. Chill for 2–3 hours or overnight.
3. Whip cream until just stiff. Add confectioner's sugar and continue to beat until stiff peaks form.
4. Fold into chilled fruit puree so that fruit streaks through cream, place in parfait glasses or desert dishes, and serve immediately.

Variation:

Blackberries, blueberries, raspberries, peaches, or any seasonal fruit can be used and sweetened to taste.

Make-It-Easy Tips:

√ To whip cream easily, chill bowl and beaters for half an hour prior to whipping.
√ When selecting a basket of blackberries, avoid any with stains, a sure sign the berries are softening or decaying.

Limited-Funds Feast

SERVES: 6–8
The Ultimate Casserole
Radish, Cucumber, and Fennel Salad
Onion Bread
Make Your Own Sundaes
Hot Fudge Sauce
Butterscotch Sauce

This menu is perfect when there are more guests than money available. It allows you to entertain graciously and successfully on a shoestring budget.

Casseroles are great standbys since they are both economical and easy. The trick is to keep them interesting. The Ultimate Casserole is full of surprises and guaranteed to feed a hungry crowd of family and friends. It's also designed to be served with just a fork and to be balanced on a lap when you have more company than table space.

Since this is a relaxed, informal meal, decorating is extra easy. Small flowering plants make an instant centerpiece—just reach for the nearest pot of African violets or begonias to brighten the table.

As always, plan ahead for a no-hassle buffet. Do as much cutting, chopping, and assembling as possible in advance. Now you are ready to begin the evening with uncluttered counters and an empty sink—which makes cleanup a snap. Assemble the casserole in advance, or even bake it, freeze it, then reheat it at dinnertime. Try doubling the recipe and freezing an extra for a future dinner. Assemble the salad and prepare the dressing earlier, too—just save the tossing for the last minute. You can also prepare the butter for the Onion Bread ahead of time, as well as the sundae sauces, which refrigerate successfully.

Line up the buffet as follows: plates, food, cutlery, and napkins. As an alternative, create a cutlery holder out of a napkin. Fold the napkin in half, fold the top flap back, one half again. Turn the napkin over, fold into quarters, and insert the utensils. (See illustration.)

A basket for the casserole is an inexpensive, pretty way to protect fingers, and a trivet protects your table top. Cutting the casserole into squares makes one-handed serving easy. Tongs do the same for the salad, and tossing in the dressing makes one less step—and one less potential spill—than serving salad dressing on the side. Pile the Onion Bread high for a bountiful look in a basket lined with a napkin or pretty dish towel.

The Cutlery Holder
1. Fold the napkin in half.   2. Fold the top flap back one half.   3. Turn the napkin over, fold it into quarters and insert the utensils.

Make Your Own Sundaes are a treat for kids of all ages. Choose whatever toppings suit your taste and your budget. The fun additions let you go with a "bargain brand" ice cream. Save this buffet-style dessert for a grand finale after all the dinner dishes are cleared out of your way.

The Ultimate Casserole

SERVES: 6–8
Preparation time: 20 minutes
Cooking time: 1 hour, 15 minutes

The bacon-based tomato sauce combined with the olives, chicken, cheese, and pasta will delight even those who usually avoid casseroles.

The Ingredients:
    6 slices bacon, diced
    1 large onion, thinly sliced
  10 large mushrooms, sliced
    1 28-ounce can crushed tomatoes, packed in puree, drained
    1 cup pimiento-stuffed olives, sliced
      Salt and freshly ground pepper to taste
    3 cups cooked chicken, diced in large cubes
    1 pound spaghetti, cooked
    3 cups grated Cheddar cheese

The Steps:
1. Preheat oven to 350°. Lightly butter large lasagne-style baking dish, approximately 11" x 14" x 3".
2. In large skillet, sauté bacon over medium-high heat until browned; remove bacon to paper towels to drain.
3. Remove all but 2 tablespoons grease from pan, and sauté onions and mushrooms until golden.
4. Add tomatoes, olives, bacon, salt, and pepper; bring to a boil and simmer 10 minutes. Add chicken and stir until thoroughly combined.
5. Meanwhile, boil pasta in salted boiling water until *al dente*; drain and rinse under cold water.

6. On bottom layer of prepared casserole, place half of spaghetti, half of chicken, and half of cheese. Repeat layers ending with cheese on top, and bake for 1 hour, or until hot and bubbly.
7. Serve cut in squares.

Variations:

Grated Swiss, Monterey Jack, or Muenster cheese can be substituted for Cheddar.

1 tablespoon chopped parsley, ¼ teaspoon dried basil, and ¼ teaspoon dried oregano can be added to taste.

If tomatoes packed in puree are unavailable, use regular whole juice-packed tomatoes; chop, drain off most of the liquid. Return tomatoes to can, and fill to the top with canned tomato puree.

Make-It-Easy Tips:

√ Pasta is rinsed under cold water to stop the cooking immediately and wash off excess starch.

√ Store mushrooms in paper bag in refrigerator, which allows air to circulate and keep them fresh.

√ Bacon dices easily if frozen.

√ Casserole can be cooked in advance and frozen for future use. Reheat frozen in 325° oven for 1 hour, or until hot and bubbly.

Radish, Cucumber, and Fennel Salad

SERVES: 6–8
Preparation time: 10 minutes

This salad also works well as part of an antipasto platter with Julienne of Carrot Salad and Green Bean and Onion Salad.

The Ingredients:

1 large cucumber, peeled, seeded, and thinly sliced
1 bulb fennel, thinly sliced with feathery top included
2 bunches radishes, thinly sliced
1 tablespoon freshly chopped parsley

Dressing:
⅓ cup olive oil
3 tablespoons lemon juice
⅓ teaspoon freshly minced garlic
⅛ teaspoon oregano, crumbled
  Salt and freshly ground pepper to taste

The Steps:

1. Place cucumber, fennel, radishes, and parsley in salad bowl.
2. Combine dressing ingredients in screw-top jar and shake well to combine.
3. Pour dressing over salad ingredients, toss, and serve.

Variations:

Salad can be prepared in advance and allowed to chill for several hours.
Sliced celery can be substituted for fennel.

Make-It-Easy Tips:

√ Fennel, also called finocchio, fenucchi, or anise, resembles celery in appearance and texture but has an anise or licorice flavor. Select compact, greenish-white bulbs with crisp green stalks. If you refrigerate bulbs in perforated plastic bags, they will keep for 5–7 days.
√ Select firm, medium-sized radishes with good red color. Avoid overly large ones, which tend to have a woody or spongy texture.

Onion Bread

YIELD: 1 loaf
Preparation time: 10–15 minutes
Cooking time: 20 minutes

The Ingredients:

Onion Butter:
2 tablespoons unsalted butter
½ cup finely chopped onion
¼ pound (1 stick) unsalted butter

Salt and freshly ground pepper to taste
1 loaf French, Italian, or sourdough bread

The Steps:

1. In skillet, heat 2 tablespoons butter; add onions and sauté over medium heat until soft and just golden; allow to cool slightly.
2. Preheat oven to 375°.
3. In food processor, blender, electric mixer, or by hand, combine onions with ¼ pound butter, salt, and pepper until just smooth.
4. Slice bread horizontally, spread with onion butter, reform into loaf, loosely wrap in aluminum foil and bake for 10 minutes.
5. Open up foil and continue to bake for an additional 5–10 minutes or until crisp and golden.
6. Serve immediately, cut in slices.

Variations:

Scallions or shallots can be substituted for onions.
¼ cup freshly grated Parmesan cheese can be added to butter mixture.

Make-It-Easy Tips:

√ It is easier to butter bread lengthwise and then cut into small slices after baking.
√ Slice bread easily with a serrated-edged knife.
√ If preparing butter by hand, make sure to soften the butter first. If you've forgotten to soften the butter, simply grate it and it will soften in a minute.

Make Your Own Sundaes

SERVES: 6–8
Preparation time: 5

A variety of sauces, ice creams to taste, and a few toppings make this a festive and inexpensive way to end this casual dinner.

The Ingredients:

2 pints vanilla ice cream
1 pint chocolate ice cream

Sauces:
Hot Fudge Sauce (recipe to follow)
Hot Butterscotch Sauce (recipe to follow)

Optional Toppings (select two or three):
Chopped nuts
Chopped toffee
Chopped fresh fruits
Liqueurs (coffee, chocolate, almond)
Cookie crumbs or granola
Shredded coconut
Chocolate chips
Whipped cream

The Steps:

1. Place scoops of ice cream in large bowl.
2. Place sauces nearby and surround with bowls of toppings.
3. Ask everyone to make his or her own sundae.

Variation:

Use all vanilla or vary ice cream flavors to taste.

Make-It-Easy Tip:

√ To scoop out ice cream easily, dip ice cream scoop in hot water before each scoop.

Hot Fudge Sauce

YIELD: ¾ cup
Preparation time: 5 minutes

The Ingredients:

6 ounces real semisweet chocolate chips
3 ounces butter
2 tablespoons heavy cream
½ teaspoon vanilla extract

The Steps:

1. In double boiler over simmering water, or heavy saucepan over low heat, melt chocolate and butter together until soft, smooth, and shiny.
2. Add cream and vanilla and continue to stir until smooth.
3. Remove from heat, stir well, and serve warm.

Make-It-Easy Tips:

✓ The sauce can be made in advance and kept warm in the double boiler.

✓ Never cover a pot in which chocolate is melting. Any excess moisture or condensation will "stiffen" the chocolate and prevent it from combining easily with the rest of the ingredients.

Hot Butterscotch Sauce

YIELD: 1¼ cups
Preparation time: 5 minutes
Cooking time: 5–10 minutes

The Ingredients:

⅓ cup (5 tablespoons plus 1 teaspoon) unsalted butter
1 cup light brown sugar, firmly packed
⅓ cup heavy cream

The Steps:

1. In small saucepan, heat butter over low heat; when melted, stir in sugar and cream.
2. Bring to a boil, reduce heat, and simmer for 3–5 minutes, without stirring.
3. Remove from heat, stir well, and serve warm.

Variation:

Sauce can be kept in refrigerator and served chilled or reheated.

Make-It-Easy Tip:

✓ Remember to firmly pack brown sugar down. (One pound of brown sugar equals 2¼ cups firmly packed.)

✓ As the sauce cools, it continues to thicken.

Country Fare

SERVES: 4
Tortilla Baskets
Addy's Chicken
Green Bean and Onion Salad
Bread
Light Lemon Pie

This budget-minded dinner saves you preparation time and cleanup chores, as well as money. It's hearty country fare, with a bit of a Mexican accent.

A simple table also saves you decorating time. Aim for a stylishly rustic look. Use any tablecloth you like, or none at all if the tabletop is pretty by itself. Napkins, opened and laid out like diamonds, make improvised place mats. Turn part of the meal itself into a centerpiece by serving the bread on a board right in the middle of the table. A round or braided loaf adds a festive flair of its own.

The breadboard and rustic motif make this a perfect time to use any wooden utensils you have—wooden dishes, salad bowls, napkin rings, or even wooden spoons for serving.

If you want to add a little more "special occasion" atmosphere, candles dress up the countryside theme with soft, old-fashioned light. Votive candles are inexpensive; they can shine on the table, or here and there around the room, in candlesticks, saucers, or even ashtrays. A selection of dried flowers or branches such as dogwood, lilac, or pussy willow enhance the country mood.

The Tortilla Baskets add the option of an unusual but budget-smart appetizer. People can enjoy them served on small plates in the living room. Remember to include little forks and lots of napkins.

The Green Bean and Onion Salad perks up the table with its splash of color. It's also a make-ahead dish that can sit in the refrigerator from two hours to two days.

Addy's Chicken teams up those classic budget-stretchers—chicken, potatoes, and onions—all in one dish for a supper-satisfying meal. Save extra money by buying a whole chicken instead of a package of higher-priced cut-up parts. It takes almost no time to easily hack a chicken into pieces with a Chinese cleaver or chef's knife. You can show off this tasty combination of flavors on an oval platter, ringed with sprigs of parsley.

Butter for the bread can get an extra touch, too. Soften it and pack it in a crock, a mug, even a wide-mouthed sugar bowl. Or put it on a plate, and brighten it with sprigs of parsley or a few leaves of watercress.

Dessert won't wear out your budget or you when it's Lemon Pie with an easy crumb crust. Bake it while the chicken simmers, or freeze it days ahead. And as long as you're using the lemon juice, you might take a minute to use the peel as a garnish. Remove the peel in a long strip with a vegetable peeler. Then wind the peel into curls or spirals to top each slice of pie.

Tortilla Baskets

SERVES: 4
Preparation time: 5–10 minutes
Cooking time: 2–3 minutes

Serve these broiled crisp appetizers piping hot.

The Ingredients:
    4 snack-size flour tortillas
    1 cup (4 ounces) grated Cheddar cheese
    2 tablespoons green chile salsa
    2 teaspoons freshly grated onion
       Garnish: Dairy sour cream

The Steps:
    1. Preheat broiler.
    2. Place each tortilla in small tart pan, or shape heavy-duty alumi-
       num foil into mini-tart pan shape. Push down in center so tor-
       tilla forms shell.
    3. Sprinkle each tortilla with 1½ teaspoons salsa, ⅓ teaspoon onion,
       and 2 tablespoons cheese. Repeat layers, ending with cheese
       on top.
    4. Broil 3″ from heat until hot and bubbly, and tortilla is crisp and
       golden. Serve immediately with dollop of sour cream.

Variations:
    Use green chile salsa available in the market or prepare salsa (see
       page 264).
    If snack-size tortillas are unavailable, substitute the larger tortillas
       and increase cheese and salsa.
    Monterey Jack cheese can be substituted for Cheddar cheese.

Make-It-Easy Tips:
    √ When placing tortillas in tart pans, push down gently to avoid rip-
       ping the tortillas.
    √ If mold forms on the surface of hard cheese, just scrape it off. The
       cheese is still good.

Addy's Chicken

SERVES: 4
Preparation time: 15–20 minutes
Cooking time: 35–40 minutes

Although the ingredients are more French than Mexican, this recipe comes from a Mexican woman who serves this inexpensive dish frequently.

The Ingredients:
    1 3-pound chicken, cut into 8 pieces
      Salt and freshly ground pepper to taste
    2 tablespoons unsalted butter
    2 tablespooons olive oil
    2 large onions, thinly sliced
    1 cup dry white wine or dry vermouth
    ¾ cup chicken broth
    2 teaspoons oregano, crumbled
    2 large potatoes, thickly sliced
      Salt and freshly ground pepper to taste

The Steps:
    1. Wash chicken, pat dry, and lightly season with salt and pepper.
    2. Heat butter and oil together in large deep skillet and brown chicken over high heat until golden. Remove chicken and set aside.
    3. Add onions and sauté over medium heat for 3–4 minutes, scraping up browned particles from bottom of pan.
    4. Add wine, allow to boil for a minute, and then add broth and oregano.
    5. Return chicken to pan, arrange potatoes on top, cover, and simmer slowly for 30–35 minutes or until chicken is tender.
    6. Adjust seasonings with salt and pepper to taste and serve immediately.

Variations:
    Chicken thighs, chicken breasts, or a combination of both can be substituted for the whole chicken.
    Sliced carrots can be added and sautéed with onions.

Make-It-Easy Tips:

√ Dish must be served immediately or the potatoes will become mushy. If preparing in advance, complete cooking through Step #4 and refrigerate the chicken and sauce separately. Reheat both, add chicken, arrange potatoes on top, and proceed with recipe.

√ Store potatoes in a cool, dry, well-ventilated place. Do not store in refrigerator. The potato starch will convert to sugar and result in an overly sweet-tasting potato. To reverse this problem, remove potato from refrigerator and sugar will convert back to starch.

Green Bean and Onion Salad

SERVES: 4
Preparation time: 15 minutes
Cooking time: 2–3 minutes
Chilling time: 2 hours or overnight

The green beans can be cooked and marinated one or two days in advance.

The Ingredients:

　　1½ pounds fresh green beans
　　½ cup olive oil
　　3 tablespoons white wine vinegar
　　2 tablespoons roughly chopped parsley
　　1 tablespoon freshly snipped dill or 1 teaspoon dried dill weed (optional)
　　2 scallion greens, roughly chopped
　　1 teaspoon Dijon mustard
　　　Pinch of sugar
　　　Salt and freshly ground pepper to taste
　　1 medium-size sweet Bermuda onion
　　1 cup cherry tomatoes

The Steps:

1. Trim ends off beans, place in large saucepan of boiling salted water, and cook for 3–5 minutes, depending on size of bean, or until just tender. Drain in colander and immediately place under cold running water.

2. In food processor or blender, process olive oil, vinegar, parsley, dill, scallions, mustard, sugar, salt, and pepper until smooth.
3. Pour dressing over beans, toss well, cover and chill for 2 hours or overnight.
4. One hour before serving, thinly slice onion, cut cherry tomatoes in half, and add to beans; gently toss and refrigerate until ready to serve chilled.

Variation:

Small tomato wedges can be substituted for cherry tomatoes; if out of season, omit entirely.

Make-It-Easy Tips:

√ When adding beans to boiling water in Step #1, add beans gradually to keep water boiling constantly.

√ Green beans should be rinsed under cold water to stop cooking process and ensure a bright green color.

Light Lemon Pie

YIELD: Two 9″ pies
Preparation time: 20 minutes
Cooking time: 30 minutes

This Lemon Pie is so creamy it resembles a cheesecake. The recipe is for two pies since it is easier to prepare two at one time. Freeze the other for a great dessert ready for last-minute company.

The Ingredients:

3 cups chocolate wafer crumbs (about 45–50 wafers)
10 tablespoons (5 ounces) unsalted butter, melted
¼ cup sugar

Filling:

1 14-ounce can sweetened condensed milk
Juice of 2 lemons (about 4–6 tablespoons)
4 eggs, separated
Pinch of salt
Garnish: Spirals of lemon peel or thinly sliced lemons

The Steps:

1. Preheat oven to 350°. Lightly butter two 9″ pie plates.
2. In bowl, mix cookie crumbs, butter, and sugar together. Spoon into prepared pans and, using back of spoon, firmly press against bottom and sides of pan. Bake 8–10 minutes. Cool slightly before filling.
3. In large bowl, mix milk with lemon juice; whisk in egg yolks until smooth.
4. In separate bowl, whip egg whites until slightly stiff. Add salt and continue to beat until stiff peaks form.
5. Gently fold beaten whites into lemon mixture, pour into prepared pie pans and bake for 20–25 minutes or until lightly golden and inserted knife comes out clean.
6. Remove from oven, cool slightly, and chill. Serve chilled with a garnish of spirals of lemon peel and thinly sliced lemons.

Variations:

To cut down on preparation time, substitute 2 prepared graham cracker crusts.

Graham crackers, ginger snaps, vanilla wafers, or any type of cookie can be used for crust.

Make-It-Easy Tips:

√ Crust can be frozen for 20 minutes, instead of baking.

√ Egg whites will not whip stiffly, if there is even a trace of egg yolk. If any yolk should fall into the whites, scoop it out with a large piece of egg shell.

√ Do not beat egg whites in an aluminum bowl or they will develop a grayish tint, unless the bowl is the new anodized aluminum.

√ If sweetened condensed milk is unavailable, substitute the following mixture: In food processor or blender, combine 1 cup instant nonfat dry milk solids, ⅔ cup granulated sugar, ½ cup boiling water, and 3 tablespoons melted unsalted butter. Process until smooth and store in covered container in refrigerator until ready to use.

√ Pie is best when served chilled. If freezing, remember to leave at room temperature for 15 minutes prior to serving.

CHAPTER THIRTEEN

SUMPTUOUS SLENDERIZING PARTIES

1. **First Night of the Diet**
   Hungarian Potted Chicken
   Toasted Rice
   Broccoli with Carrot and Lemon
       Garnish
   Light Apple Mousse

2. **Dinner from the Orient**
   Chinese Steamed Fish
   *Steamed White Rice
   Stir-fried Snow Peas, Mushrooms,
       and Water Chestnuts
   Frozen Fruits

3. **Cocktail Party for the Calorie
   Conscious**
   Warm Bloody Bull Shot
   Creamy Herb Dip
   *Vegetable Basket
   Light Liver Pâté
   Romanian Eggplant "Caviar"
   Chinese Marinated Bay Shrimp

4. **Dinner from the Famous Spas**
   Toasted Potato Shells (La Costa)
   Game Hens à l'Orange (The Canyon
       Ranch)
   Skinny Spinach Salad (The Oaks and
       The Palms)
   Mango-Lime Paradise (The Golden
       Door)

5. **Elegantly Light Dinner**
   *Chilled White Wine
   Seviche
   Poulet Citron
   Parsleyed Brown Rice
   Poireaux Braises (Braised Leeks)
   Minted Melon

* Not a recipe

HEALTHFUL LIVING, a desire for increased physical fitness and longevity, and a high regard for what we eat has produced a new wave of lighter cooking. There's less fat, less refined sugar, and less protein content to meals. This cuisine is delicate in flavor, uses a great deal of chicken and fish, and emphasizes fresh ingredients.

Entertaining in this lighter style requires inventiveness in preparation as well as presentation. The menus in this chapter are designed to convey this new fresh and wholesome approach to low-calorie entertaining. They are not limited to dieters. Attractively garnished and presented, the recipes can appeal to just about anyone as slimming alternatives.

If, however, nondieters are present, they can certainly be treated to a side dish of sour cream, some slices of bread, or even a scoop of ice cream while the dieters hopefully stick by the rules.

Nonalcoholic beverages such as the Warm Bloody Bull Shot in the *Cocktail Party for the Calorie Conscious* actually take the edge off hunger pangs. Guests can totally enjoy themselves eating all the light hors d'oeuvres such as the Creamy Herb Dip prepared with yogurt instead of sour cream.

As we have learned from the health spas in this country, garnishing, presentation, and portion control are essential to the appeal of low-calorie cooking. A forlorn piece of dried-out fish on a large empty plate will discourage the most steadfast of dieters—who will surely leave the table hungry and may reach for the nearest junk food for comfort. The same fish steamed Chinese-style as in the *Dinner from the Orient*, presented on a large platter, and beautifully garnished with greens, will appease both the eye and the appetite of a dieter.

The *Elegantly Light Dinner* emphasizes presentation of the food as well as elegance on the table. The setting of the scene can enhance the enjoyment of the evening. The freshest of flavors are combined in the Poulet Citron, using lemon juice and garlic as substitutes for salt to achieve a natural and delicate taste. The pace of this meal, as with any of the others in the chapter, should be slow and leisurely. The more time spent dining, the more satisfied the appetites, especially when the most filling ingredient is the conversation.

Carbohydrates are no longer a taboo for calorie counters. The Toasted Rice in the *First Night of the Diet*, the Toasted Potato Shells in the *Dinner from the Famous Spas*, the Parsleyed Brown Rice in the *Elegantly Light Dinner*—all make clear the idea that nutritious carbohydrates should be enjoyed as part of a well-balanced low-calorie menu.

Help and support are key factors in any low-calorie regime. The *First Night of the Diet* describes the enthusiasm we can use to help each other achieve weight loss. The background workout music, weigh-in, "before" photos, and charts can create a fun environment for guests.

Desserts in this chapter concentrate on fruit. Refined sugar provides empty calories. Honey has the same amount of calories but is considerably sweeter, so less is necessary. The real answer to dieters' desserts is to readjust the taste buds to naturally sweet fruits—plain, in compotes, whipped with yogurt, or even frozen for a cooling treat.

The following is a brief list I call Laurie's Low-Cal Larder. It includes those special ingredients I have discovered to shave off just a few more calories. I keep them in the house at all times. Remember to read the ingredient list on the package carefully before purchasing any canned, dried, or frozen foods. I make it a point to avoid those products listing sugar, salt, or MSG as a primary ingredient.

LAURIE'S LOW-CALORIE LARDER
Fresh lemon juice and vinegar
Fresh garlic or onions
Fresh herbs (I purchase when available, chop, and freeze in small plastic bags)
Variety of dried herbs and spices
Dry white wine
Mexican salsa (low-sodium)
Mustards (especially the new grainy varieties)
Unsweetened fruit juices
Milder soy sauce (salt-reduced)
No-salt canned tomatoes or tomato paste
Undiluted canned chicken or beef broth, preferably without MSG
Lots of fresh ground pepper
Low-fat yogurt
Low-fat (part-skim) Mozzarella cheese
Low-fat cottage cheese

Salt-free sparkling water or seltzer

Variety of raw vegetables for crudités: carrots, celery, radishes, broccoli, cauliflower, etc.

Variety of steamed vegetables to munch on cold, topped with mustard, to reheat, or to turn into cold or hot soups

Variety of fresh fruits: apples, pears, oranges, tangerines, and bananas in winter; melons, nectarines, peaches, plums, berries, apricots, and grapes in summer

The First Night of the Diet

SERVES: 6
Hungarian Potted Chicken
Toasted Rice
Broccoli with Carrot and Lemon Garnish
Light Apple Mousse

There's nothing quite like the buddy system to help us get through the pitfalls of dieting unscathed. When we laugh together, trade suggestions, and give each other encouragement, we reinforce our chances for success. Throwing a party to start a diet makes it something desirable rather than an occasion to think of oneself as deprived.

Starting a diet can elicit some apprehension, so set the scene for fun and encouragement. Go for vibrant colors—blues, yellows, greens— even alternating different colored napkins for a definite party mood. That helps overcome the worry that dieting has to be dull.

But shedding pounds takes determination. Have a camera ready for instant pictures—some "before" shots (for those who are willing) to compare with the slim you later on. Then set a date and *promise* to get together again for a progress check and moral support.

For party favors, how about colorful pocket-sized spiral notebooks, each dressed up with a bow? They're handy for use as food and calorie diaries, recording weight progress, and collecting a list of weight-watching tips. In fact, why not ask each guest to share his or her favorite suggestions? Trade tips for the times you get the munchies, favorite low-calorie recipes, and exercises. Exchange phone numbers for emergency help during an attack of the hungries.

Looking for role models? Hang up posters of slim and trim people—Victoria Principal, Linda Evans, Tom Selleck, or any other favorites. If your nearest teenager doesn't already have a collection of these posters, he or she can tell you where to find some.

To really get folks inspired, try some lively, exercise-oriented tapes or records, like Jane Fonda's Workout music for background music and encouragement.

You can cut calories by serving sparkling water instead of wine with this dinner, or try serving ice water with a slice of lemon in each glass.

Be sure the food is served to look as good as it tastes. The flavors and textures here are varied and delicious, so you should hear no groans of "Yuck, diet food!" If dinner is delayed, cut up raw vegetables for an easy low-calorie hors d'oeuvre.

The Hungarian Potted Chicken comes with a flavorful sauce that's thick without starch. Serve it garnished with parsley, on a pretty platter or from the skillet set on a trivet. Save some parsley to color up the rice, served in a warmed bowl alongside the broccoli with its colorful garnish of carrot and lemon.

Wind down with a delicious Light Apple Mousse—a treat for all. It's a cooling and refreshing finish to this tasty but slimming start toward successful dieting.

Hungarian Potted Chicken

SERVES: 6
Preparation time: 10 minutes
Cooking time: 45–60 minutes

This recipe comes from my friend Mara O'Laughlin's grandmother. No extra liquid is added to the dish. The juices from the onions and chicken provide a flavorful and thick sauce.

The Ingredients:
    1 3½–4 pound chicken, cut into serving pieces
    2 medium onions, roughly chopped
    1 16-ounce can tomatoes, drained and roughly chopped (use the no-salt/no-sugar brand if available)

        2 tablespoons freshly chopped parsley
        2 teaspoons sweet Hungarian paprika
          Freshly ground pepper to taste
          Garnish: Freshly chopped parsley

The Steps:

1. Place chicken in deep covered skillet.
2. Add remaining ingredients, bring to a boil, cover, and simmer slowly for 45–60 minutes or until tender.
3. Taste for seasonings, adjust as necessary, and serve hot, garnished with additional chopped parsley.

Variations:

1 large ripe fresh tomato, roughly chopped, may be substituted for the canned tomatoes.

Sliced mushrooms can be added in Step #2 if desired.

Make-It-Easy Tips:

√ Prepare a day in advance and refrigerate so that excess fat can be easily removed when chilled.

√ Sweet Hungarian paprika, sold in colorful cans, is a red powdered spice prepared from grinding chilis. The color of the powder should be bright red, not brownish, which indicates age.

Toasted Rice

SERVES: 6
Preparation time: 10–15 minutes
Cooking time: 30–40 minutes

Toasting rice in a hot oven adds nutty flavor and crunchy texture without adding any extra calories.

The Ingredients:

        1½ cups raw rice
          1 tablespoon unsalted butter
          1 medium onion, finely chopped

3 cups chicken broth
Salt and freshly ground pepper to taste
Garnish: Chopped watercress leaves

The Steps:
1. Preheat oven to 400°.
2. Pour rice onto baking sheets in single layer and bake for 10–15 minutes, shaking the pan occasionally, or until golden brown. Allow to cool.
3. Melt butter in saucepan and sauté onion over medium heat until golden. Add rice and stir to coat with mixture.
4. Add broth, salt, and pepper; bring to a boil, cover, reduce heat, and simmer for 20–25 minutes, or until tender and liquid is absorbed.
5. Serve rice in heated bowl garnished with chopped watercress leaves.

Variation:
Substitute beef or vegetable broth for chicken.

Make-It-Easy Tips:
√ Make sure the cover of the pot fits snugly. If not, place a sheet of aluminum foil on top of pot, cover, and press down to seal tightly.
√ Rice is served in a heated bowl because if hot rice is placed in a cold dish, the part that touches the dish may develop a gummy consistency.

Broccoli with Carrot and Lemon Garnish

SERVES: 6
Preparation time: 10–15 minutes
Cooking time: 2–3 minutes

The Ingredients:
4 cups broccoli florets, about 2 pounds (reserve the stems for another use)
1 large carrot, peeled and grated

    1 teaspoon grated lemon zest
    1 tablespoon fresh lemon juice
      Salt and freshly ground pepper to taste

The Steps:

1. Drop broccoli into large pot of boiling salted water; when water returns to a boil, cook uncovered for 2–3 minutes, or until just tender, but still crunchy. Drain in colander.
2. In the meantime, combine grated carrots with lemon zest and mix well.
3. Sprinkle lemon juice on drained hot broccoli, top with garnish of carrot and lemon zest, and serve immediately with salt and pepper to taste.

Variations:

Cauliflower can be substituted for broccoli.
Freshly minced garlic combined with freshly chopped parsley can be added to the garnish as desired.
Broccoli can be boiled in chicken or beef broth for added flavor.

Make-It-Easy Tip:

√ Select broccoli heads with firm, compact bud cluster, which should be green or purple-green. Avoid heads with open, yellow flowers or wilting leaves. Keep broccoli cold and humid and use as soon as possible.

Light Apple Mousse

SERVES: 4
Preparation time: 15 minutes
Chilling time: 1 hour

A refreshing and chilling treat that is only 60 calories per serving.

The Ingredients:

    1½ cups unsweetened applesauce
    1 teaspoon grated lemon rind

¼ teaspoon vanilla extract
¼ teaspoon cinnamon
Pinch nutmeg
Honey or other sweetener, in limited quantities, to taste
4 egg whites, at room temperature
¼ teaspoon cream of tartar
Garnish: Thin slices of apple, dipped in lemon juice to prevent discoloration

The Steps:

1. In a large bowl, combine applesauce, lemon rind, vanilla, cinnamon, nutmeg, and sweetener to taste.
2. Whip egg whites until foamy; add cream of tartar and continue to whip until stiff peaks form. (Do not overbeat.)
3. Gently fold into applesauce mixture.
4. Chill and serve garnished with thin slices of apple.

Variation:

For a high-calorie version, a little heavy whipped cream folded into the dessert is super.

Make-It-Easy Tips:

√ Do not prepare this dessert more than a few hours in advance or it may separate slightly.
√ The egg whites are whipped to foamy before adding the cream of tartar. The cream of tartar acts to delay the foaming action, so the whites must already by foamy.
√ If a copper bowl is available, use it to whip egg whites. Copper helps to stabilize the beaten whites.

Dinner from the Orient

SERVES: 4
Chinese Steamed Fish
*White Rice
Stir-Fried Snow Peas, Mushrooms, and Water Chestnuts
Frozen Fruits

Chinese cooking works wonders with slimming foods. It also gives us a chance to experiment with decor—some genuinely Far Eastern, some simply exotic.

Soft light, filtered and reflected, sets a mystical mood. A glass bowl of water can hold floating candles, while blossoms float among them like water lilies. Or take your cue from the steamed fish and cluster seashells on a tray or in a bowl. Use them to prop an arrangement of Chinese or Japanese fans, cloth flowers, or even chopsticks. A small candle can be very effective at the center of such an arrangement, but take care to keep flammable fans and flowers protected. A glass container for the candle shields the flame elegantly. If no one in your house has a seashell collection, don't despair. Substitute pebbles, uncooked rice, or beans.

* Not a recipe

A red tablecloth—it needn't be expensive—accentuates the Chinese mood and sets a striking backdrop for any Far Eastern utensils and accessories. Serve the fish directly from a bamboo steamer, garnished with coriander or watercress. Give the teapot a prominent place on the table. Chopsticks and graceful Chinese soup spoons are inexpensive table enhancers, and well worth acquiring when you enjoy Chinese cooking. Chopstick sets wrapped with small squares of aluminum foil and tied up with red yarn create a colorful effect for the center of the table.

Vivid napkins folded like fans take the Chinese theme a step further. Pleat them accordion-style, then fold them in half. Next, slip the folded end through a napkin ring, or tie a colorful ribbon an inch or so from the end. Lay each napkin on a plate, and open the pleats for a dramatic splash of color. (See illustration.)

To keep this meal as easy as it is elegant, both traditional Chinese steaming and stir-frying are used. The Frozen Fruits are prepared in advance, and the ingredients for the fish and vegetables should be organized and ready to assemble. While the rice cooks, the fish steams to a flaky texture. The vegetables are cooked just before serving. But don't worry; prepared in advance, this only takes about three minutes.

After a hot, steamy dinner the Frozen Fruits, served as finger food instead of the traditional fortune or almond cookies, deliver cool refreshment. It's a novel way to enjoy the natural sweetness of fruit without a drop of added sweetener—or a single added calorie.

Fan in a Ring
1. Fold the napkin in half.   2. Pleat in 1″ accordion pleats all the way to the top.   3. Fold in half.   4. Slip folded napkin through a napkin ring, or tie with a ribbon an inch from the end.   5. Lay each napkin on a plate and open up pleats like a fan.

Chinese Steamed Fish

SERVES: 4
Preparation time: 20 minutes
Cooking time: 12–15 minutes

The ingredients in this steamed fish are simliar to the Chinese Baked Fish in *Make It Easy in Your Kitchen,* but the fish is lower in calories when steamed whole and just as tasty. White fish such as sea bass, whitefish, pike, trout, snapper, or rock cod are preferable for delicate steaming. Oily fish such as mackerel or bluefish are not suitable.

The Ingredients:
1   whole fish, about 2½–3 pounds, cleaned and scaled but with head and tail still on
3   tablespoons soy sauce
3   tablespoons dry sherry
½   teaspoon sugar
1   clove garlic, chopped
2   tablespoons fermented, mashed, and drained black beans (available at Far Eastern grocery stores or by mail order)
1   tablespoon finely shredded fresh ginger
2   scallions, split and cut in 2″ lengths (green part only)
2   teaspoons toasted sesame oil
    Garnish: Coriander leaves (cilantro) or watercress

The Steps:
1. Pat fish dry with paper towels and make 3 diagonal slashes on each side of fish. Lightly spray a heat-proof platter or shallow dish that will fit into steamer with nonaerosol vegetable spray.
2. Mix soy sauce, sherry, and sugar together and pour over fish.
3. Sprinkle garlic/bean mixture over fish along with shredded ginger and scallions.
4. Place fish in steamer and steam over boiling water, for 12–15 minutes or until fish is flaky. (The timing depends on the size of the fish.)
5. Carefully remove hot platter from steamer, top with sesame oil, and serve immediately from this same dish, garnished with coriander leaves or watercress.

Variations:

For a French version of Steamed Fish, substitute lemon juice, fresh herbs, capers, and a topping of melted butter for the final step.

If black bean sauce is unavailable, it may be omitted.

Make-It-Easy Tips:

√ Ginger can easily be shredded with the fine end of a grater.

√ In general, the rule of thumb for cooking fish is 10 mnutes per inch, judging from thickest part of fish.

√ To improvise a steamer: place platter of fish on a trivet to act as a rack in a large roasting pan. Pour enough boiling water in pan to cover bottom by 1"–2" but not to touch the platter. Cover the top with heavy-duty aluminum foil and seal tightly. Place it either over low heat so that water keeps to a slow boil or in a 375° oven to bake. (Note: Inverted 2" muffin tin can also be used as a rack.)

Stir-Fried Snow Peas, Mushrooms, and Water Chestnuts

SERVES: 4
Preparation time: 15 minutes
Cooking time: 4–5 minutes

If available, the new sugar-snap peas, a cross between a Chinese snow pea pod and a green pea, can be substituted for snow peas. Sugar peas are totally edible, shell and all, and the crunchy texture is excellent in stir-fried dishes and salads.

The Ingredients:

1 tablespoon soy sauce
½ teaspoon sweetener (optional)
Salt and freshly ground pepper to taste
2 teaspoons peanut oil
¼ teaspoon finely minced garlic
½ pound snow peas, strings removed
6 mushrooms, cleaned and sliced

½ cup sliced water chestnuts, drained
2 teaspoons sesame seeds, toasted
1 teaspoon toasted sesame seed oil

The Steps:

1. In small bowl, combine soy sauce, sugar, salt, and pepper; stir and place near cooking area.
2. Heat wok or large skillet and add oil; when hot, stir-fry garlic for 30 seconds.
3. Add peas, mushrooms, and water chestnuts; continue to stir-fry for 2–3 minutes longer.
4. Add soy sauce mixture, stir to combine; add sesame seeds and oil. Toss thoroughly and serve immediately.

Variation:

Japanese or Chinese dried mushrooms, soaked in water and julienned (cut in matchstick strips) can be substituted for regular mushrooms.

Make-It-Easy Tip:

√ As in all Chinese stir-fry quick cooking, all ingredients must be assembled in advance and placed near the cooking area.

Frozen Fruits

SERVES: 4
Preparation time: 5 minutes
Freezing time: 3 hours

This mixture of cooling frozen fruits is the perfect treat to satisfy a dessert craving without lots of calories.

The Ingredients:

2 ripe bananas
2 slices watermelon
1 bunch grapes, washed

The Steps:

1. Peel bananas and immediately wrap tightly in plastic wrap or aluminum foil; freeze for 3 hours, or until ready to serve.
2. Cut away rind from watermelon, slice into spears, and wrap in plastic wrap or aluminum foil; freeze for 3 hours, or until ready to serve.
3. Wrap grapes in plastic wrap or aluminum foil and freeze for 3 hours, or until ready to serve.
4. Unwrap bananas, cut into slices, and serve immediately on platter with frozen watermelon and grapes.

Variation:

All of one fruit may be substituted for combination.

Make-It-Easy Tips:

√ Fruits will keep for 5–7 days in the freezer
√ Keep a supply of frozen fruits on hand for nutritious children's snacks or satisfying dieters' desserts.

Cocktail Party for the Calorie Conscious

SERVES: 10–12
Warm Bloody Bull Shot
Creamy Herb Dip
* Vegetable Basket
Light Liver Pâté
Romanian Eggplant "Caviar"
Chinese Marinated Bay Shrimp

A cocktail party can easily be a dieter's downfall—but not this one. With all these low-calorie treats, the party becomes a great way to entertain without later pangs of guilt. Your dieting friends will also be appreciative.

This assortment of food fills a buffet table beautifully, although you can simply place the dishes around the room on coffee tables, end tables,

* Not a recipe

or even bridge tables. For an elegant touch, accent the room with flowers in slender bud vases.

The Vegetable Basket and Creamy Herb Dip play double-duty—as low-calorie munchables and as a fresh and pretty centerpiece. The colorful vegetables look twice as lush and vibrant on a thick bed of curly lettuce leaves or deep green parsley. Arrange them on a tray or stand them in a basket, where they'll look as cheerful as a bouquet of flowers.

The yogurt-based dip rescues you from fattening sour cream. Serve it in an attractive dish or crock, and save a scallion or sprig of parsley for a garnish, either "planted" in the dip itself or dressing up a saucer underneath the dish. Another suggestion is to serve the dip in a glass bowl placed inside a hollowed-out red or green cabbage. It makes a particularly attractive presentation perfect for any dip or sauce.

The usual pâté de foie gras is just what its name means—"*fat* liver paste." But this Light Liver Pâté takes its place in a slim and trim way, without sacrificing flavor. And with its shiny glaze, it looks as fancy as it tastes. Unmold it onto a pretty plate and accent it with a spray of watercress.

Caviar and calories go hand in hand—but this Romanian Eggplant "Caviar" makes a super substitute. Surround it with crunchy crackers or melba toast in a variety of shapes and flavors.

Tiny bay shrimp are low in calories and less expensive than most seafood. Marinated in this Chinese dressing, they are a refreshing part of the hors d'oeuvres table, served on little plates with cocktail or salad forks alongside.

Alcohol is a fast way to waste calories, so guests will appreciate these zesty, unspiked, warm Bloody Bull Shots. Or serve sparkling mineral water and lime as a light, refreshing hot-weather alternative. And offer wine or wine spritzers to those who aren't counting their calories.

For a smaller party, pick and choose just a few of these goodies. But no matter how many or how few guests you have, remember that low-calorie food should look every bit as dressy as any party fare, if not more so. So get out the fancy plates and dishes, spread a lace tablecloth, runners or doilies, and choose pretty cocktail napkins. Then have yourself an elegant, guilt-free good time.

Warm Bloody Bull Shot

SERVES: 10–12
Preparation time: 5–10 minutes
Cooking time: 5 minutes

The Ingredients:
2 quarts vegetable juice cocktail (I use V-8, S&W, or a local brand)
2 cups strong undiluted beef bouillon
¼ cup fresh lemon juice
1 tablespoon Worcestershire sauce
1 teaspoon white horseradish, or more, to taste
Tabasco to taste
Salt and freshly ground pepper to taste
Garnish: Lemon slices

The Steps:
1. Heat all ingredients until hot.
2. Pour into mugs and serve with a slice of lemon floating on top.

Variations:
Substitute lime juice for lemon juice.
Spicy V-8 juice can be substituted for plain V-8, adjusting other ingredients to get the degree of spiciness you prefer.

Make-It-Easy Tip:
√ Serrated knives with narrow blades are the best tools for slicing lemons. Carbon steel knives and occasionally aluminum utensils may permanently discolor from the lemon acid.

Creamy Herb Dip

YIELD: 3 cups
Preparation time: 15 minutes

The Ingredients:

¼ cup minced scallions (green and white parts included)
2 tablespoons freshly chopped parsley
2 teaspoons freshly snipped dill or ½ teaspoon dried dill weed, crumbled
2 teaspoons freshly chopped basil or ½ teaspoon dried basil, crumbled
2 teaspoons freshly chopped tarragon or ½ teaspoon dried tarragon, crumbled
1 teaspoon finely minced garlic
2 cups plain low-fat yogurt
3 tablespoons mayonnaise
Salt and freshly ground pepper to taste
Accompaniments:

Raw vegetables:
2   boxes cherry tomatoes
1   bunch celery cut up
1   pound carrots cut up
3   medium zucchini, cut up
½   pound mushrooms, sliced
1   bunch radishes
1   bunch scallions, trimmed

The Steps:

1. In food processor, blender, or by hand, chop scallions, parsley, dill, basil, tarragon, and garlic.
2. Place in bowl, fold in yogurt and mayonnaise; season with salt and pepper to taste and chill until ready to use.
3. Serve chilled accompanied by raw vegetables.

Variations:

Any seasonal chopped herbs can be used as desired.
Dip can be also used as a salad dressing.

Make-It-Easy Tips:

√ The herbs and seasonings are chopped in a food processor or blender and then folded into the yogurt to keep the texture of the yogurt thick and creamy. Once processed, the yogurt will become thinner and often watery.

√ Crumble dried herbs between fingers before adding to recipes to release essential flavors.

Light Liver Pâté

YIELD: 9" x 5" x 3" loaf
Preparation time: 15 minutes
Cooking time: 25 minutes
Chilling time: 1–2 hours for gelatin
4–6 hours or overnight for pâté

Serve this elegant but low-calorie chicken liver pâté attractively garnished with a layer of gelatin. Or, for a quicker version, omit the gelatin and serve packed into a crock or bowl.

The Ingredients:

Gelatin Topping:
¾ cup undiluted beef broth
1 package (1 tablespoon) unflavored gelatin

Pâté:
1 tablespoon unsalted butter
1 medium onion, roughly chopped
1 pound chicken livers, roughly diced
2 tablespoons Marsala, Madeira, port, or red wine
2 tablespoons undiluted beef broth
Pinch of ground allspice
Pinch of ground cloves
Pinch of ground nutmeg
Pinch of thyme, crumbled
Pinch of cayenne pepper
Salt to taste

Garnish: Watercress sprigs
Accompaniment: Melba toast

The Steps:

1. Pour broth into small saucepan, sprinkle with gelatin, and cook over high heat, stirring until gelatin is dissolved. Do not boil. Pour into large loaf pan or similar-sized mold or dish. Chill for 1–2 hours or overnight.
2. In large nonstick skillet, heat butter and sauté onion over medium heat until just soft, about 5 minutes.
3. Add livers, sauté for 1–2 minutes, stirring constantly; add wine, broth, and remaining seasonings, cover and simmer slowly for 15–20 minutes. Cool slightly.
4. Place mixture in food processor or blender and process until smooth, or put through food mill. Cool for 30 minutes. Season to taste, place over gelatin layer, and chill for 4–6 hours or overnight.
5. Unmold pâté and serve on platter garnished with watercress sprigs, accompanied by Melba toast or other low calorie crackers.

Variations:

Calves' or beef livers can be substituted for chicken livers.
Add a tablespoon of Marsala, Madeira, port, or red wine to the gelatin mixture.

Make-It-Easy Tips:

√ Whenever you buy a chicken, freeze the livers together and soon there will be enough for a pâté.
√ Remove any yellowish skin attached to the livers before using. This skin is part of the gall sac and will give a bitter taste to the pâté.
√ To easily unmold pâté, carefully run a paring knife around the edge of the pâté, place in a basin filled with 1–2 inches of hot water, and count to ten. Place platter on top of mold, invert, and pâté will easily fall onto plate.
√ It is best to use a nonstick skillet since the amount of butter is only one tablespoon.
√ The pâté must be cooled slightly before placing atop gelatin or it will melt the gelatin.

Romanian Eggplant "Caviar"

SERVES: 10–12
Preparation time: 10–15 minutes
Cooking time: 40–45 minutes
Chilling time: 1–2 hours

The Ingredients:

2 medium eggplants
½ cup finely minced onion
2 tablespoons olive oil
2 tablespoons lemon juice
2 tablespoons freshly chopped parsley
Salt and freshly ground pepper to taste
Accompaniments: Melba toast or thin crackers

The Steps:

1. Preheat oven to 400°.
2. Wash eggplants, discard green end, place in baking pan. Pierce randomly with knife and bake for 40–45 minutes, or until soft to the touch. Cool for 15 minutes or until easy to handle.
3. Peel eggplant with sharp paring knife or vegetable peeler and mash pulp in food processor, blender, or by hand until smooth.
4. Add onion, oil, lemon juice, parsley, salt, and pepper, stir until well blended, and chill for 1–2 hours or until ready to use.
5. Serve chilled or at room temperature accompanied by melba toast or other thin crackers.

Variation:

Traditionally, the eggplant for this spread is pierced with a long fork and held over an open gas flame until scorched and browned. This method gives a smoky flavor to the spread. To achieve this without lengthy chores, place eggplant on grill over barbecue and bake until scorched on the outside and soft to the touch. Remove peel and mash.

Make-It-Easy Tip:

√ Eggplant is pierced to keep it from bursting and exploding in the oven.

Chinese Marinated Bay Shrimp

SERVES: 10–12
Preparation time: 10–15 minutes
Chilling time: 2–4 hours

The Ingredients:

  1½ pounds (3 cups) bay shrimp
  12 large mushrooms, finely chopped
  4 scallions, finely chopped (green and white parts included)
  4 stalks celery, finely chopped

Dressing:

  6 tablespoons rice wine vinegar
  2 tablespoons soy sauce
  4–5 teaspoons toasted sesame oil
  1 teaspoon freshly grated ginger or ¼ teaspoon ground ginger
  Pinch of sweetener
  Salt and freshly ground pepper to taste
  Garnish: Coriander or watercress sprigs

The Steps:

1. In large bowl, combine shrimp with mushrooms, scallions, and celery.
2. In separate bowl, whisk dressing ingredients together until smooth.
3. Pour dressing over shrimp and vegetables, toss, and allow to marinate for 2–4 hours in refrigerator.
4. Serve chilled or at room temperature, garnished wtih sprigs of coriander or watercress.

Variations:

Crabmeat can be substituted for shrimp.
½ teaspoon hot sauce, or to taste can be added as desired.

Make-It-Easy Tip:

√ Store peeled ginger in a jar, covered with dry sherry, in the refrigerator. Ginger can also be tightly wrapped and stored in the freezer indefinitely.

Dinner from the Famous Spas

SERVES: 4
Toasted Potato Shells (*La Costa*)
Game Hens à l'Orange (*The Canyon Ranch*)
Skinny Spinach Salad (*The Oaks* and *The Palms*)
Mango-Lime Paradise (*The Golden Door*)

Pampering is what spas are all about—and pampering is the mood of this dinner. Reminders of all the creams, oils, and assorted treatments should be present as the centerpiece—but in a new form. Take old cold cream jars or other low-shaped containers, wash them thoroughly, and fill them with radishes. On a new gummed label use colored marker pens to write— NO LIMITS! A large mayonnaise jar used as a container for stalks of celery and carrots can have a label reading—NO TOXINS! On a jar filled with cucumbers and zucchini spears make a label saying—ENERGY BOOSTERS! And as the perfect beverage, a large pitcher of mineral water labeled—ALL YOU WANT!

To complete the spa mood, set up a basket of four towels, each filled with cutlery and rolled and tied with new pairs of sneaker laces. Fresh herbs or greens can be added to the basket, which is capped off with a label reading—HERBAL TOWELS.

The menu is easily organized. The potatoes can be baked in advance, scooped and readied for last-minute baking. They can be served as a first course or as a side dish along with the main course.

The game hens can be totally cooked beforehand, reheated, and served attractively garnished with orange slices and parsley sprigs. The salad can be crisped and the dressing readied but tossed just before serving.

The wonderfully cooling dessert is best prepared ahead of time and allowed to chill. Top each portion with colorful slices of kiwi mixed with seasonal berries.

Toasted Potato Shells (La Costa) *

SERVES: 4
Preparation time: 5–10 minutes
Cooking time: 1 hour

La Costa Health and Beauty Spa—located in Carlsbad, California, 30 miles from San Diego—is both a hotel and spa combined. With golf courses, tennis courts, and exercise rooms, it offers all the amenities of a country club. The separate men's and women's spas provide personalized programs and diets upon request. They suggest a sound, sensible 800-calorie daily intake in a beautifully presented weight-loss routine that teaches portion control.

The Ingredients:
    2 medium baking potatoes, washed and pierced with fork
    1 tablespoon chopped chives
    1 teaspoon Parmesan cheese
    ½ teaspoon caraway seeds

The Steps:
    1. Preheat oven to 500°.
    2. Bake potatoes for 45–60 minutes or until skins are crisp and centers are done.

*Recipe courtesy of *The La Costa Diet and Exercise Book* by R. Phillip Smith, M.D. (New York: Grosset and Dunlap, 1977).

3. Cut potato in half horizontally, scoop out flesh, leaving ⅓″ nearest the skin. (Reserve potato flesh for another use.)
4. Reduce oven to 350°, return shells, and continue to bake for an additional 10 minutes, or until fairly crisp.
5. Combine remaining ingredients; sprinkle a little of mixture in each shell, return to oven, and continue to bake 5 minutes or until cheese melts. Serve immediately.

Variations:
Caraway seeds can be omitted.
Leftover potato flesh can be mashed with a small amount of yogurt and pepper for a low-calorie mashed potato.

Make-It-Easy Tip:
✓ Store potatoes in cool, dry, dark, ventilated place. Do not refrigerate or an overly sweet taste will result from the conversion of starch to sugar at cold temperatures.

Game Hens à l'Orange (The Canyon Ranch)

SERVES: 4
Preparation time: 10 minutes
Cooking time: 1 hour

The Canyon Ranch, located in Tucson, Arizona, is one of the new-style spas—no "fat farm" here! It is the perfect place for singles, or especially couples, to retreat to an unstructured atmosphere of exercise classes and walking and hiking in the Arizona desert. The dieting plan is basically low in fats, high in fiber, and contains no refined sugar. Their creative recipes are from food consultant Jeanne Jones.

The Ingredients:
2 game hens, split in half
  Corn oil
  Freshly ground white pepper
1 large onion, quartered
3 ounces frozen unsweetened concentrated orange juice, thawed
1 cup dry white wine or dry vermouth
  Garnish: Orange slices, parsley sprigs

The Steps:
1. Preheat oven to 350°.
2. Lightly rub game hen halves with oil and sprinkle all sides with pepper.
3. Place 4 onion quarters in roasting pan. Place hen halves, cut side down, atop each onion quarter and bake for 15 minutes.
4. Combine remaining ingredients, stir, pour over hens, and continue to cook for 45 minutes longer, basting occasionally.
5. Remove from oven, place hens and onion quarters on platter, spoon sauce over all, and serve hot, garnished with orange slices and parsley sprigs.

Variation:
Chicken breasts can be substituted for hens, but cooked only 30–40 minutes or until just tender.

Make-It-Easy Tips:
√ Game hens can be cooked in advance and reheated just before serving in a 400° oven until golden brown.
√ Rock Cornish game hens are now available fresh or frozen in the supermarkets. Select the smallest and lightest ones, which are the most tender.

Skinny Spinach Salad (The Oaks at Ojai and The Palms at Palm Springs)

SERVES: 4–6
Preparation time: 10–15 minutes

Under the ownership of Sheila Cluff, both The Oaks at Ojai and The Palms at Palm Springs have become well-priced retreats for singles or couples in a casual atmosphere. The diet is a sound and sensible 750-calorie regimen utilizing natural foods without additives, salt, sugar, or white flour.

The Ingredients:
6 cups spinach, washed, stems removed, torn into pieces
6–8 medium mushrooms, cleaned and sliced

1 hard-cooked egg, grated
2 tablespoons minced scallions (green and white parts included)

Dressing:
⅓ cup white wine vinegar
⅓ cup water
2 tablespoons safflower oil
2 tablespoons minced scallions (green and white parts included)
2 tablespoons freshly chopped parsley
2 tablespoons freshly grated Parmesan cheese
1 clove garlic, finely minced

The Steps:
1. Place spinach in bowl; top with mushrooms, egg, and scallions.
2. Combine dressing ingredients in food processor or blender until smooth.
3. Pour dressing over salad, toss, and serve immediately.

Make-It-Easy Tips:
√ If possible, prepare dressing several hours in advance and chill until ready to use.
√ To easily clean mushrooms, dip a paper towel into lemon juice and quickly rub mushrooms clean.

Mango-Lime Paradise (The Golden Door)*

SERVES: 4
Preparation time: 10 minutes

The Golden Door—located in Escondido, California, 40 miles northeast of San Diego—is among the most exclusive of spas (limited to 34 guests per week). Under the leadership of Deborah Szekely, the spa specializes in individual attention coupled with rigorous workouts, yoga, and other exercise routines. The diet prescribed is designed to maintain a high energy level while still achieving a significant weight loss.

*Recipe courtesy of *The Golden Door Cookbook* by Deborah Szekely, with Chef Michel Stroot (Foreman Publishing, 1982).

The Ingredients:

    2 cups mango pulp (2–3 mangoes)
    ½ cup fresh orange juice
    1 tablespoon fresh lime or lemon juice
    1 tablespoon honey (omit if mango is very sweet)
    Garnish: Kiwi slices, raspberries, or strawberry halves

The Steps:

1. In food processor or blender, puree mango pulp with orange juice, lime juice, and honey until smooth.
2. Pour into 4 individual dessert dishes and serve immediately, or chill until ready to serve, garnished with kiwi slices, raspberries, or strawberry halves.

Make-It-Easy Tips:

√ Always slice mangoes over paper towels to avoid staining.
√ Select smooth-skinned mangoes that have started to color up. Green ones may never ripen properly. A ready-to-eat mango should yield to mild pressure.

Elegantly Light Dinner

SERVES: 6
*Chilled White Wine
Seviche
Poulet Citron
Parsleyed Brown Rice
Poireaux Braisés
Minted Melon

This dinner is for that special occasion when you want to entertain in fine style without destroying your weight-watching progress—or that of your guests. It uses those low-calorie standbys—chicken and fish—in a flavorful and international style.

For a dressy dinner, your prettiest candlesticks, best china, and finest table linens add atmosphere—and no calories! All white linens lend a classic elegance to your table. The colors blue and white together denote French atmosphere, and deep reds, like crimson and burgundy, add drama. Runners add an out-of-the-ordinary look that fits the occasion. On a round table, three crisscross runners make a striking starlike pattern.

* Not a recipe

Flowers definitely belong on this table. Place one large arrangement in the center of the table—just keep it low enough so that people can see each other! Or set individual bud vases at each place to accentuate the slender look. Baby's breath adds delicacy to any arrangement and dries well for later use. And for an extra added touch, try the bottle wrap around the white wine or even a bottle of sparkling mineral water. Fold a napkin or bandana in half diagonally, then fold the bottom edge up by one-quarter two times, and tie the napkin around the bottle as an attractive table decoration. (See illustration.) It also helps to catch extra drips.

Start your dinner with Seviche served on salad plates. This colorful Peruvian version of sushi transforms fish or scallops into a delicacy—all with no added oil, gooey sauces, or even any cooking. To avoid extra steps and dishes, Seviche can be served as an hors d'oeuvre on crackers at cocktail time.

Poulet Citron is a classic French combination of chicken freshly seasoned with garlic, lemon, and parsley. Only the white meat is used, without the skin; therefore a good portion of the calories is removed. This dish is cooked quickly and served immediately. Save yourself steps at dinnertime by readying the chicken for the pan ahead of time. Give it a fresh and colorful presentation with lemon slices and sprigs of watercress.

The Bottle Wrap
1. Fold the napkin in half diagonally.   2. Fold the bottom edge up by one quarter twice.   3. Tie the napkin around the bottle and fold the points to the base.

Note: If you want to catch condensation from a chilled wine bottle, turn back one of the points over the band formed after step 2, set the bottle on the other flap and then wrap the band around the bottle. Be sure to catch the rear flap securely as you tie the napkin in a knot.

An embellished version of brown rice and a flavorful European serving of leeks—Poireaux Braisés—accompany the chicken. Both add satisfying flavors and textures. Mound the rice in a round bowl, and show off the green and white leeks on a flat plate.

Finish with a wonderfully slimming dessert of Minted Melon. It's hard to believe how melons can taste so incredibly sweet with so few calories. It's a dessert that merits as much attention as any mousse—so serve it in goblets or dessert dishes on doily-lined saucers, adorned with sprigs of mint.

Seviche

SERVES: 6
Preparation time: 20 minutes
Marinating time: 6–8 hours or overnight

This traditional Peruvian seviche is prepared less expensively with fish but can also be made with scallops. The fish must be very fresh, since it is not cooked but marinated and eaten raw. So ask at the fish market for the freshest and best fish to use for Seviche.

The Ingredients:
2 pounds very fresh fillets of fish (snapper, sole) cut into 2″–3″ strips
½ cup lime juice
1 pimiento, finely chopped
½ cup finely chopped onion
½ cup finely chopped green pepper
½ cup finely chopped tomato
1 clove garlic, finely minced
2 tablespoons freshly chopped parsley
1 teaspoon sugar
¼ teaspoon chili powder
Salt and freshly ground pepper to taste
Garnish: Freshly chopped coriander (cilantro) or parsley

The Steps:

1. Lay fish strips in shallow dish, pour lime juice over, and toss to coat. Cover and marinate in refrigerator for 6–8 hours or overnight.
2. Drain off juice, add remaining ingredients, toss well, and chill for 2 hours.
3. Serve Seviche chilled, garnished with freshly chopped coriander or parsley.

Variations:

The recipe may be prepared with bay or sea scallops if available.
Lemon juice may be used as a marinade but lime juice is traditional.

Make-It-Easy Tips:

√ Even though older limes turn from dark green to yellow, the quality of the juice remains good. Limes kept refrigerated will keep for 6–8 weeks.
√ Roll room-temperature limes between the palm of your hand and the counter, pressing down firmly; this loosens the pulp, in turn releasing the juice.

Poulet Citron

SERVES: 6
Preparation time: 15 minutes
Cooking time: 10 minutes

This low-calorie chicken utilizes fresh garlic and lemon juice as flavor enhancers.

The Ingredients:

- 6 6-ounce chicken breasts, skinned and boned and dried with paper towels
- 4 teaspoons whole wheat flour mixed with ½ teaspoon freshly ground pepper
- 1 tablespoon unsalted butter
- 1 tablespoon vegetable oil
- 3 tablespoons minced scallions (green and white parts included)

¼ cup fresh lemon juice
¼ cup freshly chopped parsley
3–4 tablespoons chicken broth
2 teaspoons freshly minced garlic
1½ teaspoons freshly grated lemon peel
   Garnish: Watercress, lemon slices, and cherry tomatoes

The Steps:

1. Flatten chicken breasts, lightly dust with flour mixed with pepper, and shake off excess.
2. In large nonstick skillet, heat butter and oil and sauté scallions for 1 minute; add chicken and sauté over high heat for 2–3 minutes a side, or until tender; remove to platter.
3. Add remaining ingredients; allow to heat through for 1 minute, pour over chicken, and serve immediately, garnished with watercress, lemon slices, and cherry tomatoes.

Variation:

Veal Scaloppine can be substituted for the chicken, but cook only 1–2 minutes per side.

Make-It-Easy Tips:

√ A powdered sugar shaker makes an excellent flour shaker for dusting meats or cake pans.
√ The chicken breasts must be flattened to facilitate quick cooking. Use a mallet, hammer, or side of a large knife.
√ A nonstick skillet reduces the amount of fats necessary and thereby reduces the amount of calories.

Parsleyed Brown Rice

SERVES: 6
Preparation time: 10 minutes
Cooking time: 35–40 minutes

The Ingredients:

2 cups chicken broth
1 cup water

1½ cups raw brown rice
   Salt and freshly ground pepper to taste
2 tablespoons freshly chopped parsley
1 teaspoon freshly grated lemon peel

The Steps:

1. In deep saucepan, bring broth and water to a boil; add rice but do not stir.
2. Sprinkle with salt and pepper, cover; reduce heat and simmer slowly for 35–40 minutes, or until liquid is absorbed and grains are tender.
3. Fluff rice with fork, stir in parsley and lemon, and serve immediately.

Variations:

Rice can be cooked with all broth and no water.
Leftover rice can be chilled, tossed with vinaigrette, and served as a rice salad.

Make-It-Easy Tip:

√ Brown rice is nutritionally superior to white rice. It is closest to its natural state, with only the hull and some of the bran removed. As with any whole grain cereal, brown rice requires a slightly longer cooking time and a little more liquid than white rice.

Poireaux Braisés (Braised Leeks)

SERVES: 6
Preparation time: 10–15 minutes
Cooking time: 35 minutes

Leeks are an extremely popular vegetable in Europe, often called the "poor man's asparagus." In the United States, they have previously been relegated to exotic status, although they are currently gaining in popularity as a vegetable rather than a seasoning.

The Ingredients:

  12 medium leeks
  1½ tablespoons unsalted butter
  ¾ cup white wine or dry vermouth
  1 tablespoon lemon juice
  ½ teaspoon Worcestershire sauce
     Salt and freshly ground pepper to taste

The Steps:

1. Trim off leeks' root ends; cut off green part, leaving only 1" of the green section. Thoroughly and carefully wash leeks under cold running water, fanning out leaves to remove all sand and grit.
2. In large skillet, heat butter and sauté leeks over medium heat, turning often, for 2–3 minutes or until barely colored.
3. Add remaining ingredients; bring to a boil, cover, reduce heat, and simmer slowly for 25–30 minutes, depending on size, or until leeks are tender.
4. With slotted spatula or tongs, transfer leeks to platter. Thicken pan juices by boiling over high heat until reduced and syrupy. Pour juices over leeks and serve.

Variation:

Leeks can also be baked in a 350° oven for 45–50 minutes, or until tender.

Make-It-Easy Tips:

√ Leeks must be carefully scrubbed under cold running water to remove sand lodged between the leaves.
√ Select leeks with tightly rolled leaves and brightly colored green tops.

Minted Melon

SERVES: 6
Preparation time: 10–15 minutes
Chilling time: 2–4 hours

Minted melon is imbued with the sweet flavor of Marsala wine.

The Ingredients:

2 ripe cantaloupes, sliced in half, with seed and strings removed
2 tablespoons Marsala wine
1 tablespoon lemon juice
   Garnish: Mint sprigs

The Steps:

1. Using melon-ball scoop, prepare 3–4 cups melon balls and place in large bowl.
2. Sprinkle with wine and lemon juice; toss gently, cover with plastic wrap, and allow to chill for 2–4 hours.
3. Serve in large goblets or dessert dishes garnished with mint sprigs.

Variations:

Honeydew, Crenshaw, or any combination of melons can be used. Marsala can be omitted if desired.

Make-It-Easy Tip:

√ Cut melons absorb refrigerator odors easily, so make sure to cover tightly with plastic wrap or aluminum foil.

CHAPTER FOURTEEN

HOLIDAY CELEBRATIONS

1. **New Year's Eve Celebration**
   Caviar Torte
   Steak Tartare
   Julienne of Carrot Salad
   Plum-Glazed Chicken Breasts
   Noodles Florentine
   Crème Brûlée

2. **Valentine's Dinner for Lovers**
   *Champagne
   Mushroom Soup for Two
   Steak au Poivre
   "Hearts" Salad
   *Baked Potatoes
   Lemon Champagne Sherbet
   *Chocolate Candies

3. **Mother's or Father's Day Family Dinner**
   Artichokes Vinaigrette
   Marinated Potted Beef
   Pasta Souffle
   Celery with Almonds
   Peach Melba

4. **Fourth of July Barbecue**
   "Parsley, Sage, Rosemary, and Thyme" Grilled Lamb
   Tomato and Mozzarella Salad
   *Sourdough Rolls
   Grilled Roasted Corn on the Cob
   Watermelon Bombe

5. **Labor Day Picnic**
   Picnic Chicken
   Red Potato Salad
   Colorful Coleslaw
   Blueberry Lattice Pie
   *Fresh Fruit

6. **Trick-or-Treat Party**
   Grape-Orange Punch
   Make-Your-Own French Bread Pizzas
   Black-and-White Cupcakes
   Pumpkin Spice Bars
   Incredibly Easy Chocolate Fudge
   Butterscotch Brownies
   *Candy

7. **Traditional Thanksgiving Feast**
   Hot Spiced Cider
   Perfect Roast Turkey
   Sourdough-Pecan Stuffing
   Glazed Sweet Potatoes
   Marmalade-Spiked Cranberry Sauce
   Spinach Flans on Tomato Rings
   Pumpkin Ice Cream Pie

8. **Merry Christmas Dinner**
   Christmas Glögg (Mulled Wine)
   Roast Beef
   Horseradish Cream Sauce
   Pan-Roasted Potatoes
   Cherry Tomato Salad in Parsley Wreath
   Quick-and-Easy Pecan Pie
   Hard Sauce
   Bourbon Balls

* Not a recipe

ALL YEAR LONG we gear up for holiday celebrations—from New Year's Eve to Christmas. We have high expectations, brimming with childhood memories of family gatherings. This section is designed to simplify holiday preparations while keeping them very special and indulging the child in all of us.

The recipes that are handed down through generations are always cherished, but the hours and hours of preparations they may require no longer are possible, given our busy lives and the demands on our time.

Normally when I entertain, I prepare light hors d'oeuvres so that guests are not full before dinner. The *New Year's Eve Celebration* menu offers an exception to this rule, since it is laden with heavy hors d'oeuvres. Dinner is often late and the champagne or wine flows freely. Therefore guests appreciate having more than light finger food available.

Valentine's Day is for couples, and the *Valentine's Dinner for Lovers* can be served on this special occasion or any night when love is the major topic of conversation.

A *Mother's or Father's Day Family Dinner* is a nice way to say thank you. Involve children in every aspect of the day, from preparing the food to setting the table to buying or even making gifts. I offer a complete menu, but if there is a food that is a special favorite of Mom's or Dad's, obviously this is the day to make that substitution.

The *Fourth of July Barbecue* and *Labor Day Picnic* are a salute to summer, so I offer Make-It-Easy recipes for a totally informal setting. The food is delicious, but it's typically only half the pleasure, since these are also occasions for out-of-door fun and games.

A *Trick-or-Treat Party* is designed to keep children safe, happy, and at home on Halloween night. They can make their own pizzas or even homemade fudge, along with playing the other traditional games.

The *Traditional Thanksgiving Feast* I've presented uses my favorite brown-bag turkey baking tip. Once in the bag, I don't have to baste or fuss. In addition, I always involve my family and friends in Thanksgiving food preparation. This is a time of sharing, and I am definitely not shy about asking for assistance with a long menu for a large group. That way I have additional time to make the table and the house look very festive.

The menu for the *Merry Christmas Dinner* is also traditional but, prepared with Make-It-Easy recipes, it is a pleasure to cook. Actually, this combination of roast beef and potatoes can be a wonderful menu any cool night of the year.

Both Thanksgiving and Christmas often require more than one meal. Guests usually finish the main meal early in the afternoon, relax for a while, and then are ready for a light supper. So, when preparing holiday feasts, I always buy a few interesting breads for late evening supper snacks.

New Year's Eve Celebration

SERVES 10–12
Caviar Torte
Steak Tartare
Julienne of Carrot Salad
Plum-Glazed Chicken Breasts
Noodles Florentine
Crème Brûlée

This great last bash of the holiday season gives us one more chance to celebrate during the chilliest, darkest days of the year. A variety of themes—last year's memories, the new year's resolutions, the finale of the holiday season—make planning and decorating enjoyable. And going buffet-style guarantees a Make-It-Easy way to serve.

Red, white, and black set a smashing color scheme. The red and white carry over from Christmas, and black adds a sophisticated touch. I use runners of red cloth to accent the table. Red and white candles carry the colors throughout the room. The Caviar Torte brings the color scheme right to the menu itself.

If you're feeling very clever or there's an artist in the family, try a clock-shaped centerpiece. Start with a styrofoam disk outlined in shiny black electric tape. Stick on black adhesive numbers and pin on black or red paper hands poised at midnight. Then mount your creation on a stick—a dowel or chopstick will do—standing in a base of styrofoam, a mound of pebbles, or even a bowl of dried beans.

If you're feeling less ambitious, fill a basket with small clocks, watches, and timers. Slip a few pages of the past year's calendar into the basket. Or line the pages end to end like a runner across the table. Leftover Christmas trimmings leave you with lots of decorating options. For starters, evergreen boughs and pinecones add color and life to any centerpiece.

Especially when the guests are family and close friends, it can be a warm experience to recall the year's events. Put out pictures and mementos of the year's milestones and good times—graduations, weddings, births, holidays, and trips. Or mark them in red on the calendar pages and ask guests to add others they can think of. An amusing party game idea is to suggest that each guest write his or her New Year's resolution anonymously and place them all in a hat. On or around midnight, the host or hostess can read them aloud and everyone can attempt to match the resolution to the guests.

It's easy to get carried away with ideas, but don't forget the practical side that also makes your party special. This menu is designed for a long, late-night party. It's really an extended cocktail hour, with lots of satisfying appetizers to last the evening.

The Steak Tartare must be prepared shortly before party time, but the torte is best done ahead and chilled. Only the topping goes on just before serving. These two dishes are placed at one end of the table, with a basket of toasted bread rounds or crackers nearby. The carrot salad can be served as part of the hors d'oeuvres or as a salad alongside the main course.

Next comes the more substantial foods: the Plum-Glazed Chicken, attractively garnished with orange wedges, and Noodles Florentine, as a side dish or for those who prefer a meatless alternative. Save yourself some kitchen hassles by having the chicken ingredients ready and the Noodles Florentine assembled in advance, ready for baking. I use a basket holder for the casserole to help protect the table and avoid burned fingers.

Forks are the only flatware needed until dessert. They may be wrapped in red and white napkins, tied with bits of Christmas ribbon, and placed in a basket or large candy jar.

Crème Brûlée, a rich and creamy make-ahead treat, is a fit ending for this feast. Individual ramekins or custard cups simplify serving, and may be carried on a tray in one trip from the kitchen.

Whatever beverages you choose, lots of glasses are a must. Plastic cups are handy, but can react with certain acidic spirits to form an unpleasant taste. And of course, include plenty of nonalcoholic choices for those who prefer it—and for those driving home.

Caviar Torte

SERVES: 10–12
Preparation time: 15–20 minutes

This is a variation on a traditional recipe that makes an especially attractive addition to the table.

The Ingredients:
      8 hard-cooked eggs, chopped
      3 tablespoons mayonnaise
         Salt and freshly ground pepper to taste
      2 bunches (1¼ cups) minced scallions (green and white parts included)
      8 ounces cream cheese, softened
      ⅔ cup dairy sour cream
      1 3½-ounce jar Danish or Icelandic Lumpfish Black Caviar
      1 3½-ounce jar red caviar
         Garnish: Lemon wedges and parsley sprigs
         Accompaniments: Toasted bread crumbs or crackers

The Steps:
   1. Generously oil or butter 9″ springform pan or pie plate.
   2. Combine eggs with mayonnaise, salt, and pepper; spread over bottom of prepared pan and top with scallions.
   3. Combine cream cheese with sour cream in blender, food processor, electric mixer, or by hand until smooth; spread over scallions, cover, and chill 3 hours or overnight.
   4. Just before serving, using black and red caviar alternately, make 6 triangle shapes so pie wedges make a red-and-black color scheme.
   5. Run knife around springform pan sides, loosen, lift off, and serve pie garnished with lemon wedges and parsley sprigs. (If using pie plate, serve torte directly from pan.) Accompany with toasted bread rounds or crackers.

Variation:

All-black or all-red caviar can be spread on top in place of the alternating colors.

Make-It-Easy Tips:

√ A wet spatula helps to spread cream layer easily over scallions.

√ Drain caviar in small strainer before spreading on top, to remove excess oil.

Steak Tartare

SERVES: 10–12
Preparation time: 15 minutes

You need the very best meat available for Steak Tartare. Ask the butcher for the leanest beef and have him grind it 2 or 3 times for you.

The Ingredients:

1 pound very lean top round steak, ground
¼ cup finely minced onion
1 tablespoon chopped fresh parsley
1 egg, lightly beaten
1 teaspoon Dijon mustard
1 teaspoon tomato paste
½ teaspoon Worcestershire sauce
½ teaspoon paprika
Dash of Tabasco sauce
Pinch of cayenne pepper
Salt and freshly ground pepper to taste
Garnish: Cornichons (sour pickles), cherry tomatoes, and parsley sprigs
Accompaniment: Pumpernickel bread rounds

The Steps:

1. Combine all ingredients, form log or mound shape, chill until ready to serve. (Do not do this earlier than 2 hours before serving.)

2. Garnish with cornichons, cherry tomatoes, and parsley sprigs and accompany with pumpernickel bread rounds.

Variations:

Fresh ground meat does not keep for a long time. Fry any leftover meat until crumbly in a skillet, add tomato sauce, and cook for a few minutes for a spicy meat sauce.

Steak Tartare may also be served as a part of a luncheon or brunch buffet.

Make-It-Easy Tip:

√ The entire recipe can be prepared in the food processor at one time but pulsated in an on-and-off rhythm just until chopped. In this case, begin with small pieces of meat and chop them yourself.

Julienne of Carrot Salad

SERVES: 8
Preparation time: 10–15 minutes

This recipe is an adaptation of a dish served at Leon Lionides's restaurant, The Coach House in New York City.

The Ingredients:

6 cups shredded carrots (about 1½ pounds)
⅓ cup capers, drained

Vinaigrette Dressing:
½ cup olive oil
3 tablespoons red wine vinegar
2 teaspoons Dijon Mustard
Salt and freshly ground pepper
Pinch of sugar
Garnish: Freshly chopped parsley

The Steps:

1. Combine carrots and capers together and chill until ready to use.
2. Combine vinaigrette ingredients together in a screw-top jar and shake until smooth.

3. Toss carrots with vinaigrette and serve immediately, or chill and serve later; garnish with freshly chopped parsley.

Variations:

If serving as hors d'oeuvre, accompany with crackers or small plates and forks.

Substitute ½ cup chopped scallion greens for capers.

Make-It-Easy Tips:

√ The food processor makes a perfect tool for shredding carrots easily.
√ Carrots with their leafy green tops remaining are more likely to be fresher than those wrapped in plastic bags.

Plum-Glazed Chicken Breasts

SERVES: 10–12
Preparation time: 10–15 minutes
Cooking time: 40–45 minutes

The Ingredients:

  1 cup plum jam or preserves
  6 tablespoons red wine vinegar
  ¼ cup finely chopped scallions
  ¼ cup soy sauce
  2 tablespoons freshly grated ginger or 1½ teaspoons dried ground ginger
  1 teaspoon dry mustard
    Pinch of ground cloves
    Pinch of cayenne
 10 chicken breasts, split in half
    Garnish: Orange slices

The Steps:

1. Preheat oven to 375°. Select a baking dish that can hold the chicken in a single layer and cover it with aluminum foil to save on messy cleanups.
2. In small saucepan, combine plum jam with vinegar, scallions,

soy sauce, ginger, mustard, cloves, and cayenne. Heat, stirring constantly until smooth.

3. Arrange chicken pieces in single layer, skin side down, in baking dish.
4. Brush half of sauce over chicken and bake for 20 minutes, basting occasionally.
5. Turn chicken and brush with remaining sauce; continue to bake for 20–25 minutes longer, or until tender and glazed.
6. Serve hot, garnished with orange slices.

Variations:

One whole chicken cut in 8 pieces can be substituted for the chicken breasts.

After baking, chicken can be placed under broiler for 2 minutes to further caramelize the color.

Make-It-Easy Tip:

√ Store peeled ginger in dry sherry in a covered jar in the refrigerator.

Noodles Florentine

SERVES: 12
Preparation time: 20 minutes
Cooking time: 45 minutes

This extra rich casserole is hearty, filling, and best of all can be assembled in advance.

The Ingredients:

    20 ounces medium-wide noodles
     6 tablespoons unsalted butter, at room temperature
     2 pints dairy sour cream
     4 10-ounce packages frozen chopped spinach, thawed and squeezed dry
     6 eggs
  1½ cups freshly grated Parmesan cheese
   ½ teaspoon Worcestershire sauce

Pinch of nutmeg
Salt and freshly ground pepper to taste
1–2 tablespoons unsalted butter

The Steps:

1. Preheat oven to 350°. Generously butter 9" x 13" x 2" pan or similar-sized baking dish.
2. Drop noodles into boiling salted water and cook until just done; drain and place in large bowl. Immediately toss with butter, coating noodles well. Add sour cream and continue to toss.
3. Squeeze any excess moisture out of spinach and set aside.
4. Beat eggs with squeezed spinach until smooth. (This can be done in blender, food processor, with electric beater, or by hand.)
5. Toss noodles with spinach-egg mixture to combine. Add 1 cup of cheese and continue to stir. Season with Worcestershire sauce, nutmeg, salt, and pepper and pour into prepared pan.
6. Top with remaining cheese and a few tablespoons butter cut into tiny bits; bake for 45 minutes, or until hot and bubbling.

Variation:

Four 10-ounce packages frozen chopped broccoli, thawed, can be substituted for spinach.

Make-It-Easy Tips:

√ If casserole is not being used immediately, it can be refrigerated after assembly and baked when ready to use. If doing ahead, be sure to bring to room temperature before baking.
√ If using a glass baking dish, reduce heat by 25°.

Crème Brûlée

SERVES: 8–12
Preparation time: 20–25 minutes
Cooking time: 1 hour

Crème Brûlée sounds complicated, but in reality it only requires a few steps and can be made a day or two in advance. The best part of Crème Brûlée is that it is an instant winner. Forget the diets, however. It is best to make the dessert a day ahead. Chill it overnight, prepare the caramel topping the morning it is to be served, and allow to chill again.

The Ingredients:
1 quart heavy cream
6 tablespoons granulated sugar
8 egg yolks
2 teaspoons vanilla extract
1 cup light brown sugar, firmly packed

The Steps:
1. Preheat oven to 350°
2. In large saucepan, scald cream by heating until bubbles just begin to form around edges of pan and steam escapes. Do not allow to boil or cream will scorch. Add sugar to cream and stir until sugar is completely dissolved.
3. In separate bowl, beat egg yolks until lemony in color. Add a little hot cream to eggs, stirring constantly and then gradually add remaining cream, whisking until smooth. Add vanilla and pour mixture into 8 ramekins, Pyrex custard cups, or a 10″ shallow baking dish.
4. Place dish or cups in roasting pan filled with 1″ of hot water and bake 35–40 minutes for ramekin dishes or custard cups, 50–60 minutes for 10″ baking dish, or until inserted knife comes out clean. Remove from oven, cool, cover with plastic wrap, and chill for 4–6 hours or overnight.
5. Preheat broiler to high.
6. With the back of a spoon, push brown sugar through a strainer and sprinkle on top of custards about ¼″ thick; broil 4″–6″ from broiler until sugar has caramelized, about 3 minutes, watching very carefully, and turning dish as necessary to avoid burning. Cool and chill again.
7. Serve Crème Brûlée chilled.

Variation:
A vanilla bean can be sliced open, added to the cream that is scalded for Step #2, and removed before proceeding with recipe. If using vanilla bean, omit extract.

Make-It-Easy Tips:

√ When cooking with egg yolks, it is important to introduce hot liquids gradually, to avoid curdling the eggs.

√ Cooking the custard in a hot-water bath prevents the custard from curdling or overcooking.

√ To keep very fresh, store brown sugar in a tightly closed plastic bag in freezer. Bring to room temperature before using.

Valentine's Dinner for Lovers

SERVES: 2
* Champagne
Mushroom Soup for Two
Steak au Poivre
* Baked Potatoes
"Hearts" Salad
Lemon Champagne Sherbet
* Chocolate Candies

It could be Valentine's Day, an anniversary, or just the fact that the kids are visiting Grandma and Grandpa. Lovers don't need an excuse to make their own private holiday. Here is a dinner you can prepare for your favorite person without getting too tired to enjoy the rest of the evening. You can even cook it together.

The table setting should be very simple—the emphasis is on the couple, not the decor. A white tablecloth with red napkins will set a Valentine mood. Napkins can easily be folded accordian-style and slipped into

* Not a recipe

Napkin Fan
Begin with a crisp napkin 17–18″ square.   1. Fold napkin as shown with
some overlap.   2. Accordion fold in sharp creases 1½″ wide starting from the
left.   3. Place napkin in glass and fan out.

champagne glasses, fanning out over the top. Three roses traditionally
say, "I love you." And what romantic dinner is complete without soft
candlelight? Either tall thin tapers or even lots of inexpensive small votive
candles all around the house will set the mood for romance.

The soup can be prepared in advance and reheated at serving time.
Bake the potatoes in a 375° oven, or even a toaster oven, for about 1 hour
and 15 minutes. Don't worry if they overbake; the skins will get even
crispier and the centers will become powdery-soft. The salad greens can
be readied and chilled, and the dressing prepared and left at room temperature. This leaves plenty of time for setting the table—and making
sure you look your best. Having your ingredients ready will make the
steak especially easy to prepare.

The bottle of champagne looks extra-special wrapped in a white napkin
(see illustration of bottle wrap on page 161) and set on a trivet. And
speaking of champagne, be sure to leave a little for the Lemon Champagne Sherbet, which is made just minutes before serving. Spoon the
sherbet into chilled goblets or dessert dishes, set them on doily-lined
saucers, garnish with lemon slices, and perhaps a few Valentine's choco-
lates on the side. Then, back to the candlelight!

Mushroom Soup for Two

SERVES: 2
Preparation time: 15 minutes
Cooking time: 25 minutes

The Ingredients:

4 tablespoons (½ stick) unsalted butter
½ pound mushrooms, roughly chopped
1 small onion, roughly chopped
1½ tablespoons all-purpose flour
1½ cups chicken broth
  Salt and freshly ground white pepper to taste
1 tablespoon dry sherry
½ cup half-and-half
  Garnish: Freshly chopped parsley

The Steps:

1. Melt butter in a Dutch oven or large saucepan. Sauté mushrooms and onions until just golden.
2. Sprinkle flour over mushroom-onion mixture and stir well until absorbed.
3. Add broth, salt, and pepper, and taste for seasonings. Bring to a boil, lower heat, and simmer 20–25 minutes.
4. Add sherry and cream and heat until just warm.
5. Pour into blender or food processor and pulsate just until smooth. Taste, and adjust seasoning if necessary. Serve hot, garnished with parsley.

Variations:

Mushrooms may be sliced and sautéed and the soup served without pureeing.
Beef broth can be substituted for chicken broth.

Make-It-Easy Tips:

√ Raw mushrooms should be stored in a paper bag, which is porous, to keep them fresh.
√ The freshest mushrooms are closed around the stem by a thin veil, with no blemishes.

Steak au Poivre (Pepper Steak)

SERVES: 2
Preparation time: 10 minutes
Cooking time: 6–10 minutes

The Ingredients:
2 tablespoons black peppercorns, coarsely cracked
2 individual steaks, 1"–1½" thick, completely trimmed (shell, club, or fillet)
1 tablespoon unsalted butter
1 tablespoon vegetable oil
Salt
3 tablespoons port wine
2 tablespoons strong beef broth
3 tablespoons heavy cream
Garnish: Freshly chopped parsley

The Steps:
1. Lay cracked pepper on sheet of waxed paper and press pepper into both sides of steaks.
2. Heat butter and oil in large skillet; when melted, sear steaks for 2–3 minutes on each side, seasoning with salt on each side.
3. Add wine and cook for an additional 2 minutes. With slotted spoon, remove steaks to warm platter.
4. Add broth and stir to scrape up browned particles; cook over high heat until liquid is slightly reduced.
5. Gradually add cream, stirring until sauce is smooth and thickened; pour sauce over steaks and serve hot, garnished with freshly chopped parsley.

Variations:
Steak au Poivre can be served traditionally over butter-fried slices of French bread.
Marsala or Madeira wine can be substituted for port wine.

Make-It-Easy Tips:
√ To crack peppercorns easily, place in plastic bag and pound with mallet, cleaver, or heavy object.
√ Both the club steak (also called Delmonico) or the shell steak (also

called New York strip, Kansas City strip, or strip steak) are tender cuts of meat from the short loin of beef with the tenderloin parts removed. These cuts, as well as the fillet strip, which is the tenderloin itself, can be successfully used for Steak au Poivre.

√ This recipe is for medium-rare steaks. If rarer steak is desired, sear only 1–2 minutes in Step #2; for medium to well done, sear for 3–4 minutes per side.

"Hearts" Salad

SERVES: 2
Preparation time: 10 minutes

Serve this mixture of "hearts" salad for Valentine's Day. It is an expensive mixture of vegetables that should be reserved for a special occasion.

The Ingredients:
    4 canned artichoke hearts, drained
    4 canned hearts of palm, drained
    1 small bunch watercress

Vinaigrette Dressing:
    7 tablespoons olive oil
    2 tablespoons red wine vinegar
    1 teaspoon Dijon mustard
    ¼ teaspoon curry powder
    Pinch sugar
    Pinch paprika
    Salt and freshly ground white pepper to taste

The Steps:
1. Slice artichoke hearts in half and place 4 halves on each plate.
2. Slice hearts of palm and distribute evenly.
3. Break off watercress sprigs and place on plates decoratively; chill until ready to serve.
4. When ready to serve, combine vinaigrette ingredients together and mix well. Pour small amount of dressing on each salad and serve on chilled salad plates.

Variations:

The salad may be tossed with the dressing in a bowl and then distributed evenly between the two plates

Hearts of celery may be substituted for the more expensive hearts of palm.

Cooked frozen artichoke hearts may be substituted for the canned ones.

Make-It-Easy Tips:

√ Curry powder provides enough spiciness so that very little salt is necessary—a good tip for those on a salt-restricted diet.

√ Salad dressing can be prepared in advance and refrigerated until serving time.

Lemon Champagne Sherbet

SERVES: 2
Preparation time: 5 minutes

This cooling dessert must be served immediately. Enjoy champagne with dinner and save just ⅓ cup for this fabulous froth.

The Ingredients:

1½ cups lemon sherbet
⅓ cup champagne
½ teaspoon grated lemon peel
Garnish: Thin lemon slices

The Steps:

1. Place sherbet, champagne, and lemon peel in blender or food processor; process until smooth and ready.
2. Pour into stemmed goblets, wine glasses, or dessert dishes and serve immediately, garnished with lemon slices.

Variations:

Frozen lemon yogurt or lemon ice cream, if available, can be substituted for sherbet.

For a nonalcoholic version, substitute lemon-flavored soda or even ginger ale.

Make-It-Easy Tip:
√ The froth can be prepared with white wine, but it is the bubbles that give the dessert its frothy effervescence.

Mother's or Father's Day Family Dinner

SERVES: 6–8
Artichokes Vinaigrette
Marinated Potted Beef
Pasta Soufflé
Celery with Almonds
Peach Melba

Long before Mother's Day and Father's Day were introduced in this country, the custom of Mothering Day arose in England. It was a time for children to visit Mother, bake her a soft "simnel cake" made of fine white flour, and in return receive her blessing. While simnel cakes have gone out of fashion, mothers and fathers alike are sure to appreciate a dinner served in their honor. It's a particularly thoughtful way to show your love when presents don't seem to say all you feel.

Here is a dinner with all the looks and tastes of a special meal, yet it can easily be served family-style. Enjoy it in the evening or as a midday Sunday dinner.

Fresh flowers are traditional, and an excellent selection certainly is available in May and June. Another creative centerpiece suggestion is a collection of toys—dolls, trains, miniatures, or whatever is available, clustered at the center of the table. Cards or a gift can be set at Mom's or Dad's place. And for extra family touches, include parents' baby pictures or family pictures from past years. It might be a fun time to show slides or home movies after dinner.

Like the flowers, fresh artichokes will be in season. Be sure to cut the stem straight across the bottom so that the artichokes will stand up, and provide large enough plates to accommodate the uneaten part of the leaves. Enjoy the artichokes while the beef simmers, the soufflé bakes, and the almonds sit chopped and ready for cooking. That way no one gets stuck alone in the kitchen.

With a little supervision, children can help prepare this meal. Junior cooks can be delegated to help mix the vinaigrette, toast the almonds, and, best of all, assemble the Peach Melba for dessert.

Artichokes Vinaigrette

SERVES: 6–8
Preparation time: 15 minutes
Cooking time: 30–45 minutes
Chilling time: 2–4 hours or overnight

Artichokes are at their peak in May, although you can find them in the markets year round. Even if your family is only 6, by all means boil enough artichokes to have extras cold for lunch the next day. Once cooked, artichokes will keep for several days covered in the refrigerator.

The Ingredients:
Water
1 teaspoon salt
8 medium to large artichokes
1 lemon, cut in half

Vinaigrette (yields 2 cups):
1 cup olive oil (or ⅓ cup olive oil and ⅔ cup corn, safflower, or soy oil)
6 tablespoons red wine vinegar (or lemon juice)
2 tablespoons minced parsley
1 tablespoon minced chives or scallion greens
1 teaspoon chopped capers (soft)
1 teaspoon Dijon mustard
½ teaspoon dry mustard
½ teaspoon freshly minced garlic
Pinch of sugar
Salt and freshly ground pepper to taste

The Steps:

1. Wash artichokes. Slice off stems 1" from base and remove small bottom leaves. Cut off about 1" from top of artichoke. Trim tips of leaves easily with a kitchen scissors to avoid prickles. Rub cut side with cut lemon half.
2. Select deep kettle large enough to hold all artichokes standing upright (or use 2 large pots). Fill with enough water to cover artichokes, add salt, bring to a boil, and plunge artichokes into water. Cover and boil gently for 30–45 minutes (depending on size of artichokes), or until base can be pierced easily with fork.
3. Drain thoroughly upside down and chill for 4–6 hours or overnight.
4. Meanwhile, prepare vinaigrette by combining ingredients in food processor, blender, or small jar, blending or shaking until smooth. Chill until ready to use.
5. Serve each chilled artichoke on a large plate with a small cup containing about ¼ cup of salad dressing and enough room for the uneaten parts of the leaves.

Variation:

Artichokes can be served hot with melted butter plus a splash of brandy, or lemon-flavored butter if desired.

Make-It-Easy Tips:
√ If time permits, soak artichokes in cold water plus a pinch of vinegar or lemon juice for half an hour, to remove any lurking dirt or bugs. This will save time on washing chores.

√ To steam artichokes, place upside down in steamer, and steam until tender, about 45–60 minutes. (No need to drain.)

√ Any seasonal herb can be added to vinaigrette as desired: basil, dill, tarragon, oregano, or a combination.

Marinated Potted Beef

SERVES: 6–8
Preparation time: 15 minutes
Marinating time: 6 hours or overnight
Cooking time: 3–4 hours

It's easiest to marinate the roast a day in advance.

The Ingredients:
    4 boneless chuck roast, brisket, tri-tip, or other beef for potting
  3½ cups red wine (about 1 bottle)
    ¼ cup brandy
    1 carrot, sliced
    1 small onion, sliced
    2 tablespoons freshly chopped parsley
    1 teaspoon thyme, crumbled
    ¼ teaspoon ground allspice
      Salt and freshly ground pepper to taste
    1 tablespoon unsalted butter
      Salt and freshly ground pepper to taste

The Steps:
1. Marinate beef in wine, brandy, carrot, onion, parsley, thyme, allspice, salt, and pepper in bowl or shallow dish so that meat is covered with marinade; cover and marinate 6 hours or overnight in refrigerator, turning once or twice.
2. Remove meat from marinade and pat dry on paper towels.

3. Heat butter in Dutch oven or deep skillet; when melted, sauté beef on all sides until brown.
4. Discard accumulated fat, add marinade, bring to a boil, cover, and simmer for 3–4 hours, or until meat is tender.
5. Remove meat from sauce and set aside on heated platter.
6. Continue to cook sauce in pan over medium-high heat, reducing until slightly thickened, about 20 minutes.
7. Defat gravy, season to taste with salt and pepper, and serve meat hot, sliced, with sauce spooned over.

Variation:

½–1 teaspoon minced garlic can be added to the marinade.

Make-It-Easy Tips:

√ It is best to prepare the beef a day ahead, remove any fat, slice, and reheat wrapped in foil with the sauce reheated and served on the side.

√ A quick method of defatting gravy is to chill in freezer for 30 minutes and easily remove the congealed fat with a spoon.

√ For a quick thickener, blend 2 teaspoons potato starch or cornstarch with 1 tablespoon cold water; add to sauce and stir until thickened. Gravy can also be pureed in a food processor or blender, or through a strainer.

√ When chopping parsley by hand or in a food processor, make sure it is thoroughly dry so that the pieces will separate easily and not adhere to each other.

Pasta Soufflé

SERVES: 6–8
Preparation time: 15 minutes
Cooking time: 1 hour

This is a variation of a recipe given to me by the famous caterer Milton Williams.

The Ingredients:

¼ pound unsalted butter, softened to room temperature
4 ounces whipped cream cheese
1 pint dairy sour cream
3 eggs
1 tablespoon lemon juice
1 teaspoon sugar
½ teaspoon Worcestershire sauce
    Pinch of paprika
    Salt and freshly ground pepper to taste
4 cups water
1 teaspoon powdered or 1 cube chicken stock base
8-ounce package fine noodles

The Steps:

1. Preheat oven to 350°. Generously butter 1½ quart soufflé dish.
2. In food processor or blender, combine butter, cream cheese, sour cream, eggs, lemon juice, sugar, Worcestershire sauce, paprika, salt, and pepper and process until smooth. Pour into large mixing bowl.
3. Bring water and chicken stock base to a boil, add noodles, and cook for 5 minutes; drain without rinsing.
4. Add noodles to butter mixture, toss to combine, pour into prepared baking dish, and bake for 1 hour. Serve immediately.

Variations:

To serve as a dessert, omit salt and paprika and add 2–3 tablespoons lemon juice, an additional egg plus ¼ cup sugar. Proceed as above and serve hot with fresh berries or other fruit and a sprinkling of powdered sugar.

Vegetable variations: add 2 tablespoons corn kernels, chopped zucchini, or other vegetables for a colorful variation.

Make-It-Easy Tip:

√ If timing is off and it is necessary to hold the soufflé, leave oven door shut and reduce heat to 300°; it will keep for an additional 45–60 minutes.

Celery with Almonds

SERVES: 6–8
Preparation time: 10–15 minutes
Cooking time: 4–5 minutes

The Ingredients:

3 tablespoons unsalted butter
4 cups celery, thinly sliced
1 8-ounce can water chestnuts, drained and sliced
3 scallions, finely minced (green and white parts included)
¼ teaspoon minced garlic
½ cup slivered almonds, toasted

The Steps:

1. In a large skillet, melt butter and, when hot, add celery; toss well, stirring constantly for 1 minute.
2. Add water chestnuts, scallions, and garlic and continue to cook, stirring constantly for 2–3 minutes, or until just cooked but still crunchy.
3. Add almonds, toss, and serve immediately.

Variations:

Shallots or onions can be substituted for the scallions.

Make-It-Easy Tips:

√ Celery can be easily sliced in a food processor.
√ Toast nuts easily in a toaster oven or under a broiler, watching carefully, until brown.

Peach Melba

SERVES: 6–8
Preparation time: 20 minutes
Chilling time: 1 hour

A traditional favorite, prepared Make-It-Easy style.

The Ingredients:

Sauce:
    1 10-ounce package frozen raspberries in syrup, thawed
    1 10-ounce jar currant jelly

    4 fresh ripe peaches, about 1 pound
    1 tablespoon lemon juice
    2 pints vanilla ice cream
    ⅓ cup slivered almonds or pine nuts, lightly toasted

The Steps:

1. Prepare melba sauce by pureeing raspberries in food processor or blender until smooth. Mash puree through sieve to remove seeds. Place puree and currant jelly in small saucepan and heat, stirring constantly until jelly has melted. Chill for 1 hour or until ready to use.
2. Peel peaches easily by dropping into boiling water for 1 minute; then promptly remove peel. Slice peeled peaches thickly and sprinkle lightly with lemon juice to prevent discoloration.
3. Place scoop of vanilla ice cream in tall goblet or parfait glass, top with peach slices, spoon a little melba sauce over, and sprinkle tops with toasted almonds. Serve immediately.

Variation:

If fresh peaches are not in season, use thawed frozen unsweetened peaches.

Make-It-Easy Tips:

√ The sauce may be prepared several days in advance and kept in the refrigerator.
√ Select firm yellow or creamy-colored peaches that yield to slight pressure. Avoid green ones (which will not ripen) or those with bruises or spots indicating possible decay.

Fourth of July Barbecue

SERVES: 6–8
"Parsley, Sage, Rosemary, and Thyme" Grilled Lamb
Tomato, Basil and Mozzarella Salad
*Sourdough Rolls
Grilled Roasted Corn on the Cob
Watermelon Bombe

July 4th is both our country's birthday and our midsummer holiday. That gives our celebration the themes—one patriotic and one plain summer fun.

Red, white, and blue tablecloths and napkins, in solids or checks, reflect the day's theme. Small American flags can make a centerpiece, either bunched bouquet-style or even mingled with a vase or pitcher of fresh flowers. Napkins can be paper for a casual look, or cloth rolled up and tied with appropriately colored ribbons or heavy yarn. For an alternative, straw place mats give a rustic look, or crisscrossing cloth runners give an unusual touch to the table.

It's no wonder a barbecue has become so popular for this day—it allows you to avoid a hot kitchen. The grilled lamb gives us both the traditional barbecue and a change from the usual hamburgers, hot dogs, and chicken. Sourdough rolls, or any variety of roll desired, can be warmed on the edge of the grill if you like, then served in a basket lined with colored napkins or a square of red gingham. The tomato salad will carry the color theme even further if served on a blue plate or set on a blue tablecloth.

It's hard to think of a more all-American treat than corn on the cob. Keep pot holders or oven mitts handy for easy husking. Little corncob holders are inexpensive, make corn neater to eat, and help prevent burned fingers.

The Watermelon Bombe is another variation on a tradition. Not everyone likes watermelon, but this one is made of ice cream. And who can turn down ice cream on the Fourth of July? But resist the urge to show it off too early. It should stay in the freezer until serving time.

Because of the summer sun, people will appreciate all the help they can get in keeping cool. If there are no trees, umbrellas will help. And folks of all ages will enjoy a plentiful variety of cold drinks.

"Parsley, Sage, Rosemary, and Thyme" Grilled Lamb

SERVES: 6–8
Preparation time: 20 minutes
Marinating time: 4–6 hours or overnight
Cooking time: 40 minutes

This recipe, courtesy of Myron Falk, requires a butterflied leg of lamb. Ask the butcher to bone the leg of lamb, leaving it open like a large jagged and lopsided piece of steak.

The Ingredients:
 1 5–6 pound leg of lamb, butterflied with fell (tough outer skin) and any excess fat removed

Marinade:
 1 cup olive oil
 ⅔ cup lemon juice

  3 cloves garlic, crushed
  2 bay leaves, crushed
  6 sprigs parsley
1½ teaspoons ground sage
1½ teaspoons dried rosemary, crushed
1½ teaspoons dried thyme, crumbled
    Salt and freshly ground pepper to taste

Sauce:
  ½ cup beef broth
  ¼ cup red wine
  2 tablespoons chopped shallots (or white part of scallions)
  1 teaspoon ground sage
  1 teaspoon dried rosemary, crushed
  1 teaspoon dried thyme, crumbled
  3 tablespoons unsalted butter
  3 tablespoons chopped parsley

The Steps:

1. Place lamb in flat dish; combine marinade ingredients and pour over meat; marinate 4–6 hours or overnight, covered, in refrigerator; bring lamb to room temperature before cooking.
2. Preheat broiler or outdoor grill to high.
3. Drain meat, reserving marinade, and sear over hot grill on both sides; lower heat to 450° or 500° (or if outside, raise grill slightly). Cook for 20 minutes a side, basting occasionally with marinade. (Lamb should be pink on the inside and crusty on the outside, with an internal temperature of 145°.)
4. In saucepan, combine beef broth, wine, shallots, sage, rosemary, and thyme, and ½ of reserved marinade; boil until reduced to ½ cup; add butter and parsley and stir until smooth.
5. Slice meat on the bias and serve with sauce on side.

Variations:

Lamb can also be served with mint jelly on the side.
Leftover lamb can be used cold for sandwiches the next day with mustard on dark rye bread.

Make-It-Easy Tips:

√ Crush rosemary easily in a mortar and pestle or place it between sheets of waxed paper and roll a rolling pin over.
√ Marinade can be prepared in advance and refrigerated overnight.

✓ In Step #1, meat can be marinated in a jumbo plastic storage bag, securely tied, to facilitate turning without getting herbs and garlic on your hands.

✓ Remember to ask the butcher for the lamb bone, which can be frozen and used for stock or soup making.

Tomato and Mozzarella Salad (Pomodori e Mozzarella)

SERVES: 6
Preparation time: 10 minutes

Serve this salad whenever tomatoes are at their peak and fresh basil is plentiful.

The Ingredients:
        6 medium-sized ripe tomatoes
        ¾ pound Mozzarella cheese, as fresh as possible
     4–5 tablespoons good olive oil (Italian is preferable)
     6–8 fresh basil leaves, washed, dried, and coarsely chopped
        Salt and freshly ground pepper to taste

The Steps:
1. Cut tomatoes in half horizontally and remove seeds by gently squeezing. Cut tomato halves in small cubes and place in bowl.
2. Cut Mozzarella in similar-size pieces and combine with tomatoes.
3. Toss with oil and basil, season with salt and pepper, and gently stir to combine.
4. Serve salad at room temperature or slightly chilled.

Variations:
If fresh basil is unavailable, do not substitute dried basil in its place. It is better to use freshly chopped parsley to bring out the flavor of ripe tomatoes.

Tomatoes and Mozzarella can be thinly sliced, presented in alternate slices, and garnished with basil leaves and a drizzle of olive oil.

An extraordinary variety of Mozzarella cheese, called Buffalo Mozzarella, has a wonderfully creamy texture and special flavor. Available only in Italian groceries or specialty cheese shops, it's very expensive; but if you're looking for an incredible treat, it's worth a try.

Make-It-Easy Tips:

√ A serrated-edged tomato or bread knife is an invaluable tool to use when cutting tomatoes.

√ To ripen tomatoes at home, store in a warm location away from direct sunlight, standing flat stem end down in a plastic bag with a few holes punched through. The natural ethylene gas of the tomatoes speeds up the ripening process.

Grilled Roasted Corn on the Cob

SERVES: 6–8
Preparation time: 10–15 minutes
Cooking time: 15–20 minutes

Use any seasonal fresh herb or combination of fresh herbs desired.

The Ingredients:

12 ears corn

Herb Butter:

6 ounces (1½ sticks) unsalted butter
⅓ cup freshly chopped herbs (chives, parsley, basil, etc.)
Salt and freshly ground pepper to taste

The Steps:

1. Light outdoor grill and allow coals to heat thoroughly.
2. Pull husks away from cob, leaving them attached at stalk end; remove silk with brush, and wrap husks back around corn. Soak in cold water for 10–15 minutes.
3. In food processor, blender, electric beater, or by hand, process butter and herbs until smooth and creamy.
4. Turn back husks of corn, place each ear on piece of heavy-duty

aluminum foil, spread corn with about one tablespoon butter, and wrap husks around corn again.

5. Wrap each foil packet securely and roast ears directly on hot coals, turning occasionally for 15–20 minutes or until tender. Unwrap and serve corn hot.

Variations:

Garlic, onion, or any flavor butter can be substituted for herb butter.

Corn can be husked, wrapped in strips of bacon, secured with skewers, and grilled on a rack until bacon is crisp and corn is golden and tender.

Corn can be cooked indoors in a preheated broiler.

Make-It-Easy Tips:

√ The corn is soaked to prevent burning or drying out.

√ Buy the freshest corn possible and it will be the sweetest. Once corn is picked, the sugar in the kernels starts converting to starch.

√ The tip-off for freshly picked corn is the stem. If damp and pale green, corn is freshly picked. After 24 hours, the stalk turns opaque; longer than that, it becomes brown.

√ Always refrigerate corn until use.

Watermelon Bombe

SERVES: 10–12
Preparation time: 10–15 minutes
Freezing time: 1–2 hours

This is the latest version of watermelon ice cream. It may not taste like the original—but it certainly looks like it and is sure to bring smiles. It's cool, refreshing, and amusing. Clear out enough space in the freezer to fit the bowl in comfortably.

The Ingredients:

1 quart (2 pints) green ice cream or ices (pistachio, mint, lime, etc.), softened for 10 minutes

1 quart (2 pints) red or pink ice cream or ices (peppermint, strawberry, or raspberry), softened for 10 minutes
3 ounces chocolate chips

The Steps:

1. Line rounded 5- and 6-cup bowl (such as a metal mixing bowl) with plastic wrap, overlapping sides. Layer green ice cream 1″– 2″ thick on bottom and up sides of bowl, and freeze until hard.
2. Fold chocolate chips into softened red or pink ice cream and fill cavity of mold with mixture; cover completely with plastic wrap and freeze until hard, 1–2 hours.
3. Open plastic wrap to expose top surface, place platter on top of bowl, and turn bowl and platter over. Remove remaining plastic wrap, slice in wedge-shaped pieces, and serve immediately.

Make-It-Easy Tips:

√ The bombe can be prepared up to four weeks in advance.
√ The plastic wrap lining in the bowl is essential if you wish to unmold the bombe easily.

Labor Day Picnic

SERVES: 6–8
Picnic Chicken
Red Potato Salad
Colorful Coleslaw
Blueberry Lattice Pie
* Fresh Fruit

Labor Day is almost everybody's day off, and it seems only fair that it should be the cook's day off too! Make-ahead picnic fare is a great way to guarantee a good time with a minimum of fuss. You'll have no more to do than transfer the finished product from refrigerator to picnic basket, with perhaps a simple tablecloth or sheet, napkins, plates, cups, and cutlery. And since no one seems to mind paper plates and plastic forks at a picnic, cleanup can be Make-It-Easy, too.

Labor Day also marks a transition from summer to fall, reflected in the contents of the picnic basket. Blueberry pie is generally a summer treat, while the Red Potato Salad shows a hint of fall color. A basket of fresh fruit makes a pretty and edible centerpiece, as well as a healthy alternative to potato chips and other "junk" foods found so often in a typical picnic lunch. Some summer fruits are still available in early September, and the first early apples may even be on the market. I also bring along a bunch of multicolored balloons to provide a splash of color and a feeling of festivity.

Plastic dishes with tight-fitting lids make packing secure and serving a snap. Many cities have restaurant supply stores, open to the public, which sell a wide variety of inexpensive, disposable containers. On the cleanup end, a large plastic bag keeps litter under control.

If picnic tables are unavailable and you prefer a smoother, more cushiony surface than a cloth spread directly on the grass, try a blanket or even exercise mats for padding. Wrap each napkin around a fork and a Wash'n Dri towelette—a handy addition since the chicken is messy finger food. A colored rubber band can hold each package together. Then pack along some extra napkins, just to be on the safe side. Once the cloth is laid out, a napkin package can be placed on each plate. Napkins and plates in contrasting outdoor colors add a casually pretty touch.

Of course, picnics are not just for food. They're for outdoor fun besides. Why not pack along a basket of games? Frisbees, a football, a soccerball, and potato sacks are great active fun, while board games like chess, checkers, or Scrabble are appreciated by others (especially if a little rain moves your outdoor picnic inside).

* Not a recipe

And while fall may be on the way, Labor Day can be a hot, sunny, thirsty day. Pack lots of cold drinks so your supply doesn't fall short. And remember the insect repellent—ants, mosquitoes, and bees don't take the day off.

Picnic Chicken

SERVES: 6–8
Preparation time: 15 minutes
Cooking time: 50 minutes–1 hour

The Ingredients:
2 whole chickens, split in quarters

Marinade:
¾ cup olive oil
¼ cup vegetable oil
6 tablespoons red wine vinegar
⅓ cup minced scallions (green and white parts included)
⅓ cup Dijon mustard
¼ cup freshly chopped parsley
1 tablespoon drained and chopped capers (optional)
½ teaspoon dried tarragon, crumbled
Salt and freshly ground pepper to taste

The Steps:
1. Pat chicken dry on paper towels and place in shallow dish.
2. Combine marinade ingredients in food processor, blender, or by hand; process until just smooth.
3. Pour mixture over chicken and marinate at room temperature for 1–2 hours. (Chicken can be marinated overnight in the refrigerator.)
4. Preheat broiler.
5. Remove chicken from marinade, place on rack, and broil 3″–4″ from heat, basting occasionally with marinade, for 15 minutes per side, or until tender and golden.
6. Cool, wrap securely in foil, and chill.
7. Serve chicken chilled or at room temperature.

Variations:

Chicken can be grilled outdoors over a charcoal fire.

Lemon juice can be substituted for vinegar.

Make-It-Easy Tip:

√ Longer shelf life increases the strength, saltiness, and dryness of mustard. But mustard will never "go bad." It may become dry or darken, but it will not mold or mildew. Once opened, refrigerate.

Red Potato Salad

SERVES: 8–10
Preparation time: 15 minutes
Cooking time: 20 minutes
Chilling time: 1–2 hours or overnight

No need to peel these potatoes. The bright color and nutritious peel add to this simply prepared salad.

The Ingredients:

20 tiny or 10 medium red potatoes, washed well

½ cup chopped scallions (green and white parts included)

Vinaigrette Dressing:

¾ cup olive oil

5 tablespoons lemon juice

2 tablespoons freshly chopped parsley

1 tablespoon Dijon mustard (smooth or grainy style)

1½ teaspoons freshly minced garlic

Salt and freshly ground pepper to taste

The Steps:

1. Place potatoes in pot of boiling, salted water; cover pot and cook potatoes until fork-tender, about 15–20 minutes for small size and 20–25 minutes for medium. (Do not overcook.) Drain, run under cold water, and allow to cool. Cut potatoes into small wedges and place in large bowl. Top with scallions.

2. Combine dressing ingredients in food processor, blender, or small jar and process or shake until smooth.
3. Pour dressing over potatoes and scallions, gently toss well, and chill for 1–2 hours or overnight. Serve cold or at room temperature.

Variations:
New potatoes can be substituted for red potatoes.
Sautéed, chopped, and drained bacon bits can be added if desired.

Make-It-Easy Tip:
√ Store potatoes in cool, dark, dry place but *not* in the refrigerator because the cold will cause the potato starch to convert to sugar and produce an undesirably sweet taste when cooked. Avoid potatoes with a greenish tint; they can be bitter and often toxic.

Colorful Coleslaw

SERVES: 6–8
Preparation time: 15 minutes
Chilling time: 2–4 hours or overnight

Serve this salad attractively arranged in a large bowl or on a deep platter.

The Ingredients:
½ large head green cabbage
½ large head red cabbage

Dressing:
1 cup mayonnaise
1 cup dairy sour cream
2 tablespoons lemon juice
1 tablespoon freshly snipped dill or 1 teaspoon dried dill weed
½ teaspoon capers (optional)
Salt and freshly ground pepper to taste
Garnish: Freshly snipped dill

The Steps:

1. Shred both cabbages separately, placing each in separate bowl.
2. Combine dressing ingredients in small bowl, whisk to combine, pour half over each kind of cabbage, and toss separately.
3. Arrange each half separately in large bowl or on lettuce-lined platter and chill for 2–4 hours or overnight.
4. Serve salad chilled, garnished with additional snipped dill.

Variation:

Chopped chives can be substituted for snipped dill.

Make-It-Easy Tips:

√ When selecting cabbage, avoid ones with separate leaves growing below the head from the main stems. These cabbages often have a stronger flavor and coarser texture.

√ When shredding cabbage in food processor, always use the slicing disc.

Blueberry Lattice Pie

SERVES: 8
Preparation time: 15 minutes
Cooking time: 45 minutes

The Ingredients:

1 package refrigerated folded pie crust or 1 package deep-dish frozen pie crust
3½ cups fresh blueberries
¾ cup light brown sugar, firmly packed
3 tablespoons all-purpose flour
1 tablespoon grated orange rind
1 tablespoon orange juice
2 tablespoons unsalted butter, diced
Garnish: Whipped cream

The Steps:
1. Preheat oven to 400°.
2. Unfold pie crust and place in 9″ pie pan (or use frozen pie crust, unthawed). Trim bottom crust even with edge of pan.
3. In large bowl, combine berries with brown sugar, flour, rind, and juice. Gently toss to combine. Spoon filling with prepared crust and top with butter bits.
4. On floured board, lay out remaining refrigerated pie crust. (If using frozen crust, thaw slightly, carefully remove from pie tin, and place on board.)
5. Cut 8 one-inch strips and lay 4 over filling, across pie, about 1″ apart. Repeat with remaining 4 strips in opposite direction. Trim strips even with pie edge. Turn bottom crust up over ends of strips and press firmly all around to seal edges.
6. Place pie on cookie sheet and bake for 45 minutes or until golden brown on top.
7. Serve garnished with whipped cream.

Variations:
If fresh blueberries are unavailable, substitute two 16-ounce packages frozen unsweetened blueberries, thawed and drained.

Blackberries, strawberries, raspberries, peaches, and other seasonal fruits can be substituted for blueberries.

Lemon rind and juice can be substituted for orange rind and juice.

To bake as a two-crust pie, place second crust on top of filling, fold edges of top crust under bottom, press down, and flute with fork. Cut slits in top crust to allow steam to escape.

If picnic is indoors, serve pie warm, topped with vanilla ice cream.

Make-It-Easy Tips:
√ Remember to pack the pie in box or basket to keep it safe. Cut at picnic.

√ To avoid a soggy crust, do not prick bottom crust before filling.

√ To prevent excessive browning on edges of pie crust, cover edges with strips of aluminum foil.

√ Use kitchen scissors to easily trim edges of pie crust.

Trick-or-Treat Party

SERVES: 12–16
Grape-Orange Punch
Make-Your-Own French Bread Pizzas
Black-and-White Cupcakes
Pumpkin Spice Bars
Incredibly Easy Chocolate Fudge
Butterscotch Brownies
* Candy

Here is a Halloween party that satisfies the needs of both children and adults. First and foremost, it keeps children safe inside, which puts parents' minds at ease. At the same time, it lets children have their Halloween fun, while sneaking some real food in among the traditional Halloween sweets.

A brightly colored sheet will do for a table covering. Or use an inexpensive vinyl tablecloth and let the children draw on it with felt-tip pens.

* Not a recipe

No cutlery is necessary, but children will need plenty of napkins. A variety of colorful washcloths or inexpensive bandanas makes a handy napkin substitute. Spread out in a row of overlapping diamonds, the washcloths or napkins will make a bright and colorful border on the table.

A basket of apples makes a cheerful, seasonal, and healthy centerpiece. Children may have fun bobbing for apples in a large kettle of water—but be prepared for some mopping up afterwards.

Even your kitchen broom can moonlight as a witch's flying machine, dressed up with a black crepe paper bow and standing in a corner surrounded by pumpkins. Is she a bad witch or a good witch? The children will know for sure if they find her paper hat filled with candy for a Halloween cornucopia. The costume and decorating hats found in stores will work, with one side of the brim cut or folded straight to keep it from rolling.

As for the pumpkins, their usual Halloween dress-up includes a carved grin and a candle inside. But pumpkin carving is time-consuming, and candles are dangerous among all those flammable costumes. If you really want to carve your own pumpkin, consider lining it with plastic, then filling with goodies. If you compromise by painting a face with black markers, the pumpkin will stay fresh for later use in made-from-scratch pumpkin pies (*not* a Make-It-Easy recipe, but tasty!)

Besides the usual children's party games, youngsters will enjoy making their own pizzas. Top the bread with sauce and cheese, and put them on a tray or cookie sheet on the table. Next to the tray, place dishes of assorted toppings. Each child can choose his or her favorites, then set the finished creation on a cookie sheet for baking.

Grape-Orange Punch is a cold, colorful, even good-for-you treat. For extra color, ice cubes can be made from grape and orange juices. This also keeps the flavor from being diluted as the ice melts.

Baking will be simplified if the Pumpkin Spice Bars and Butterscotch Brownies are made in advance and frozen. And the fudge is so easy that your children can make it with very little help. They'll be proud to serve their friends a treat they made themselves.

Grape-Orange Punch

SERVES: 12–16
Preparation time: 5–10 minutes

Serve this punch in a large bowl with a ladle or in a large pitcher.

The Ingredients:
1½ quarts (48 ounces) grape juice, chilled
1½ quarts (48 ounces) orange juice, chilled
4–6 ice cubes
1 pint orange sherbet

The Steps:
1. Combine juices in bowl or pitcher and mix with ice cubes.
2. Just before serving, add sherbet in spoonfuls and serve immediately.

Variation:
Combine grape juice and apple juice for a Grapple Punch topped with orange or lemon sherbet.
For an added treat freeze orange juice in ice cube trays and use in place of ice cubes and sherbet.

Make-It-Easy Tip:
√ It is best to chill the jars of juice separately rather than find room in the refrigerator for a large and cumbersome punch bowl.

Make-Your-Own French Bread Pizzas

SERVES: 16
Preparation time: 10 minutes
Cooking time: 15 minutes

These pizzas are just as much fun at an adult party! Have each guest assemble a pizza of his or her choice.

The Ingredients:

> 4 sourdough, French, or Italian flutes (the smaller breads measuring 12")
> 4 tablespoons (½ stick) unsalted butter
> Pizza Sauce (recipe follows)
> 32 slices Muenster cheese
> 1 cup freshly grated Parmesan cheese

Toppings:
Crumbled sautéed sausages
Pepperoni slices
Sautéed sliced mushrooms
Sautéed strips of green pepper
Sautéed sliced onions
Sliced black olives

The Steps:

1. Preheat oven to 450°.
2. Slice bread in half horizontally, then cut each piece in half vertically, resulting in 4 open-faced pieces. Lightly butter each slice.
3. Place 1½–2 tablespoons pizza sauce on each piece, top with 2 slices Muenster cheese, and sprinkle with 2 teaspoons Parmesan cheese. Have each guest add topping desired.
4. Place assembled pizzas on cookie sheet and bake for 5 minutes.
5. Increase heat to broil and continue to broil pizzas until hot and bubbly.
6. Serve immediately, taking care they are not too hot for young children.

Variations:
English muffins, or even bagels, can be substituted for bread.
Bread can be slightly hollowed and sauce used as a filling.

Make-It-Easy Tip:
√ Despite the popularity of Mozzarella cheese for Italian food, I find the cheese that melts most evenly and quickly is Muenster; but Monterey Jack, Swiss, Cheddar, or even Mozzarella can be substituted.

Pizza Sauce

YIELD: 3¾ cups
Preparation time: 10–15 minutes
Cooking time: 30 minutes

The Ingredients:
      2 tablespoons olive oil
      ½ cup finely minced onion
     42 ounces (1½ large cans) crushed tomatoes packed in puree
     1½ teaspoons finely minced garlic
      1 teaspoon sugar
      1 teaspoon dried oregano, crumbled
      1 teaspoon dried basil, crumbled
        Salt and freshly ground pepper to taste

The Steps:
   1. Heat olive oil in deep, heavy saucepan and sauté onion over medium heat until just soft, about 3–4 minutes.
   2. Add remaining ingredients, stir to combine, bring to boil, reduce heat, and simmer over low heat for 30 minutes, or until smooth and slightly thickened.
   3. Puree in food processor or blender until smooth, and chill until ready to use.

Variations:
Sauce can be used without pureeing.

Use sauce as a topping for chicken or veal parmigiana, or as a basic marinara sauce for Italian cooking.

Tomatoes can be pureed before adding; Step #3 is then omitted.

If tomatoes packed in puree are unavailable, use regular whole juice-packed tomatoes; chop, drain off most of the liquid. Return tomatoes to can, and fill to the top with canned tomato puree.

Make-It-Easy Tips:
   √ Sugar is added to cut the acidity in the canned tomatoes.
   √ Garlic is added with the liquid for a more subtle flavor. If sautéed with onions, the garlic will brown and often take on an acrid and bitter flavor.

Black-and-White Cupcakes

YIELD: 24
Preparation time: 15 minutes
Cooking time: 20 minutes

The Ingredients:
    8 ounces cream cheese
    1 egg
    1 tablespoon sugar
      Pinch of salt
    6 ounces semisweet chocolate bits
    3 cups all-purpose flour
    2 cups sugar
    ½ cup (2 ounces) cocoa
    1 tablespoon baking soda
    1 teaspoon salt
    2 cups water
    ⅔ cup vegetable oil
    2 tablespoons white vinegar
    1½ teaspoons vanilla

The Steps:
1. Preheat oven to 350°. Generously butter muffin tins (24 cups) or line with paper or foil baking cups.
2. In food processor or electric mixer, process cream cheese with egg, sugar, and salt. Pour into bowl and fold in chips.
3. In separate bowl, sift flour with sugar, cocoa, soda, and salt. Add water, oil, vinegar, and vanilla and beat until smooth. (Use food processor or electric beater to achieve a smooth texture.)
4. Fill muffin cups ⅔–¾ full with cocoa mixture, then drop in 1 tablespoon cheese mixture on top of each. Bake for 20 minutes or until cake tester comes out clean.
5. Cool 10 minutes in pan, remove, and serve immediately; or freeze until ready to use.

Variation:
Chopped nuts can be added to cream cheese mixture.

Make-It-Easy Tip:

√ To save extra time and steps, prepare cream cheese mixture in food processor and pour out into bowl; then, without washing food processor bowl, blend cocoa mixture.

Pumpkin Spice Bars

YIELD: 20–24 bars
Preparation time: 20 minutes
Cooking time: 30–35 minutes

The Ingredients:

4 ounces (1 stick) unsalted butter, softened
1 cup dark brown sugar, firmly packed
¾ cup canned pumpkin
1 egg, lightly beaten
½ teaspoon vanilla extract
1 cup all-purpose flour
¾ teaspoon ground cinnamon
½ teaspoon baking powder
¼ teaspoon baking soda
¼ teaspoon ground ginger
¼ teaspoon ground nutmeg
¼ teaspoon ground allspice
Pinch of salt
Garnish: Sweetened whipped cream and chopped pecans

The Steps:

1. Preheat oven to 350°. Generously butter 9″-square baking pan and lightly dust with flour.
2. In large mixing bowl, cream butter and brown sugar together; add pumpkin, egg, and vanilla and continue to beat until smooth.
3. Sift dry ingredients together and add to batter.
4. Pour batter into prepared pan and bake for 30–35 minutes.
5. Cool for 5–10 minutes, cut into bars, and serve warm with sweetened whipped cream and a sprinkling of chopped pecans.

Make-It-Easy Tips:

√ Batter may be easily blended with an electric mixer.

√ To keep flour and other grains insect-free, add a bay leaf in each package and seal shut in airtight plastic bags.

Incredibly Easy Chocolate Fudge

YIELD: 16 bars
Preparation time: 10 minutes
Cooking time: 5 minutes
Chilling time: 2 hours

The Ingredients:

18 ounces (three 6-ounce packages) semisweet chocolate chips
1 14-ounce can sweetened condensed milk
½ cup finely chopped walnuts or pecans
1½ teaspoons vanilla
Pinch of salt

The Steps:

1. Line 8″-square pan with waxed paper.
2. In top of double boiler, or in heavy saucepan over very low heat, melt chocolate with milk.
3. Remove from heat and stir in remaining ingredients just until smooth. Pour into prepared pan, spread smooth, and refrigerate until firm, about 2 hours.
4. Place chilled fudge upside down on cutting board, peel paper off, and cut with sharp knife into small squares.
5. Serve immediately or store in airtight container.

Variations:

Nuts can be omitted if desired.

For Butterscotch Fudge, butterscotch chips can be substituted for chocolate chips.

Make-It-Easy Tip:

√ Never cover a pot in which chocolate is melting. Any excess moisture or condensation will "stiffen" the chocolate and prevent it from combining easily with the rest of the ingredients.

Butterscotch Brownies

YIELD: 16 brownies
Preparation time: 15–20 minutes
Cooking time: 20–25 minutes

The Ingredients:
   6 tablespoons unsalted butter, softened
   1 cup dark brown sugar, firmly packed
   1 egg, lightly beaten
   ½ teaspoon vanilla extract
   ¾ cup all-purpose flour
   1 teaspoon baking powder
     Pinch of salt
   ¾ cup chopped pecans

The Steps:
   1. Preheat oven to 350°. Generously butter 8"-square baking pan and lightly dust with flour.
   2. In large mixing bowl, beat butter with brown sugar with electric mixer or by hand until smooth and fluffy.
   3. Add egg and vanilla; beat until smooth.
   4. Sift flour with baking powder and salt into separate bowl; add dry ingredients and nuts to batter, and spread into prepared pan.
   5. Bake for 20–25 minutes, or until golden.
   6. Cool for 10–15 minutes in pan and cut into bars.

Make-It-Easy Tips:
   √ Freeze the squares uncut; later slice into squares while semifrozen for easier cutting.
   √ If you've forgotten to soften the butter, grate it and it will soften quickly.

Traditional Thanksgiving Feast

SERVES: 10
Hot Spiced Cider
Perfect Roast Turkey
Sourdough-Pecan Stuffing
Glazed Sweet Potatoes
Marmalade-Spiked Cranberry Sauce
Spinach Flans on Tomato Rings
Pumpkin Ice Cream Pie

Our Thanksgiving menu has come a long way since the Pilgrims roasted a meal of wild turkeys. Now it's rich with generations of tradition and regional favorites. Here's a real American menu—drawn from all corners of the country.

No colonial cook ever heard of roasting a turkey in a paper bag, but it's a sure and easy way to keep the bird moist and flavorful without bothersome basting. You save time (and a few calories, but on Thanksgiving who's counting?) by using the clear, seasoned liquids from the pan in place of thickened gravy.

The Pilgrims first enjoyed turkey in New England, but the stuffing in this menu combines sourdough from the West and pecans from the South for a great cross-country combination. Don't worry about having extra—you can bake it separately for later use.

At the first Thanksgiving, the Pilgrims had not learned how to turn cranberries into a tangy treat, although their native American neighbors knew how to sweeten them with maple syrup. Here the zingy Northern berries team up with oranges from Sunshine Country to add zest to your turkey—all without tedious chopping or grinding.

Two vegetables are included, and both add color to the table. The traditional cuisine of the Southeast inspires the glazed sweet potatoes, while the Spinach Flans reflect Southwestern tastes.

I serve steamy mugs of fragrant hot cider alongside. Here apples from the North Country's autumn are spiced in the New England style, while some sunny citrus flavors add a special touch.

Early Americans never enjoyed a pumpkin pie quite like this one—which is a pity, since we're told that George Washington, among others, dearly loved ice cream. Prepare this pie up to two weeks early and freeze it.

As for decor, a natural fall harvest mood is the prettiest and simplest without excess ornamentation. Table coverings of soft creamy or rich earthy tones warm up the harvest look. Fill a bowl or basket with nuts, gourds, squash, fruit, or any combination. Decorate the room with bouquets of dried flowers. But the best centerpiece will be the turkey itself—plump and roasted to a golden brown.

While these recipes minimize the kitchen fuss without undoing tradition, perhaps the best time-saver of all is very much a part of the traditional Thanksgiving spirit. Guests often ask what they can bring, or how they can help. Why not share some recipes with those who kindly offer?

Hot Spiced Cider

SERVES: 10
Preparation time: 5–10 minutes
Cooking time: 5 minutes

The Ingredients:
2 quarts apple cider or apple juice
1 cup orange juice
5 tablespoons lemon juice
2 tablespoons sugar
2 tablespoons allspice berries
2 teaspoons ground nutmeg
4 cinnamon sticks
4 cloves
Garnish: Thin orange slices; 1–2 tablespoons rum to taste (optional)

The Steps:
1. In large kettle or deep saucepan, combine ingredients; bring to a boil and stir until sugar is dissolved.
2. Strain cider into pitcher and serve in warm mugs with a thin slice of orange and maybe a splash of rum.

Variation:
Sugar can be omitted if desired.

Make-It-Easy Tips:

√ Traditionally "sweet cider" was fresh juice that had fermented only a brief time and therefore was only slightly alcoholic. Today, what we purchase as "sweet cider" is exactly the same as apple juice, pasteurized and totally nonalcoholic. By all means, substitute apple juice (filtered or nonfiltered) for cider in this recipe. Hard cider is juice that has finished the fermentation cycle and is higher in alcoholic content.

√ Spices can be wrapped and tied up in cheesecloth and boiled with remaining ingredients. No straining necessary: just remove bag of spices, squeeze out excess moisture, and discard.

Perfect Roast Turkey

SERVES: 12–16
Preparation time: 25–30 minutes
Cooking time: Approximately 5 hours, 15 minutes

Although my complete Thanksgiving menu serves 10–12, I've written a recipe for a larger bird, to ensure lots of delicious leftovers. Remember, for health reasons, always stuff a turkey at the last minute, just before placing in the oven. Bacteria can grow if a bird is stuffed and held for too long.

The Ingredients:

    1 turkey (14–16 pounds) (hen is preferable)

Marinade:
    1 cup oil
    1 onion, thinly sliced
    3 tablespoons lemon juice
    2 tablespoons freshly chopped parsley
    2 cloves garlic, minced
    ½ teaspoon oregano
    Freshly ground pepper

    3–4 tablespoons unsalted butter, softened
    1 teaspoon paprika
    Salt and freshly ground pepper to taste

    1 large heavy brown paper bag (nonrecycled), available at the grocery store

    2 13½-ounce cans chicken broth

    2 onions, chopped

    Accompaniment: Sourdough-Pecan Stuffing (recipe to follow)

The Steps:

1. Wash turkey well, clean out cavity, and pat dry with paper towels.
2. Prepare marinade by combining ingredients. Marinate turkey in marinade for 12–14 hours in refrigerator, making sure marinade goes under skin and into cavity.
3. Preheat oven to 325°.
4. Remove turkey from marinade, lightly pat dry with paper towels, and stuff cavity and neck area with prepared stuffing (see following recipe). Discard marinade. Truss with needle or skewer and tie securely. Massage bird with 1–2 tablespoons butter all over; sprinkle with paprika, salt, and pepper.
5. Place open brown paper bag on table, seam side up. Butter inside of bag with remaining butter and place turkey in bag, breast side down and with drumsticks at open end. Neatly fold over edge of bag, staple shut or clamp closed with metal clamp, and place on rack in roasting pan.
6. Place chicken broth and onions in bottom of roasting pan and roast for 4 hours.
7. Cut bag open, remove and discard; turn turkey and roast an additional 1 hour and 15 minutes.
8. Remove from oven and allow to rest 15 minutes at room temperature before carving or removing stuffing.
9. Strain liquids from pan. Remove fat with straining device, and serve clear liquids in a gravy boat alongside turkey and bowl of stuffing.

Variations:

For giblet gravy: For 1½–2 hours boil neck and giblets with 2–3 cups canned chicken broth, 1 roughly chopped carrot, 1 onion, and a few sprigs parsley. Remove vegetables, chop giblets, and shred neck meat into broth. Season with concentrated liquid or powdered poultry stock if desired; add salt and freshly ground pepper to taste and 1 teaspoon tomato paste for added sweetness and color. Add giblet gravy to defatted pan juices in a saucepan, thicken with 2–3 tablespoons instantized flour, and stir until smooth and slightly thickened.

Fresh turkeys are the most flavorful. Frozen turkeys can be substituted but avoid those that are "butter-basted." They are sometimes basted with saturated fats and additives. Read the label carefully.

Make-It-Easy Tips:

√ If turkey is frozen, the best and safest method of thawing is in the refrigerator 2–3 days, depending on size.

√ The bird can be marinated in a jumbo food storage bag and easily turned without messing your hands.

√ When stuffing a bird, do not pack the stuffing tightly. Stuffing expands as it cooks.

√ To test for doneness, place meat thermometer in hip joint. It should register between 180° and 185° and juices should run clear. If juices are red, bird needs more roasting.

Turkey Timetable (Stuffed)
(Reduce roasting times by 30 minutes for unstuffed birds)

Size of Bird	Oven Temperature	Total Cooking Time
4–8 lbs.	325°	2½–3½ hours
8–12 lbs.	325°	3½–4½ hours
12–16 lbs.	325°	4½–5½ hours
16–20 lbs.	300°	5½–6½ hours

Sourdough-Pecan Stuffing

YIELD: 2½–3 quarts
Preparation time: 15–20 minutes
Cooking time: 5 minutes

The Ingredients:

2 quarts (8 cups) cubed stale sourdough bread
4 ounces (1 stick) unsalted butter
1 cup minced onion

    1 cup minced celery
    ¾ teaspoon powdered thyme
    ¾ teaspoon sage
    ¾ teaspoon marjoram or oregano
    1½ cups coarsely chopped pecans or walnuts
    ¼ cup freshly chopped parsley
    ¼–⅓ cup chicken broth

The Steps:
1. Preheat oven to 300°.
2. Dry out bread cubes on cookie sheets for 10–15 minutes. Watch carefully to avoid burning.
3. In large deep skillet, heat butter and sauté onion and celery over moderate heat just until soft, about 5 minutes.
4. Add thyme, sage, marjoram or oregano, salt, and pepper and mix well.
5. Pour over bread cubes, add nuts and parsley, and stir until well mixed. Add enough chicken broth to barely moisten bread.
6. Place in bowl, cover, and chill until ready to stuff bird.

Variations:
Bread crumbs can be substituted for cubes.

For New England-style stuffing, add 1 cup diced peeled tart apple in Step #5.

To bind stuffing together, a beaten egg can be added to Step #5.

Make-It-Easy Tips:
√ It is easiest to prepare stuffing a day in advance and stuff chilled stuffing into bird just before roasting.

√ Any remaining stuffing can be placed in a buttered dish, covered with foil, and baked separately for 45 minutes to 1 hour.

√ Immediately remove cooked stuffing from leftover bird, wrap, and refrigerate separately to reduce risk of food poisoning.

Glazed Sweet Potatoes

SERVES: 10
Preparation time: 15 minutes
Cooking time: 45 minutes

What we buy under the label "yams" are actually sweet potatoes in two varieties: a dry-fleshed yellow one with a pale brown outer skin, and a moist-fleshed orange one with a reddish-colored outer skin. The latter variety is best suited for this recipe.

The Ingredients:

    8   medium sweet potatoes
    1½ cups dark brown sugar, firmly packed
    ¼   pound (1 stick) unsalted butter
    ½   cup orange juice
    ¼   cup golden raisins
    3   tablespoons Grand Marnier or other orange-flavored liqueur
        Garnish: Orange slices

The Steps:

1. Drop sweet potatoes in salted boiling water to cover, and cook covered for 15–20 minutes, until tender but still firm. Drain, cool, and peel. Cut lengthwise into ¼"-thick slices.
2. Preheat oven to 350°. Generously butter 1 large or 2 smaller-size baking dishes.
3. Lay potatoes in prepared baking dish, overlapping slightly.
4. In small saucepan, combine brown sugar, butter, and juice; bring to a boil, stirring until smooth. Add raisins and Grand Marnier and stir to combine.
5. Spoon over potatoes, bake for 30–35 minutes, basting occasionally, until golden and glazed.
6. Serve hot, garnishing each portion with orange slice.

Variations:

1–2 tablespoons grated orange rind can be added if desired.
1–2 tablespoons slivered crystallized ginger can be added if desired.

Make-It-Easy Tips:

√ To save time and easily peel potatoes, instead of waiting for potatoes to cool, wear heavy-duty gloves.

√ Recipe can be assembled a day in advance; bake just before serving.

√ Do not store raw sweet potatoes in refrigerator. They should be stored in a humid, well-ventilated area. Once cooked, of course, they should be refrigerated.

Marmalade-Spiked Cranberry Sauce

SERVES: 10
Preparation time: 15 minutes
Cooking time: 5 minutes
Chilling time: 4–6 hours

The Ingredients:

1 large juice orange
6 whole cloves
Fresh orange juice
1 pound fresh cranberries
1 cup granulated sugar
½ cup cold water
½ cup orange marmalade
1 tablespoon lemon juice

The Steps:

1. Remove a coin-size piece of peel from orange and stud it with cloves.
2. Grate remaining rind of orange and measure out 2 tablespoons.
3. Juice orange and add enough fresh orange juice to equal ⅓ cup liquid.
4. In large heavy saucepan, combine cranberries, sugar, water, studded peel, rind, and juice; bring to a boil and cook over moderate heat for several minutes, or until berries have stopped popping.
5. Remove from heat and discard studded peel; add marmalade and lemon juice, stir to combine, and cool; then chill in refrigerator.

Variation:
Thawed frozen cranberries can be used to enjoy this recipe all year long.

Make-It-Easy Tip:
√ The cranberries will explode as they pop, so stand back—and loosely tent the pot with foil for protection.

Spinach Flans on Tomato Rings

SERVES: 10
Preparation time: 15 minutes
Cooking time: 35–40 minutes

Spinach flans—vegetable custards called *timbales* in France—make a particularly attractive presentation especially when served on ripe red tomato slices.

The Ingredients:
    3 tablespoons unsalted butter
    1 large onion, finely chopped
    2 10-ounce packages frozen chopped spinach, thawed and thoroughly squeezed dry
    1¼ cup half-and-half
    6 eggs
    ½ cup Gruyère or Monterey Jack cheese, grated
    2 tablespoons freshly grated Parmesan cheese
       Salt and freshly ground pepper to taste
       Pinch of freshly ground nutmeg
    10 tomato slices, cut ¼" thick
       Garnish: Watercress

The Steps:
1. Preheat oven to 350°. Generously butter ten 5-ounce custard cups, porcelain ramekin dishes, or timbale molds.
2. In large skillet, heat butter and sauté onion for 5 minutes over medium-heat, until soft. Add spinach and continue to cook for

2–3 minutes longer, until thoroughly combined; allow to cool slightly (about 5 minutes).

3. In large bowl, beat half-and-half, eggs, cheeses, salt, pepper, and nutmeg and stir until well mixed. Add spinach and stir to combine. Distribute mixture among cups, place cups in shallow roasting pan with 1″ boiling water, and bake for 35–40 minutes, or until custard is set.

4. Loosen custard from sides of each mold with sharp knife. Lay tomato slices over tops of molds, invert, and set attractively on platter garnished with sprigs of watercress.

Variations:

If time permits, 3 pounds of fresh spinach can be used, cooked, covered for 4–5 minutes, drained thoroughly, and roughly chopped.

If molds are unavailable, bake in a large deep-dish pie shell, invert on a platter, and garnish top with slices of tomatoes.

Make-It-Easy Tips:

√ Molds can be brushed with oil or coated with nonaerosol vegetable cooking spray.

√ Fresh nutmeg is preferable to ground nutmeg, which loses its potency and flavor on the market shelves.

√ Custard is baked in a warm bath to keep an even temperature throughout.

√ To prepare in advance, bake flans in the morning and reheat by covering with foil and setting in hot water in a 350° oven for 10 minutes. Or cover the baking pan with foil and set on back of stove to keep warm until serving.

Pumpkin Ice Cream Pie

SERVES: 10
Preparation time: 15 minutes
Freezing time: 30–60 minutes

The Ingredients:

Gingersnap Crust:
25 gingersnaps (1½ cups) crushed

5 ounces (5 tablespoons) unsalted butter, softened
⅓ cup granulated sugar

Pie Filling:
1½ cups canned pumpkin
½ cup granulated sugar
½ teaspoon cinnamon
¼ teaspoon ground nutmeg
¼ teaspoon salt
⅛ teaspoon ground ginger
⅛ teaspoon ground allspice
1 quart vanilla ice cream, softened
½ cup chopped pecans (2¼-ounce package diced pecans)

The Steps:

1. Crust: Crush gingersnaps; reserve 2–3 tablespoons for topping; mix crumbs with butter and sugar in bowl and press into 9" pie plate. Chill.
2. Pie Filling: In large bowl, combine pumpkin, sugar, cinnamon, nutmeg, salt, ginger, and allspice and mix well.
3. Fold pumpkin mixture into softened ice cream, stir in pecans, and spoon into pie shell; sprinkle with reserved crumbs.
4. Freeze uncovered for 30 minutes, or until set. Cover with plastic wrap or foil and keep frozen until ready to use.
5. Remove from freezer 10 minutes before serving, cut into wedges, and serve icy cold.

Variations:

Chopped walnuts can be substituted for pecans.
1 teaspoon pumpkin pie spice can be substituted for all the spices.
Vanilla wafers, zwieback crackers, or any type of plain cookie desired can be substituted for gingersnaps.

Make-It-Easy Tips:

√ Pie can be frozen for up to two weeks.
√ Filling can be easily combined in food processor or blender.

Merry Christmas Dinner

SERVES: 8–10
Christmas Glögg (Mulled Wine)
Roast Beef
Pan-Roasted Potatoes
Horseradish Cream Sauce
Cherry Tomato Salad in Parsley Wreath
Quick-and-Easy Pecan Pie
Hard Sauce
Bourbon Balls

Christmas is that special holiday when, no matter how busy we've become all year, we tend to gather at home. Add to this the chilly weather of December, and you have the perfect time to heat up the oven for traditional favorites—like roast beef and potatoes—that take a minimum of preparation and bake slowly to perfection.

An extra plus comes from all those Christmas trimmings. When the whole house is fully decked out for the season, your table will need little more to set the scene for a holiday dinner. It's easy to use what's at hand. Candles surrounded by pinecones or boughs make a quick and lovely centerpiece, and some Christmas tree ornaments provide a shiny accent. Or include some oranges—a traditional Christmas stocking-stuffer.

Red ribbons can tie your napkins, with perhaps a sprig of holly slipped under the bow. Holly leaves also make a festive garnish, especially for dessert. The berries can give food a bitter taste, however, so substitute some cranberries instead. Besides holly berries, it's wise to keep yew berries, poinsettia, and mistletoe away from the table. They may be pretty, but beware—they're poisonous!

Luckily, lots of very edible holiday color is available for the table. The Cherry Tomato salad proves that food can look Christmasy, yet be healthy and nonfattening, all at the same time. (We have to save some calories for the Pecan Pie!) Make it the night before to save steps on Christmas day.

The recipe for Christmas Glögg, the traditional Swedish holiday punch, adds cranberry juice, an American touch that adds zest and extra holiday color. The pronunciation stays Swedish, though—a sound somewhere between "gloog" and "glurg".

The Bourbon balls can be made weeks before the holiday season reaches its hectic climax, to sit quietly mellowing while you're busy shopping, wrapping, and mailing. Serve them after dinner with coffee, or wrap them up as special holiday house gifts direct from your own kitchen.

Christmas Glögg
(Mulled Wine)

YIELD: 3 quarts
Preparation time: 10–15 minutes
Cooking time: 15 minutes

This traditional Swedish mulled wine is always a big hit with the addition of American cranberry juice. Prepare enough, but warn guests that because the wine is warmed, it's more powerful than it seems.

The Ingredients:
>   2 cups cranberry juice
>   2 cups water
>   1 cup sugar
>   ½ lemon, sliced
>   6 allspice berries
>   4 whole cloves
>   2 cinnamon sticks
>   ⅛ teaspoon ground cinnamon
>   ⅛ teaspoon ground ginger
>   Pinch of nutmeg
>   2 bottles red wine (I prefer claret)
>   ½ lemon, sliced
>   ½ orange, sliced
>   ¼ cup raisins
>   Accompaniment: Cinnamon sticks

The Steps:
1. In large saucepan, combine cranberry juice, water, sugar, ½ lemon, allspice, cloves, cinnamon sticks, cinnamon, ginger, and nutmeg; bring to a boil, stirring often, until sugar is dissolved. Boil over medium heat for 15 minutes. Strain through cheesecloth or very fine strainer and set aside.
2. When ready to serve, heat cranberry base, add wine, lemon slices, orange slices, and raisins; heat until warm but do not boil. Pour into punch bowl and serve warm with ladle, and accompanying cinnamon-stick stirrers.

Variation:

Lemon slices, orange slices, and raisins can be omitted for a clear punch.

Make-It-Easy Tips:

√ To avoid straining, tie up spices in cheesecloth before adding to the base in Step #1. When boiled, discard cheesecloth and proceed.

√ Base may be prepared 2 or 3 days in advance, through Step #1, and refrigerated until ready to use.

√ If available, serve wine on a heated tray to keep at warm temperature.

Roast Beef

SERVES: 8–10
Preparation time: 10 minutes
Cooking time: 2–2½ hours

The roast suggested for this menu is the eye of the standing rib. It may be called by different names in your area, such as Spencer roast or rib-eye roast. Make sure to ask the butcher to leave a thin layer of fat around the roast to keep it tender and create a crusty exterior when roasted. The meat should be about 3″–4″ in diameter in the center section, and it is not rolled or tied.

The Ingredients:

6–8 pound eye of the rib roast, left at room temperature 2 hours
1 clove garlic, smashed and peeled
Salt and freshly ground pepper to taste
2–3 tablespoons all-purpose flour
1 cup beef broth
½ cup red wine
Accompaniment: Horseradish Cream Sauce (recipe follows)

The Steps:

1. Preheat oven to 450°.
2. Rub roast with garlic, sprinkle with salt and pepper, rub with flour, and place on rack in roasting pan, fat side up.

3. Roast meat for 20 minutes or until well seared. Reduce heat to 350°, insert meat thermometer in fleshiest part of meat, and continue to roast for 14–15 minutes per pound—or until thermometer registers 120° for rare, 130° for medium-rare, 140° for medium, and 150° for well-done.
4. Remove from oven and allow roast to rest for 20–30 minutes before carving.
5. Remove rack and skim off excess fat from pan. Place pan over heat, add broth and wine and cook, stirring to mix browned particles from bottom of pan into sauce. Boil until thickened, season with salt and pepper to taste, and serve alongside sliced meat, with horseradish sauce on side.

Variation:

Roast can be served cold in the summer, sliced on a platter with Mustard Sauce (see page 50)

Make-It-Easy Tips:

√ A meat thermometer is the only safe way to be sure of the correct degree of doneness. It is an inexpensive item that can ensure the success of an expensive cut of meat.

√ Remember that the roast continues to cook as it rests, so be sure to remove it from the oven at the correct internal temperature.

√ After searing, a 6-pound roast will take 1½ hours to cook while an 8-pound roast can take up to 2 hours.

Horseradish Cream Sauce

YIELD: 2 cups
Preparation time: 5 minutes
Chilling time: 1 hour

Prepare this sauce according to taste. Increase the amount of horseradish at your own risk!

The Ingredients:

1½ cups dairy sour cream
½ cup prepared white horseradish, drained

> 1 teaspoon Dijon mustard
> Salt to taste

The Steps:
1. In medium-size bowl, combine ingredients together until smooth.
2. Cover and chill for at least 1 hour before serving.

Make-It-Easy Tip:
√ To prepare with fresh horseradish: Peel and cube horseradish root, chop in food processor until just grated. Add 2–3 tablespoons lemon juice or white vinegar, 1 teaspoon dry mustard, ½ teaspoon sugar, and proceed with recipe.

Pan-Roasted Potatoes

SERVES: 8–10
Preparation time: 5–10 minutes
Cooking time: 1 hour, 15 minutes

It is beneficial to oven-roast potatoes without peeling, since so many nutrients are in the skin. It also saves extra KP duties for the family.

The Ingredients:
6 large baking potatoes, well scrubbed and cut into 3 sections; or 12–16 new potatoes, well scrubbed.

The Steps:
1. Drop potatoes into boiling salted water and boil 10–15 minutes, or until barely tender; drain well.
2. About 1 hour before roast is done, add potatoes to pan, coat well with drippings, and roast until golden brown, basting occasionally with drippings.
3. Serve hot, alongside slices of roast beef.

Variation:
Parboiled, peeled onions can be added.

Make-It-Easy Tips:
✓ If roast needs longer cooking time, it will not harm the potatoes to be overcooked.

✓ When roast is removed from oven to rest and pan juices are boiled down, place glazed potatoes on separate pan in warm oven until ready to serve.

Cherry Tomato Salad in Parsley Wreath

SERVES: 8
Preparation time: 10–15 minutes
Chilling time: 2 hours or overnight

This attractive presentation makes this holiday dish worthy of serving all year long.

The Ingredients:
    2–3 large bunches parsley, large stems removed
    1 quart cherry tomatoes, stems removed, washed and dried

Vinaigrette Dressing:
    ½ cup olive oil
    3 tablespoons red wine vinegar
    2 teaspoons freshly minced parsley
    ½ teaspoon Dijon mustard
    ½ teaspoon freshly minced garlic
    Pinch of sugar
    Salt and freshly ground pepper to taste

The Steps:
1. In large ring mold, pack down parsley tightly, cover with foil, and refrigerate for 2 hours or overnight to firm into shape.
2. Slice tomatoes and place in medium bowl.
3. Combine vinaigrette dressing ingredients together in food processor or blender, or in small bowl with whisk. Pour dressing over tomatoes and gently toss.
4. Unmold chilled parsley onto a platter, tapping to release parsley onto plate. Place tomatoes in center and serve immediately, or chill until ready to use.

Variations:

Tomatoes can be served whole to save preparation time.

Substitute chopped fresh basil, dill, chives, or a combination of green herbs for parsley.

Make-It-Easy Tip:

√ Tomatoes can be marinated in vinaigrette for several hours in the refrigerator.

Quick-and-Easy Pecan Pie

SERVES: 8
Preparation time: 10 minutes
Cooking time: 45–50 minutes

Pecans are strictly an American nut. George Washington carried pecans in his pocket throughout the American Revolutionary War. They are traditionally raised in the Southern states but now grow in California too.

The Ingredients:

½ cup white sugar
½ cup dark brown sugar, firmly packed
½ cup light corn syrup
2 ounces (¼ cup) unsalted butter, melted
3 eggs, well beaten
1 cup pecan halves
1 9″ unbaked pie shell (if frozen, thawed)
  Accompaniments: Vanilla ice cream, hard sauce (recipe follows), or whipped cream.

The Steps:

1. Preheat oven to 375°.
2. In large bowl, mix together sugars, syrup, and butter.
3. Add eggs and pecans, stir well, and pour into pie shell.
4. Bake for 45–50 minutes, or until set and golden.
5. Serve warm or at room temperature with accompanying hard sauce, vanilla ice cream, or whipped cream.

Make-It-Easy Tips:
√ Pie can be prepared in advance and frozen successfully.
√ Store nuts in freezer to keep fresh.
√ Store brown sugar in a tightly sealed jar once box is opened.
√ When measuring sticky liquids like corn syrup, rub the cup with oil and the syrup will pour out easily.

Hard Sauce

YIELD: 2 cups
Preparation time: 10 minutes
Chilling time: 2 hours

Hard Sauce is the traditional accompaniment to English plum pudding, but it can be served year round to flavor hot fruit puddings or pies or to give as an unusual house gift. It is easy to prepare in a food processor, blender, or electric mixer.

The Ingredients:
½ pound (2 sticks) unsalted butter, softened
2 cups powdered sugar
2 tablespoons brandy or rum
1 teaspoon vanilla extract
Pinch of salt
1 teaspoon grated lemon rind (optional)

The Steps:
1. Cream butter and sugar together, adding sugar to butter gradually for softness.
2. Add brandy or rum, vanilla, salt, and optional lemon rind and process until light and creamy.
3. Pack hard sauce into crock and refrigerate until hard, about 2 hours.
4. Serve atop pie.

Make-It-Easy Tip:
√ If you've forgotten to soften the butter, grate it and it will quickly soften.

Bourbon Balls

YIELD: 70
Preparation time: 20 minutes

These bourbon-laced candy/cookie combinations are a dessert and after-dinner drink in one. Prepare a large batch, wrap in an attractive container, and give as a gift with a copy of the recipe enclosed. Remember to prepare 2 weeks in advance to allow them to "ripen" and become really flavorful.

The Ingredients:

1½ cups confectioner's sugar
1 teaspoon unsweetened cocoa
   Pinch of powdered instant coffee
⅓ cup light corn syrup
⅓ cup bourbon
1 teaspoon vanilla extract
1 12-ounce box vanilla wafers, crushed
1½ cups pecans, chopped
1 cup raisins, chopped
½ cup confectioner's sugar
1 teaspoon unsweetened cocoa

The Steps:

1. In food processor, blender, or by hand, combine 1½ cups confectioner's sugar, with 1 teaspoon cocoa and pinch of coffee; add corn syrup, bourbon, and vanilla and stir to combine.
2. Add crumbs, nuts, and raisins and continue to process until mixture holds together.
3. In separate bowl, combine ½ cup confectioner's sugar with 1 teaspoon cocoa and set onto a flat plate.
4. Shape pecan mixture into 1″ balls and roll them in the sugar-cocoa mixture.
5. Store in airtight container until ready to serve.

Variations:

Chopped walnuts can be substituted for pecans.
Chopped dates or apricots can be substituted for raisins.

Make-It-Easy Tips:

√ Get the family involved in this fun holiday activity.

√ Wrap the balls in small plastic bags tied up with ribbon in plastic jars attractively labeled, or even miniature cans or crocks.

Emergency Substitutions

**When You Are
Out Of:**   **Substitute:**

Buttermilk, 1 cup   1 cup fresh milk plus 1 tablespoon vinegar or
                             lemon juice allowed to stand 5 minutes.

                             1 cup plain yogurt.

Sour cream, 1 cup   ⅓ cup melted butter plus ¾ cup sour milk.
                             (To make sour milk, use ¾ cup whole milk
                             plus 2½ teaspoons lemon juice or 2¼
                             teaspoons white vinegar. Let mixture stand
                             10 minutes.)

                             1 cup plain yogurt or sour half-and-half (but
                             only in cooked, not in baked dishes).

*Light cream (18%),
1 cup*   Add 3 tablespoons melted butter to ⅞ cup of
                             undiluted evaporated milk. (Evaporated milk
                             is homogenized milk dehydrated to half its
                             original volume.)

Whole milk, 1 cup   ½ cup evaporated milk plus ½ cup water =

                             1 cup skim milk plus 2 tablespoons melted
                             butter =

                             1 cup reconstituted nonfat dry milk plus 2
                             tablespoons butter =

                             1 cup skim milk plus 1 tablespoon cream =
                             (or in baking substitute 1 cup fresh fruit
                             juice).

Heavy cream (36%),
1 cup
¾ cup milk plus ⅓ cup melted butter (for baking and cooking only).

Half-and-half (10%),
1 cup
⅞ cup milk plus 1½ tablespoons melted butter.

Yogurt, 1 cup
1 cup sour cream or sour half-and-half (though they have a higher fat content).

Baking powder,
1 tablespoon
1 teaspoon baking soda plus 2 teaspoons cream of tartar (1 teaspoon baking powder = ⅓ teaspoon baking soda plus ½ teaspoon cream of tartar).

Unsweetened baking
chocolate, 1 square
3 tablespoons unsweetened powdered cocoa plus 1 tablespoon butter or shortening.

Cake flour, 1 cup
¾ cup plus 2 tablespoons all-purpose flour plus 2 tablespoons cornstarch.

Self-rising flour, 1 cup
1 cup sifted flour plus 1¼ teaspoons baking powder and a pinch of salt.

Thickener
1 tablespoon cornstarch = 2 tablespoons flour + 1 tablespoon arrowroot = 1 tablespoon potato starch = 4 teaspoons quick-cooking tapioca = 3 egg yolks.

Honey, 1 cup
1¼ cup sugar plus ¼ cup water (liquid).

Light corn syrup, 1 cup
1 cup sugar plus ¼ of the liquid called for in the recipe boiled together until syrupy = ¾ cup honey = 1¼ cup molasses = ¾ cup maple syrup. Lower temperature to 350° with honey to prevent excessive browning.

Confectioner's sugar, *1 cup*	⅞ cup granulated sugar whirred quickly through blender or food processor with 1 tablespoon cornstarch.
Superfine sugar	Grind granulated sugar in food processor or blender, pulsating until as fine as necessary.
Breadcrumbs, 1 cup	¾ cup cracker crumbs.
Cayenne, ⅛ teaspoon	4 drops hot pepper sauce.
Lemon juice, *1 teaspoon*	½ teaspoon vinegar.
Canned tomatoes, *1 cup*	1½ cups fresh chopped tomatoes, simmered 10 minutes.
Jerusalem artichokes	Water chestnuts = jicama.
Pine nuts	Slivered almonds.
Dry mustard, *1 teaspoon*	2½ teaspoons prepared mustard.
Raisins or dried *currants* (for baking), *1 cup*	1 cup finely chopped soft prunes or dates.

MAIL ORDER GUIDE

EQUIPMENT AND GADGETS

Williams–Sonoma
P.O. Box 3792
San Francisco, California 94119

Zabar's
2245 Broadway
New York, New York 10024

The Professional Kitchen
18 Cooper Square
New York, New York 10003

Walter Drake & Sons
Drake Building
Colorado Springs, Colorado 80940

Figi's Collection for Cooking
Marshfield, Wisconsin 54449

The Cook's Magazine
1698 Post Road East
Westport, Connecticut 06880

Colonial Garden Kitchens
270 W. Merrick Road
Valley Stream, L.I., New York 11582

Kitchen Bazaar
4455 Connecticut Avenue, S.W.
Washington, D.C. 20008

The Wooden Spoon
Route 6
Mahopac, New York 10541

The Chef's Catalog
Professional Restaurant Equipment
for the Home Chef
725 County Line Road
Deerfield, Illinois 60015

Chef's Warehouse
Box M
Montpelier, Vermont 05602

Chinese
The Chinese Grocer
209 Post Street at Grant Avenue
San Francisco, California 94108
Call toll free: 800-227-3320

Hungarian and German
H. Roth and Son
1577 First Avenue
New York, New York 10028

The Bremen House
218 E. 86th Street
New York, New York 10028

Paprikas Weiss
1546 Second Avenue
New York, New York 10021

Schaller & Weber
1654 Second Avenue
New York, New York 10028

Indian and Middle Eastern
Bezjian Groceries
4725 Santa Monica Boulevard
Los Angeles, California 90029

India Gifts and Foods
1031 W. Belmont Avenue
Chicago, Illinois 60650

K. Kalustyan
Orient Export Trading Corporation
123 Lexington Avenue
New York, New York 10016

Italian
Todaro Brothers
555 Second Avenue
New York, New York 10016

Il Conte di Savoia
555 W. Roosevelt Road
Chicago, Illinois 60607

Manganaro Foods
488 Ninth Avenue
New York, New York 10018

Mexican and Latin American
Casa Moneo
210 W. 14 Street
New York, New York 10011

Spices
Aphrodisia
28 Carmine Street
New York, New York 10014

House of Spices
76–17 Broadway
Jackson Heights, New York 11373

General
Balducci's
424 Avenue of the Americas
New York, New York 10011

Gaspar's Sausage Company
(for Portugese sausages)
P.O. Box 436
North Dartmouth, Massachusetts 02747

Ferris Fine Foods (for cheese)
P.O. Box 5412
Madison, Wisconsin 53705

The Country Store
P.O. Box 9983
St. Paul, Minnesota 55199

MAXIMUM FREEZER STORAGE TIMES

The chart below answers the question "How long can I freeze . . . ?"

The maximum storage times reflect foods stored at 0°F. or below. If foods are stored in a freezer that is being constantly opened, maximum storage times should be slightly shortened. Remember to wrap tightly, seal closed, and label and date each package clearly. Fruits and vegetables are not included since they require blanching, steaming, and other complex techniques to freeze.

FOOD	MAXIMUM STORAGE PERIOD	TIPS
Breads Quick Breads and Rolls	3–4 months	–Rolls freeze well in food-storage bags. –Slice and butter French, Italian, or sourdough bread; wrap in foil, and it can go from freezer to oven to heat.
Cakes and Cookies	4–6 months	–Freeze frosted cakes before wrapping for 1 hour or until cake can be easily wrapped without damaging frosting.

FOOD	MAXIMUM STORAGE PERIOD	TIPS
Cakes and Cookies (*continued*)	4–6 months	–Use pure vanilla extract rather than the artificial, which tends to turn bitter during freezer storage. –Freeze bar cookies uncut; slice easily semi-frozen.
Cooked Casseroles, Soups, or Stews	4–6 months	–Freeze in foil-lined casserole with enough foil to overlap and cover the top; when frozen solid, remove and return to freezer; reheat in same casserole. –To reheat: uncover and heat for 45 minutes to 1 hour or until hot and bubbly.
Dairy Products Butter	6–9 months	–Unsalted butter keeps longer.
Cheese (Hard)	4–6 weeks	–Tends to become crumbly after freezing.
Cheese (Soft)	4–6 weeks	–Freeze Brie and other creamy cheese in wedge shapes when just perfectly ripe and runny.
Cream, Heavy	2–4 months	–Freeze in tightly sealed containers not quite full (leave a small amount of air space at the top). Thaw in refrigerator and use for whipping, not at the table, since it tends to separate when frozen.

FOOD	MAXIMUM STORAGE PERIOD	TIPS
Eggs		
–Whole	9–12 months	–Do not freeze whole eggs in shell; beat lightly and freeze in a labeled container.
–Egg Yolks	9–12 months	–For future use in sweet dishes, add 1 tablespoon light corn syrup; for non-sweet dishes, add 1 teaspoon salt.
–Egg Whites	9–12 months	–Freeze egg whites, one in each square of an ice-cube tray; when frozen, remove from tray and store, dated, in plastic food-storage bags.
Ice Cream	1–2 months	–Ice cream with a very high percentage of cream can be stored longer.
Milk	3–4 weeks	–Freeze in its own container or storage container.
Buttermilk	3–4 weeks	–Freeze in container and thaw in refrigerator.
Fish & Seafood (Raw)		
Fatty Fish (mackerel, salmon, striped bass, trout, tuna, etc.)	2–3 months	–Freeze whole fish, which has been gutted and cleaned, tightly sealed in foil.
Lean Fish (flounder, haddock, halibut, sea bass, sole, etc.)	4–6 months	–Fish should be frozen as fresh as possible.
Seafood		
–Clams	2–3 months	–Steamers and quahogs should be steamed opened and frozen in juice; cherrystones

FOOD	MAXIMUM STORAGE PERIOD	TIPS
		should be packed in liquid to avoid toughening.
–Crabs, Lobsters	2–3 months	–Freeze after boiling or steaming. Pick out meat and freeze in small portions.
–Oysters	2–3 months	–Pack in liquid to avoid toughening.
–Scallops	2–3 months	–Most scallops are only available frozen and must be cooked immediately without refreezing.
–Shrimp	4–6 months	–Freeze either raw or cooked.
Herbs	9–12 months	–Wash, dry, and chop herbs; pack into tightly sealed containers or wrap in foil packets. Use directly from freezer, without thawing.
Meats (Raw) Beef and Lamb		
–Roast	4–6 months	–Trim excess fat before freezing.
–Steaks and Chops	4–6 months	–Remove supermarket wrap and tightly rewrap each steak or chop individually.
–Ground	2–3 months	–Save preparation time by packing meat in the form in which it is to be cooked, e.g., patties, loaf, or ½- to 1-pound packages for ground beef dishes.
Liver	Not advisable to freeze	–Highly perishable.
Pork		
–Ground	1–2 months	–Freeze in small patties to use for oriental dishes.

FOOD	MAXIMUM STORAGE PERIOD	TIPS
–Roast & Chops	2–3 months	–The storage time for pork is less than for beef and lamb; therefore, freeze in small quantities.
–Sausages	1–2 months	–Freeze wrapped tightly in foil or plastic wrap.
Meats (Processed)		
Bacon	1 month	–Remove from package and freeze in family-size portions.
Frankfurters	1 month	–Remove from package and wrap individually for quick defrosting.
Ham	1 2 months	–Freeze deli slices in small packets; the texture may become mealy.
Nuts		
Salted	Should not be frozen	–Salt may absorb moisture and make nuts sticky.
Unsalted	9–12 months	–Freeze in small plastic bags.
Pies		
Baked Fruit Pies	2–4 months	–Cool thoroughly, cover, and freeze.
Custard Pies	Do not freeze	–Custards will separate.
Ice Cream Pies	*See* Ice Cream	
Poultry (Raw)		
Chicken or Turkey (Parts/ Cut-up)	6–9 months	–Always remove supermarket wrap plus excess fat before freezing.
Chicken or Turkey (Whole)	9–12 months	–Remove giblets from poultry and freeze separately.

FOOD	MAXIMUM STORAGE PERIOD	TIPS
Duck and Geese	6 months	–After cleaning the bird inside and out, tie the legs and wings close to the body and wrap tightly (the bird will take up less freezer space).
Giblets	2–3 months	–Remove from bag and wrap in foil or plastic wrap.
Livers	2–4 weeks	–Chicken livers have a short freezer life.
Salads	Do not freeze	–Greens will wilt.
Soups Stock	3–4 months	–Freeze in ice-cube trays, remove, and place individual cubes in plastic storage bag. Add stock cubes to soups and stews for heightened flavor.
Cream Soup	Not advisable to freeze	–Cream soups tend to separate after thawing; whisk while reheating to make smooth again.

Index